Books by Ron Glick:

Godslayer Cycle

One
Two
Three *(July, 2015)*

Chaos Rising

Tarinel's Song
Immortal's Discord

Oz – Wonderland

The Wizard In Wonderland
Dorothy Through the Looking Glass
The Wonderful Alice of Oz *(January, 2015)*

Trivia Books

Ron El's Comic Book Trivia Volume 1
Ron El's Comic Book Trivia Volume 2
Ron El's Comic Book Trivia Volume 3
Ron El's Comic Book Trivia Volume 4
Ron El's Comic Book Trivia Volume 5
Ron El's Comic Book Trivia Volume 6
Ron El's Comic Book Trivia Volume 7
Ron El's Comic Book Trivia Volume 8
Ron El's Comic Book Trivia Volume 9
Ron El's Comic Book Trivia Volume 10
Ron El's Comic Book Trivia Volume 11
Ron El's Comic Book Trivia Volume 12 *(Obtober, 2014)*

Nonfiction

U.S. Political Prisoner Since 2004

U.S. Political Prisoner Since 2004

The True Story of an Innocent Man Detained As a Political Dissident In Kalispell, Montana

by

Ron Glick

Ron Glick / 3

In Dedication

Mary Alice and Vera Jane,

For believing in the truth.

Copyright © Ron Glick, 2014
ISBN #: 1502340364 - ISBN-13 #: 978-1502340368

Ron Glick / 5

Table of Contents

Foreword..9

Chapter 1...19

Chapter 2...45

Chapter 3...69

Chapter 4...89

Chapter 5...116

Chapter 6...142

Chapter 7...169

Chapter 8...185

Chapter 9...208

Chapter 10...229

Chapter 11...258

Chapter 12...281

Chapter 13...310

Afterwards..332

Appendix 1...342

Appendix 2...372

Appendix 3...410

About the Author...429

Foreword

When any government, or any church for that matter, undertakes to say to its subjects, "This you may not read, this you must not see, this you are forbidden to know," the end result is tyranny and oppression no matter how holy the motives.

- Robert Heinlein, 1940

No law shall be passed impairing the freedom of speech or expression. Every person shall be free to speak or publish whatever he will on any subject, being responsible for all abuse of that liberty...
- Montana Constitution, Article II, Section 7

In spite of what anyone may think, this book is very hard for me to write. Not because it is untrue or even because of the subject matter being so radical. Instead, it is because every time I tell my story, I feel like I am spreading lies about myself. It is not a good feeling, and it leaves me sick every time I have to open myself up for this kind of scrutiny. There is also the ever present fear of further retaliation for speaking out. But I have reached a point where I just cannot remain silent any longer.

A great many people have tried to silence me, to suppress what I am presenting within this volume. They have convicted me of a heinous act to discredit and undermine anything I have to say – it is so much easier to say, "He is a convicted felon, so don't listen to him" than to give me the credibility I should be entitled to. But what people forget is that all of what I am speaking of in this biography happened before there was a conviction, and much of it happened before there was ever a charge filed against me. This is the story of political corruption and how I became a political prisoner in my own country for standing up to it. And it is a story that could very easily be your own if you ignore the forewarning provided herein.

People talk about feeling shame for their past – shame for things they have done and for which they wish they could undo. But no one talks about the shame associated with having to talk about things that are not true, but that people automatically assume are. In all my years, I have never met anyone else who talks about feeling shame for being accused of something they did not do. I am confident that this is not a unique phenomenon; I in no way believe I have somehow evolved an entirely new kind of emotion. But it is certainly not an aspect of shame that is ever talked about.

And I do feel shame. I do. Every time I am compelled to talk about this, I feel it. But it is not shame for anything I have done – it is shame for having to tell people something about myself that is not true, for having to open myself up for prejudice and bigotry for something about myself that has been made up by other people about me. It is hard to express beyond that, but it is a feeling I cannot escape.

I feel it as I write these words, and I imagine I will feel it for the rest of my days. Even if I could somehow be exonerated, this will always be hanging over me. In today's information age, there will always be a scarlet letter out there with my name attached to it. And there will always be people who would rather believe me guilty, if for no other reason than to validate their own wicked views of the world. I have become a poster child in the community I find myself confined in, and I have no idea how to ever escape it.

So what do I feel ashamed of? It can be summed up in two words:

Sex offender.

For me, they are not words of truth – they are a false label imposed over me to undermine any support I might gain in fighting a corrupt regime. But they are powerful words all the same.

The words have a pretty broad meaning, but every invocation of them creates negative feelings and repugnance. It used to be rapists, and molesters, and pedophiles, and so many other words. Now all of these and more have been dubbed under one easily classified label, and in doing so, every offender – regardless of how minor or serious the offense may or may not be – are now grouped with the full-fledged maniacs like Joseph Duncan. If you urinate in an alley, you are now classified with serial rapists.

In American society, just having these words attached to your name is enough to convict you. Varying statistics show that over fifty percent of sexual assault allegations are false in America, but to the general public, the mere mention of the accusation is equal to one hundred percent guilt. And conviction rates for this kind of crime are nearly equal to the court of public opinion. Simply put, if you are accused, there is a ninety-nine percent chance that you will be convicted – at least in Flathead County, Montana. It will not matter if you are innocent. It will only matter that you were accused. And even if you somehow escape being prosecuted or convicted, if someone says you molested a child – true or not – the accusation alone can destroy you.

Before I fell under this scrutiny myself, I often heard the term, "Where there's smoke, there must be fire." And I hate to admit it, but I held similar beliefs. I was a youth advocate, and if I heard a child say they had been molested, I automatically shifted into defense mode. I believed the child because – to my mind – I could not conceive of a child ever lying about something like that.

To put it bluntly, I was wrong. I was naïve, and corrupt authorities in Kalispell, Montana, were able to take advantage of my naivety to brand me as a sex offender in order to stop my own legal challenges against their corruption. And they were able to do it through abduction, terrorism and outright manipulation of the the legal system through an entrenched Good Ol' Boy Network that holds absolute power over a blind public. It turned out it is pretty easy to create a political prisoner in the United States if you convince the public that a dissident is actually a child molester. And remember – the accusation alone is enough to have the public believe it.

When you hold absolute power, you can threaten witnesses without fear of reprisal. When you control the courts, you can legitimize abduction of children by calling it child welfare. When you own the prosecutor's office and court clerk, you can have documents filed at 4am to have someone arrested to get them off the street to stop a lawsuit – even if they are in another state. When you run the jails, you can keep that person locked up indefinitely without a trial or hearing while you run around terrorizing everyone in their life and to give you time to manufacture witnesses against them – to make sure that when a trial is held, it is a kangaroo court where everyone does exactly what you want – because you control what can happen to *their* lives. And when you are in charge of who represents the accused, and the public defenders are all assigned by the same court that is in your pocket, there is absolutely no hope that the truth will ever be presented to a jury.

For almost ten years now, I have been a political prisoner in my own country because of being naïve. Because I held personal belief in my own integrity and knew I was incapable of ever harming a child, it was simply inconceivable to me that a child would ever say I had. But I knew nothing of the kind of corruption that ran rampant in Kalispell, or in Montana, in general. I did not account for how a child could be taken from her home and scared into saying whatever she had to in order to go back home. And I knew nothing of the psychology involved with how children are raised to follow the direction of anyone in authority – even if what that person says to do is wrong.

Unfortunately, by the time all of this became crystal clear to me, it was too late. Even when I was arrested, I held to the belief that they could not convict me. I stubbornly held – even after sitting for sixteen months in jail without a trial or probable cause hearing – that sooner or later, I would get the truth out there and they would be exposed. Again, my naivety and trust in the *illusion* of truth and justice worked against me.

As consequence, I spent five years incarcerated – almost two years in jail, and over three years in prison. Ironically enough, under Montana law I was eligible for parole before I ever saw trial, since after serving one quarter of one's sentence, one becomes eligible – and I spent sixteen months in jail before I ever saw trial (on a five year sentence, fifteen months meets that requirement). But I was subsequently sent to prison because I would not confess to the false allegation against me. And when I finally saw the parole board, I was denied parole twice because I refused to confess. I have since been subjected to over five years of probation (when I was only sentenced to a suspended sentence) at the time of this writing, and have another ten years to look forward to. And during it all, I continue to be victimized and given harsher restrictions than anyone else – all because I refuse to admit to a crime I did not commit. All because I sued Kalispell and the power players in this town, and they cannot abide that someday I might win free of their false conviction.

I mean, it all makes sense in a warped way – so long as I maintain my innocence and continue to look for ways to overturn my conviction, I remain a very real threat to the powers-that-be. If I ever overturn my conviction, if I ever prove my innocence, they become exposed as the true criminals. And that is a very dangerous proposition for them.

I had hoped that when the time came for me to write this book, my story would be done. That I would be writing a story of what happened, how I continued fighting and – most of all – how I overcame the impossible odds mounted against me. But the more time that passes, I realize that day may never come. And so I am going to write this so that at the very least there will be a record of the truth – a record that will survive my death.

I also know that writing this at this juncture just opens me up for more retaliation. I could find myself back in jail again over this. But I need to do something – and I would like to know that at least there is one place I can send people to look for what the real truth is.

I will be drawing material from several places for this book. A lot of the content in here will be modified from online posts I have written, for example. In scripting this, I imagine a lot of this will not read like a narrative. I will be quoting laws and judicial precedents, as well as other legal material. And I will be including scanned content from materials I have managed to reacquire in recent years. I hope that in presenting this, that it will at least be cognizant enough to be able to be followed. But I, of course, welcome any feedback and suggestions in how to better organize what is contained herein. I will be the first to admit that I am too close to this topic to write objectively, so by all means – please do not hesitate to ask.

One more note for this foreword: One of the many restrictions that was uniquely placed upon me that does not exist for any other individual convicted within the State of Montana that I can find is that I am forbidden by court order to use the real name (or publish any identifying information, which would include the initials) of my alleged victim. It is standard practice to not identify minors or victims in court records, substituting initials for their true names, but no such law exists outside a court. However, I alone am forbidden to name the person who accused me – My sentence was modified six years into it to include that condition that I cannot publish nor maintain any record using any identifying information of my alleged victim. And as my alleged victim is over eighteen, this convention is no longer appropriate, either.

Please do not mistake my raising this point to in any way suggest that a victim of a crime is not entitled to a certain amount of privacy. I actually hold to European practice that not even criminal offenders or suspects should be publicly named.

But this being said, there should not be blanket protection for individuals who bring forth accusations simply by virtue of making such an accusation – not when (as previously mentioned) statistics prove that over fifty percent of accusations made are false. If there is going to be a right to publicize the name of a man or woman accused of a crime, then there should rightfully be the right of the accused to not only confront his accuser, but also to speak out in the same public forum against them. In law, as I mentioned, this is permitted through using initials to protect minors and victims – but as I am prohibited from even using *initials*, one has to ask why such an extreme measure is being used in my instance?

Keep in mind, as well – before there was *ever* a prosecution, the alleged victim's and family member's names were published on the Internet. In fact, their names can still be found in archive records if you search for the original posts – and because they are archive records, I could not change them if I wanted to (search for "Another Case of Gov Abuse" for evidence of this –

GeoCities (where this was originally posted) is a now-defunct website where I made an initial appeal for public support, but the site exists solely as an archived record now, which means it cannot be edited by anyone – including myself). Consequently, the order actually only prohibits me from creating *new* material, since this original information has been searchable on the Internet since 2003 – it is a moot point, but it makes it harder for people who might support me to actually research the truth.

If there had been a general crime committed in this instance, there would be no need to write this book and therefore no need to mention anyone's name in any kind of public disclosure like this. However, since there is – by virtue alone of my own protests of innocence coupled with the evidence presented in this book and elsewhere – there should be no restriction upon my relating the true names of the individuals involved. And Montana law agrees, since there is no law which prohibits anyone else in the State of Montana from naming people involved in their criminal cases. But there is a court ruling that specifically bars me alone from doing so, even though there are clearly sources that are beyond my control that already name the person whom I am currently forbidden to name.

To avoid the legal infraction, I will be adhering to the court order so the corrupt authorities cannot use this as an excuse to incarcerate me again. Who knows – maybe they will blame me for the site I have no control over and still do it, since they may claim that they were unaware the site existed. It is hard to predict the form – reasonable or otherwise – that their retaliations take. But of course, anyone is able to go to the Internet and get the real information – and I encourage you to do so, in the interests of full disclosure.

I do not violate the law by telling you that the information is out there – I am only forbidden in naming these people myself or maintaining any source where they are named; I do not maintain the archive of Geocities, and therefore this court order is ineffective and pointless – it exists solely in an effort to harass and frustrate me personally in a way that no one else is. This is but one of many examples of disproportionate treatment that I have been forced to endure, and it is my hope that collectively you will see that the disparate attention and restrictions applied in my case alone are cause to question the validity of all that has been done to me.

I will be reprinting the content of this original posting, albeit, with my alleged victim's name substituted. For instance, Daughter 1 will refer to my alleged victim, since she is the eldest. The only other name I will redact is that of her sister out of respect that she is still a minor at the time of this writing, whom I will call Daughter 2. Other than these changes, I will endeavor to post everything in as close to its original content as possible. And that includes full disclosure on all names and identifying information necessary to expose the truth.

I should also note before I leave this topic – the United States and Montana State Constitutions protect freedom of expression. They entitle any citizen of the United States to say whatever they want about any subject or person, so long as in doing so they do not deliberately spread false information intended to harm another or breach national security. It should be noted that this is the reason no law exists that prohibits anyone else in the country from naming people involved in their criminal prosecutions – because freedom of speech trumps it. This is a basic, inalienable right – yet I alone have been censured in what I can say.

As you continue to read, you might ask yourself why such a blatant violation of civil liberty has been inflicted upon me – what exactly are these people afraid that I will say? This is not the only example – but it is a pretty obvious one that needs little documentation to back it up, since everyone knows that we are supposed to have freedom in this country. Right?

I encourage you to ask this question – and keep asking it. And while you are at it, by all means please start asking your federal representatives and law enforcement agencies why Montana is being allowed to treat American citizens like this. If enough people ask, maybe – just maybe – some day we might get an actual answer. I only pray it comes before I die. And as you will see later on, one person has already died to cover up what these people do not want you to know.

Chapter 1

Frank Garner. Ted Lympus. Peg Allison. Ed Corrigan. These are real names of very real criminals hiding under the cover of official titles and positions in Kalispell and Flathead County, Montana. These are members of an elite Good Ol' Boy gestapo network of corruption that has been entrenched in this area – a small subset of a larger problem persistent throughout Montana as a whole. And just as their names are real, so is my own.

My name is Ron Glick. My name is real, and so are the names of most of the people in this book (with a noted exception barred by unconstitutional court censorship, and one other for respect to her being a minor at the time this is written). Likewise, everything in this book is true. Before the events of this volume, I was a single father and a community leader. All I ever wanted to do with my life was to use what moderate skills I had to improve society and bring people together. I had my ups and downs – and I certainly was not wealthy enough for my community-minded pursuits. But as a single dad with a disability, I wanted to give back and make the world a better place. Unfortunately, in doing so I ran afoul of people who did not want someone like me out in the world working against their own corrupt interests.

I was never anyone exceptional before any of this – I was not a celebrity, expert in my field, nothing of especial noteworthiness. I had a rough upbringing – surrounded by alcohol and addiction from my parents (father and step-father), I was left to my own devices on where to draw any kind of morality from. And for me, that moral compass came from comic books.

Spider-man's "with great power must also come great responsibility" was a ruling mantra of my life. Superman's inability to lie was another. From comic books I drew inspiration, hope and an unquenchable desire to help others. I could look to my own life, see the pain and misery I lived through, and see the heroes in comics overcome even worse obstacles to arrive at victory – just so long as they persevered in the name of what was just, they would eventually prevail. Sans any genuine concept of right or wrong from my parents, comics were the guidepost by which I modeled my life.

No, I was not running around in spandex – but I was living up to the ideals of truth, justice and the American way of life in every breath I took. Even today, after all the years I have suffered as a US political prisoner, I continue to reach out and help others. That is the one thing about me these criminals posing as authority figures can never do: they cannot take away from me who I really am. And who I am – in spite of what they want others to believe – is a good person.

Like many who are reading this, I worked in a wide variety of jobs over the years, ranging from general labor, to retail, to debt collection, to telemarketing. I tried my hand at several personal businesses along the way, primarily retail oriented, but I tried publishing once, also. I even created and operated several nonprofit charities. Learned early on that I enjoyed working with and helping people, and this is the direction I took my life, always moving forward over the occasional bump in the road.

I became a father at 21 while living in Bakersfield, California. I raised my son John with his mother until he was five, and then we were on our own from that time after we moved to Montana. I settled originally in Polson, but by 2000, we had moved to Kalispell. I had opened a youth recreations program in Polson in 1997, and moved it to Kalispell that year. By 2003, I and my then-girlfriend Mara Pelton had opened a business, Arcadia, to coordinate with the youth program. But it was then that this story came to an abrupt halt – because it was then that the true face of Kalispell showed itself.

This is a story of not only corruption, but how a good person's life can be destroyed by falsehoods and manipulation of people in positions of power. It is a story of the true darkness that far too many people possess, both those in affluence and those who do not care who they hurt to gain it. Worst of all, it is a story of what happens when people allow themselves to be blinded by propaganda, specifically that people allow themselves to be indoctrinated into the belief that they live in a free society with guaranteed civil liberties.

I was not a radical. I was not a terrorist, or troublemaker, nor did I have a criminal record of any kind. My whole life I had prided myself that I was a law abiding citizen and would never be a burden to society. In fact, even when I became disabled in my twenties, I spent fifteen years trying to find ways to not rely on government support as best I could. So imagine my surprise when I was not only accused, but convicted of a heinous, unthinkable crime. None of it was true – and it staggers me to this day how many people believe it is true simply because other people say it is – but when people have absolute power to do whatever they want outside the law, people will bend to the popular belief just so they do not stand out. It is sad that a country based on standing together against oppressive rule would bow so meekly to it two hundred years later.

Abraham Lincoln once said, "The trouble with too many people is they believe the realm of truth always lies within their vision." In other words, too many people think they know the truth even when they do not. If you always believe the first thing you hear or believe what you want to believe rather than search for what is really going on, then truth does not lie within your vision no matter what you may think. Of course, there are too many people out there who deliberately encourage people to believe in the mistruth, also – so it is a slipper slope. I guess all I can ask is that anyone reading this follow President Lincoln's wisdom and consider that the truth is not always so simple.

Another way of looking at it is to look to a quote attributed to Samuel Clemins: "A lie is far easier to believe, for it can be molded to the ear of the listener. Truth, by comparison, is far more rigid and less likely to be believed." To put it another way, lies can be told to be what someone wants or expects to believe – but truth is unalterable and not as pleasant to hear. As you read this book, I ask you to keep this thought in mind: it represents the road of least resistance to believe that our government is filled with honest, honorable and trustworthy people who work to preserve our rights above and beyond all else, and that someone accused or even convicted of a crime could only be so if what is said against him is true. It is far harsher to hear that people in power are corrupt and manipulative, and that people you may have supported or even assisted in getting elected are lying to you in order to protect their own criminal misconduct. But just because the latter is not as pleasant to hear, it nevertheless is the truth in this instance and I would appreciate if you, as the reader, will set aside your own personal prejudices and opinions in order to consume the content of this book with an ear tuned for truth rather than preference.

Ironically enough, before all this, I was just about as patriotic as you could imagine. I voted every election, I contributed to political campaigns and I openly promoted the ideals of American civil liberties. I am a compulsively honest person by nature, and honor was more important to me than anything else. Most importantly, I did my absolute best to pass these morals down to my son, inspiring through my own dedication to my country and its ideals a belief in the American way of life.

But I was naïve. It was all a lie. Because there are no civil liberties in this country if the government does not want you to have them. They are not guaranteed as we are raised to believe – they are conditional. So long as you live your life quietly, meekly, and most of all do not stand up to your "betters", you will be allowed to believe you have freedom and liberty. But if you do just the opposite – if you stand up and demand these rights, you can just as easily have them stripped from you.

If you are wealthy or in a position of political power, you can walk all over anyone else's liberties without repercussion. And even if you are exposed for some crime or another, you will not face legal consequences. If you do not believe this to be true, I ask you to look at all the sexual scandals in the last couple of decades American politicians have been caught in and ask yourself why they were never arrested for actions that would sent anyone else to prison. When a mayor has sex with an underage intern, why is their worst consequence to simply not be reelected in the next term?

I realize this is a harsh viewpoint, but let me tell you what happened to me and how I came by this hard-earned knowledge. Then perhaps you will better understand why I have come to see it as an inescapable viewpoint.

By 2003, I had been a youth advocate for nearly seven years. I ran a youth recreations program, originally called The Flipside CCG, and later renamed to The Outpost CCG, that promoted educational activities with youth to inspire independence and self-worth. My nonprofit promoted educational games and activities amongst youth to provide better alternatives than to leave restless minds to create their own forms of entertainment, which too often resulted in vandalism or worse. My work as a youth advocate was an extension of this work.

I should note that in spite of all my work, I had been listed as being physically disabled since I was 22. In 1990, I was diagnosed with a rheumatoid variant disease, which is a chronic joint pain disease, that would progressively become worse as I grew older. For almost twenty years I resisted the label of being disabled though, and always looked for ways to work and support myself so I would not have to fall back on support from the government for disability. I did initially receive funds from California state when I lost my first job because of the disease, but that lasted for less than a year and I refused to seek federal disability after that. My youth program and business that I will be talking about throughout this were just my latest efforts to not become fully disabled, as I hoped to support myself through them.

Beginning in 2002, I partnered with Mara Pelton, who had been my girlfriend at the time, to open a for-profit business called Arcadia in downtown Kalispell. Part of the reason for this business' creation was to provide a full-time facility for The Outpost CCG to operate from, since at that point we had some rather disastrous partnerships with local businesses and the organization existed mostly as a mobile tutorial program. But Arcadia's location also (unintentionally) placed me within a block of where teenagers gathered downtown during evening hours. These kids were known as the Third and Main Crew for where they hung out – and my business was located between Third and Fourth Street on Main Street in Kalispell, Montana.

Within a few months of setting up Arcadia, I became aware of abuses perpetrated against teenagers by members of the Kalispell Police Department. Aside from being told of atrocious acts of abuse from police officers by teenagers in my youth program, I personally witnessed police officers hit and shove teenagers, try to persuade them to have sex and generally bully and harass them out of what I could only see as a sense of elevating their own personal egos. And this is just what I have *seen* – the stories that reached my ears made these instances pale by comparison.

There were a couple instances that stood out quite clearly in my mind even to this day.

There was a time I saw a teenage girl forced into the back of a police car and driven away when she refused to "date" one officer ("date" used in the context of a prostitute's services, not going out to see a movie). I had been standing a short distance away and heard the officer proposition the girl, asking her if she wanted to go on a date with him, his head nodding toward his police car. She responded with, "F--- off, perv," which prompted the officer to reach around behind the girl's neck and propel her to the back of his car, open the door and shove her inside before peeling off. It all happened so fast, I was just too stunned to react.

When I asked about what happened later, I was told by a friend of the girl that she was driven to the edge of town where the officer threatened to have her arrested if she did not have sex with him, and that she had complied. The girl herself was too ashamed to even talk about it.

Another instance involved another girl who I witnessed enter the police station (I was there helping another teenager file a police report regarding a separate issue), fearful that if she went home, her mother would beat her. The officer who met her in the lobby told her that a parent could do whatever they wanted to a child in Montana, that her mom could beat her within an inch of her life if her mother wanted to, and she probably deserved just that. The officer even went so far as to say that if she were his daughter, he would have beaten her "black and blue" (his words) long ago.

Keep in mind that Montana law requires any report of abuse or fear of abuse to be referred to Child and Family Services[1].

1

Needless to say, the girl fled the station in tears and I seriously doubt there was ever a report made.

These kinds of stories circulated for a few month before I ever witnessed anything on my own. Ironically enough, they were happening less than a block from my youth center. But I – to my own shame – ignored the complaints initially because I thought they were just kids trying to escape accountability for their own misconduct.

At first, I never went out to witness anything because I believed that no police officer would do the things that were being reported to me. I just could not believe it could be true. I told the teenagers to file reports with the police department if this was going on, and when they refused, I took it as a sign the stories were being fabricated. After all, if there were a handful of rogue cops acting out against teenagers, I could not conceive that anyone else in the department would permit this if they knew about it.

Not until I saw it myself. And then I began to stand up and defend these kids who had no other voice.

———————

See Appendix 1, MCA § 41-3-201.

Needless to say, power corrupts and absolute power corrupts absolutely. No one in authority ever paid the least bit of attention to reports I filed, and attempting to talk to police officers directly were met with belittling attitudes and redirected blame onto me ("Why would you be hanging out with teenagers if you weren't doing what you are accusing officers of doing?"). Eventually, my vocal outcry against the abuse made me a target, as well.

Sometime in mid 2002, just before we opened Arcadia, as I recall, there was a rumor that reached Mara from a childhood friend, Chantel Beasley. See, prior to dating Mara, I dated a girl named Melissa Turner (Turner being her married name) and Chantel was her ex-husband's sister. Therefore, when Chantel came forward with an allegation that I had molested Melissa's daughter, there was the assumption that Chantel had been told this by my ex-girlfriend, who I did not exactly have the most amicable break up with. This story was accompanied with a warning from Chantel that I was dangerous to have around Mara's children and that Mara needed to break up with me to get me away from Mara's girls.

After hearing about this, I personally went to Child and Family Services myself to make sure to make it a matter of record that none of it was true. CFS confirmed that they had received a report, and though they would not confirm who had made the report, they did confirm that it was not from the child's mother (Melissa). But it caused a rift between Mara and I, since she believed what Chantel had told her, no matter how much I protested it.

For several months, Mara's and my relationship was rocky. We broke up and got back together more than once for various reasons, though to this day I believe the biggest underlying reason was this nebulous accusation.

Ironically, we were out at a bar one night and ran into Melissa. When told about the story and the harm it had caused, Melissa did not hesitate in telling Mara that there was no truth to the story whatsoever, and that the story had not come from her. It turned out that her daughter had been molested by a sitter, but this happened over a year after Melissa and I broke up. When she heard the story about me, she had asked her daughter if any of it were true, and even her daughter confirmed none of it was true.

Confronted with this, Chantel admitted that the story had not come from Melissa, and – in fact – Chantel had never even asked Melissa about it. Chantel claimed that the person who told her was trusted, so she never felt the need to ask Melissa.

Now, keep in mind – Chantel was the aunt to Melissa's children and saw Melissa regularly. So Chantel had more than enough opportunity to check the details of this allegation with Melissa and her daughter before ever going to Mara with it. But not only did Chantel not try to confirm the information, but she went directly to Mara, warning that I was dangerous and that she needed to get away from me.

Even in spite of the fact that Chantel would not confide who had told her this damaging story – and even in light of Melissa confirming that the story was not true – the time spent with Mara believing this story had caused trust issues between us. After speaking with Melissa, Mara admitted she no longer believed the story, but it had done its harm to us as a couple.

It was not until much later that we learned where the story had come from – Chantel admitted months later, amidst all the tumult of the later allegation, that the person who had told her was Mara's father, Jerry Nezat. According to what Chantel finally admitted, Jerry called her on the phone and told her that I had molested Melissa's daughter and I had probably already molested Mara's two daughters. Chantel claimed that she had only acted to defend Mara's daughters, but honestly when Chantel had the opportunity to confirm the story before spreading such a malicious lie and refused to do so, it clearly indicates that there was some other motivation involved.

To this day, I believe Chantel had been encouraged by Jerry to *not* talk to Melissa about this allegation. Knowing Jerry as I do, I can imagine him telling Chantel that he was relating something he had learned in confidence and that Melissa would be hurt if she found out her "trust" had been violated. Personally, if someone told me something disastrous about someone else, then accompanied it with, "but don't tell so-and-so that you know", I would either keep it to myself or confront the person about it. I would certainly not go out of my way to tell others that it was true without having some kind of confirmation. But Chantel was clearly more motivated in spreading gossip than any real concern about whether she was causing harm to someone for no reason.

I cannot even begin to speculate what could have made any person think it was acceptable to spread this kind of malicious rumor without even a shred of evidence from the people who were supposedly involved, but Chantel did all of this – and she did so without any remorse. Perhaps there was some kind of promise or incentive offered to Chantel, but since I do not personally know of any, the only conclusion I can reach is that Chantel is just a wicked person who took perverse pleasure in spreading malicious rumors and hurting other people through them. It is far too common that people are motivated in hurting others simply to give themselves a sense of empowerment or to make their own lives seem so much better by comparison. And without any other contradicting information, this is what I have to conclude was Chantel's reason for her participation in this farce.

However, what is significant about this earlier allegation is who started it: Jerry Nezat. And what makes it significant is what eventually came to light surrounding the later allegations, as well. See, after the later allegation was made, it came to my attention that Mara's parents, Jerry and his wife, Dixie, had actually been coming into my business while I was away and telling anyone who would listen that I was molesting Mara's daughters, amongst other defamatory remarks about me – and this had been going on since at least December of 2003 (keep in mind, the allegation that was later made originated six months later) – it could have been going on longer, but this was the earliest date I could verify later, that it had been going on before Christmas of 2002.

I was told by people who had been hearing this that they just disregarded it and did not give it any credence. But because it was Mara's parents, they did not want to cause trouble by alerting me about it. Instead, they were apparently telling Mara, who would tell them that none of it was true, that it was just how her parents were and that they should just ignore her parents when they talked like that.

But what Mara did not do was tell me about it. I did not hear about any of it, since Mara apparently took it upon herself to "shelter" me from it.

This was not all Mara was sheltering me from, either. As I mentioned, Mara indicated to others that this was just how her parents were, and apparently, her parents had been starting rumors like this for Mara's entire life. Jerry and Dixie had ruined at least three other men's lives over this kind of false allegation, and they had tried to ruin a fourth before they attacked my own. All because they did not approve of the men in their daughter's lives. But to explain all of this, I need to go into detail of Mara's own troubled relationship history.

Before I begin with this, something should be said about Jerry's and Dixie's beliefs, and what they were looking for from their daughter. The Nezats held to the Old World practice of arranged marriages. There is certainly nothing wrong with the institution of arranged marriage, but from everything I have learned about them, Mara's parents were only interested in this tradition in hopes of using their daughter to gain financial reward through marrying her to a wealthy man. This was demonstrated by who they tried to arrange to first marry their daughter, and throughout Mara's life, it seemed to be a major underlying motivation for their objections to the choices their daughter made.

In pursuit of this tradition though, when Mara was thirteen, her parents offered her to a local clergyman, Ray Frye, to marry. Mara reported to me that Ray was always very respectful to her and never did more than hold her hand and play games with her like chess. He did ask Mara if she would like to marry him when she was older, but he never tried to consummate such a relationship. From everything I know from Mara, Ray was always a perfectly respectable gentleman in every way.

While Ray was in good standing in the community, the Nezats reaped financial gain from Ray. Reportedly, he would pay for trips for Mara and her parents so that he could spend time with Mara in a chaperoned capacity, and he would give expensive gifts to her parents. There were also other financial exchanges that occurred – open-ended loans and the like – though if Mara knew the specifics of these, she did little more that allude to them with me.

The problem with all of this was Ray was apparently married. Now, whether he was already engaged in a divorce at the time, or whether he started the divorce after beginning to court Mara was never made clear to me. But regardless, Ray's ex-wife, Jeri Frye, became an accomplice with Dixie later on – and this became the first instance where Mara's parents demonstrated a propensity for making up sexual impropriety as a weapon to sever their daughter from men they disapproved of.

At some point, Ray fell into disfavor. Jeri made allegations against Ray in the divorce that he had molested their daughter, Tiffany. These reports were not initially substantiated, but Jeri made a point of circulating the information around Ray's church, which ended up with Ray losing his job. Ray fell into destitution as this false allegation ruined his career. For a time, apparently, he even stayed on the Nezat's couch. But he no longer had the finances to give the kinds of gifts that he had before, and this made him fall into disfavor with Mara's parents.

It was after Ray lost his job and was left homeless that Dixie met with Jeri Frye. From the story, I gathered that this meeting occurred at least in part over frustration over Ray taking up residence on the Nezat's couch, but this may have just been an impression I got from the story itself. When Dixie talked about Ray being on their couch, there was a definite slur to the way she talked about it, and I had the impression that Ray was living with the Nezats before Dixie met with Jeri.

According to Tiffany years later, Dixie and Jeri met with young Tiffany (who at the time was about eight years old) and told her that Ray intended to take Tiffany out of the country if he won custody in the divorce, and if that happened, she would never see her mother again. Young Tiffany was then told that the only way to stop this from happening was to affirm the story Jeri had made in the divorce and to make an allegation that Ray had touched Tiffany in her private areas. With this fear as a motivation, Tiffany recited a story Jeri and Dixie gave her about Ray reaching over her and touching her one time inappropriately (this will all sound very familiar soon enough).

The advantage of this kind of story, of course, is that it cannot be disproved by any kind of physical evidence. By claiming that Ray had only touched his daughter, there was no physical trauma that could be measured, and DNA evidence was useless because he was around his daughter constantly. Nevertheless, based upon this allegation, Ray reportedly went to prison for seven years for molesting his daughter.

Years later, when Tiffany was sixteen or seventeen, she ran across Mara at a foster children event. By that time, apparently, Jeri had lost custody of Tiffany for reasons I was never told, and Tiffany was in the Child Protective Service's system as a foster child. Mara at the time was also involved in this as a foster mother herself (remember, there was at least a five year age difference between Mara and Tiffany).

Tiffany confessed to Mara that the story against Ray had not been true, and that as a little girl, she had only said what she did because her mom and Dixie had scared her into believing that if Tiffany did not say what she did, that Ray would never let her see her mother ever again. Tiffany, of course, had not been told that the consequences of this story would mean she would lose her father instead, and she lived with the guilt of what had happened for nearly a decade at that point. Tiffany asked Mara if Mara thought that her father could ever forgive her, and Mara assured Tiffany that Ray would understand. At last report, according to Mara, Tiffany and Ray had been reunited and were rebuilding their relationship. But clearly, they had lost years because of Jeri and Dixie's malicious lie.

A few years after Ray went to prison for allegedly molesting his daughter, when Mara was fifteen or sixteen, she dated someone named Joe Carter. Dixie did not approve of Joe, it seemed. Mara told me she believed that the dislike stemmed from Joe and her dying their hair for Halloween one year. Apparently, Dixie considered this act to be proof that Joe was not a good influence, and when Mara would not break up with Joe, her mother took measures to make it happen.

Without any evidence to support anything of the kind, Dixie got ahold of a school directory listing contact information for other students' families and school staff, including teachers and the principal. She proceeded to call every person she could reach on this list to tell them that supposedly Joe was being molested by workmen down the road from his home – apparently there was some implication that this was a consensual thing for Joe, since he kept going back supposedly. Only after calling as many people as she could reach did Dixie then call Joe's mother, Adele Carter.

When I learned of all this, I reached out and spoke directly with Adele herself, who by then was a practicing attorney in Plains, Montana.

According to Adele, she had avidly defended her son against Dixie's false allegations, but the damage had been done by Dixie calling everyone else first. Joe was called into the principal's office to ask about the allegations just so Joe could deny them. The parents of other kids in the school asked their own children if they knew anything about the allegations, which spread the information amongst the student population. As a consequence, Joe earned the reputation of being a boy-toy and his remaining two years of high school were miserable, being bullied, dumped in trash cans and other malicious abuse from fellow students. Prior to all of this, Joe was apparently pretty popular – but afterward, Joe became a pariah in school.

Needless to say, Joe broke up with Mara over this, which was exactly what Mara's mother had wanted. And Mara's own reputation around school became tainted as well, as students began saying that Mara and her mother were crazy.

In spite of all of this, Mara finally found a new boyfriend in her senior year of high school, Jared Salois (pronounced Sal-o-way). This high school romance advanced to the point that the two married after high school, and they had two daughters, though the second daughter died tragically. But Jared was an underachiever – while Mara tried to better her life by going to college, Jared would stay at home playing video games all day. And, needless to say, his lack of success drew negative attention from Mara's parents.

Mara told me that Dixie never approved of Jared and rarely had anything good to say about him. But by this time, Mara had developed something of a thick skin against abusive comments on men in her life coming from her mother and largely ignored these malicious barbs. To me, it seems from things that Mara told me that she probably stayed with Jared as long as she did out of spite to her mother. But whether this is true or not, Dixie finally found a message that did penetrate whatever guards Mara had against the lies she knew her mother capable of.

As an aside, during the course of their relationship, Mara and Jared had two daughters – Daughter 1 and a younger girl. The youngest girl died tragically when she choked on a toothpaste cap. I mention this only in the briefest capacity to explain later when I reference Mara's third daughter why there is no further mention of her second.

About the time that Daughter 1 was three, Dixie began telling Mara that Jared was cheating on her – with a thirteen year old at work (I believe it was a fast food restaurant). Meanwhile, unbeknownst to Mara at the time, Dixie was also telling Jared that Mara was cheating on him. For whatever reason, neither talked to the other about these issues, but the trust in their relationship was destroyed over these allegations. Both Jared and Mara have said that the allegations were not true, though notably after they divorced, Jared did begin dating a thirteen year old – someone he eventually took up into Canada to marry. In all fairness, it is my understanding that Jared has insisted that he never started being with his future wife though until after his divorce from Mara, and though I can only report what I know, it is somewhat convenient in my mind that it was a thirteen year old he ended up with after the specific allegation made by Dixie.

Keep in mind that Mara knew the majority of all of this proceeding information – with the exception of the story that Dixie had told Jared that she had been cheating on him, as well –

when we began dating, and that we were together for a year and a half before she ever acknowledged any of this to me. Had I known about any of this, what came after would have been viewed in a completely different light, but Mara never told any of this to me, nor did anyone else. And even when she became aware that her parents were turning their malicious lies in my direction, she made a concerted effort to keep me from finding out.

When asked why she did not tell me any of this, Mara told me that she was afraid if I knew about her parents' past behavior, or even about the current efforts to malign me, that I would break up with her. I told her in response that had I known, it would have had them I expelled from our lives, not her. But her fear of my leaving her only aided her parents in eventually laying the foundation for the destruction of my own life. If I had known any of this, I could have acted to defend myself. I would have seen their actions as a warning that they were gearing up to do to me what they had done to others in the past. But Mara insisted on keeping me ignorant, and so I proved vulnerable to their machinations.

After she divorced Jared, Mara eventually met her second husband, Tim Pelton. Tim, it turned out, was a masochistic person. I have had personal dealings with the man, and some of the abuses and manipulations he heaped upon his wife and children were horrendous. So I cannot defend this man as being undeserving of the Nezat's negative attentions, but there certainly was no justification for some of the things they did to try to distance Mara from him.

Tim entrenched himself into Mara's life pretty strongly. Even before the two were married, Tim insisted on adopting Daughter 1. Towards this end, he approached Jared – who by this time had begun dating his future wife – and threatened to report him for molesting his thirteen year old girlfriend if Jared 1 did not sign away his parental rights to Daughter 1. Jared was never a strong person, and he bowed to the threat, signing the document provided to him and then fleeing to Canada with his girlfriend. Tim then pushed through his own adoption of Daughter 1.

Remember, Tim and Mara were not married at this point – but clearly Tim wanted a control over Mara that was absolute, and by doing this, he made absolutely certain that Mara would have to marry him. After all, he was now the legal father of her child. This is possibly the most manipulative and controlling thing I have ever witnessed in years of working around dysfunctional and abusive relationships, but Mara went along with it, so clearly Tim had his hooks in her – hooks that remained solid enough until he could impregnate Mara with her third daughter.

Daughter 1 readily confirmed that Tim Pelton was very abusive to her through the years that followed – pushing her head into the wall, punching her with all his strength in the stomach, even holding a gun to her head at one point threatening to shoot her. Notably, none of this was ever investigated when reported, but these were consistent and ongoing demonstrations of the level of abuse that Tim heaped upon Daughter 1. Mara told me that on more than one occasion, Tim tried to strike her, as well, but she reportedly managed to avoid his physical abuse. Unfortunately, Mara did little to stop the abuse against Daughter 1.

Ironically enough, it was this abuse that finally broke apart Mara's second marriage. It was witnessing Tim striking Daughter 1 in the stomach that finally gave her the reason to evict him from her home and file for divorce. But by then, Daughter 1 was eleven, meaning she had suffered through eight years of physical abuse from Tim Pelton.

Mara and I had been friends before her divorce, and though there had been a mutual attraction between us, Mara remained faithful to Tim and I never pressed her for anything. Even after she began her divorce, Mara and I did not immediately act upon our attraction, either. To tell the truth, at the time I had been interested in another girl and the pursuit of that relationship was where my attention lay.

However, Tim's behavior following the filing for divorce forced Mara and I closer and closer together. He made very direct and specific threats – recorded on Mara's answering machine – that if she were not with him, he would not let her be with anyone else. It was very obvious that he was threatening to kill Mara. As her friend, I made it a point of being there for back-up whenever Tim came around. Tim meanwhile sabotaged Mara's vehicles and left threatening notes on her front porch. Fearful of being alone with her girls in the country, Mara began staying at my place in town.

This close proximity broke through Mara's and my mutual reservations after about a month, and on Halloween of 2001, we officially began dating. It is a memory I will always cherish, because there were no words spoken – we just began holding hands at some point while we were walking our kids around for Trick or Treat. To this day, I do not know who reached out to the other first. It just seemed that our hands found each others' as we were walking. But that night we made love for the first time, and I consider that the date when we first started seeing each other romantically.

Of course, Tim tried to accuse Mara of her and I being together while they were married, but there was never any truth to this. Mara and I were only friends prior to her divorce. But it did not stop him from spreading malicious lies to the contrary.

In the early days of the divorce, Mara's parents seemed to like me. I was financially successful – I had a good paying job working for a debt-to-debt collection agency and ran a nonprofit youth program on the side. I was a well-respected member of the community with a great deal of potential for improving my life. And all of this was in spite of the physical limitations of my chronic joint pain disease. Mara's parents certainly took advantage of my financial stability by "borrowing" money pretty regularly – money, I might note, that I never had returned. But as I saw it, this was family, so I was never really concerned at the time.

During this period, the Nezats were pretty dedicated to speaking poorly about Tim, which was to be expected. But notably, they tried on more than one occasion to have me convince Mara to not let her daughters have visitation with Tim. To support this idea, Jerry told me that Daughter 1 had confided in him that Tim had tried to have sex with her, though he urged me not to mention it to Daughter 1 or Mara because Daughter 1 had told him in confidence, and he claimed Daughter 1 would not trust him if she knew he told me. In spite of this caution, I took the concern to Mara and then together we asked Daughter 1 about the allegation. Daughter 1 vehemently denied it, and therefore nothing else was done.

Remember earlier I said this was something I could see Jerry telling Chantel – to not tell Melissa about her daughter's alleged molestation? This is why I say I can see him telling her this – because in a similar circumstance, he had told me the same thing regarding Tim. In the same position, I went after the truth rather than spread this kind of thing – Chantel did not do that. Guess that just shows you Chantel's character.

In hindsight, this was really the first glimpse I had of the Nezat's dishonesty, but at the time it was an isolated instance and Mara told me that her father was just trying to look out for his granddaughter. I accepted this at the time, but wish in hindsight that I had not.

Also around this time, Jared Solois came back into Daughter 1's life. He had had no contact with his daughter since giving up his parental rights when she was three, but upon learning through Mara in a chance encounter that she was divorcing Tim Pelton, he revealed to Mara the threats and manipulations that Tim had engaged in to get Jared to release his parental rights. Jared expressed a desire to get to know his daughter again, and Mara discussed the idea with me. I agreed it was important for Daughter 1 to have a relationship with her birth father, and so Mara agreed to let Jared begin having visitations with Daughter 1.

Of course, this did not sit well with the Nezats. Within a month of Jared starting to have visitation with Daughter 1, both Jerry and Dixie came over to my home and tried to convince me that Jared would molest Daughter 1 if he was left alone with her. They claimed to have seen Daughter 1 sitting in Jared's lap and that his hands were roaming over her body inappropriately, including rubbing between her legs. They also asserted that Jared had an interest in thirteen year old girls, and at the time, Daughter 1 was only a little younger than that.

I again reported this allegation to Mara, who yet again dismissed it as just her father trying to protect her granddaughter. I recall that Mara said that her parents had never forgiven Jared for supposedly cheating on her during their marriage. By that time, Mara had been told by Jared that he had not actually cheated, but Mara made it appear that her parents did not know the truth of this. And yet again, I trusted Mara's take on the situation and did nothing about it.

This should have been my second red flag. It after all was the second time that Mara's parents had specifically created false allegations of sexual impropriety against men in Mara's life. But I allowed my trust in Mara to overshadow what should have been warnings that I was just as capable of being falsely accused of something like this. But, as they say, hindsight is twenty-twenty, and by the time I realized I was at risk, it was too late.

A great deal could be said here of Mara's own culpability in protecting her parents, too – remember, in each instance I went to her and she minimized what her parents were doing. And – as was later revealed – she had been fully aware that this was the way her parents dealt with every other man in her life up to this point, so there was no reason to believe that I would be treated any different. But Mara kept silent and let it happen. Take what you will from this.

Meanwhile, time passed and I lost my job over an ethical challenge with my boss, and though I still had the youth program that worked through partnership with a local business, apparently this loss began to have me shine less favorably to Jerry and Dixie. When the Outpost's partnership fell apart because of Tim Pelton's own manipulations – specifically befriending the business owner, Paul Beaver, who I was partnered with and undermining the partnership we had – I became even more tarnished in their eyes. I am told this is when they first began spreading malicious rumors about me. Notably, this was when the false allegation was made up about me with Melissa's daughter. As you may recall, this allegation proved itself false but was not linked back to the Nezats until after they had leveled the allegation involving Daughter 1 against me.

Right around this time, Mara received a settlement from an accident she had been in and she offered to use the money to create a business to partner with the Outpost CCG and create a permanent site for the youth program. This business was, of course, Arcadia. Mara wanted to help establish a gaming and collectibles business, but had absolutely no experience in how to do so. I, on the other hand, had years of experience and contacts to set up such a business. And so with her investment and my expertise, we entered into business together.

For future purposes, I should explain how the business was organized. Mara and I formed a corporation under the name Multiverse Enterprises, and seeded ownership of Arcadia to the corporation. I owned sixty percent of the shares in order to maintain a single block of controlling interest – though nine percent of the shares were considered held in trust for our children (three percent each). Mara was given thirty percent shares for her investment, and ten percent were held in reserve for selling to future investors (notably we sold maybe three shares in this way, so there was still well over nine percent of the shares unowned). In spite of the share structure, Mara and I had a separate agreement that we would always consider the business assets to be fifty-fifty ownership between us, so that any profits not distributed to other shareholders would always be equally divided between us, regardless of what the paperwork of the corporation dictated.

Upon initially setting up the business, the Nezats' opinion of me shifted back to the positive for awhile. Apparently they viewed the idea of entrepreneurship to be a positive move forward for our future lives – and of course, they could continue to "borrow" money from me if I was financially successful. But the business – as is common with any new start-up – did not immediately become profitable, and within six months of starting up Arcadia, the negative attacks on my character resumed – this time with their actually entering my business and spreading their malice to my customers and employees.

One of the first things the Nezats started doing once they decided to start running this negative campaign was to convince Mara that the division of the corporate shares were not fair. They convinced her that she should have controlling interest of the corporation because she had provided the start-up capital, and continued to hold a second job at Wendy's to pay our personal bills.

I reminded Mara that her investment was gone before we ever opened up the doors for business – we had even opened the doors early in order to start getting money back in. By the point her parents began ceding doubts about ownership in her mind, the business was maintained solely upon my own expertise to keep cash flow moving through the business and that the business only paid me a stipend that covered the bills her own paycheck could not. I also reminded her that investors rarely owned a controlling interest in a business (pointing out the much larger finances that would be raised if we had sold the ten percent stock shares over what she had invested) because the money alone did not make money – that it took knowledgeable investment of that money to make a business successful. That was what I provided – and why we had agreed at the beginning that I should maintain the controlling interest of the corporation. Finally, I reminded her that in spite of the shares, we had agreed to split any profits of the business so the corporate structure was irrelevant.

None of this mattered to Mara once her parents had inserted their manipulative thoughts into her mind though. She insisted I had played upon her ignorance, that she should be given controlling interest of the corporation, implying – though never outright saying – that I had the ability to steal the business from her at any time I wanted. As another red flag of dangers to come, I should have seen this for what it was – Mara was wanting to distance herself from me. Whether she realized what she was doing or not, since this all came from her parents, it was what she was doing. Her parents wanted her to be able to evict me from the business, especially in light of the ideas they were trying to get to take hold that I was molesting her daughters.

Remember – this particular campaign to accuse me started in December, 2002. The allegation that the Nezats eventually managed to get Daughter 1 to cooperate with supposedly occurred in July, 2003. So there was over six months between the initial allegations made by the Nezats that I had supposedly been molesting Mara's daughters before Daughter 1 ever made an allegation against me. The fact that these accusations preceded any actual allegation from the supposed victim by over six months should have been a huge factor in determining the allegation's credibility, but of course this detail was always overlooked.

The initial rumor that the Nezats started against Melissa Turner's daughter was not put to rest until sometime in October, 2002, when I found Melissa and she affirmed to Mara that the accusation was complete fabrication. As best I can tell, at that time, I was considered "in favor" with the Nezats, so they were not actively spreading the story any longer at that point. By my best ability to determine, they did not start up again until December, 2002, and they changed their tactic from spreading the first story – that had by that time been reported to them as disproved – to starting to tell stories that I was molesting Mara's daughters.

As this story progresses, I hope you will keep this timeline in mind – the Nezats were actively engaged in trying to convince people from sometime in early-to-mid 2001 that I was a child molester. Their first story remained as a point of conflict between Mara and I for nearly a year before I could find Melissa, who could prove there was no truth to it. So there had been barely two months between the time the original doubt was set aside and the Nezats started a new sequence of stories. And all of this preceded the actual allegation against me by over six months.

Chapter 2

Historically, December 7, 1941, is known as the day that would live in infamy, since this was the day that Japan launched a surprise attack on Pearl Harbor in Hawaii, as well as a broad campaign across the Pacific theater. For me, the day that will live in infamy will always be July 9, 2003 – this was the day the surprise attack was launched against me, the day that signaled my own downfall.

This is not to say that on this morning, the Nezats woke up and decided on this plan of attack. No, this date was preceded by a series of lesser events, things that individually were seemingly unimportant, though in the larger scale of things, it represented threads in a greater tapestry that I could not see at the time. In hindsight, there were certain things that raised red flags, but nothing that specifically said, "Mara's parents are going to set you up for a false sexual assault charge against Daughter 1."

As I write this next section, I need to make something clear: I have no real ill will towards Daughter 1 for what she did back then. The truth is, I understand that what started as a simple plan of trying to get her mom and birth dad back together grew into fear as she found herself threatened by people in authority. She was scared and she was trying – in her own misguided way – to protect herself from the harm that others held over her head. So even though I can never abide her lying or what she did at the bequest of others, I cannot really say that I wish her ill for her part in it back then.

Daughter 1 was a thirteen year old girl following directions of people in authority whom she believed in. When she lied, she did so without real understanding that what she did was wrong because she was conditioned to do what her elders and people in authority told her to do. This is not to say that she was incapable of making other choices – her younger sister certainly did when presented with the same conundrum – but I do at least understand what she was going through. Though I do resent that she did not come forth with the truth once she was out from under their thumb, I have to imagine that spending five years being conditioned by the authorities using her as a pawn had something to do with that, as well.

So as this and later areas lay out, no matter how animous or negative I may appear when presenting the information, it is not done with any desire to will harm or consequence upon Daughter 1. I will endeavor to present the information in as impartial a capacity as possible, but there are bound to be those who try to twist my words and claim I am trying to cast blame upon her. The truth is, I do not blame Daughter 1 – I blame all the people who manipulated and threatened her. Am I disappointed in her? Certainly. Am I discouraged that she did not have the strength of character to do the right thing then or since? Absolutely. But do I hate her for what she did? No, not at all.

This being said, it is important to understand that Daughter 1 was not completely uninvolved in events that led up to July 9. In fact, to this day, I believe there was a mixture of motivations that led to her agreeing to cooperate, not the least of which were her own unrelated feelings towards me personally.

There is no other way to say this other than to say that Daughter 1 had a crush on me. She was a thirteen year old girl and I was a reasonably attractive older man in her life. Not understanding her own sexuality yet, it was natural for her to develop an attraction towards me, and as I became aware of it, I spoke routinely with Mara and our family friend, Carrie Beth Mountjoy, about them. I was convinced it was simply something to accept as part of her natural growth into maturity. But some of her interests did cross the line, and it is those things that I suppose I should maybe have been more concerned about. But again, I trusted in those around me for guidance, and intended to simply not make a big deal of them at the time. I did not want to embarrass her – I only wanted what was best for her, and her emotional development was important to me.

Basically, even before Mara and I began to date, I had sensed that Daughter 1 had a crush on me. Whenever she was part of a gaming event I hosted for the youth program, she was always hanging around me, smiling, laughing and trying to get my attention. It was pretty obvious to just about anyone who saw it, including Mara. At one point when Daughter 1 was maybe ten or eleven, long before Mara and I were dating, Mara even gave me a print picture from Daughter 1 that was tinted blue, joking with me that I liked blue-skinned girls (because I really liked the character Chiana on the science fiction show, Farscape, who was played by Gigi Edgley). It was given in humor and I laughed at it, but it demonstrates that others saw how obvious Daughter 1's crush was towards me.

After Mara and I started dating, Daughter 1 was around me a lot more often, and her affections graduated from getting my attention to wanting to have physical contact with me when she was around. She was about eleven at this point, and I saw the open affection as a sign of acceptance, not of anything dastardly. She would hold onto my arm, or hug me, or sit on my lap. When I would lay down on the couch, she would often lay down beside me. In fact, this started a competition of sorts between Mara's daughters and my own son as to who could get beside me on the couch first. I never felt there was anything wrong with physical affection in these instances, because I was after all assuming a step-father role in Daughter 1's life, though this casual acceptance turned out to be a mistake on my part later on.

As winter of 2002 set in, it had become something of a race amongst the kids to who could lay beside me under the blanket on the couch in the back office whenever we were there during the day, since there was only a space heater in the office to keep warm. This was also where the computer was, and we had downloaded a lot of cartoons for the kids to watch, so this became something of a family room for them to watch things. So if there was no one in the store – or if it was slow and we had someone to watch the front – and the kids wanted to watch something, it was not uncommon for me to take the kids back into the office to watch cartoons.

As time passed though, Mara clearly began to see Daughter 1's affections as a concern. Whether this was because of a bug in her ear from the Nezats or residual concerns from the false story about Melissa's daughter, I cannot say. I will admit that I was probably a bit blind to how it looked to Mara, since I never saw Daughter 1 as anything more than a step-daughter, a child whose budding sexuality never even crossed my mind. But looking back, I can say that if she had been older, I probably would have seen her affections with more intimate intent that I saw them as at the time. After all, if an adult girl were always holding my hand, or wrapping herself around my arm, or wanting to snuggle in my lap, I probably would have seen her as someone who was really into me. But – like I have said over and again – I just did not see Daughter 1 in that way – I saw her as a child seeking love and affection from a parent – and so it just struck me as the actions of an affectionate child.

I mentioned before that Mara continued to work at Wendy's to help with personal bills while I ran the store. But she worked the opening shift, which meant she had to be into work by 5:30 a.m. To allow for this, and since we only had one car at the time, we had to drive into town as a family by 5 a.m. This meant the rest of us – Mara's daughters and my son – were all really tired and would go to the store and sleep for a few more hours before the kids had to get up for school.

Occasionally, if the kids could not sleep, they would come back into the office to watch cartoons while I tried to nap. Sometimes it would be one, sometimes all three. But it was not something I really discouraged, since if they were quiet, I could still get some rest before having to open the store. In hindsight, I think that Daughter 1 made more visits to the back room than any of the others, but again, it just was not something of great concern and it was not something I was particularly concerned over. As the weather warmed up, they would sit in a chair in the room rather than laying down, but when it was cold, it just made sense to let them cuddle where it was warm. I was not bothered by any of the children laying under the blanket with me, and Daughter 1 was just one of the kids to my mind.

At this point, it's important to mention something that happened with Daughter 1 that revolved around a birthday party she attended in or around April, 2003, for her friend Chelsea. It was going to be an overnight slumber party at the local Outlaw Inn. Chelsea's mother was the chaperon for the party, and even though there had been some question as to how she could afford a suite for the night when she was not working, we had no reason to question that it was going to just be a fun time for all the girls involved. And so Mara and I agreed to let Daughter 1 go, and dropped Daughter 1 off around 3 or 4 p.m., as I recall.

Later that night, Daughter 1 called the store and asked to come home because she felt sick. At the time, our store was staying open until 10 p.m., so when we received a call at around 8:30 p.m., we still had a lot of people in the store. I remember Mara asking Daughter 1 to wait until the store closed, but that Mara reported that Daughter 1 just cried, saying she wanted to come home right then. It was decided that since Mara was involved in a game, that I would go to pick up Daughter 1.

I arrived at the Outlaw Inn just before 9 p.m., and asked the desk clerk what room the girls' party was in so I could go back and pick up Daughter 1. I remember that the clerk seemed more than a little defensive about the idea of one of the girls being picked up. He insisted that anyone who was not a guest was not allowed back to the rooms (which upon reflection was very odd, since the Outlaw Inn actually had people renting rooms on a month to month residency as tenants), and so called back to the room. Assured that Daughter 1 would be right up, I sat down and waited.

As I sat there, I remember that the clerk never left the counter and kept looking over in my direction. After a few minutes passed, I remember a second clerk coming up and talking with the first, and that the clerk kept looking over in my direction as he talked. At the time, I remember thinking that they just did not trust someone sitting alone in the front lobby after dark. It was an excessive reaction, but I just thought the clerk was paranoid.

After twenty minutes and Daughter 1 had not come up to front, I once again approached the clerk and asked after her. The clerk was obviously nervous when I asked again if I could just go back and get her. He did not at first want to call back again, but when I demanded to talk to his manager, he did. The clerk kept turning away as he talked, trying to keep me from hearing some of what he was saying. I became suspicious of what was going on and insisted on talking to Chelsea's mom and took the phone from the clerk.

The background noise on the other end of the phone was deafening. It took more than once for me to get Chelsea's mom to understand who she was talking to, but when she did, she kept talking away from the phone to someone else. When I asked what the noise was, she insisted that the girls were watching a movie, though to my ear, the background noise had too much discord to be a movie. It sounded like a loud raucous bar more than anything else. When I asked about Daughter 1 coming up front, Chelsea's mother acted surprised that I was there, as if she did not know that anyone had come to get Daughter 1, or even that Daughter 1 had even called anyone to come get her. Chelsea's mom then made a few attempts at getting me to go ahead and let Daughter 1 stay, since she was just lying in front of the "movie" with the other girls and clearly not sick. I asked to talk to Daughter 1 myself, but this just made Chelsea's mom talk away from the phone again. Finally, after several efforts to dissuade me, and never actually letting Daughter 1 come to the phone, Chelsea's mom just said, "okay" and hung up the phone.

It was pretty obvious to me at that point that something was going on back in the room. My conclusion though was that Chelsea's mom was drunk and did not want me to come back and see her like that while she was supervising a dozen or so teenage girls. It was not an issue to me though so long as I was able to just get Daughter 1 and take her home.

At any rate, since the clerk would still not tell me the room number, I went and sat back down to wait. But another twenty minutes passed with no appearance by Daughter 1 and I got back up to once again demand of the clerk to tell me what room the girls were in, because by that point I was really worried that something had happened to Daughter 1. It was just as I was starting to talk to the clerk this time that Daughter 1 entered the lobby though.

There was clearly something amiss. Daughter 1, who was normally a bright and chipper girl, was very solemn and withdrawn. Worse, her hair was wet, and her clothes clung to her damp skin. I immediately hugged her and found her shivering.

I asked her what was wrong, but Daughter 1 insisted that she was just sick and wanted to go home. When I asked why her hair was wet, she said she had gone swimming. I knew she had not brought a swimming trunk though (because we had been told the pool would be closed at night), and asked how she had done that without a suit. She said that she had borrowed a swimsuit from

Chelsea. This explanation hardly made sense since Chelsea was a larger girl and Daughter 1 was tall and slim – any suit of Chelsea's would have hung off of Daughter 1. But I did not argue this, since she just shivered all the harder as she stood there and I knew I needed to get her home.

In Montana, April is still pretty cold, though at the time we were having fairly warm days even if the nights could be bitter. The plan though had been for Daughter 1 to be inside all night, so when she was dropped her off for the party, she did not have a jacket with her. Now, with the sun down and the night's cold set in, even in the lobby Daughter 1's shivering was really bad. So I gave her my own jacket to keep her warm and led her out to the car as quickly as possible.

The entire trip back across town was in silence. Daughter 1 would not answer any questions as to what they were doing or even what movie they had been watching. Remember, this was a girl who not only loved being around me, but was an extremely outgoing girl who loved to talk and talk. So her sullen behavior was very atypical. And I just could not understand that if she had been displaying these symptoms why she would ever have just gone swimming. Also remember, I had waited forty minutes in the lobby, and Daughter 1's hair and skin were freshly wet – which meant that if she had gone swimming, she had to have done so right before coming to the lobby. None of it made sense, but Daughter 1 was not answering any questions, and she was obviously not feeling well. So for me, getting her home and to bed was the most important priority.

By the time I made it back to Arcadia, the store was closed and everyone was waiting for Daughter 1 and I, so we could all go home. All the way home, Daughter 1 was silent and withdrawn, but both Mara and I chalked it up to her not being well. But as I recall, Mara was even more upset with Chelsea's mom for letting Daughter 1 swim when she was clearly this sick.

That night, Mara tried to talk to Daughter 1 about what had gone on at the party, but all Daughter 1 would reportedly do was cry and lie in her mom's arms. I was not part of this conversation, since Mara wanted to be alone with Daughter 1 and I let them. I can therefore only report what Mara reported to me later about that night.

Of peculiar note, Mara reported to me also that Daughter 1 had her first menstruation a couple days later.

Immediately following this night, Daughter 1 wanted nothing to do with Chelsea for quite awhile. She was clearly upset with Chelsea, and it also came to light that not all of Chelsea's friends had been invited to the party, and that apparently some of the girls who came to the party were not even regular friends of Chelsea's, just girls she knew from school. At first, it seemed that Daughter 1 was just mad on behalf of the friends who had been excluded from the party, but when Mara and I later compared a list of who had and had not been invited, there was a specific pattern: all the girls who had been excluded had weight problems and were unattractive, while the girls who did attend were all thin and attractive.

This was only compounded by another inconsistency. Roughly a week after the party, Chelsea came to the store to find Daughter 1. Chelsea wanted to talk to her because they were apparently not getting along, and Chelsea wanted to make up for whatever was wrong between them. Chelsea confirmed that not all of her friends were invited, and this was the reason she said Daughter 1 was mad at her. But of particular interest were two things Chelsea said: First, she made a comment about how since Daughter 1 had not stayed until morning, she had not gotten any of the party favors like the other girls did, and, second, she said that it was too bad that Daughter 1 had not brought a swimsuit so she could have gone swimming with the other girls.

Remember, Daughter 1 had specifically said that *Chelsea* had loaned her a swimsuit to go swimming as answer for why her hair was wet...

There was also a friend of Daughter 1's who was clearly traumatized by something around that time, as well. Without explanation, this friend cut off all her hair – literally shaved it down to stubble – without any logical reason. Daughter 1 only offered up one cryptic clue – that her friend did not want to be pretty anymore.

Another issue of note that began to crop up about a month later was that money began to disappear from the register in Arcadia – and not small amounts, either. By the time we finally narrowed down who had been stealing, we had lost over two hundred dollars. Both Daughter 1 and my son, as well as a couple volunteers, had access to the drawer, and I began to systematically do random checks on the balance in the register when each worked. Eventually, it was inescapable that the only common denominator to the thefts was Daughter 1.

When confronted, Daughter 1 denied it and we never did get the money back. As soon as she was found out, though, the thefts stopped. Between her being the only common person on the register during each theft, and that the thefts stopped once she was confronted, we knew she had been the one. But we never did get the money back from her, and searching her personal areas did not reveal it.

Sometime in January, 2004, there was a major scandal in Kalispell. One of the town leaders, Dick Dasen – and at least part-owner of the Outlaw Inn – was exposed as running a prostitution ring through the Outlaw Inn and through a couple neighboring hotels in the south part of town. Originally, the newspaper article reported that Dasen and his sons were arrested for the prostitution ring, but within a day or two, the allegations against Dasen's sons were dropped and Dasen alone remained accused. This specifically affected me because my cousin, Kim, happened to be married to Dick's son, Jeremy, even if she did keep her distance from the rest of the family, except for our grandma. I had never met Dick, but I had met Jeremy a couple of times. In spite of this, I never did confront Jeremy over any of this, largely because Kim did keep such an estrangement from the rest of us, but also because I was not free for much longer after this story broke.

Specifically, one part of the story stuck out – that Dasen had a practice of offering young virgins to visiting businessmen, and that he would hold all night "de-virginizing" parties at the Outlaw Inn for this purpose. It also came to light that Dasen had several "kept" girls around town – women whom Dasen paid their bills and such in order to have sexual relationships – and that Chelsea's mom was one such girl. It turned out that the reason Chelsea's mom could always pay her bills while not working was that Dasen was covering them for her.

The only reason any of this was investigated was because the mother of one of the girls from one such party made a report to the state level Child Protective Services. I personally had known about Dasen's prostitutes being run through the Outlaw for years (though not about the minors) since I had known another of Dasen's kept girls, who happened to be the sister of a girl I dated for awhile. And I also knew that the Kalispell Police Department was turning a blind eye to it – in spite of reports – because Dasen was giving the Chief of Police, Frank Garner, and select officers access to the girls for free. I even confirmed this later with one of the prostitutes herself. But what was even more troubling is that apparently reports had also been made to the county Child and Family Services for a couple of years, and they had been ignored. Since I knew about the protection racket running through the KPD, I can only assume that someone within that local CFS office was also getting some kind of perk for their assisting the cover-up.

At the time this story broke, I was in Goldendale, WA, working on setting up a satellite youth program there. But Mara was still in Kalispell, and I still had quite a few contacts in town to follow this issue up, especially when it became obvious that this affected Daughter 1. According to officials in the Child and Family Services who were investigating the complaint, the common practice for the "de-virginizing" parties was for Dasen to gather a group of young, virgin girls, dress them up in make-up and nice clothes, and then present them to businessmen who were visiting from out of town. The girls who participated would be held overnight to help cover-up any physical signs and in the morning were supposed to be paid for their cooperation and silence. Presumably, this is what Chelsea was talking about when she mentioned "party favors" that Daughter 1 missed out on because she left early.

Now, having given all the facts, it is necessary to go into speculation of what really happened. I do not like doing it this way, but since Daughter 1 has denied all efforts to answer what happened the night of the party, though, all we have is conjecture. And all of this is critically important to Daughter 1's motivations. We know for a fact that *something* happened that night – since if nothing else, the swimming issue could not be explained away – but whenever Mara or I would try to get Daughter 1 to answer questions, she just clammed up. But it was not for the better part of a year until the final clue – the issue with Dasen's child prostitution parties – came to light that let us assemble the likelihood of what happened that night.

With this new information, it seems pretty obvious what happened that night – but again, it is just reasonable conjecture. We may never know what really happened in full detail that night unless someone steps forward and provides the specific details.

And my reports of this to CFS were clearly ignored, I imagine in light of Daughter 1 by that time already being used as a pawn against me.

Once it was revealed that Dasen had hosted child sex parties at the Outlaw Inn, it became obvious that Daughter 1 had been invited to one by Chelsea's mom, since she was, after all, one of Dasen's "girlfriends" in the community. Now this is not to say that Dick Dasen specifically participated or even had anything to do with this individual party – clearly the staff were involved, since they had been acting so shady that night, as well. But it was too much of a coincidence that the description of Dasen's parties provided to me by CFS fit the evidence of that night to completely dismiss that possibility.

What now seems obvious is that Chelsea used her associations through the middle school, friends and any attractive girls she thought would be interested, and invited them to an overnight party under the pretense of it being her birthday party, excluding friends who would not have appealed to these businessmen (after all, a chevalier does not offer ugly prostitutes to his clientele). In reality, it was an adult party – which was why the background noise in the room sounded more like a bar when I spoke with Chelsea's mom that night. The girls would have been dressed up with makeup and nice clothes and presented to these adult men.

Apparently, at some point in the night, Daughter 1 no longer wanted to participate. The experience so traumatized her that she wanted to come home, and – if Chelsea's mom's reaction was any indication – her call to be picked up was done in secret. Once I arrived, people started scrambling to try to cover things up. At this point, I don't think the clerk's first call was to the room, at all – I believe it was to whoever the second clerk was that came up a few minutes after he got off the phone, ie, calling for backup.

For whatever reason, they did not actually call the room until my second time talking to the clerk. At that time, Chelsea's mom did not even seem aware that I was out in the lobby and certainly did not know that Daughter 1 had called to be picked up. At this point, she began trying to talk me into leaving Daughter 1 until morning, but only after she kept talking to someone away from the phone for suggestions. And when I asked to talk to Daughter 1, she apparently felt trapped and hung up on me.

Whoever the culprits of this party were, they spent the next twenty minutes cleaning Daughter 1 up. They bathed her – probably washing off makeup and, if there was blood, trying to clean this up, as well. Daughter 1 was clearly told to say she had gone swimming with a suit borrowed from Chelsea to explain why she was wet. This is why Daughter 1's skin and hair were so freshly wet when she came into the lobby. The whole process must have been rushed, as they did not even wait long enough for Daughter 1 to properly dry off.

Evidence suggests that all of this happened after Daughter 1 had sex, though. Mara had been molested herself as a child by her older brother, and reported that within a couple days of being raped for the first time that she started her first period. I also spoke with medical doctors and confirmed that it is very common for per-menstrual young girls to start menstruating after having sex for the first time. Daughter 1's own menstruation conforms with the premise that she had been engaged in sex the night of the party – whether voluntarily or forced remains in question.

Another factor that Mara and I consider to confirm this premise is the missing money from Arcadia in the following month. As Mara pointed out to me, a couple hundred dollars would be what an abortion would cost. Daughter 1 had never stolen before, and never after, to the best of my knowledge. But something compelled her to steal over two hundred dollars from the family's business right after this party – which means that she was either involved in very short-lived and high-cost drug habit or she was paying for something really important – like an abortion to help hide what had happened to her the night of the party. Or possibly to another of her friends.

Although this is all a long and drawn out story that would on the surface seem unrelated to the premise of this book, it does actually relate.

Remember that the day of personal infamy for me was July 9, 2003, which was five days after Independence Day on July 4th. A couple of days before the holiday, Mara and I had been sitting around talking about plans for the holiday with our kids. In spite of the Nezats still being around, Mara really did not like spending time with them on most holidays, though I remember that was a particularly strong resistance that year to the idea of spending the holiday with them (never did learn why, though I imagine it might have had something to do with their spreading negative gossip about me, something Mara was keeping from me at the time).

In rejecting Mara's family, we turned to talking about mine. I said I likewise did not want to spend the holiday with my own mom, to which Mara asked about my grandmother. I responded that it was more likely that my grandma would be spending the holiday with "Kim and the Dasens".

As soon as I said this, I remember Daughter 1 jerking straight up and asking in a shocked tone, "You're related to Dick Dasen?" I told her I was through marriage, that my cousin Kim was married to his son, Jeremy. Daughter 1's only reaction that I recall was, "Oh." But it was clear that something about it bothered her, though it just did not stand out at the time as significant. Yet she had reacted to the Dasen name, and on her own came up with "Dick Dasen".

Now keep in mind that I had been around Mara and her daughter for years and know I had mentioned this before. It was not a secret, nor anything that had been kept from Daughter 1. In fact, she had met Jeremy before when my Uncle Mark, Kim's dad, had considered hiring her at his insurance office. Kim and Jeremy had pulled up outside the office and I have a specific memory of introducing Daughter 1 to them. It was not like we hung out with the Dasen's, but there was no way that Daughter 1 did not know this. Yet clearly it was something she had forgotten.

But of particular note was that I had said, "Kim and the Dasens", and Daughter 1's question was *specifically* about Dick Dasen. Now, I cannot recall whether there had ever been a conversation about Dick specifically around Daughter 1, but the fact that I mentioned Kim and her married family, and Daughter 1's shock was related to someone who had not even been named, it seems there was something about the Dasen name that clicked that connection. And as it had been mentioned innumerable times in the past, it had to have been some kind of recent issue that made it so poignant to her.

I remember at the time that Daughter 1's reaction had shocked me, but like so many other seemingly unimportant issues, it fell into the recesses of memory without any real reason to dwell upon. At least, not until I was forced to go through my memories looking for reasons for everything that had happened after-the-fact.

The first real sign of concern I had was sometime in May or June, 2003, but even with that hanging in my mind in July, the Dasen issue still did not stand out. Remember, none of these individual instances raised any greater concerns because I thought each instance was isolated, and in most cases, any concerns I had I thought were quickly resolved.

But in May or June, Mara said something that raised personal concern. Specifically, she asked me to promise her that if Mara and I ever broke up, I would not date Daughter 1 when she was older. I have to admit – the request came completely out of left field and I was flabbergasted by it. It did not have any conversation leading up to it other than, "Can I ask you something?"

I remember that my first thought was that Mara was planning to break up with me – the significance of Daughter 1 being included in the request escaped me for a moment. So my first response was defensive – I told Mara that if we were broken up, she had no say who I would or would not date. Then as I realized that she was specifically asking me not to date Daughter 1, my reaction shifted to the defense that I could never conceive of a point where I would even be presented with that possibility. After all, in what reality would Daughter 1 and I even be associating if Mara and I broke up?

Again in hindsight, I realize Mara must have been seeing more in Daughter 1's behavior than I was. Mara had always been insecure in our relationship, though – always concerned about the possibility of my ex-girlfriend, Melissa, reappearing and me leaving to be with her again. There was also another friend, Carmen, whom I had admitted to pursuing at the time Mara and I got together, but nothing had ever come of that – though this did not stop Mara from being afraid that if Carmen ever expressed an interest, I would for some reason leave Mara for her. Ironically enough, in the latter instance, Carmen had told me after I started dating Mara that if we ever broke up, Carmen wanted to be with me – but I did not leave Mara for Carmen, so obviously these fears were misplaced.

And this was how I saw Mara's request about Daughter 1 – this was an unreasonable manifestation of fear that now had come to encompass even her own daughter as a threat to our staying together. It was not any more true than the prospect of my leaving her for another woman, but it was still a fear Mara had, apparently. Even more ironically though, it was Mara who ultimately cheated and left me, not the other way around.

At any rate, Mara only brought this up once, and it was something I dismissed from my mind. She did not express to me the reasons for her fears, and admittedly, I am drawing a conclusion based upon information I have reflected upon since. Mara herself never did explain this beyond that night.

Do not get me wrong – I saw the affection Daughter 1 had towards me, but I never saw it as overly inappropriate at the time. I understood what it was like to have a teenage crush, and the last thing I wanted to do was hurt her feelings. I felt it was an innocent affection that was harmless, actually believing that calling her out for her affection would hurt more through embarrassment than any unrequited affection on my part would do.

There was also the issue that I was not alone in her affections, either. Or at least, I was not alone in her *perceived* affections. Daughter 1 was very popular with the teenage boys at Arcadia, and she had begun to accept tokens of affection from them. There was clearly no real interest in her towards the boys, but she seemed to have to no trouble accepting gifts from them. This prompted the necessity of my having to take her aside around this time and tell her that this was not appropriate conduct, that unless she had real feelings towards someone, it was not right for her to take gifts and give them false hope. I remember that this conversation was the first of several I had to have with Daughter 1 about inappropriate conduct over the next few weeks though.

It was a couple weeks later that my own denseness was pierced by Daughter 1's behavior. We were in the basement of Arcadia for a reason I do not recall, but while we were down there talking, Daughter 1 leaned into me for a hug, which – as I have mentioned – was not all that uncommon. My placement in the room though was that I was close up to the wall and her hug was forceful enough, that it pushed me back into it. I am not saying she shoved me into the wall, only that the wall was close enough that when she leaned into me strongly, it was natural for me to fall back against the wall.

As she realized I could not back out of the hug, Daughter 1 pulled me tighter still, and buried her head into my chest. I recall it striking me that she must be upset over something, and so I returned the hug, not really sure what was bothering her, but silently letting her hug me. In hindsight, this would have been a few weeks after the April incident, so in hindsight I believe there could have been a connection – but if there was, it is something I can only guess at.

It was not until I realized that she was pressing her groin into mine that I first became concerned. I noted it, but did not immediately see anything untoward in it. I honestly thought she was just trying to get closer, and dismissed my initial concern.

But the first push was followed by her actually moving her groin against me, and that did raise a concern, since my body actually began to react to it. This worried me greatly, since I had never before had a sexual reaction to her closeness, but here with her grinding her warmth against me, my body reacted unconsciously. I realized then, as now, that I had no control over this reaction, but it still bothered me a lot. It still bothers me as I write this, in fact. It is disturbing to have your body react in a way you have no control over, and in this instance, it was completely contrary to anything I could ever have wanted.

I will admit that I was shocked, both by the obvious sexual advance Daughter 1 was making, and I spent several seconds in confusion trying to figure out whether she even knew what she was doing. But after I recovered from this confusion, I remember telling her that I was supposed to be her stepfather and this was not appropriate. She then backed away and we left the basement.

The whole thing continued to bother me, though, and I went to a mutual friend of Mara's and mine, Carrie Beth Mountjoy, to talk about it. I told her what had happened in the basement and that I was really bothered by my own unconscious reaction to Daughter 1's proximity. Carrie Beth assured me I had done nothing wrong, and that Daughter 1 was maturing into the kind of girl I was often attracted to – a slim, petite young woman – so even on an unconscious level, it made sense that I would react to Daughter 1 pressing up against me in that way. Carrie Beth said she would talk to Daughter 1 about it, and I agreed that this was probably the best way to handle it.

A few nights later though, something else happened. I never did find out whether Carrie Beth had talked to Daughter 1 before this or not, but it was clearly related to what had happened in the basement. Around this time, our family's schedule was pretty tight. We would drive into town at 5 a.m., and not get home until ten-thirty or eleven at night. We had enough time each night for either the girls or my son to take a bath and get ready for bed, so we alternated them on the nights. Because Daughter 2 was five and needed someone to help bathe her, and to save time, she took her bath with Daughter 1.

It was on a night a couple nights removed from the basement incident when the girls were in the bathroom for their bath that this happened. As Mara and I lay in bed waiting for the girls to finish, Daughter 2 came rushing out of the bathroom wrapped in a towel crying that there was a large spider in the tub. Without hesitation, I jumped out of the bed and raced into the bathroom to remove the arachnid (I don't kill spiders unless I know they might be poisonous, and this was just a large sand spider).

I picked up a cup and collected the spider, and turned to take it out of the bathroom. But what I saw shocked me for a moment – Daughter 1 was standing behind the door so that only I could see her. But she was completely nude, without a stitch of clothing and making no effort to cover herself! Towels were hanging behind her on the door, so it was not that she could not reach for a towel – she *wanted* me to see her like that. Both girls knew that Mara would not come in to take care of the spider – since Mara was deathly afraid of spiders – and so she knew that I would be the one who came in. And she had to have spent the several minutes while I was engaged getting a glass and then collecting the spider just standing there. Completely naked and *waiting* for me to see her.

Of course, none of this really occurred to me at the time. I just thought she had not had time to cover herself in time and that it was accidental. But again, with the evidence I at the time ignored and in connection with everything else I later thought back on, it was obviously not as innocent as I originally took it to be.

After a moment's shock, I just turned and left the bathroom and took the spider outside. I returned to bed and did not say anything to Mara, since – yet again – I was trying not to embarrass Daughter 1.

A few nights later, another incident happened at Arcadia, though. At the time, I had been working with Daughter 1 on a game deck idea for a squirrel deck for *Magic: the Gathering*. Mara sat across the table from Daughter 1, and I was sitting beside Daughter 1, helping her with her game play. I was constantly leaning over to look at Daughter 1's cards, and after awhile, this began to hurt my hip and back joints (remember, I have a chronic joint pain disease), and so at one point I tried to lean against Daughter 1's chair, though her leg was so close to the edge of the seat and it was the only thing I could lean on.

My right hand settled on Daughter 1's leg just up from her knee. I was not putting my full weight into the lean, just basically balancing myself so I would take some strain off of my joints as I leaned. I did not actually grab her leg, either; as I recall, initially only my fingers were in contact with her jeans.

As I was focusing on Daughter 1's cards, I was surprised when her hand reached over and grasped tightly to the last two fingers of the hand resting on her leg. This, of course, took away half the weight I was leaning on her leg and so I allowed my palm to rest on her leg instead. Again, I was not too concerned by this, since it was fairly common for Daughter 1 to want to hold my hand.

It was not until Daughter 1 began to pull my hand up her thigh that I became concerned. It was not an immediate concern when I first felt it, as I just thought that maybe my weight was uncomfortable where it was and let her guide my hand to a new position. Again, I was focused on the card game and was not really committing any real concentration to what was going on below the table.

But after a few insistent tugs and pulls, my attention was drawn to what Daughter 1 was really doing – she was trying to draw my hand up towards her groin.

I became very self-conscious since Mara was sitting across the table and I really did not know how to respond to this. I tried to pull my hand gently away, but Daughter 1 had a firm grip on my fingers. She was insistent upon what she wanted, and she clearly did not want to let go of my hand. And as she continued to pull me up her leg, I was really becoming worried. To this day, I don't know what possessed her to try something so brass with her mom sitting across the table, but I will tell you that it was very unnerving.

Finally, I did not have a choice but to pull my hand free forcefully, then – trying to mask what had just happened – I put my arm around the back of Daughter 1's chair as I continued to try to help her finish the game.

But Mara noticed something had happened. As soon as the game was over, Mara took Daughter 1 into a side room to talk. It was not anything sudden or abrupt, but when I saw they were talking alone, I remember entering the room to ask what was going on, and Mara just smiled back saying that she and Daughter 1 were just talking. I shrugged and left.

It was not until later that night that Mara told me what the conversation was about. Mara had indeed noticed something strange when I suddenly pulled my hand from below the table and reached around behind Daughter 1's back. It concerned her enough to pull Daughter 1 aside and ask if I had ever tried to touch her inappropriately, to which Daughter 1 insisted I had not. But – in a typical teenage reaction – she did try to divert blame for the contact at the table, saying sometimes when I touched her, I made her uncomfortable.

Now, keep in mind – ninety percent of physical contact between Daughter 1 and I were initiated by her towards me, not the other way around. I would certainly return a hug or other contact if she initiated it, but I was not normally reaching out to her. So if Daughter 1 were supposedly feeling uncomfortable by contact between us, why was she always trying to make contact with me?

At any rate, this prompted me to have another sit down for the second time with Daughter 1 the next day about what was and was not appropriate. This was within the first week of July, as there were only a few days from this instance and the infamous July 9.

I took Daughter 1 by herself – since I really did not want to embarrass her in front of her mom – and told her what Mara had told me. She admitted to having said that, but I reminded her that I was not the one making most of the physical contact between us, she was. I even reminded her about the basement and what had happened at the table. Daughter 1 acknowledged that sometimes she did not know what was proper and what was not. I told her that if she did not want physical contact between us, I would agree to this – but it required her to not be always sitting in my lap, or holding my hand, or always giving me hugs. She agreed to follow these limitations.

But Daughter 1 did not follow what she agreed to. If anything, her efforts to elicit physical contact from me increased. She was even more affectionate than before, but this time, I was not returning the affection. If she hugged me, I would either act impassively to it or gently push her away. If she tried to hold my hand, I would pull away. There were a couple of times she even tried to sit in my lap. The first time I got back up, but the second time she did so while we were with others, and so I quietly endured it so as not to embarrass her. During these last few days, she was not trying to be sexually intimate, but clearly she was trying to get me to back out of the agreement to not touch her. There was even an instant the morning of July 9 when she was holding onto my arm so tightly that the mother of the boy I was teaching a game to actually made a comment about it.

It should be noted that after my arrest, I tried to get contact information for people who saw this behavior, but it was Mara's refusal to turn over business records after she had been arrested and released herself that barred me from doing so. And of course, while being in jail, I was powerless to find these people on my own.

At any rate, all of these instances led up to July 9 – and though in hindsight, these all seemed important clues, none of their significance impacted me until well after the accusation that destroyed my life.

Chapter 3

There were a couple more thing leading up to the infamous date of July 9, as well as an issue that came up almost immediately after. The first is so closely linked to what happened that day, I have chosen to put it into this chapter rather than the preceding one. But the second, having happened literally years before, did not really fit well into the preceding histories, and so it is being provided here as background. Finally, the third component involves investigations, of a sort, conducted outside the control of the local authorities.

The first specific sequence had to do with the Nezats though rather than anything directly involving anything that revolved around Daughter 1, so perhaps it is better presented separately. This will likely come across as a short aside to the rest, but considering its significance to the overall history, I think it is does deserve its own discussion.

In the latter week of June, 2003, the Nezats began making requests to take Daughter 1 alone to their home for a day. Prior to this point in time, Mara's parents had never asked to see one of their grandchildren alone. In fact, I cannot recall a time when they ever even asked to have both girls out to their place without Mara or I there, either. But before, when they wanted to see their grandchildren, it was always a request to see both. Never before had they ever asked for just one.

The first request raised no real concern, since the Nezats asked for Daughter 1 to visit to help Dixie to do yard work. This seemed a task that Daughter 2 might have been too young for, and Jerry also made the comment that they could not handle both girls while they were working. Again, this seemed reasonable and Mara and I did discuss it. However, since our schedules were so full – leaving home early and coming home late – there just was no time to make a special trip out to the Nezat's home when they would be awake to comply with the request. After telling this to Jerry and Dixie, I had thought this would be the end of the issue.

Obviously, if that *had* been the end, it would not have even been noteworthy. However, we received a similar request two days later – again asking to have Daughter 1 brought out alone, this time to help Jerry with work on their house (they had been building a new home for as long as I knew them, so there was always work to do in that regard). This time however, I was the one who received the request and I remember that not only was there a request for Daughter 1 to visit alone, but Dixie specifically asked in the background of the call for Mara to drive Daughter 1 out there. The significance of this part of the request did not strike me until later, but there was a distinct interest in making sure I was not the one driving Daughter 1 out.

I rejected this new request for the same reason that Mara and I had discussed, that neither of us had time to bring Daughter 1 out. I remember very specifically that Dixie took the phone and argued with me about this, saying that Mara and I both did not need to be at the store to run it – but we did have a tournament that night, so we actually did have to be at the store that night. And so I rejected this argument, as well. I ended the call telling her I would talk to Mara about it and see what she said, but I knew before I asked what Mara's response would be.

Now, in all fairness, Dixie's request was not inaccurate. We did have a tournament that night that both Daughter 1 and Mara regularly participated in, but Daughter 1 had said from the beginning that she liked the idea of visiting her grandparents for the day. It was Mara who really raised the obstruction here with her reasoning that we did not have time when we talked about it.

But the truth is, Mara got off work around 2 pm, and the tournament would not start until six. So there was plenty of time for her to drive Daughter 1 out to her parent's place and be back in time for the tournament – and Daughter 1 wanted to visit her grandparents more than be at the tournament. But it was not an unmanageable thing – it was just something Mara did not want to do, and she would not voice what her real reasons were.

This is not to say that I argued with Mara on this. I agreed with her and went along fully with her decision. And had I known the real truth of what was going on behind the scenes, I would have never even considered Daughter 1 visiting her grandparents. But I did not have all the information, and I simply followed Mara's lead on this.

It was at this point that red flags first started getting raised for me, though. The two different requests – once for gardening and now for help with building the house – were too disparate to be the real reason for the Nezats to want to have Daughter 1 visit. And when I mentioned this thought to Mara, this was also where I first saw Mara being a little hedgy about having Daughter 1 visit her parents. She did not say anything specifically; she just acted a little guarded when it got brought up, especially when I mentioned that her mother wanted her to be the one to drive Daughter 1 out.

Once I learned of the things that Mara had been keeping from me about her parents, this reaction made sense. Clearly, Mara was beginning to see warning signs of prior behavior – and remember, Mara knew about her parents coming into Arcadia to spread malicious rumors about me, as well, so she was already forewarned that her parents had set their target on me. But she chose to remain silent on her real reasons for her reluctance and so I was not given the opportunity to protect myself, as will be explained soon.

At any rate, after this second request, Mara's parents began to call almost every day to ask again – and each time it was with a different request, everything from helping Dixie with chores around the house to picking up scrap wood from trees that had fallen down from winter. And every time after this, the requests were routed through Mara, and each time her only response was that we did not have time to drive Daughter 1 out to their home.

On the morning of July 9, this all came to a head. Since Mara's excuse up to this point had always been that *we* did not have time to drive Daughter 1 out, *the Nezats* decided to come into town to pick her up themselves.

At ten thirty in the morning, I was sitting at a table teaching one of our young players how to play the game, *Warlord: Saga of the Storm*. His mother was sitting watching on his side of the table, and Daughter 1 was sitting at my side, her arms wrapped snugly around my left arm, and her head leaning on my shoulder. At one point, the young man's mother made a comment about Daughter 1 really loving her "daddy", to which I remember commenting that she was not actually my daughter, but that she was really affectionate. Daughter 1 just smiled and snuggled closer.

As a reminder, remember that Daughter 1 had specifically asked for me not to be in close contact with her, that she had told Mara that it supposedly made her uncomfortable. This, of course, had been in response to Mara pressing her about her conduct under the table while playing a game a few nights before this, and her conduct since – increasing her amount of personal contact with me – pretty much showed that this was not what she really wanted. She only said that, it seems, to satisfy her mother's concerns.

I obviously do not know what was specifically said between mother and daughter on that night, but Daughter 1's reaction was not what her actions demonstrated in the days that followed, so clearly she had felt pressured in some way to ask for the contact to stop. Upon reflection, I can see Mara confronting Daughter 1 about her own attentions towards me and trying to have her daughter stop doing so. Remember, Mara had recently confronted me about some imagined future where Daughter 1 and I would possibly date, so clearly she was threatened by her own daughter's affections towards me. So this does not seem too inconceivable to me.

However, in compliance with Daughter 1's request, I had largely stopped returning the affection. I did my best not to call her out in front of others – and Daughter 1 quickly learned that she could be more expressive towards me around others because I would not do this. If we were alone, I could rebuff her, but I could not do the same thing in public without embarrassing her.

This was what was going on that morning – Daughter 1 was taking advantage of my being in front of a young man and his mother to affectionately hold onto my arm and lean on my shoulder, knowing I could not ask her to stop without openly embarrassing her. To this day, I honestly believe she was still trying to make some kind of advance on me in the last few days, and she was trying to get my forgiveness with the increased amount of affection she was directing towards me. Though none of this latter day affection was at all sexual like it had been before, it was most definitely more than she had ever directed to me before.

Regardless of whether I was embarrassing her, though, I think it was also pretty obvious that I was rejecting her, as well. No matter how much she leaned into me, sat on my lap or whatever else, I made a point of not returning it as I had before. I had told her I would not, and no matter how unbalanced that was with her, I was committed to keeping my word not to. I will admit that it was quickly approaching a point when I knew I would need to have another (third) sit-down alone with Daughter 1. At the time

I was just hoping (naively) that she would just get the message and stop.

Of course, this was the morning destined to change everything – so that opportunity never came.

Shortly after ten thirty that morning, the Nezats showed up at Arcadia, making their request to have Daughter 1 visit alone again. This time, I seem to remember that the request was just to "help out" Dixie with things needing to be done around the house, so it was essentially the chores request being recycled. Both girls were of course excited to see their grandparents, but when they made the request to have Daughter 1 go out alone, Daughter 2 started to cry. This did not dissuade Mara's parents though – they were insistent upon taking Daughter 1 only.

There was some effort to console Daughter 2, as I recall, but it was only lip service – promising that next time they would take Daughter 2, instead. But it was really dismissive in the way it was said, so even at the time I knew it was only designed to placate Daughter 2.

Daughter 1 was extremely excited at being able to go out to spend the day with her grandparents, though to be honest, I still do not know whether it was just excitement to got out there or to get away from the chores her and my son were assigned to help around the store. Since both John and Daughter 1 were teenagers, Mara and I had agreed to give them small tasks around the business to help organize – mostly just sorting cards. But Daughter 1 had always balked at being asked to work at anything, which is one reason it was so surprising that she wanted to go work for her grandparents.

This was the point where red flags really went up for me. Something was not right here – not only had Mara's parents shown up on their own at a time they *knew* Mara would be at her day job, there was just something in the way they were acting that raised my hackles. I have a very distinct memory of the hairs on the back of my neck going up and a shiver going down my spine when they asked me if they could take Daughter 1. Even after I agreed, I remember a distinctly sick feeling in my stomach.

I should have listened to my senses that day, but I did not. I knew something was going on, that there was something no one was telling me. But I had no reasonable excuse to not let the Nezats have their granddaughter. Mara's only objection to Daughter1 going for the day with her grandparents had been that we could not drive her out there – and now her parents had come to town on their own. And since Mara had not given me her *real* reasons, in the end, I just did not have a logical reason to deny the request. And even though I *knew* something was wrong, I just had no way of knowing exactly how *bad* it was going to be.

Daughter 1 was really excited to go, and I have to admit – I liked doing things that made the kids like me. To this day, I can remember how her face was lit up at the prospect of going when she turned to me to get permission – and how elated she was when I said yes. And once I said yes, Daughter 1 bounced up, gave he a huge hug, then raced into the back to get a few things to take with her. And after they had the consent to take Daughter 1, the Nezats wasted no time in taking her, either. Within less than ten minutes of getting permission, they had rushed Daughter 1 out the door and were gone.

As it was related later, the Nezats did not take Daughter 1 immediately home. Mara called me from her work later to let me know the Nezats had brought Daughter 1 into Wendy's for a shake, informing her that they had Daughter 1. I remember Mara's call being more a question of me whether I had really given permission than just telling me. I told her that yes, they had come in and I had let them take Daughter 1. I recall asking, "Why, is there a reason I shouldn't have?" Mara just dismissed this question and got off the phone – but her tone had only stirred up the nebulous sick feeling I had that something was wrong. But again – I had nothing more than a *feeling* to act on, since Mara would not tell me what was really going on. It was pretty clear from Mara's call though that she had not wanted the Nezats to take Daughter 1.

As I have been told, Daughter 1 never actually did any work at the Nezats, either. She initially went to our house (located about half a mile from the Nezat's own home on the same property) to get a few things, then spent the day "playing with [the Nezat's] cat". And while this was going on, Dixie was shadowing Daughter 1 talking to her, though Daughter 1 never relayed what Dixie was talking to her about. This was the only explanation I ever received of what was going on for the first six hours of Daughter 1's visit to the Nezats'.

Meanwhile, Mara and I went about our normal work at the store after she got there after 2 pm. Around 4 pm, we left to set up a new business bank account. And it was upon our return from that venture – just after 5:15 pm – that my world collapsed. And I will be covering these circumstances in much greater detail as this narrative continues.

The other detail that is important to convey about events prior to July 9, 2003, is that Daughter 1 did recant her allegation, and did confess to confusing a suppressed memory with what had really happened. In the next chapter, I will be presenting a verbatim post that I made for public support, wherein this issue is discussed – but I think it's important to talk about it at least briefly first to demonstrate that the information presented in that original plea for help is no longer entirely accurate, as I no longer entirely believe this was a mistaken memory – I believe Daughter 1 may have drawn upon the details of what she witnessed, but I do not believe at this point that she ever truly believed it had happened to her at that point in time.

Basically, when Daughter 1 was three years old, Mara separated from Jared Salois. Jared and Mara had a family friend (whose name I only ever knew as "Shane") who came over one night to offer his "sympathies" over Mara's and Jared's break. Taking Shane's token concern at face value, Mara let him into her home where she and Daughter 1 were.

In short order, Shane's true purpose came to the fore and he attempted to force himself on Mara. Apparently, Shane must have held some attraction for Mara, but while she was with Jared, she had been off-limits. With Jared out of the house, he felt he could have his way with Mara. As reported by Mara, he had not been there long before he grabbed her from behind and tried to force himself on her.

In the course of the struggle, the two ended up on the family couch, with Shane grabbing Mara from behind and reaching with one hand under her shirt, and the other being forced down her pants. No matter how much Mara struggled, she could not break free of Shane's grip.

Daughter 1 witnessed the entire exchange. Shane never had the decency to even make sure Mara's child was out of the room. At first, Daughter 1 huddled to the side of the room, squatting and rocking back and forth, according to Mara. But after a time, Daughter 1 actually got up, took a hard plastic toy ball she had, and smashed it into Shane's head.

As Shane reached to push away or strike Daughter 1, Mara was finally able to break free (with one less arm holding her, she gained leverage, it seems) and she was able to get away from Shane and turn on him. Mara says she at that point turned on him and began hitting and kicking at him, until finally he was beaten unconscious. She then dragged him onto the porch and shut the door. Mara told me that at first, she thought she had killed Shane, but when she looked outside sometime later, he was gone.

As is the case with so many victims of sexual assault, Mara never reported the incident. But considering that Daughter 1 later confirmed the details of the assault, I have no reason to disbelieve Mara about this.

Mara also relayed that Daughter 1 never spoke of the assault, either, but that years later – when at a yard sale, Daughter 1 saw a hard plastic ball identical to the one she had used against Shane. Without any explanation, Daughter 1 took the ball and threw it hard. When Mara asked Daughter 1 why she had done that, Daughter 1 had no explanation. This story was also confirmed by both Daughter 1 and Mara.

Months after Daughter 1 made the allegation against me (conveniently in October, 2003, *after* the original investigations were closed in September, 2003), Mara drew the connection between the description Daughter 1 had been giving about me and what she had witnessed as a child. The details of the assaults described were amazing similar – both occurred on a couch with a hand down the pants and another up the shirt, for instance, not to mention that by pure chance, the pattern on the couch in our office was the same common pattern where Mara's assault happened.

When Mara made this connection, she decided she needed to confront Daughter 1 about it. Mara wanted me present, and at my insistence, we also had another couple of friends present, Jeff Berna and Tasha Bordeaux. By this point, I had absolutely no trust in Daughter 1, and the last thing I wanted to do was give her more ammunition to claim I did something to her. After all, I was acting under the belief that she had already claimed Mara was lying to "protect" me to authorities during the investigation. (Note: It turns out this was just another lie told by law enforcement at that point in time, though later after this time, Daughter 1 did assert a similar claim against her own mother at the bequest of CFS.)

So with four adults present, Mara asked Daughter 1 if she remembered the assault. When Daughter 1 said she did not, Mara began to relate the story in detail. Shortly after Mara began to talk, Daughter 1 sat down against the wall and began to rock back and forth, holding her knees tightly – the exact position Mara later said she was in during the first part of Shane's assault. About halfway through Mara's account, Daughter 1 began to recite the story herself, filling in details Mara had left out. In essence, reminding Daughter 1 of the story brought the memory fully to the surface.

When Mara finished, she pointed out similarities between Shane's assault and the allegation Daughter 1 had made against me. It was at this point Daughter 1, incidentally, remembered that the couch patterns were the same, which Mara confirmed. Then Mara explained what a repressed memory was – about how when someone is traumatized, the memory sometimes is hidden, and that when it does start to come back to the surface, it does not always come out fully. Mara then asked Daughter 1 whether it was possible that this was what had happened here – whether her own memory of Shane's assault had somehow been transferred onto me when only part of the memory returned.

With this information, Daughter 1 did not hesitate – she unequivocally stated, "Ron didn't do this to me." She went on to relate that now that she recalled the memory in full, she knew that it was not me that had done this to her, that the version where she saw me assaulting her was not real – that it was just me superimposed over her memory of Shane.

At this point, though the criminal and CFS investigations were closed, Mara and I still had a lawsuit against her parents for a multitude of malicious things they had been doing towards us after Mara insisted on standing beside me during this fiasco. So I asked Daughter 1 if she would be willing to write a statement clarifying where her allegation had come from, and she agreed to do so.

Keep in mind – at this point, everything I was saying in the lawsuit – and one of the specific claims for damages against the Nezats – was that they had made up the story and made Daughter 1 go along with it. By asking Daughter 1 to write this statement, I was essentially giving the Nezats clemency for one of the claims for damages against them in the suit.

After a few days and Daughter 1 had not provided the requested statement, I asked again. Daughter 1 told me she did not know how to write the statement, and asked me for help. I told her I could help her put it into an affidavit format, but I needed a witness present if I did that. When Daughter 1 agreed, I arranged that night (October 18, 2003) to have Carrie Beth Mountjoy be present in the room while Daughter 1 relayed me details and I transcribed them into an affidavit. There were several different versions created, as each time I printed out a copy, Daughter 1 had a correction she wanted made. But eventually, the copy represented what she said were her true statements, and she signed the document in front of Carrie Beth and I.

Incidentally, later, as her story changed – after she was abducted and threatened by authorities – Daughter 1 claimed that I created this affidavit and forced her to sign it. Daughter 1 insisted that Carrie Beth was never present and that, if Carrie Beth was saying she was there, that Carrie Beth was lying. However, Carrie Beth's own police interview (which is included in Appendix X) clearly establishes that she was there – even though Carrie Beth herself had long since abandoned supporting my innocence, she specifically stated that she was present and that there was no coercion on my part in getting Daughter 1 to sign the affidavit, which consisted of her own statements, not mine.

Sorry to say, this is only one of the many lies Daughter 1 was forced to tell while under threat from the authorities in Kalispell, Montana. I will go into more detail on this later.

The final issue needing clarification here is of Mara's own efforts to seek out the truth. Immediately upon having learning of Daughter 1's allegations against me – even though she herself has said repeatedly that she did not believe them – Mara did the proper and responsible thing in setting up a counselor for Daughter 1 to discuss the alleged sexual assault. The counselor selected as Edith Paxman, a Licensed Clinical Social Worker practicing in Kalispell.

It should be noted that setting Daughter 1 up with counseling was never suggested to Mara by either CFS or the KPD, to the best of my knowledge. Having been a survivor of child and sexual abuse herself, Mara had on her own sought out counseling for Daughter 1 knowing that this was critically important to someone enduring this kind of trauma. Mara had said repeatedly before and after that she did not believe Daughter 1, but irregardless of her personal beliefs, she still set up the appointment promptly to make sure Daughter 1 received whatever support she needed, in the off-chance Mara herself was mistaken. Personally, I think this is one of the best and most mature decisions Mara could have made and in spite of all she did wrong along the way, I believe Mara deserves credit for doing the right thing at this juncture, even if it went against her own beliefs.

However, without being influenced or under the control of either the Nezats or any authorities, Edith's own inquiries into Daughter 1's allegations tore apart her story almost immediately. After just one forty-five minute session with Daughter 1, Edith stated quite frankly that she believed Daughter 1 was lying, as well. And Edith had very specific and clinical reasons for this assessment.

For the record, much of this was relayed to me third-person by Mara, but I was also able to listen in on phone calls between Mara and Edith (with Mara's consent) to help fill in some details. So some of this is second-hand, but it is intermixed with my personally overhearing details from Edith which confirmed the details that Mara related to me.

To begin with, Edith noticed that Daughter 1 related the alleged incident without any trauma or emotion. According to Edith, if Daughter 1 had genuinely been assaulted as she alleged, there would have been tears or some kind of distress visible in Daughter 1's voice, but there was nothing of the kind. In fact, Edith commented that Daughter 1 was actually in an upbeat mood during their interview. Remember, the Nezats claimed that Daughter 1 was crying heavily when she related the story to them, so it was not as if Daughter 1 were somehow emotionally detached – from Edith's account, Daughter 1 told the allegation to her as if it were just a story she were telling.

Another cue that Edith picked up on was that Daughter 1 was using words she did not understand. The example given to me was the word "fondled", ie, I allegedly "fondled" Daughter 1's breasts. Edith asked Daughter 1 if she knew what "fondled" meant, but Daughter 1 could not provide a definition. Then Edith asked Daughter 1 to use it in another sentence, and again Daughter 1 could not. According to Edith, this was not the only such word, but it was the example given to me.

Months later, Daughter 1 made a comment to her aunt, Evonna McCumbers, about this incidentally. Daughter 1 told her aunt that no one believed her because, "Grandma made me use too big of words." This was as close to an admission as anyone ever heard that Daughter 1 had been coached by Dixie Nezat in what to say, but Edith noticed the issue right there at the beginning, which certainly says something for Edith's objectivity.

Notably, Carrie Beth Mountjoy made a similar observation in the weeks that followed about her own conversations with Daughter 1, saying that Daughter 1 was using really big words that were not part of her normal vocabulary when she would talk about the alleged assault with Carrie Beth. I remember Carrie Beth gave me an example, but to be honest, I cannot recall what example she gave me, though it was not "fondled".

The third thing Edith noticed was that Daughter 1's story changed whenever Edith challenged any details in the story. Daughter 1 was apparently quick witted and was always fast in filling in any gap that Edith noticed, but Edith noticed that it Daughter 1's use of these fast-answer fixes could end up contradicting her original story.

For example, according to Edith, Daughter 1's original allegation had no resolution – which is to say that Daughter 1 described that I supposedly touched her, but never said how the incident came to an end. Yet when pressed for details, Daughter 1's filling in the blanks ended up contradicting her own story.

By Daughter 1's account, I – a 35 year old man and fully awake – had encircled her in my arms and was supposedly molesting her – but she had never provided an actual explanation as to how the encounter ended. Apparently, this is an important issue for a victim of assault, as their "survival" of the assault is typically a large part of their recounting. In Daughter 1's case, it was completely absent – all Daughter 1 related was the alleged contact, but not how the contact ended. In other words, did she break away, did I get up and leave, did I just lose interest after the alleged five second foundling, etc? By what Edith told Mara, all Daughter 1 was relating was the story without a resolution for how the story ended. It would be like saying someone shot a gun at you, but offering no explanation as to how you survived (did he miss, did he only wing you, did you have to go in for surgery, etc?).

Noting this hole in Daughter 1's story, Edith asked Daughter 1 how she got away. According to Edith (and this is a conversation I overheard), initially, Daughter 1 was confused by the question, and Edith explained that I was a much larger and stronger person than she was, so if I were doing all this to her, how did the assault stop? Daughter 1 reportedly just said, "I got up and sat in the chair," to which Edith asked, "And he let you?" Daughter 1 simply responded, "Yes." Edith then asked, "What did Ron do about your getting up?" Daughter 1 said, "He just laid there." Next, Edith asked, "Did he talk to you or ask you to come back?", and Daughter 1 responded, "No." So Edith said, "So you just got up, he didn't try to stop you and he didn't say anything after you got up and sat in the chair?", to which Daughter 1 confirmed the details. At this point, Edith asked, "Were his eyes open or closed?" and Daughter 1 responded promptly, "Closed, I guess," to which Edith asked, "Could he have been asleep?" According to Edith, Daughter 1 – by my guess realizing she had been trapped – sunk back into her seat pouting and muttered, "I guess he could have been asleep."

As you may recall, Daughter 1 had insisted from the very beginning of her allegations that I was awake and talking to her. With Edith directing questions to come at it from a different direction – outside the actual context of the story Daughter 1 had been coached into telling – Daughter 1 was caught off guard and made admissions that directly contradicted the original story. Daughter 1 could not explain why I just let her get up and walk away, nor could she explain why I did not try to stop her or bring her back. She tried to fill in plausible answers, ie, he just laid there, and no he did not try to get me to come back (because that would have suggested the assault or attempted assault lasted longer than her original five second claim), but what she ended up doing was contradicting herself. Whereas a normal person drawing upon recollection would have taken a moment perhaps to draw upon the memory, Daughter 1's efforts to fill in the blank were quick and impulsive, without any effort to try to conform them to her original story – which Edith had already found flaws in.

The final detail that Edith provided was statistical information that had no specific relationship to her interview with Daughter 1. As Edith put it, men do not just start molesting children at age 35. This is the kind of deviant behavior that exists in an individual from a young age, and progresses through their lifetime. There had never been an allegation of child molestation against me – by any child, ever – and to suddenly start at age 35 was unheard of. By Edith's account, it was inconceivable for me to have made the decision to molest a 13 year old girl for the first time at age 35, and combined with Daughter 1's own flawed accounting of the alleged assault, Edith was of the opinion that Daughter 1 was lying and that she was being coached to say what she had said.

This, by the way, was one reason I am sure the KPD spent such an inordinate amount of time contacting family and friends during my sixteen month pre-trial incarceration, in an effort to find some prior conduct that would counter this kind of conclusion. But there was no prior conduct anymore than there was a current assault – I was not a child molester then, nor have I ever been, so there was no record to find. I may have some of the worst family members in history, what with their preferring to cast dirt for their own personal ego-stroking, but there was never a credible claim of me ever molesting a child, simply because nothing of the sort ever happened.

Collectively, Edith's opinion was that she did not believe Daughter 1 was being honest because she had no emotional trauma, used words in her story she did not understand, and that she creatively filled in gaps in the story with details that contradicted her original accusations. She further asserted that the fact that I was 35 years old at the first time any such allegation had ever been made greatly diminished the credibility of the accusation, and Edith's own observations of Daughter 1 only supported this standard. And remember – this was Mara who took Daughter 1 to see Edith, not me. I had absolutely no involvement in this exchange, either as a decision-maker or anything else. In fact, to this day I have never even met Edith Paxman. I had no capacity to influence her findings, and therefore her determinations were completely her own.

I also want to connect this to what has previously been related. I have previously detailed how the Nezats had initiated allegations that I had molested Melissa Turner's daughter (disproved by Melissa herself) and that I had supposedly been molesting Daughter 1 for somewhere around a year before the allegation made by Daughter 1 herself. It is completely improbable – with the Nezats creating false stories about me for over a year before this incident, one such story involving Daughter 1 herself – that I would suddenly decide that it was a good idea to do exactly what I had been accused of. It's akin to saying, "So-and-so is a murderer because he shot some guy," then So-and-so going out and shooting someone just because it sounded like a good idea.

I was either a child molester before while the Nezats were claiming I was, or I was not. Since all possible evidence – and according to Edith every psychological paper ever written – demonstrated I was not, something else was going on. And to have the Nezats then involved with Daughter 1's supposed "admission" is extremely questionable – they had already made up two separate stories before that had not been true, but somehow when they can get their granddaughter alone for a night, suddenly they stumble on a *real* case of molestation? Sorry, but it is far more credible that they were looking for a way to continue with their pre-existing efforts to make up an allegation against me – just as they had with so many before me – and they convinced Daughter 1 to go along with it.

The reason I am connecting this is to set up what happened next. After her conversation with Edith about Daughter 1's story, Mara confronted Daughter 1. In the basement of our business, Mara told Daughter 1 what Edith had told her, and asked Daughter 1 why she was doing this. According to Mara, Daughter 1 said, without any preamble, "I want you and my dad back together, and that can't happen if Ron is here." When Mara told Daughter 1 that there had been problems between her and Jared long before I had ever been in the picture, and that there was no possibility – even if I were not around – that she and Jared would ever get back together, Daughter 1 reportedly just burst into tears and was inconsolable. By Mara's description, Daughter 1's reaction was far and above any reasonable response to being told that her mother and father were not going to get together.

Remember, Jared Solois – Daughter 1's natural father – had only recently come back into Daughter 1's life. There was certainly no romantic interest remaining between Mara and Jared, nor had Jared made any efforts to even discuss this with Mara. This idea had been put in Daughter 1's mind by someone – that if I were not with Mara, that Mara could get back together with Jared – and under the circumstances, the only people that had the opportunity or motive to tell Daughter 1 something like that were the Nezats.

Some incentive had to have been offered to Daughter 1 to get her to lie for the Nezats – and with Daughter 1 blurting out to her mother that she was doing this because she wanted her dad back in her life within a week of her original allegation, it seems inescapable that this was the incentive given. As I will relate in the next chapter, it is important to understand that Daughter 1's original agreement to make this accusation against me included a promise from the Nezats to not involve law enforcement. By all accounts, Daughter 1 agreed to cooperate with this story under the promise that it would be used as leverage to get Mara to end our relationship – not to actually escalate it to send me to prison or be convicted of a crime. Unfortunately, when Mara stood up to her parents and told them she did not believe the allegation and would not leave me – even under threat of having the Nezats have her children taken away – the situation escalated and Daughter 1 was swept along in the wake of the criminal case. And once she had made this accusation, clearly Daughter 1 realized she could not back out of it without getting into trouble herself.

Having set forth all of this, it is now time to relate the specific events of July 9, 2003.

Chapter 4

Some of this chapter will be redundant, I am sure. But there is a sequence of events that specifically happened on July 9, 2003, that goes beyond the simple allegation made against me. There were many subtle nuances and issues of the evening that cast quite a bit of color to the background of the allegation, and I believe it is important enough to provide a single chapter where this day's events can be read in one place.

As mentioned previously, prior to July 9, Mara's parents, Jerry and Dixie Nezat, had spent weeks trying to get their eldest granddaughter, Daughter 1, alone at their house. They had spent well over a year before this trying to spread malicious rumors that I had been molesting other children, as well. So this day did not just happen randomly – the Nezats did not just happen to have come into town and taken their granddaughter out to their house as part of a normal routine. This was deliberate and it was premeditated, and it was so out of their normal pattern of behavior, that even Mara was not willing to let them take Daughter 1 under the circumstances. But I did not know Mara's reasons because she chose not to share them, and I had no reason not to allow this, and so I gave them permission to take her.

Incidentally, if I had been molesting Daughter 1 as the Nezats had been alleging, one would think I would not want her alone with her grandparents in the first place. After all, people who actually commit sexual assaults operate from a position of control and manipulation, and they do not let others have control over their victims if they have any say in the matter. But the Nezats came to me specifically and I did not try to stop them from taking Daughter 1 – hardly the conduct of someone trying to keep secret the molestation of a child. But I digress.

The morning of July 9, 2003, was a common Wednesday – we had come into town that morning and Mara had gone on to work as normal. As a reminder, we came into town around 5:30 am so Mara could open Wendy's, leaving myself and the children (Mara's daughters and my son, John) at the store. The kids had gone to sleep separately, and as I recall, I think John came back to watch some cartoons in the office where I was resting, but the girls had slept until I woke them around 9:30 am as we got ready to open the store around 10. Incidentally, being as it was summertime, none of the kids would lay under blankets with me on the couch at this time – that had stopped sometime in April as the weather warmed up. This is significant about an element of Daughter 1's allegation, which will be clarified later.

Roughly a half hour after opening the business for the day, a couple of our regular customers – a mom and her son whose names now escape me – came in to take me up on promises of free lessons in a game called *Warlord: Saga of the Storm*. A card game lesson can typically take as long as an hour, so they had come in early in the day so the son could have the time to learn and then play the game some with others. Our store was arranged with several long tables, and so the mom and son sat on one side, while I sat down on the opposite side.

Within a few minutes of beginning the lesson, Daughter 1 came over and began watching the lesson, and soon thereafter entwined her arm around mine and leaned into me. I distinctly remember the mother commenting that Daughter 1 "really loved her Daddy", and I had commented that she really was not my daughter, but that Daughter 1 was really affectionate.

As readers of the previous chapters will know, at this point, Daughter 1 had told her mother that *my* physical contact was making her "uncomfortable" and I had spoken with Daughter 1, telling her that since she was the one who most often initiated these kinds of contact, that she needed to not do that. I agreed to not hug her or reach out to her, but she had to agree not to, as well. She agreed at the time, but that did not last through the day of the agreement before she was doing things like what she was doing that morning – coming up to me and hanging on me, sitting on my lap, or just generally being close and touching me in various different ways.

Daughter 1 was an incredibly bright girl, as well. She quickly learned that if we were alone, I could shrug off her contact, but that I was far less inclined to do so if we were around other people. I think she must have known on some level that I was reluctant to just outright embarrass her, so she could be amorous towards me when we were in the store around customers much more than she could be if we were alone. And this is precisely what she was taking advantage of that morning – she was wrapped around my arm and leaning into my shoulder for close to fifteen minutes before the Nezats came that morning – and she even snuggled tighter when the mom across the table commented about how she really loved her "Daddy". But short of calling her out publicly, I felt all I could do was endure the attention until I could once more talk to her alone.

Another important thing to note here is that Daughter 1's behavior is not typical of someone who is supposedly been assaulted. Daughter 1 as soon as that evening insisted that she was "scared" of me, and that she was terrified at the prospect of being alone with me. And yet that very morning, she was leaning on me and showing very open affection. This is another indication of her coaching – clearly, she was told she either needed to or at the very least *say* she was afraid of me in order for her story to have come kind of impact.

Maybe it was just a reaction to something the Nezats told her, like, "If you say this, you know Ron is going to hurt you," or perhaps it was just an internal fear that she knew she was lying and she was afraid of some kind of consequence because of her years of physical abuse from her adopted father, Tim Pelton. Or maybe it was something that was manufactured as part of her scripted story. It is hard to say, since I have never been given a satisfactory answer for this blatant contradiction. But it is important to note how contrary Daughter 1's actual behavior was from what she said later that night.

At any rate, at 11 am that morning, Jerry and Dixie showed up at the store, coming in through the rear door. They knew that Mara worked at Wendy's until 2 pm during the week, so they were well aware that I would be at the store alone with the children. It was fairly obvious that they had come into town (more than a half hour drive) with the specific intention of picking up Daughter 1 – after barely five minutes of pleasantries, they were already asking to take Daughter 1 with them.

When they came in, it could not have escaped their attention that Daughter 1 was snuggling into my shoulder, either. The way we were sitting, Daughter 1 and I were facing the front of the store – since the Nezats came in through the back entrance, they were able to approach us unseen since the back door is not always able to be heard from the front of the store.

As a basic idea of the store's layout, there were two rooms between the back door and the front of the store, an entryway and then a kitchenette area, which together took up perhaps a hundred feet. The back office, which figures prominently into this history, opened off the back entryway and did not connect with the rest of the store, except that windows from old construction existed between the office and bathroom (ie, no real privacy in the office – the office was an add on to the building and the original back windows were still in place along the original brick wall).

Though the doors between the entry, kitchenette and front of the store were routinely kept open (since deliveries sometimes came in through the back door), it was possible to enter the back of the store without anyone in the front knowing – and this is what the Nezats did that morning. Whether they deliberately entered quietly, or my involvement in teaching the game distracted me so that I did not hear them, I could not say – but what I can say is that neither Daughter 1 nor I knew that the Nezats were in the store until they announced themselves after entering the front area of the store, behind both Daughter 1 and I. Which meant there could not possibly have been any misunderstanding of the open affection Daughter 1 had been displaying towards me – something I am certain must have irritated them as it underscored the stories they had been trying to spread about me.

As soon as Daughter 1 heard her grandparents, she immediately leaped up in excitement to greet them. It was not uncommon to have the Nezats drop in and visit with their granddaughters while they were in town, yet Jerry made a comment as part of his greeting this time that they had just gotten into town when they dropped by. Jerry did claim that they had errands to run before leaving town, but this proved to be a lie, as I will elaborate soon.

As I explained, niceties were exchanged and I provided introductions to our customers as I excused myself to speak with the Nezats, while they immediately moved to sit at the back table closest to the door where they entered the front room. Their demeanor was good-natured, and there certainly was nothing in their manner to suggest that they had any ulterior motive to drop by. Only in hindsight did the idea that they had dropped by before their errands asking to take their granddaughter stood out – as I said, it was not uncommon for them to drop by while in town, but it was almost always in the afternoon *after* they had run errands and after Mara had arrived from her job at Wendy's.

Of note, later in the afternoon was also the time period where it was most likely that I would be out running errands for the store, and the Nezats could spread their dissent amongst our clientele without my knowing, which is another reason they would never come by in the mornings when only I was running the store. Dropping by in the morning, before Mara was there, was unheard of – but it was not something that stood out to me at the time. I suppose the idea that they were there to get just one of their granddaughters was the one oddity that overshadowed everything else.

It is obvious now that their coming by in the morning – when *Mara* would not be there – was a calculated maneuver. They must have known that Mara would not let them take Daughter 1 alone, and in spite of all the garbage they spouted about me, they knew I was a very amenable person. This is why when Jerry or Dixie wanted to "borrow" money (I emphasize this because lending money to the Nezats was always a one-way exchange – I never actually ever got paid back for what was borrowed), they would always ask to talk to me alone rather than with Mara present. I was the easier mark – the one who was more likely to acquiesce to their requests. Ironic in a way, considering how far they went to convince others that I was a deviant.

As I mentioned, Jerry offered a brief explanation that they had come into town to run "errands", which they intended to do on the way out of town. But without missing a beat, Jerry said that since they were in town, they thought they could drop by and pick up Daughter 1, since Mara and I had not been able to drop her off ourselves. The excuse offered was that Dixie – who did in fact have health issues – needed help with gardening work, and they needed Daughter 1 to help her. And Dixie herself made a point of saying that they *were* her grandparents and had the "right" to pick up their granddaughter if they wanted to. There was a definite undertone suggesting that I did not have any right to refuse their request (since after all, I was just the boyfriend), but at the time I was not sure if it was intentional or not. Upon reflection, after what happened later, I now clearly believe it was.

Daughter 1's younger sister wanted to come along, but Dixie immediately interrupted the little girl (who at the time was six years old, I believe) and told her that Daughter 1 and her had to do "hard work" and that they could not watch Daughter 2. Daughter 2 was heartbroken and began to cry, to which Dixie promised to take her "next time". Ignoring Daughter 2's continued tears, Dixie turned to me and asked again if they could take Daughter 1. Daughter 1 herself was bouncing with excitement and asked me also if she could go.

I have mentioned before and I reiterate here. Something raised my hackles at this point, and the intensity with which Dixie stared at me when she asked raised an inner red flag for me. I remember hesitating for a second or two, trying to reason out what could be wrong with the request, but I could not think of any reason to deny it. Ultimately, it was Daughter 1's excitement to go that was my deciding factor – she really wanted to go, and I did not really want to disappoint *her*.

And so I agreed.

As anyone reading this must know, this was the tipping point – this was point at which things could have been completely avoided, if only I had known a fraction of what the Nezats' past conduct had been. But in spite of the bad feelings I had about the situation, I had no reasonable justification to deny the Nezat's request. It bothered me how they snubbed Daughter 2 in their zeal to get me to agree to take Daughter 1, it bugged me that I had a gut reaction that something was wrong with the whole situation, but I just had no logical reason to say no – and logic won out. In hindsight, I should have gone with my instincts that something was wrong, but I did not. And as consequence, I gave leave to the Nezats to obliterate my entire life.

At any rate, once permission was obtained, the Nezats wasted no time in rushing Daughter 1 from the store. I recall that Daughter 1 wanted to get a few things before leaving, and Dixie told her to hurry as "Grandpa wanted to get going." Within a couple of minutes of getting my leave to take Daughter 1 with them, they were all three gone from the store. In total, I believe the Nezat's visit could not have lasted more than ten or fifteen minutes, to be honest. Once again, very unusual, as they had never before been in such a hurry to get away as they were that day.

And of course, they left with Dixie barely giving more than a cursory hug to the crying Daughter 2, leaving me to find a way to comfort her after they were gone. Needless to say, the lesson was sidetracked as I spent the next half hour with my son and I trying to console Daughter 2.

At this point, the Nezats made a beeline for home, stopping only long enough at Mara's work to let her know that they were taking Daughter 1 with them – Daughter 1 later related that they only stopped in the first place because *she* wanted to talk to her mom and get something to eat. Had Daughter 1 not made the request, the Nezats would have simply driven Daughter 1 straight to their house without pause.

Remember, Jerry had specifically said they had come into town to run errands and was picking up Daughter 1 before running them. However, as soon as they *had* Daughter 1, there was no stopping to do anything other than meeting Daughter 1's request to get something to eat and talk to her mom before leaving. Also, as I pointed out in an earlier chapter, this visit prompted Mara to call me, challenging whether the Nezats had really gotten my permission to take Daughter 1. I mentioned before and I reiterate here – there was something in the way Mara asked that suggested I had done something wrong, but of course, Mara would not elaborate.

By Daughter 1's later recounting, there was never actually any work done at the Nezat's house. Basically, Daughter 1 was given free reign to run around the house and property and play all day, with the exception that Jerry apparently took Daughter 1 by our house to get a few things of hers. The door had been locked, but Daughter 1 had revealed to Jerry how to open her bedroom window, a fact that became relevant later on.

Daughter relayed that she spent part of the day chasing the Nezat's cat, but otherwise provided nothing specific about what she did all day – however the one thing she did say repeatedly was that Dixie was always following her, talking to her. But when asked what Dixie was saying, Daughter 1 would never answer – she would just shrug and say, "I don't know." Knowing Daughter 1 as I did, I knew this was not a case of her not remembering – it was her way of avoiding talking about something she did not want to.

Meanwhile, the day for me at the shop proceeded pretty routine. It never crossed my mind to worry about anything, or to think that anything foreboding was on the horizon. I worked at the store, kept the kids (customers and our own alike) entertained, and sorted cards. When Mara got off work at 2 pm, she did only asked briefly if I had heard from Daughter 1, which I had not. Otherwise, even Mara seemed content with going about daily routine around the store.

Around 4:30, Mara and I left to go set up a new bank account. Our business accounts with the bank we were with had been problematic, and we were switching banks. We left Carrie Beth Mountjoy in charge of the store and we were gone for approximately forty-five minutes.

When Mara and I returned around 5:15 pm, Carrie Beth gave us a message that Dixie had called. In hindsight, I remember Mara having a panicked look on her face as she asked Carrie Beth if something was wrong. Carrie Beth said there was nothing wrong, and that Dixie had even specifically told her, "It's nothing important. Just have her call when she gets back."

As an aside, I have no idea why Mara got the panicked look on her face. Whether she had a suspicion all along that this was what her parents were up to, or whether she thought something might have happened to Daughter 1, I cannot say. To be honest, with everything else that came piling down upon us immediately after, I never did ask her about it. I know she had not wanted Daughter 1 alone with the Nezats – though I did not connect the dots at the time. Mara's constant reasoning not to have Daughter 1 go with the Nezats, coupled with the Nezats' obvious circumventing Mara to get permission, pretty much told that story. Plus there was the call to me from work to ask if I really let Jerry and Dixie take Daughter 1. Now with the panicked expression, I think Mara was fearful of what her parents were up to – but she would not tell me, and because she did not, she left me vulnerable.

Mara did a couple of small things, as I recall, then called Dixie. I do not believe more than five minutes passed between arriving back and Mara placing the call. I had gone up front at first, then gone into the back to get something and remember Mara sitting down in the middle room with a shocked look on her face. I remember stopping at looking at her puzzled just as she said, "I want to talk to [Daughter 1]. I want her to tell me this herself." At that point, a feeling of dread overtook me – I knew something was clearly wrong, and I was fearful of what had happened. I had no clue that it involved an allegation against me, but I could tell something was really, really wrong.

At any rate, Mara waved me away to talk privately and I returned to the front of the store. It bothered me incredibly that whatever was going on, Mara was not wanting to que me in on it, and it was as I sat in the front room that I began to get an inkling that something had been said about me. Call it a paranoid instinct, or simple reasoning, but as my mind raced over what was happening, it seemed inescapable that the discussion between Mara and her mother was about me. Even my imagination though could not go so far as to create what was really being said – but it was then that I began to realize that Dixie and Jerry were up to something, and it was some kind of plot against me.

In about fifteen minutes, with several moments when Mara's voice could be heard even behind the closed door, I went back into the middle room. Mara looked up at me and said, "I need to talk to Ron about this and I'll call you back." She then hung up and walked me back out to the front room, where Carrie Beth waited.

With Carrie Beth and I both there, Mara revealed what had been said. Dixie had immediately told Mara upon getting on the phone that she needed to pack up all of her and the girls' belongings and move out of her house and into the Nezats', that she needed to get as far away from me as possible or the Nezats would call CFS on her (Keep in mind, the threat *preceded* any kind of explanation). When Mara asked why she was saying that, Dixie blurted out that I had molested Daughter 1 and that neither Mara nor her daughters were safe around me, then repeated the threat. Mara says she told her mom that she was not going to just move out of her home, and she wanted to hear this from Daughter 1 (the point in the conversation I overheard). Dixie refused to let Mara talk to her daughter, and Mara says that most of the conversation consisted of arguing with Dixie to let her talk to Daughter 1. When Mara told her mom that she was going to drive out there to see Daughter 1, Dixie told her she could not come to see her daughter, and Mara says Jerry's voice yelled from the background that he would shoot anyone – including Mara – if they tried to come out to their house.

As I understand it, that first phone call only contained some small details – that I had "felt up" Daughter 1 while lying on the couch in the back office. No time frame, no suggestion of exactly had supposedly happened. Just barely more than that I had molested Daughter 1 and that Mara and her daughters needed to move into the Nezats' house immediately.

As I heard all of this, I was stunned. I of course knew I had never molested anyone – much less Daughter 1. I *worked* with kids every day, and this was absolutely the *last* thing I could ever imagine doing. And I had just cleared myself (with Mara) of the false allegation against me about Melissa's daughter a few months before, so I genuinely thought this nonsense was done and over with. (As the reader may recall, at this point, we had no idea who had actually started that rumor – we had originally thought it was Melissa, but Melissa herself exonerated me, and it would still be weeks from this point when we learned that it had actually been Jerry Nezat).

I remember opening my mouth to talk, and then I became intensely aware that we were standing in the front room of the store. There were a few people in the front, but no one was close enough to hear anything, but I immediately realized we did not need to be speaking about this up front. With this in mind, I quickly turned and led Mara and Carrie Beth into the back office. As I walked quickly to the back, I remember thinking to myself that I needed to say something – but I had no idea what exactly to say.

When we got back to the office, I was still overwhelmed by the accusation. To be honest, there was not a great deal of thought that went into my words – I remember that my mouth just started rambling, trying to make sense out of everything. My initial thought was that the accusation was something that had supposedly happened that day, and I remember saying that

Daughter 1 was not even back in the office with me that day – John had been.

Then I began trying to make sense of the accusation, trying to reason why Daughter 1 would have said this. The last time I could remember lying on the couch with her was months ago, and there had certainly never been anything done by me, and Daughter 1 had never indicated that there was.

As you may recall, as recently as a week before this, Daughter 1 had a conversation with Mara where she was *specifically* asked whether I had ever touched her inappropriately, and Daughter 1 denied that forcefully. That was when Daughter 1 claimed that *my* contact (hugs, etc) made her uncomfortable, but that was as far as her accusations went. Now – something that could only have happened months ago was being said to have happened? None of it made sense.

I remember Mara asking if I thought I could have touched her while asleep, and I remember a huge sense of guilt hitting me at the thought. At the time, it seemed the *only* possible explanation. I could not conceive of Daughter 1 making something like this up, and I knew I had never deliberately done anything to her. With a sick feeling in my gut, I confessed that this was the only thing that could have happened.

With this in hand, Mara called Dixie back (From this point on, Mara was never left alone when she was on the phone with Dixie - Either myself or Carrie Beth were with her at all times, and often the phone was held so we could hear what Dixie was saying). Mara immediately renewed her demand to talk to Daughter 1, but Dixie claimed Daughter 1 did not want to talk to Mara. Mara called that "ridiculous" and once again insisted on talking to her daughter. I remember Mara saying, "That is a very serious accusation, and I deserve to be able to ask my own daughter about it." But still, Dixie refused to let Daughter 1 on the phone, and only kept repeating that Mara was going to lose her girls if she did not leave me immediately.

This back and forth went on for over an hour. Mara kept insisting on talking to Daughter 1, Dixie kept refusing to let her come to the phone. Mara said that if they did not let her talk to her daughter, she would call the police, and Jerry reasserted that he would shoot anyone "coming down his driveway", even the police. Under no circumstances, he insisted, was anyone going to see Daughter 1.

Let me reiterate: Jerry and Dixie Nezat were holding their granddaughter hostage, and threatening to *shoot* anyone who tried to come out to talk to her about a supposed molestation, *even the police!* Needless to say, the Nezats were in a standoff, and none of us knew what to do about it.

After that first hour, Carrie Beth asked if Daughter 1 would agree to talk to her – as a family friend, she insisted she was impartial and she considered herself a close friend of Daughter 1. Dixie initially refused, once again saying no one could talk to Daughter 1, but Daughter 1 herself spoke up from the background at the mention of Carrie Beth's name, saying she wanted to talk to her. Dixie went away from the phone for several seconds, saying something mumbled to Daughter 1, but then she came back and agreed to let Carrie Beth talk to Daughter 1.

Carrie Beth kept the phone to her ear during her conversation, so all any of us heard was Carrie Beth's part of the conversation. But Carrie Beth did relay what was said. Daughter 1 first came on and assured Carrie Beth that she was okay, and that Grandma and Grandpa were just "protecting" her. When asked, she did finally provide details of the alleged incident though:

By Carrie Beth's account, Daughter 1 said that while lying in the back office watching cartoons, I had put my hand (not specified which) up her shirt. Daughter 1 said she pulled it out and then I put that same hand down her pants, which she said she also pulled out. And then I stopped.[2]

Up to this point, Carrie Beth said Daughter 1 had seemed perfectly calm and normal, as if nothing was going on. Then she heard Dixie say something unintelligible in the background, and suddenly Daughter 1 began to cry into the phone. Carrie Beth said it seemed to her to be a fake cry, and in her opinion, it was very obvious that Daughter 1 was crying on cue because Dixie told her to.

Carrie Beth continued on to ask if I had hurt her, and Daughter 1 said no. She asked Daughter 1 if I had ever told her not to talk about this to anyone, and again, Daughter 1 said, no. Carrie Beth noted that as she continued to talk to Daughter 1, the fake crying disappeared again and Daughter 1 just began talking normal again.

This conversation ended, as I understand it, because Dixie took the phone away from Daughter 1 saying something to the effect of, "Okay, you've heard enough," at which point the phone was passed back to Mara, as yet again the back and forth arguing went on – Mara insisting on seeing her daughter, and the Nezats threatening to shoot anyone who came into their driveway.

As Mara continue to argue, I talked with Carrie Beth about what Daughter 1 had said. Carrie Beth was not at all hesitant in her conclusions – she knew Daughter 1 was being controlled, and recited the fake crying as an example of this. Daughter 1 was not really upset – afraid, certainly, but not upset. She did not cry until Dixie said something in the background, and then she only cried for a few seconds and forgot herself again as she continued talking to Carrie Beth. Carrie Beth specifically said she believed that Daughter 1 was clearly acting, putting on a performance.

---

[2] This represented the first version of the allegation against me. I note this, as I will refer readers back to this description several times.

And from how she described it and what I have learned since, I obviously agree. But at the time, I was just confused.

Mara argued for awhile longer, and finally hung up the phone, saying she needed to think about what to do. Several threats had been made by Mara that she would call the police, but she really did not want it to get to that level, she said – she did not want her dad to "go to jail for shooting a cop."

This threat, by the way, was really the *only* thing keeping any of us from calling the police in the beginning – even back then, so many cases of school violence and public standoffs had happened, and the thought of Jerry and Dixie getting in a shootout with law enforcement and Daughter 1 possibly getting caught in the crossfire terrified us all. All any of us could see was the police being forced to open fire on Jerry while he tried holding them off, and Daughter 1 being killed by stray bullets. Or worse, Jerry using Daughter 1 as a shield...

At any rate, it was at this point – almost ninety minutes after the allegation had been voiced against me – that Mara finally came clean on her family history. She confessed that her parents had been making up false sexual abuse stories about men in her life since she was in high school, starting with Joe Carter when Mara was in tenth grade. She also confessed that after being raped by her brother (a story I knew about in part at this point), that Dixie had covered up for him, blaming her for making up a story about him. As Mara put it, when Mara was really a victim, Dixie went out of her way to punish her, but when she was happy, Dixie would go out of her way to ruin it.

This was the first time I ever knew anything about Dixie and Jerry deliberately making up false stories about others. True, they had told me stories about Tim and Jared, but Mara had minimized those to being just mistakes by her parents. And I had accepted the explanation. Hindsight is twenty-twenty, they say, and I truly wish I had not trusted Mara so much – I should have taken concern away from the false stories about Jared and Tim, but because Mara deflected the blame, I did not.

I remember asking Mara why she would ever have kept something like this from me. I felt angry, betrayed and turned against. Here was the woman I had spent years trying to set up a family with, and she had purposefully kept information about a genuine and realistic threat to my welfare from me. She knew what her parents were doing, knew about Jerry and Dixie's history, and *had to have known* that sooner or later, they would do the same thing to me that they had done to every single other man in her life. Mara's only answer had been that she thought if I had known, I would not have dated her.

I do need to explain something briefly here – at this point in time, Mara and I were at a rocky place in our relationship. On more than one occasion, I had slept on the floor because I could not sleep beside her. I had called off our relationship completely a couple weeks before, but we were still living together, and Mara was dedicated to winning me back. The reasons were rather emasculating, and I will likely go into the reasons later in this biography, but for now, the only thing that is relevant is that we were not in a stable point in our relationship to start with when this accusation was made.

At this point, the night of the accusation, I would have said we were back together – but learning this, it sent it right back the other direction. I could not trust her or believe in her, knowing she intentionally put me in harm's way and never warned me about it. When I first interviewed with the police, I even told them that Mara and I were no longer together because of this. Within a week, after all the emotional damage had a chance to sink in, I did forgive her and we began working together toward trying to fix the problems in our relationship and in what the Nezats had caused. But if I am being absolutely truthful here, I have to admit that this was not a good period for Mara and I to begin with, and this whole thing only made things exponentially worse.

At any rate, after making this admission and my own admittedly less-than-positive response about being lied to and set up, Mara decided she needed to talk to someone else about what to do. So at my suggestion, she called her counselor, ie, therapist, and related what was happening. At first, she just left a message, but her counselor did call her back within a half hour or so. But after hearing what was going on, her counselor really only had one thing to say: if Mara did not call the police, she would. See, under Montana law, a counselor is required to report to law enforcement any report of suspicion of assault – and Mara had just relayed that Daughter 1 was not only accusing me of sexually assaulting her, but the Nezats were threatening to shoot people.

Upon her counselor's recommendation, and with my support, it was at this point that the sheriff's department was first called – at roughly 8 pm, approximately three hours after the initial call was returned to Dixie. Mara specifically called the sheriff department to report that her parents had kidnapped her daughter and were threatening to shoot her if she came out to try to see Daughter 1. The sexual assault report was actually secondary to the immediate crimes being committed by the Nezats.

Of interesting note, Dixie and Jerry had been holding their granddaughter hostage for three hours, threatening to shoot anyone who came to see her – including the police – and not *once* tried to call the police themselves over this alleged sexual assault. In the end, it was Mara who called – and then only because she had been told to do so by her counselor, over the fear that her daughter was going to end up getting shot in some ridiculous stand-off with law enforcement. And by the end of the evening, they had been making threats to shoot police for over six hours.

The next three hours were involved with calls between the sheriff's department (the Nezat's residence was in the county, ie, unincorporated region) and the police (because the alleged assault supposedly happened in the city). According to the authorities, the Nezats renewed their threat to law enforcement to shoot anyone – including peace officers – who came out to their house, and they spent another three hours trying to negotiate to have the Nezats let them interview Daughter 1. Finally, around 11pm, the Nezats agreed to bring Daughter 1 in for an interview – but only if the police promised they could take Daughter 1 back to their home afterwards.

Incidentally, though the sheriffs department repeatedly said they could not safely send out an officer to retrieve Daughter 1 because the threats of being shot, the Nezats *never* faced charges for the threats to law enforcement, nor did they face charges for kidnapping. They voluntarily left their home and drove Daughter 1 into town, but were allowed to leave immediately afterward without incident. In hindsight, there was an inordinate amount of attention paid to the alleged accusation of me molesting Daughter 1 that night and very little to the kidnapping and lethal assaults made against law enforcement that night. I ask the reader to consider: With the Nezats *literally* threatening to *kill* people, *including* law enforcement officers, how is it that the only person *anyone* in law enforcement could focus on that night was me?

Another point of interest is that I have never been permitted to see the sheriff report for that evening, though the police report makes absolutely no mention of the threats, the three hour negotiation with the Nezats, nor the kidnapping charges Mara insisted on pressing against her parents. Everything ended up directed at me, and the Nezats' own criminal conduct was completely overlooked. In effect, because the Nezats were acting against *me specifically*, they got a free pass – a pattern that would emerge repeatedly over the next few months.

That night, when the police reported that the Nezats were bringing Daughter 1 in for an interview, Mara and Carrie Beth rushed over to the police station to intercept them. Carrie Beth reported that when she saw Daughter 1, she was guarded on both sides by her grandparents, with her head bowed and her arms crossed defensively in front of her. Carrie Beth rushed forward and gave Daughter 1 a big hug, but Jerry immediately reached over and grabbed Daughter 1's arm, pulling her forcefully from Carrie Beth's grasp (an action that bruised Daughter 1's arm, incidentally), with Dixie barking, "You can hug her if you ever get her back," or something to that effect, with Jerry saying something about not trusting Carrie Beth (remember, I was not there and this is just what was reported to me). The Nezats then rushed Daughter 1 into the police station.

The interviews that happened inside the police station really need their own chapter to discuss, particularly Daughter 1's. The transcript of Daughter 1's interview is included as Appendix 3. But there are some specific details that need to be discussed here.

As I understand the sequence of interviews, Jerry and Dixie were called in (together) for an informal interview, then Daughter 1 was called in for a recorded interview, followed by Mara. There is no actual record of the Nezats or Mara being interviewed that night – I only know about the interviews because both the Nezats and Mara told me they had been interviewed. This is an interesting factoid about the evening, as once again, there was an excessive amount of interest focused on Daughter 1's accusation against me, and no record made of the other people surrounding the accusations – including the crimes committed by the Nezats that very evening.

At this point, Daughter 1's account of the alleged molestation changed for the first and second time, all in the same interview. As time progressed – often in response to contradictions in her own story – her story would change again, but this is the first time the story changed – and it did so within hours of first telling it. The officer conducting the interview of Daughter 1 was Myron Wilson (a later defendant in my lawsuit that sparked the girls' kidnapping), and this is the story told then:

Daughter 1 reported that while lying on the couch with me in the back office of Arcadia, I put my hand down her pants. At first, she claimed my hand touched her vagina when asked by Wilson, but she changed that a few minutes later to say I had come "really close".

The interview was in fact led in several places by Officer Wilson when he wanted it to go a specific direction – for instance, Officer Wilson suggested that I had reached over the top of her and that Daughter 1 had been the one to pull my hand out of her pants, both of which Daughter 1 just agreed with. It was also Wilson's suggestion that she got up herself and walked away from the alleged assault (an element notably Daughter 1 left out of her account to Edith Paxman the following week), which Daughter 1 also went along with. Officer Wilson also put forward the idea that I was awake, and that I had been talking to Daughter 1 – again, something Daughter 1 never mentioned herself – although interestingly enough, within minutes of agreeing with Wilson that I was talking to her, when asked if I said anything to her, Daughter 1 responded, "No."

This was the extent of her second accusation – that I had just started reaching into her pants. All the other details were provided by Wilson, to which she went along with. This is significant, because she had *previously* told Carrie Beth that I had reached under her shirt and after pulling my hand out, then put the same hand down her pants.[3]

But then Wilson *also* asked if I had ever touched her up top – an element that Daughter 1 had made absolutely no mention of

---

3 I place this footnote primarily as a marker of the second version of Daughter 1's accusation, to compared to version 1 and 3, marked with their respective footnotes.

during the interview. Daughter 1 had specifically and *only* described me putting my hand down her pants – and when Wilson asked her if I had ever made any other advances to her, Daughter 1 had repeatedly said, "No." But the moment Wilson asked about her top, Daughter 1 immediately chimed in with that I touched her there at the *same time* I was supposed to be going down her pants. Now her story changed that I had been touching both her breasts with my left hand (which, she was lying on) while my right hand went down her pants. Incidentally, the designation of right and left hands was provided by Wilson, not by Daughter 1 – but as with all suggesting and leading comments, Daughter 1 just went along with it.

For the record, this makes the third change in Daughter 1's story. Though it is closer to the version told to Carrie Beth earlier in the evening, it is markedly different, as well. In the version told to Carrie Beth, I had used the same hand – first up her shirt, and then down her pants – and that she had pulled my hand out of her shirt before it went down her pants. In this version, I was using both hands simultaneously.[4]

Of extreme importance to this third version – which became the "official" version for some time supposedly – Daughter 1 made very specific allegations that I used my left hand – which she was lying on top of – to touch both of her breasts (in the later interview with Edith, Daughter 1 said "fondled", but she did not use that word here). Anyone who takes time to review basic human anatomy would realize that this is an absolutely physical impossibility. The human elbow can only move at a forty-five degree angle. If my arm were lined up to fondle one of Daughter 1's breasts, I would have to have raised it *straight up* to have fondled the other – but the forty-five degree angle of the arm

---

4 Again, I provide this footnote primarily as a marker to the third alteration of Daughter 1's allegation, to be compared to the first and second versions, each noted with their own footnote.

would not have allowed for this. Without knowing which breast I originally was supposed to have fondled, my arm, when moving away, would have either reached Daughter 1's shoulder or her stomach – but *not* her other breast. Literally, to accomplish the feat Daughter 1 described, I would have to have had an extra joint somewhere along my forearm – and I challenge anyone to find such an impossible malformation on my body.

This detail became a sticking point that led to Daughter 1 creating yet another variation of the incident later on, but it is critically important to this point in my accounting – not only did Daughter 1 change her story three times in the same six hour period, but her last account (with the help of misdirected coaching from Wilson) actually described a physical act that no human being would have been capable of without breaking their forearm in half (and good luck on motor control if that were done).

All of this sets a very clear a distinct pattern regarding Daughter 1's allegations that night. To Daughter 1, this was a new story – one that she was taking direction and guidance from the very beginning. The Nezats wanted to keep Daughter 1 isolated and away from everyone – including law enforcement. They had her alone for twelve hours before they were convinced to bring her in, and even then it was over objections that they wanted to keep her alone until at least the next day. Plainly, they were not confidant that Daughter 1 had nailed down the details enough, and that much proved true.

Still seeking outside guidance into what to say, Daughter 1 was extremely susceptible to Wilson's leading interview. When Wilson offered details that Daughter 1 had not come up with, she latched onto them and agreed readily to try to conform. She said yes to almost everything he suggested, and even came back and contradicted things later on in the same interview because she was not able to keep track of all the details. What came out of the Wilson interview was two separate, distinct stories, both of which ran completely contrary to the original story told earlier in the evening. All because Daughter 1 was not certain of the details she was supposed to be relaying, and she mistakenly believed that Wilson was going to go over the same details that her grandparents had already established.

I mentioned earlier that it was clear from the way Daughter 1 acted that she was not expecting to be taken into the police. The Nezats avoided calling the police themselves and fought against the authorities being involved, even going so far as to threaten to shoot police who tried to approach the house, so it was pretty obvious they did not want to involve the authorities, either – at least not until after they had Daughter 1 for a full day (and who knows, maybe longer). This is *not* the conduct of someone who is stumbles upon a sexual assault allegation – these are the actions of people desperate to control the situation. And why exactly would anyone need to control this kind of thing?

To me, it is blatant – the Nezats assured Daughter 1 that police would not be involved, and began to panic when the simple threat against Mara did not work. They had the expectation that if Daughter 1 said I had molested her, Mara would rush out at the Nezat's bidding in heartbeat – but Mara did not trust them, and so they began to panic. And the more they were pressured, the more outrageous their panic became. It took six hours to talk them out of their den, and they did so with extreme reluctance. Clearly they did not want to bring Daughter 1 in to make a statement, and I believe it is because they promised Daughter 1 that the police would not be involved. They simply were not prepared for that eventuality, and did not have enough time to coach Daughter 1 in what to say. Since Daughter 1 was still to unsure of things, she looked to an authority figure to guide her, and the consequences were very obvious contradictions.

In any other situation, the contradictions would have discredited Daughter 1. But the authorities were hellbent on nailing this crime on me, even urging the Nezats to bring Daughter 1 in at 11 pm at night to make a statement. Any statement could have been taken the next day – there was no reason to take the statement that night. The only reason to have Daughter 1 brought in at night would have been to return her to her mother – so why were the authorities so insistent upon focusing on this particular investigation so late at night?

To me, there is only one answer – it is why the police ignored the kidnapping and felony assault crimes of the Nezats, why they insisted on interviewing first Daughter 1 and then Mara so late at night, and it is why Wilson tampered with Mara as a witness, threatening her and knowingly providing her false information about my having an alleged criminal history of child molestation. It was because the authorities wanted to lock in control over this investigation and make sure this particular accusation pushed through. And as time pressed on, the reasoning became even more apparent – they saw an opportunity to take down someone who had been a thorn in their side for close to a year. The one person standing up and defending the youth of this town from Kalispell Police Department abuse was me – and now they had a shot at taking me down. True or not, they did not care. This was something they wanted, and they were willing to throw all other consideration to the wind to get it. Break the law, let others break the law – who cared, so long as they could frame me for this crime.

After Daughter 1's interview, Wilson took Mara into the interview room. Having viewed Daughter 1's tape, I was able to see the first few seconds of this interview, but the tape was shut off and only comments about there being no actual rape were discussed. However, Mara reported that Wilson made some very specific threats against her – he told her that I had a prior criminal record of child molestation, and that if she did not help the police department convict me, that he would have her children taken away by CFS! First, I had *no* prior criminal history whatsoever, much less a record of child molestation, but Mara believed Wilson – because he was a police officer. Based on his threat, she agreed to take her daughters and go into hiding.

At any rate, after the interview was over, Daughter 1 was allowed to leave with Mara and Carrie Beth, much to the fury of the Nezats. Carrie Beth reported that Daughter 1 was in a very upbeat mood upon being released, that she was skipping and laughing all the way back to the store. Specifically, Carrie Beth described Daughter 1's behavior as that of an actress who just finished a play and was unwinding. All in all, Carrie Beth said Daughter 1's behavior was completely out of place for someone who had just supposedly related being sexually assaulted to the police.

Mara only told me at the store that she needed to make sure I had no contact with Daughter 1 during the investigation, that she was going to go stay with a friend so that did not happen, and that she would call me once they got settled to tell me what happened. But she never called me that night. Nor did she call me immediately the following day. At that point, I began calling around looking for her, scared at that point because I had no idea what was going on. At the single lowest point of my life, Mara of all people was *hiding* from me? It was inconceivable.

Finally, about midmorning on the 11th of July, Mara called me to ask me to stop trying to find her. When I asked why she was doing this, she explained to me that she "knew" about my past. I, of course, had no idea what she was talking about. When asked, she admitted that Wilson had told her that I had a criminal history of molesting other children. I knew there was no such record, but Mara did not believe me. I had to go obtain print outs of both my state and national criminal history before Mara would believe me.

It was blatantly clear that Wilson had intended to use this misleading information to drive a wedge between Mara and I, and to tamper with Mara as a potential witness. Mara had gone into the police station believing her parents were making this up and getting Daughter 1 to somehow go along with it – she walked out believing I was a serial child molester and was hell bent on my guilt.

Wilson's plan had almost worked. If Mara had not called me to tell me to stop bothering her friends, I would never have known about any of this and I would likely have been arrested much sooner. Mara proved vital as my own defense worked up, as well – putting me in contact with Adele Carter, Joe Carter's mom, and providing me specific names and information about the Nezat's prior faux accusations. She also would likely have disregarded Edith Paxman's observations, because for those twenty-four hours, Mara believed I had molested her daughter. Without any of this, I would not have been able to gather what information I have.

Of course, in the end, authorities still turned Mara against me, but that happened months later down the line...

Chapter 5

It is important to note that this is the point where things began to shift from a personal vendetta by my girlfriend's twisted parents to a political issue involving the local authorities. This is the point where something personal became public, and where the corrupt authorities in Kalispell, Montana, began to manipulate things. This is the point where players like Frank Garner, Peg Allison and Ed Corrigan began to tamper with witnesses, records and circumstances in order to advance their own corrupt agenda. It never should have gone down like this – it could all have resolved itself if these people did not feel they needed to "teach a lesson" to the "upstart" who had the audacity to stand up to them.

As mentioned, immediately following the initial allegation on July 9, Daughter 1's story began to fall apart very quickly. Her story was not standing too well on its own on that night alone, but in the days that followed, it only crumbled faster. But even after that night, Daughter 1's interview with Edith Paxman completely discredited her story. Daughter 1 had told three different versions of the alleged offense in the same evening – two of which were filled with Myron Wilson leading her to get the responses and story *he* wanted – and then demonstrated a very mercurial story with Edith, leading to Edith's ability to critically undermine the aspects of Daughter 1's allegation. By all accounts, with everything that happened in the days immediately following this allegation, the accusation was proved to be unfounded and the investigations were closed – and would have stayed closed if not for the corrupt interests of local authorities like Frank Garner.

Remember, Daughter 1's interview was done at 11 pm, at a time when Daughter 1 had already dealt with six hours of stress and anxiety by her grandparents, the Nezats, holding her hostage and threatening to shoot people. This is far from an ideal situation to sit a witness alone in a room – and certainly not an impressionable thirteen year old girl. But Wilson wanted the charge pressed against me and for whatever reasons he had, did not want to wait for the next day when Daughter 1 could be brought in after an evening's rest.

I think it is important to reiterate why Wilson had a reason to come after me specifically. For nearly a year at this point, I had been advocating against police brutality and assaults against minors who gathered on Main Street in the evenings. I had witnessed not only physical and verbal assaults and bullying from officers, but in one instance I had even witnessed a police officer take a thirteen or fourteen year old girl by force when she refused to accept his sexual advance. I also witnessed a police officer tell another young girl that she should go home and get beaten by her mother because she deserved it. Not only had I seen this things myself, but I was helping minors gain a voice and begin to speak out against this abuse. I was on my way to becoming a huge thorn in the side of these abusive officers, and this allegation made against me by Daughter 1 represented a golden opportunity to remove me as a threat.

Plain and simple, the Kalispell Police Department knew my name and when an opportunity came up to get a criminal charge of this nature brought against me, everything else took a back seat. The police and sheriff ignored the kidnapping and felony assault committed by the Nezats, and chose to drag a very emotionally drained barely-teenager into a back room to interrogate her in order to make sure that they could pursue a criminal investigation against me.

I cannot speak for why Wilson chose this tactic specifically. Whether he was an officer who had been guilty of the abuse against the teenagers on Main Street or was simply stepping up to defend his fellow officers, I do not know. I know that I never personally witnessed anything done by Wilson, nor was his name ever dropped to me by the youth who talked to me about the assaults against them by police officers (though, in all fairness, most of these reports to me did not include the offending officer's name). There is the concept of the "Blue Shield" – an unwritten standard amongst American police officers across the country to stand up and protect other police officers, even protecting their fellow officers' misconduct and criminal activity – and this could have been all this was. There is no mistaking that officers from the Kalispell Police Department were committing criminal actions, and I was a "civilian" who was challenging their misconduct – so this is entirely credible as a possible motivation.

However, Wilson's bias was plain that night when he fabricated to Mara that I had a prior history of child molestation and threatened to have her girls taken away if she did not collaborate the allegation, not to mention how he deliberately led the interview with Daughter 1. He set out from the beginning to taint the following investigation, and his manipulation of Daughter 1 and Mara, at the very least, forever corrupted the inquiry that followed.

Following Edith Paxman's critique of Daughter 1's story, she once again changed her story. Remember, up to this point, she was implacable that I was awake. In the interview with Wilson she had said that I was both talking to her and *not* saying anything to her, which in itself was contradictory within the same interview. But when she spoke with Edith Paxman, she specifically stated that I stayed on the couch when she just "got up and walked away", and that I said nothing to her for several minutes. When pressed, she insisted my eyes were closed as a justification for why I did not try to get her to come back to the couch or even keep her from leaving – which again was contrary to what she had told others previously – and Edith pressed on this point, getting Daughter 1 to state that I could have been asleep. Armed with this information, Mara had obtained an admission from Daughter 1 that she was saying all of this as part of a scheme to reunite Jared (her birth father) and Mara (her mother).

To continue the chain of events, no one did anything immediately with the allegation. Mara disappeared, and my primary focus that first day – aside from being stressed in general by the false accusation – was trying to figure out why. And the police department did not contact me for an interview until July 11, two days later. Which meant two sleepless nights worrying about what was coming.

I knew some kind of follow-up was forthcoming – and I am sure there was a certain amount of plotting here, letting the anxiety of the allegation weigh no me before actually interviewing me. After all, if they could make me suffer for awhile, stew in my own juices, so to speak, all the better, I imagine. To be honest, I was expecting a police officer to show up and just arrest me, so when I was called by Detective Doug Overman, I was almost relieved – except that he wanted to interview me in person at the police station. Once again, I remember the fear of being arrested gripping me – this time, literally asking me to walk over and turn myself in.

I should point something out at this point – something I will go into in greater detail later, but nevertheless deserves reference here: Montana does not have an active grand jury system. The process exists in the lawbooks, but it is not practiced actively anywhere that I know of in Montana. Instead, Montana relies primarily upon an information system, which is to say, the prosecutor files a charging document called an "information" in which they present the accusation along with supporting evidence to a judge, who then issues an arrest warrant. There is no practice of preliminary challenge nor any controlling measure to provide defense of anyone accused in Montana – if the prosecutor, an agent of the government, decides to file a charge against you, they alone have the view of the court and you will be arrested. Period.

Keep in mind, this system is even further bastardized in Kalispell. All the Flathead County prosecutors ever file is a statement saying a crime was committed and universally, the court issues the arrest warrant – no evidence required. This is all part of a very dysfuntional criminal justice system that completely foregoes the pretense of being innocent until proven guilty. In Kalispell, Montana, once charged, you *are* guilty – it is just a horse and pony show after this to take you through a pretense of prosecution.

This being said, law enforcement can arrest and hold an individual for seventy-two hours before being required to formally charge the person. Which means that anyone can be arrested upon the moment an accusation is made, and then held until the prosecutor's office can file charging documents. Whether it is fortunate or unfortunate, I have now been in the legal system for over ten years, and have witnessed hundreds of instances of sexual assault charges – and in nearly every case I am aware of (with only one notable exception that the person accused had to be identified afterwards because the victim had been a stranger), the person charged in Flathead County is arrested the moment an allegation is made, or as soon thereafter as possible. The police do not wait for the prosecutor to decide whether to prosecute – once they have a victim, they make an arrest. Period.

Not realizing this as the normal pattern, I still walked in on July 11 with the expectation of being arrested. When I was interviewed and released, it came as a shock – it was not what I expected. And in hindsight, I now realize that it was not the authorities' standard procedure, either.

Knowing what I do now, I cannot help but think there was some expectation that I would run away, ie, flee, once the initial allegation was made. When I was still there two days later running my business as usual, I think there was an expectation that calling me in to rattle me would possibly generate this reaction. And again, when it did not, only then do authorities realize they were really going to have to investigate the case. This is reflective in the police reports – there are noticeable gaps in the investigation that have no genuine purpose other than that the investigating officers were waiting for something – and the only thing I can imagine they were waiting for was to see if their scare tactics would run me out of town. And I believe now that they were simply giving me rope enough to hang myself with – hoping their problem would just solve itself by scaring me out of town.

Remember – I was innocent and had no reason to believe that this false accusation would stand. I was fearful of being arrested, certainly, but I was known to readily joke at the idea of getting a free bed and three square meals for a day – and then suing them for false arrest after. I was invested in proving my innocence, and running away never even crossed my mind. I had not done anything wrong, so why would I run away? Perhaps a guilty man would have – but I was not a guilty man.

At the time of the initial interview with Overman, I had not yet heard from Mara, so the issue of the tampering had to wait for the next interview on July 17. But I made it clear from the initial interview that I was innocent and that I had not molested Daughter 1. I declined submitting to a polygraph, because I had prior experience with polygraphs – having taken two in the past and failed both when I was telling the truth. With this history, I had no intention of leaving my innocence to what I saw as a defective method of truth-telling. I was also asked to take a voice-stress analysis test, but considering I just had two sleepless nights, stressed to no end over my future, I could not imagine my voice not registering stress. As I told Overman, "I've just had two sleepless nights and days, and my entire life has been turned upside down – of course I'm stressed!"[5]

Notably, this interview was initiated with reading my rights and advising me on my right to counsel, and to have one appointed if I could not afford one. I stated I could not afford one, but was promptly told I could not have a lawyer appointed to me unless I was charged, which at that point I had not. In other words, even though I was read my Miranda Rights, they were discarded immediately. I have since learned that this is common practice of the Kalispell Police Department – interview after reading the Miranda Rights, but never provide counsel. In conducting legal research since, I now know that any evidence collected after an accused requests counsel is inadmissible – but of course, this is Kalispell, and even my own attorney, Eduardo Gutierrez-Falla, later refused to make this argument on my behalf. But it is notable that this is how the interview occurred – even if Overman deliberately omitted this challenge I raised.

Of additional note, Overman specifically asked my consent to have the interview recorded, and he even pointed out to me where the hidden camera was in the room. But his later report does not reflect that this interview was recorded. It is my suspicion that this recorded interview was deliberately withheld for the precise reason that I asked for counsel and was denied.

At any rate, after this interview, Overman did nothing else immediately. He made no effort to contact Mara or Daughter 1 or any other witnesses until Monday of the following week (July 14th). Once again, I believe this delay was deliberate, as the police department was waiting to see if I would flee. Remember, typically, a person accused of sexual assault is not given any

---

5 The complete Kalispell Police Department reports are available in Appendix 2 for review.

leeway – they are promptly arrested before they have the chance to run. But that was not done here – and the delays between the initial interview of Daughter 1, and then waiting for the weekend after my interview sends a pretty clear signal that the KPD was giving me the chance to run. I did not, of course, but this seems to me to be what they were expecting.

On Monday afternoon, Overman finally called Mara in for an interview. Mara at this point asserted that she did not believe Daughter 1, and provided several substantial reasons, though only part of them are reflected in. Mara reportedly told Overman that Daughter 1 had herself stated that she was only doing this to get her and Daughter 1's birth father, Jared Salois, back together, and that her parents had been making up false allegations against men in her life since she was a teenager. Yet the only allegation that shows up in Overman's report is that Mara believed her daughter was being coached.

Remember, the clear motivation of the police department's interviews was to establish my guilt, not to provide potentially exonerating information. Knowing what the full content of these interviews were makes it difficult to draw any other conclusion when information regarding an actual admission of the so-called victim or specific details about the Netzats having a history of making false reports that had extended back twenty years at that point were notably omitted.

In law, this is known as exculpatory evidence, ie, evidence which tends to exonerate someone of a crime. In this instance, the Kalispell Police Department consistently throughout this affair suppressed information from their records which would disprove the allegation or discredit the source from which the allegation came, and only recorded information which would not undermine their ultimate goal: to convict me of child molestation. As public servants, it is the responsibility of law enforcement to investigate reports of criminal conduct, but the expectation is that they seek the truth of the charge – not to manipulate the facts they gather to push through the allegation.

By this point, Overman had already received half a dozen reasons to disbelieve the accusation. Though the record itself did not reflect the events of the evening, he knew from my own interview and Mara's that the Nezats had kidnapped Daughter 1 and threatened to shoot anyone – including law enforcement – the night of July 9th. It was also reported that the Nezats had a long-standing history of making up false allegations against men in Mara's life, and Mara had provided examples of this to Overman during her interview. Finally, Overman was told that Daughter 1 had specifically admitted to Mara that she had only made the allegation as part of a scheme to get her parents back together. Yet none of these details ever made it into the official police reports – and anyone reading this account should be asking by now why that is.

Overman's next interview was of the Nezats on July 16th, incidentally *before* he interviewed Daughter 1 on the same day. As discussed later, there was a reason why Overman talked to every conceivable person he could before he re-interviewed Daughter 1, and this flew in the face of any kind of logical investigation. Nevertheless, Overman must have thought he finally had fished a bone out of the quagmire of this investigation when the Nezats made up yet *another* false story: now they insisted that Chantel – the friend of Mara's who had previously helped spread the rumors about me supposedly molesting Melissa Turner's daughter – had dated me, and that I had molested *her* daughter, also names Melissa. Clearly, the Nezats were reaching here – I had never dated Chantel, and to the best of my knowledge, she did not even have a daughter named Melissa. But remember, this had been how they operated for over twenty years: making up one false allegation after another. And now they had made up a new one right in front of the investigating officer!

Subsequently, though this is not in precise chronological order, Overman conducted an interview of Chantel weeks later as part of a last desperate effort to preserve this investigation on July 28th – Chantel denied ever having dated me. She then admitted she had not been told of any allegations against me by her friends Mara or Melissa.

It is quite notable that the statement does not say Chantel was not told allegations against me *at all* – only that she had not been told by her friends. This leads me to believe that she did tell Overman that Jerry had told her what ended up being a false allegation, but as has been consistent throughout the reporting process, Overman omitted this exculpatory information. Personally, I have not had the opportunity to speak with Chantel since seeing these reports for myself, though, so it is only speculation based upon Overman's conduct in other areas of this investigation, specifically covering up details which discredited the accusation against me.

Incidentally, by the time Overman had conducted Chantel's interview, Mara and I had confronted her about where her original story of my supposedly molesting Melissa's daughter had come from and, when pressed, she confirmed that it had been Jerry Nezat who called and told her this story. According to Chantel, she had said Jerry had urged her to help him "protect" Mara from me because Mara would not believe the story if it came from him.

The next interview in sequence was of Daughter 1 the following Wednesday (July 16th), a full week after the initial report was made. Keep in mind – though Daughter 1 had been interviewed the night of the initial report, an actual investigation – one that was based upon actually pursuing an real criminal report – would have been initiated by the investigating detective seeking to conduct his own interview of the accusation, ie, interviewing the alleged victim himself. First. Before anyone else was interviewed. To conduct a proper investigation, a detective needs to conduct his own inquiry, and that *starts* with the person making the accusation. Yet Overman waited for a full week – after interviewing myself, Mara and the Nezats – before arranging an interview with the alleged victim.

Again, this procedure of the Kalispell Police Department makes no sense if the objective had been to make an actual investigation of a crime. But clearly, that was not the objective here – no one actually cared about the actual accusation; they only cared about convicting me to get me out of the way. They used the investigation as a pretense to dig for dirt on me, not to actually investigate whether a crime had been committed.

Having had several conversations with Overman, I believe that he is a very intelligent man – and though he was tasked with making sure this charge stuck, I think he must have seen the same defects in Wilson's interview as I have pointed out. Why would he want to interview a so-called victim who had already demonstrated that she could not stick to a consistent story in the space of a single interview? If the point was to convict me of this crime, they could not give her the latitude to contradict herself even further – and it is for this reason that I believe that the Kalispell Police Department did not initially arrest me, and why they tried to see if scare tactics would send me running out of town. It is also why Overman interviewed Mara and I before conducting another interview of Daughter 1. He wanted to fish, to gather information he could use to shore up his investigation, since Daughter 1's interview was clearly not really all that credible in the first place. It was only when every other method was exhausted that he finally went back to interview Daughter 1.

This interview on July 16th though proved critical – it was here that Daughter 1 admitted to Overman that she could not say whether I was awake or asleep. Under law, to commit a crime, one must have what is commit an act knowingly, purposely or negligently, which is to say, he or she must be aware of what he is doing. An involuntary act – an act taken while unconscious, for example – lacks the prerequisite that the offense was committed knowingly.[6] So when Daughter 1 stated – to the investigating officer – that she could not say whether I was awake or not, she immediately made it impossible to prosecute, since there could be no proof that any deliberate act was made by me.

Now, remember – although I initially believed this to be the case when the accusation was first made, it was not what I believed to be true at the time, nor is it what I believe now. But I was more than happy to accept if the police department agreed to dismiss the charges upon this admission by Daughter 1. After all, regardless of how the investigation was dismissed, its ongoing status was extremely harmful to my family, my business and my life in general. Mind you, I was not aware of any of this until October, so I still spent several months with the potential threat of arrest and prosecution hanging over my head even *after* Overman had received this admission from Daughter 1.

In spite of receiving evidence that made the pursuit of prosecution impossible, Overman still arranged for a follow-up interview with me on July 17, 2014. Overman was still pursuing the criminal investigation, seeking to illicit some kind of confession from me. I maintained my innocence, of course, and Overman's spent the bulk of the interview trying to illicit some kind of sympathetic confession from me, which is to say, he was trying to "identify" with me by saying things like, "I can understand your interest in [Daughter 1] – she's an attractive

---

[6] See MCA § 45-2-103 and the supporting definitions in MCA § 45-2-101 included in Appendix A.

young girl," and, "Just touching [Daughter 1] really isn't that big of a deal – it's not like you had sex with her".

I was appalled by this, even though I did not know at the time that this was a kind of investigative strategy. I did not have any sexual interest in Daughter 1, and really only saw her as a child, so even the idea of seeing her as an attractive young girl really never entered my mind before this. Of course, I saw that she was developing – Mara and I had conversations about things like training bras and Daughter 1 having her first period, after all. But none of this made me see Daughter 1 sexually – she was growing up, and that is really the only way I saw her. So as Overman tried to lay sympathetic groundwork to try to evoke some kind of admission from me, it had exactly the opposite effect – I threw it back at him and told him that was disgusting.

It was also during this interview that I made it clear to Overman that I was aware that Wilson had lied to Mara, and told her that I supposedly had a criminal history of child molestation. Overman pulled back the sheets of the file to show me there were no such records in the casefile, and stated he did not know why Wilson would say that since clearly there was no such history. He even went so far as to say he did not think that Wilson would say something like that, suggesting that Mara was just trying to cover up her own reasons for her believing me guilty. But as has been said, once I went and obtained the police records, Mara became a staunch supporter for over eight months after this, so the lie about my having a prior record was clearly what had intimidated Mara.

Overman left the issue saying he would talk to his "Chief" (ie, Police Chief Frank Garner) about it and get back to me, but no one ever did follow up with me on this report to Overman, and there is not even mention of it in the police report. As I have said before, anything that either exonerated me or cast question upon this investigation were omitted from the official record, so this is really no surprise beyond what I have already noted.

Realizing that the police department was not open to even discussing this issue, that essentially they were taking the preemptive position of denying it even happened, I decided it was time to make an official objection to this conduct. And so on July 18, 2003, I issued the demand letter against the City of Kalispell which I have since called "the shot heard across Montana". This was the letter that officially called out the misconduct of the Kalispell Police Department and called for damages for the witness tampering and harassment. It was the precursor to the lawsuit, the abduction of Mara's daughters and my own eventual incarceration.[7]

Years later, on January 5, 2012, I would write the following about this letter as after I recovered this record:

Though the initial false allegation had preceded this, this letter is what exploded things beyond a quiet investigation into what eventually became revealed to be the Great Montana Conspiracy's existence. This was the volley that started the escalation that became the war; This was the shot heard across the State of Montana, and what initiated the broad attacks upon my person, first by various City officials and offices, later by County agencies, and eventually by State representatives. This is it – proof positive that nine days after the initial allegation was made on July 9, 2003, months before the lawsuit was filed on November 18, 2003 (or its precursor Petition on October 30, 2003), and even further from the actual charges being brought against me on February 20, 2004, this was the first effort I made to return fire. And this was what eventually led to my defeat and my imprisonment as a US Political Prisoner...

I look back at this letter, and it is hard to believe that I was ever so naive or gullible. I honestly believed in writing this letter

---

7 A copy of this letter can be viewed in Appendix 2.

that I was dealing with a rogue police officer. I could not conceive that the entire police department, much less the City, County and State would step up to defend the abuse by that officer. Nor could I conceive that the United States government would turn a blind eye to the abuse, as well, nor that I would become a US political prisoner.

This is it – the abuse may have pre-existed this letter, but just as the Fort Sumter incursion that started the War Between the States (aka, the US Civil War) was preluded by years of abuse against the southern states, so too was this the act that took this conflict beyond the simple investigation that – it turned out later – would have fallen apart on its own merits within weeks of writing this letter without the harsh consequences that followed.

There is something I need to say here. This letter was never actually anything more than a bluff early on. It was designed to make a record of KPD's misconduct in hopes that they would not tamper with any future witnesses. As the letter states, at the time I believed Myron Wilson to be a rogue officer, that he was acting alone and the KPD's only fault was in trying to shelter a fellow officer. I had no idea of the actual level of corruption present within the police department or even the city and county itself. My feelings at the time were that if the City of Kalispell were made aware of this travesty of justice, that they would oversee the police department and make sure that the rest of the investigation was handled properly.

This of course is not what happened, but that had been my genuine intention at the time. I really did not have any interest in suing Kalispell at that point – I believed the City would back down rather than have this kind of conduct exposed, and that was the only reason I wrote this letter. I still believed that a fair, impartial investigation would exonerate me, because I knew I had committed no crime. Call it naivety or whatever you like, but the concept of an entire government being corrupt just seemed inconceivable to me at the time, and I genuinely believed in the American system of justice. And just because one officer had overstepped his legal authority by threatening a witness was no reason for me to believe that this was anything more than an overzealous police officer trying to fill a quota of some kind. Clearly, I was wrong.

Incidentally, this letter did get a response from the KPD – I was called in for a separate interview with Sergeant Greg Burns. Of interesting note, Kalispell Police Department does not have an Internal Affairs Department as most law enforcement agencies have. The purpose of an Internal Affairs Department is to provide unbiased reviews of police misconduct – IA officers are typically not work with other police officers and are therefore, in theory, free of any loyalties or conflicts of interest. In KPD's case, however, their own officers investigate complaints made – and this is why Burns sought to interview me on behalf of his department, to create an illusion of investigation while actually continuing to protect his fellow officer.

Apparently, the letter sent to the City had supposedly triggered an internal investigation of Myron Wilson's conduct, but this interview with Burns was not really directed at Wilson's conduct – it was purely an intimidation angle to try to underscore the claim I made for damages in my letter to the City. All Burns kept badgering me about was why I felt I had been damaged, how I had chosen the amount of my damage claim, etc. He also kept reiterating that Wilson was authorized to do whatever he needed to do in an investigation, and my complaining about it was a waste of time. The pretense that this was an internal investigation of misconduct was just that – a pretense. Burns wanted me to back down off the complaint, and he used this interview to intimidate me.

Of course, had this been an actual internal investigation, Burns would have interviewed Mara, who was the person who had relayed the complaint to me. She never was – Mara was never called in to be asked about what Wilson said to her. Burns' efforts to rattle me, as I have said, was a cover story for trying to intimidate me to not pursue the claim I had made against his department and his fellow officer. In effect, this was the second tier in the KPD's blue shield defense, ie, police officers defending other officers from any criminal misconduct – the first being Overman's general denial of Wilson's conduct.

It was shortly after this that I was contacted for the first time by Tana Ryggs with the Montana Municipal Insurance Agency. She made it clear that the City had forwarded my claim to her for resolution, but that she was not willing to discuss settlement while there was a pending investigation with the police department. This will become significant later, but it is important to note here – especially in that it came almost immediately after Burns attempted to intimidate me into dropping the claim.

Also during this period, Adjutant City Attorney Richard Hickle (acting as official counsel for the City in response to my July 18 demand letter) began sending letters, as well. These correspondence were irregular, but essentially, it was creating a foundation of conduct further denying the actions of Wilson. So in effect, this was the third tier of the KPD's defense – and the first real effort of the City to step in and defend Wilson's conduct.

Finally, another general set of circumstances that began at this point and continued throughout the following months is that my business, Arcadia, began receiving a successive group of harassments from the City and County. It began with a letter from the City denouncing a banner ad we had posted over our door (claiming city ordinance prohibited outside displays, while my neighbor business had a dozen wind socks hanging from their awning).

Before I go further into this, I should point out that there is actually no ordinance requiring a business license in Kalispell.

Though it is recommended that one in business get a fictitious business name statement with the state's secretary of state office, there are no taxes nor regulatory fees to actually run a business in Kalispell, and so no business licenses. Arcadia was owned by Mara's and my corporation, Multiverse Enterprises, Incorporated, but there was actually no documentation with the City or County itself that listed me as the business owner, much less the sole owner. But in each of the following instances, everyone contacted our business asking for me *by name*. The only connection the City or County actually had regarding me owning and running this business was with the Kalispell Police Department and my letter to the City, and even then, it demonstrated that Mara and I co-owned the business – just as we co-owned the corporation. So the fact that each instance that follows was preceded by specific requests asking for contact with me by name is a clear indication that these following events were connected to the claim I had made against Kalispell.

At any rate, I complied and took down the banner, but a couple days later we received a visit from a police officer, who came into the business with his hand on his pistol (in a room with several teenagers and adults present) asking for me by name. I honestly believed the officer was there to arrest me (and so did everyone else in the room), but it turns out he was only there because "the Chief" (ie, Frank Garner) had sent him over to talk to me about getting a bike rack in front of our business. Incidentally, this had been something I had been trying to get the City to approve since we had opened the business a year before, but because our storefront ran right up to the sidewalk, the City would not let us put a bike rack out front. When I pointed this out to the officer, he looked deflated – especially when I asked if he could help me get the permission I had not been able to get.

Keep in mind, there is no ordinance nor regulatory reason in Kalispell, Montana, for a police officer to come to a business about a bike rack. At best, this would be something the City would issue a fine over (if it was assumed that there was obstruction of a city walkway), but there was no *legal* reason for a police officer to come in and talk to me about this. Further, there was a toy shop a few blocks north of us who also had the same issue with bikes not being parked in a bike rack and when I inquired, they had never even been talked to in all the years they had been in business. This was harassment, pure and simple – the officer came in with his hand on his pistol, for crying out loud! And when I came back with a logical response to the officer's complaint, it defeated the whole purpose of the visit.

However, since I took the officer into the middle-back room (where the kitchenette was), his visit was clearly responsible for our next visit – from the Flathead County Health Department. A representative of the health department came into Arcadia (once again asking for me by name) a couple days later with a pre-prepared citation against our business – alleging that we were selling food from the back kitchen without a health permit. Clearly, the officer saw the kitchen and made an erroneous referral that we were preparing food for sale, and the health department came in with the citation already in hand. However, when the representative made the accusation, we flatly denied it – because we were not serving anything to the general public from the kitchen. Mara was intimately familiar with health code laws, and we did not even serve water to anyone from our faucets. When we proved that there was nothing actually being done like this, the representative was left standing there dumbfounded, mumbled an apology, and kind of slinked out of the store.

Next came the most persistent visit – from the Flathead County Fire Marshal's Office. The Assistant Fire Marshal Jim Stewart called me on the phone, asking for me once again by name, and requested an appointment for an "annual inspection". This investigation consisted of walking through the business and creating a list of alleged fire code violations, upon which we would be required to have a follow-up investigation to confirm we had done all the required actions. This initial list was complied with, but when Stewart returned, he simply created a new list of so-called violations, ones that were increasingly more expensive. We again complied with this second list, and upon the third inspection, yet another list of alleged violations were "discovered", and these included even rewiring the entire building! Needless to say, the purpose here was to create a continuously escalating cost burden upon our business until they could finally get leverage to just shut us down for noncompliance.

Incidentally, as this level of harassment escalated, I circulated our business by several blocks, contacting other businesses and asking if similar demands were being placed upon them. Without exception, each business said though they were inspected, the demands of the fire marshal were never as wide-sweeping and expansive as the ones made against our business. In fact, the most the fire marshal ever did for other businesses was just to make sure their fire extinguishers were functional.

On the third inspection, I finally confronted Stewart about why he had asked for me by name. Since there were no actual business records in Kalispell, and there had been no prior contacts, there should have been no reason to ask for me by name. I pointed out to him that his visit followed almost immediately upon the heels of the prior visits and my belief that someone in the Kalispell Police Department was the one who had sent him. Stewart balked, and fumbled something about having a note on his desk to call my business and ask for me, but claimed he did not know who had left the note. But a few minutes later in the conversation, he made a comment that since his office was with the County, that he was not required to follow up with a request from "Frank", but that he still had to do an inspection, regardless, because that was required by county ordinance. Essentially, what Stewart admitted to was that he did get a recommendation from Police Chief Frank Garner, but that that was not really the reason for the inspections. This may have been a justifiable answer for the first inspection, but not for the two follow-ups and the increasingly costly repairs needed to stay in business.

All of this went on between July and October of 2003, essentially at the same time as I believed that the police investigation was ongoing – It is difficult to put in precise alignment with the interviews, however, which is why I mention these in the context.

At any rate, approximately a week or so after the interview with Overman, Mara asked Chantel Beasley to come into Arcadia. Keep in mind, we had no idea at this point that the Nezats had created a new allegation about me supposedly molesting Chantel's daughter – we were just trying to independently track down who had really been responsible for the allegation made against Melissa Turner's daughter, since we suspected that it was Dixie Nezat. Our intention was to provide proof to the police department that the Nezats had manufactured this allegation against Daughter 1, just as they had made up the one against Melissa's daughter.

When Chantel came, we took her to the back office and Mara confronted her with the knowledge that we had spoken to Melissa – who had emphatically denied that I had ever touched her daughter, and had even written up an affidavit saying as much. Chantel's body became stiff as she realized we had tracked down Daughter 1, and at first she was completely silent. Mara told Chantel that she knew there were only so many people in their lives that they shared between myself and Chantel – and that was limited to Mara herself, Melissa and the Nezats. Mara mentioned that her mother had made up these kinds of allegations before and mentioned Joe Carter, at which point Chantel chimed in, "It wasn't Dixie who called me." Pressing on this, I asked, "So it was Jerry?" Chantel did not answer, just saying she did not want to be involved in any of this. It was pointed out to her that she already was because she had come to Mara with this lie, but all Chantel continued to say was that she was just telling her friend what she was told, and it was not her fault that it was not true.

After a few minutes, I got called out of the office and Mara visited alone with Chantel. Before I could return, Chantel left so I was not able to ask more of her. But Mara later told me that Chantel had admitted to her that Mara's dad had called her up one day and told her that she needed to help him get me away from Mara's children before I could molest anyone else like I had Melissa's daughter. I never knew why Chantel did not just go to Melissa to verify this, considering she was Melissa's ex-sister-in-law and had regular contact with Melissa for visiting her niece and nephew (Melissa's children), but she did not.

Irregardless, Chantel had apparently been scared at being dragged into anything like this and made excuses to leave as soon as she could after I left the room. But what she had left behind was an unalterable fact: Jerry Nezat had been the one who had told Chantel the story about me supposedly molesting someone else in the past – and it was for this reason I believe that the Nezats felt they could rely on Chantel to support the story about me supposedly molesting her own daughter. Whether it was because she had been "found out" by Mara and I, or whether she just genuinely was not willing to lie to the police, I cannot say – but as the record demonstrates, she was not willing to back up the Nezats' story about her own daughter.

The only other interview conducted in the investigation was that Chantel Beasley on July 28, 2003. This was really a last ditch effort to find something else to pursue the investigation on since plainly the hope of using Daughter 1 had fallen apart. But, as the record reflects, and as I have previously stated, Chantel was not willing to lie and told Overman that she had never dated me and I had not molested her daughter.

This ended the investigation – the police department had nothing else to go on. There was no credible allegation against me because Daughter 1 had kept changing her story and had finally claimed that she could not tell if I was awake or asleep, removing the intent requirement of commission of a crime. But the file still remained open September, presumably in hopes that someone would give them something else they could pursue. But at last, Overman filed a closing record on the investigation on September 4, 2003, specifically stating that the case was "suspended pending further evidence."

This statement is important for three reasons:

First, suspended is not the same as closed, but the Kalispell Police Department had evidence that if the alleged incident happened, there was no intent present. So there is no possible way they should have been able to pursue anything, because with this evidence, there *is no crime*. Consequently, the case should have been "closed", not "suspended". All my inquiries into the status of this investigation, by the way, was that it had been closed – not suspended. That it was only suspended is a direct link to the intentions of the Kalispell Police Department's desire to find a way to make this case – in spite of evidence which exonerated me, they had every intention of keeping this investigation open indefinitely.

Second, there was no possibility of "further evidence", nor was any ever provided. The entire allegation hinged upon the accusation of Daughter 1, who had declared that she could not say that there was intent to the alleged crime. There were no witnesses, no additional allegations of further misconduct, nothing. This comment was actually the embodiment of the KPD's efforts to dig for evidence even after they received evidence that exonerated me. They were still looking – months later – for further evidence, and though they officially suspended the investigation at this point, they were obviously still reaching, trying to find something to act on.

Finally, third, the investigation was reopened months later *without* any new evidence. They just started actively trying to dig again. And their reasons were because I was after the police records of the investigation, which I will go into in a moment.

At any rate, on September 18, 2003, Mara received a letter from Child and Family Services stating that their own investigation of Mara's exposing Daughter 1 to unreasonable risk, ie, to a child molestation, were "unsubstantiated".[8] Remember, we had not been informed of the police department's investigation had been closed yet, so Mara and I saw this as the first step in finally putting all of this behind us.

It was not until the first week in October that we received the first indication that the police investigation had been closed. Doug Overman had been shifted by this point to be a liaison officer with the Kalispell Middle School, which conveniently was where Daughter 1 went to school in the fall. Mara ran into Overman while picking Daughter 1 up one day, and he told Mara that the investigation had been closed – specifically telling Mara that it was his belief that if the alleged incident did happen, it happened while I was asleep. Upon learning this, I followed up with Daughter 1's school counselor, Mary Jane Foxx, and other school staff, who had also been told this by Overman over the preceding weeks. I then confirmed with the Kalispell Police Department that the case was closed. Finally, I called Tana Ryggs with the Montana Municipal Insurance Agency, who also confirmed that it had been reported to her that the investigation was closed and no charges would be filed.

---

8 A copy of this letter can be viewed in Appendix 2.

So, coupled with the letter from CFS, we had every reason to believe the worst of this was behind us. All that was left was for us to try to put our family back together. Towards this end, around October 10th (this is an estimate, since the exact date escapes me), Mara and I met with both John's school counselor (whose name I cannot recall) and Daughter 1's to discuss what steps we could take to reunite the family. Remember, up to this point, Mara and her daughters were living separately from me, and coming out of these months of turmoil, I had some genuine trust issues with Daughter 1. So it was believed that the school counselors would be a place to start in discussing ways to reestablish the family bonds that had been shattered by all of this.

It was during this meeting that Mara had a shocking recollection. She admitted that the details of Daughter 1's accusations had always sounded vaguely familiar, and it was at this time she announced that she now remembered why – this was when she told the story of how Shane had attacked her when Daughter 1 was three years old, and how the incident Daughter 1 had described was almost verbatim that of the incident she had witnessed as a child. To this day, I do not know if Mara deliberately withheld this until that point, or whether this was a genuine sudden recollection in the midst of our meeting.

I have detailed all of this previously (see Chapter 3), including Mara's confronting Daughter 1 and Daughter 1's follow-up affidavit, so I will not go too much into detail. I am only mentioning it here again to place these events in chronological order. It is additionally important to point out that in what came next, Daughter 1 had actually fully recanted her original allegation – so there was not even the *claim* of a crime being committed. And Daughter 1 had recanted her allegation over a month and a half *after* the police investigation had closed. So there was nothing really to be gained by me at that point – except the truth.

Another thing I did following the discovery that the police investigation had been closed was to send a letter to Richard Hickle officially requesting the police records of the investigation. I wanted to see if the Nezats' and Wilson's comments had been recorded. In September, Mara and I had jointly filed a lawsuit against the Nezats, and this was more as a request for discovery in that lawsuit than a demand related to the City complaint. When Hickle did not respond to the letter, I visited him personally in his office, requesting the records in person. Hickle refused, claiming that I needed to make requests per Montana law, specifically MCA § 44-5-214[9], which required that any such request be made directly to the department who held the records, which in this case was the Kalispell Police Department.

Armed with this information, on or about October 28, 2003, I made my infamous request directly to the Kalispell Police Department. I say infamous, because this was the day I first met Frank Garner face-to-face, and the day he had the "closed" investigation reopened.

---

9 See Appendix 1 for text of this law.

Chapter 6

Of all the details I have written so far, this chapter contains the most emotionally frustrating for me. It details the crux of everything that came after – and it represents the days when my firm, previously-intractable faith in America and my rights to civil liberties were abolished. Before the events of this chapter, I still held onto the belief that I was an American citizen, entitled to all the rights and liberties associated therewith. After this, I became aware that I had no rights – I was not a citizen, or even a person under the law, and I clearly was not entitled to any kind of dignity. It was here that I first began to see that I had not been dealing with one corrupt officer and a department (and City) trying to loyally protect him, but that I had actually been antagonizing an entire criminal enterprise masquerading under the color of official government.

Maybe all that had happened previously should have forewarned me, but I was wearing my rose-tinted glasses, blinded by my sincere and genuine belief in the American dream. And the events that followed could not have left me more disillusioned.

As mentioned previously, I had been informed by Adjutant City Attorney Richard Hickle that I needed to make request of the police department directly for their records. Every indication was given to me by Hickle that if I went to the KPD with an official request, that I could obtain records of the investigation there. I returned to my business to tell Mara what I had been told and requested that she accompany me to the police station – having had some degree of legal experience, I knew better than to approach the police department – whom I had made a demand for damages against – without a witness being present. This being said though, I had not expected the scene that followed.

I made a copy of the applicable law and went with Mara to the Kalispell Police Department. I met and spoke with receptionist and told her I was there to make a formal request for the records of the criminal investigation against me. The receptionist at first seemed very cooperative – right up until I she asked my name. I can still remember her eyes going wide and her mouth hanging slack for a fraction of an instant as it registered who I was. I really had no idea at first why she would react the way she had, but after a moment's panic she asked me to hold a moment and picked up the phone to call someone.

Mara and I were standing right there, and though the receptionist was clearly trying to talk low into the phone (very odd behavior for someone who is simply calling back to get someone to help me), I could hear most of what she said. I heard her say that Ron Glick was at the front counter, pause, then say, "He's asking for records." Then after a moment, she repeated, "He's here right now," as she cast a look up at me, then away again. She broke away from the call for a moment and said, "This isn't something we do. You need to talk to the city attorney." I responded that I had just come from seeing Richard Hickle, and produced the law that I had copied, telling her this is what Hickle told me, that the police department was the one who was required to produce records. The receptionist went back to the phone, and actually covered the mouthpiece and turned away, so what she said next I could not make out. But after a couple of minutes, she put down the phone and told me someone would be right out to talk to me.

Having had experience with the police department in the past, I was used to being made to wait. I really expected to wait at least fifteen or twenty minutes, but someone came around the corner in the back almost immediately. He paused just briefly to look at the receptionist, who said, "That's him" as she nodded at me. Then the man turned to me and said, "Mr. Glick, you are not getting any records. And I don't appreciate you harassing [girl's name here – I genuinely don't remember it] about it."

I once again relayed to this person that I had just spoken with Richard Hickle, who had pointed me to the applicable law. I tried to show it to him, but he brushed it physically aside on the counter, saying, "You can put that away. I don't care what the Code says, you are not getting access to your file." I then asked him under what legal right he was keeping the records from me, and he responded, "Under what legal right? Because I say so, that's what legal right!" Realizing I was not getting anywhere with this person, I then asked to speak to his supervisor – only then did the man say, "I *am* the Chief!" Up to this point, he had not identified himself at all, simply met me aggressively refusing to release any records – it was not until I asked to speak to his supervisor that he identified himself.

The conversation went downhill from there. Garner proceeded to tell me that he was not required to turn over any records to an active investigation. I reiterated that the case was closed and had been for weeks (at this point, I believed the case had been closed the first week of October, not a month earlier on September 4, 2003) – and that I had been told it was closed by no less than five separate parties. Garner said he did not care, that he was "reopening" the case and sending it to the county attorney (ie, prosecutor's office) with recommendations to prosecute.

I was dumbfounded, and felt a pit opening up in my stomach at that. The case had been *closed* – I had finally gotten the chance to breathe a sigh of relief, and now I was being led to believe that just to keep the records from me, Garner was going to reopen the case and push for prosecution of the case. I fumbled over what I was saying next, I will admit, but I pointed out to him that the law did not make exclusion for active investigations – it was very specific: An individual may inspect *any* criminal history record information maintained them by the criminal justice agency maintaining the record. There was no exception for any records that were part of an ongoing investigation. All Garner said was, "I don't care." He then told me that if I did not leave, he would have me arrested.

I had no idea what to do but leave. Here I was – just asking for records of an investigation that had been closed at the time of my request – only to have the case reopened *just* because I asked for the records. Worse, I was now going to be prosecuted for it.

Keep in mind – now as I have a much broader understanding of the situation, I realize this was not about keeping the records from me, so much as it was that Garner thought I was there to get the records to file a lawsuit against his department. Remember, I was not looking for the records for that reason – and at that time, I really had no genuine interest in suing the police department. The investigation was done, I was walking away without a charge, and as far as I was concerned, the case was done except for any settlement with the Montana Municipal Insurance Agency. But Garner never even asked why I wanted them – he clearly did not want me having them, because he was fearful that I was preparing to sue him and his department. This was therefore nothing but a strong-arm tactic designed to stop the lawsuit, not to actually keep the records from me, per se.

Let me reiterate – what Frank Garner did on the afternoon of October 28, 2003, was criminal. He obstructed a legal request for records and essentially tampered with official records by withholding them.[10] These records were publicly accessible under the law, ie, available to a member of the public (specifically myself) and Garner deliberately purposely impaired the availability of that record to me. Frank Garner obstructed the availability of a public record and this is a felony in Montana.

---

10 See Appendix 1, MCA § 45-7-208(c).

Further, official misconduct – which is to say criminal conduct by a government official – is also a felony.[11] Therefore by committing the first felony, Frank Garner had in effect committed a second at the same time by virtue of his status as a government official. And in this instance, Garner actually tripped three areas of this particular law, making it three separate felonies – failing to perform a duty he was required to do by law (ie, make his department's records available), knowingly perform an act he knew was against the law (ie, tampering with public records), and for the purpose of his own interests or the interests of others performs an act in excess of his lawful authority (ie, obstructing access to records to protect himself and officers under his authority from liability under a lawsuit).

In effect, Frank Garner committed four felony acts within the space of a few minutes. This was only the first set of many crimes Frank Garner would commit in the course of the next several weeks, but this *was* the first acts that Garner committed directly himself that I knew of. Remember, two others had previously told me they had been sent by Frank Garner to harass my business (which, by the way, also triggered the exact same criminal acts – since Frank Garner was abusing his authority to have others harass me and my business, he was committing official misconduct on multiple counts even before this date).

And whether I recognized it for what it was at the time or not, this was a whopper. The top official in the Kalispell Police Department, Police Chief Frank Garner, had just committed four felony offenses punishable by up to ten years in prison or a fifty thousand dollar ($50,000.00) fine for each offense - in my personal presence – *just* to block my filing a lawsuit against him and his department. There was no question that someone else could have been *claiming* to have been acting under Garner's authority – there could never be a hearsay claim made here, no

---

11 See Appendix 1, MCA § 45-7-401.

third party *saying* they were sent by Frank Garner. This was Frank Garner *himself* committing four simultaneous felonies *right in front of me!*

As I say, I did not realize at the time exactly how monumental this was at the time. All I could focus on was that I was once again under threat of going to prison for a crime I had already been cleared of. Which I am sure is precisely what Garner was out to do – he wanted to rattle my cage, to scare me into running away and hiding. Well, he scared me – he definitely did, I will not deny that. But personally, I do not run away when I am afraid – I stand up and fight back.

The real irony at this point is that if Frank Garner had just followed the law that day, there would never likely have ever been a lawsuit against him or his department. I was settling the case with the City's insurance and my own risk was completely nonexistent at that point in time. All I wanted the records for was Mara's and my action against the Nezats. The problem, as I have come to understand since, is that Frank Garner and his fellow Good Ol' Boys had been above the law for so long, they knew it did not apply to them. They broke the law on a regular basis and did not care – who was ever going to hold them accountable after all?

It is just like Garner said to me: "Under what legal right? Because I say so, that's what legal right!" And what he said was true – the only law that mattered was what Garner and his fellow corrupt authorities said. The Kalispell Police Department, the City of Kalispell and yes, even the County of Flathead, were and remain nothing more than an organized gang who go around Kalispell and beat down the people they don't like and shelter others they favor from any actual consequences for their misconduct. And of course, no one in government in Flathead Count is *ever* accused of a crime, because anyone and everyone in control of actually filing any criminal charges is part of the very corrupt network that allows this to happen in the first place!

This is the kind of thing I came to understand in the weeks and years that followed – and my confrontation with Garner that day was the first time a crack in my unshakable faith in the American system of justice began to form. I had been exonerated by what I at the time had *thought* was a fair investigation. Since seeing the actual police records, I know it was not nearly as fair as I had thought at the time, but nevertheless it was what I perceived at the time. And now, here I was being exposed a second time to the exact same thing which I had already been cleared of. And I began to fear that this was something that could *always* be hung over my head if I made waves of any kind.

My problem at the time was that though I certainly had doubts forming, I was still a steadfast believer in the ideal enunciated by Martin Niemoller:

*First they came for the Socialists, and I did not speak out —
Because I was not a Socialist.*

Then they came for the Trade Unionists, and I did not speak out—Because I was not a Trade Unionist.

*Then they came for the Jews, and I did not speak out—
Because I was not a Jew.*

Then they came for me—and there was no one left to speak for me.

Niemoller was saying that all citizens needed to speak out against injustice when it occurs, or the rights of others would be lost if they did not. In my case, I held to the belief at the time – and voiced it quite readily – that if I bent over and let Frank Garner and his department deprive me of my rights, that I would only be letting them go on and treat others worse later on.

Hand-in-hand with Niemoller's philosophy was Edmund Burke who is accredited as saying, "The only thing necessary for the triumph of evil if for good men to do nothing." And above all else, I saw myself as a good man – and that Frank Garner – if not Hitler-esque evil, per se – was certainly the real criminal in this situation. He recklessly disregarded the law to protect himself and was denying me my rights under the law – and once again threatening my own liberty and peace of mind.

Call it a crusader's complex, call it white knighting, call it whatever you like – but at the time I genuinely believed that I needed to stand up for more than myself – after that night, I believed I needed to stand up to make sure that people like Frank Garner could not victimize others later down the line. Clearly, I was much more self-confident of my chances of success then – but I cannot deny that this was very much a central part of my mindset at the time. I genuinely believed that as a good man, I had a duty to make sure the evil personified by Frank Garner and his corrupt police department did not prevail.

I began initially by making phone calls, followed up by a new rash of letters when no one would take my calls – to City Manager Chris Kukolski, to Mayor Pam Kennedy, and even to Richard Hickle. But I knew I was spinning my wheels at this point.

With this in mind, I also knew I was a bit out of my depth – I did not know that Garner was specifically violating the law. I still had a shred of belief that Garner would not do something outright illegal, and I needed to know what authority he was acting under. So I consulted an attorney who specialized in freedom of information. This attorney (whose name I honestly cannot recall after all this time) advised me that no, Frank Garner did not have any legal right to withhold the records, active investigation or not. He then advised me that if the police department was not willing to voluntarily release the records, then I would have to file a petition with the local district court.

Based upon the advice of this attorney, on October 30, 2003, I filed the opening volley in what would eventually evolve into the civil lawsuit against the City of Kalispell and Kalispell Police Department. It started out as a simple petition for production of records – but behind the scenes, it was so much more.

Meanwhile, Frank Garner did not immediately deliver on his promise to reopen the police investigation on October 28, but he did send a complaint to Child and Family Services to have *their* investigation reopened, as well. None of us knew this initially – I certainly was only acting under the premise that the KPD investigation was open, and that it was being sent to the county attorney's office. But CFS assigned an intern, Kori Taylor, to clandestinely recontact witnesses in the case to see if anything new could be dug up.

I later realized why he did this – CFS had the police records I had requested as part of their own investigation, the one that had been closed on September 18, 2003. Frank Garner had stopped me from obtaining the records from his department, but he did not want me obtaining them from CFS. It simply did not occur to me that CFS and the KPD would be sharing records, but when I learned later that Taylor had the original police records during her own investigation, the reason to have CFS reopen their own case became apparent. And since CFS was not a criminal justice agency, I could not use the same law to obtain the records from them – if they wanted to keep me from records of an active investigation, there was literally nothing I could do about it. A closed investigation would have been a different story. But Garner made sure CFS' case was open to keep me from the same records he was blocking.

Only upon my filing a request for the records in court did Garner act upon his threat to have the KPD's investigation reopened and sent to the county prosecutor.[12] Apparently, Garner felt his threat to do so would be enough to intimidate me – until I proved I was not abandoning my efforts and filed a petition in court to compel the records' production. Incidentally, the district court – and even the city attorney – ignored this filing almost entirely. The only response the Kalispell City Attorney ever made was to have Hickle send me a copy of my criminal record, which consisted of nothing more than identifying information since I did not *have* a criminal record. But his office never filed a response to the petition in court, and the district court ignored it altogether.

I should note here that this initial filing was not against any specific person – it was only against the City of Kalispell, the City Attorney's Office and the Kalispell Police Department. Later, the individuals would be added when this case elevated to a full complaint, but at the beginning it was just the divisions of government whom I was seeking to compel to produce the records. It is also important to note that this initial petition was served by Mara, who took the initial opening document with the accompanying summons[13] and served the City, the City Attorney and KPD. I accompanied her to act as backup in case she encountered any problems, but mostly this just consisted of me helping her navigate the city building and find the right person to serve for the City itself. Whenever she performed service itself

---

[12] As evidence of this, please note the date at the top of each page of the police report included in Appendix 2. These copies are from the Flathead County Attorney's Office, as transmitted by the Kalispell Police Department after being printed by Greg Burns on October 30, 2003, *after* I had filed the initial petition and had it served upon the police department.

[13] For anyone who does not understand what a summons is, it is a cover document that declares to the defendant or respondent of a legal action that they are being sued, their time they have to respond, and an official notice that failure to respond could result in a default judgment against them. It is a document issued by the court clerk's office when any new case is opened or when new defendants or respondents are added to a case. This becomes critical later on, which is why I pause here to explain.

though, I stood well back – down the hall in each instance – so it could not be said that I was in any way affecting service myself.

Meanwhile, Stewart with the Fire Marshal's Office was still conducting his escalating inspections, as well. Following the third list of demands from Stewart (which was in early November, I believe), and it became clear that our landlord had no intention of rewiring the building to comply with his latest demands, I sent a letter to Richard Hickle demanding that the harassments stop. It was plain what the plan was – to persistently harass me and my business and to eventually get the leverage to shut us down – and I told Hickle if he or any city/county official harassed me further, I would just file the lawsuit.

Ironically enough, I never heard from Stewart again. But as replacement, I kept getting insulting letters from Hickle himself, not only denying the City's responsibility for the KPD's conduct but also inferring that I was guilty of what I was being investigated for. Finally, pushed into a corner and feeling I was just going to keep being harassed by one division of government or another, I decided on November 18, 2003, to do what I had never really planned to do in the first place: I filed a lawsuit in the petition case, naming the City of Kalispell, Kalispell Police Department, Kalispell City Attorney's Office, Frank Garner, Myron Wilson, Doug Overman, Pam Kennedy, Chris Kukolski, and Richard Hickle.

Incidentally, I initially sought to file the original petition in the justice court, ie, the lower court which I had been told handled claims against the City. However, when I went to file it, I was told the that the district court had jurisdiction over these kinds of petitions, and so I filed the original petition in district court with the Flathead County Justice Court's heading. When I went back to file the complaint, I neglected to change the heading, and so it also has the justice court's heading, even though it was filed in the Eleventh Judicial District Court of Montana. This is why there is a discrepancy in the heading of the complaint. I should note also that the original petition is not being withheld by my choice – it is a document that I have been forbidden access to by the district court, who will not provide me access to my original lawsuit file for reasons that will be explained later, and I have not been able to obtain it anywhere else.

Of course, nothing is ever easy when dealing with this issue, and Frank Garner's allies began to complicate things this time around. When I went to file the complaint with the district court, I knew I needed additional summons since I had added new defendants (Garner, Wilson, Overman, Kukolski, Kennedy and Hickle). However, the deputy court clerk I spoke to, April Coen, refused to issue me any new summons. Initially, she seemed more than willing to issue new summons when I told her I needed to file this complaint in the case file already opened and to have new summons issued. But her demeanor changed when she looked at who I was suing (or perhaps it was my name across the top, who knows). She immediately changed her story, and said she could file the complaint, but summons had already been issued in the case and no new summons could be now. I knew this was not true, and tried to argue with her about it – but she refused to budge, just telling me that I needed to talk to an attorney if I did not understand court proceedings.

Remember, this is both tampering with official records and official misconduct again – pursuant to Montana Rules of Civil Procedure Rule 4, the deputy clerk *must* issue any summons presented for issuance, regardless of whether they are original parties or added to the action later.[14] For the clerk to refuse to issue a summons represents not only tampering with the official records of the proceeding by impairing the integrity of the document I was seeking to have filed, but also official misconduct since the clerk was failing to perform a mandatory

---

14 See Appendix 1, 25-20-Rule 4(c)(1)

duty, taking an action forbidden by law, and doing so to give the corrupt officials being sued an advantage. Once again, a sequence of four simultaneous felonies committed by yet another official, this time at the county government level.

Needless to say, there was something going on behind the scenes by this time. Peg Allison, who was the Clerk of Court for Flathead County's Eleventh District Court, was complicit by this point and had left instructions to not permit the progression of my claims against the City of Kalispell. As time progressed, I even received letters from Peg Allison openly admitting to tampering with official records – again with complete impunity because she knew she would never be held accountable for her felonious criminal conduct. The clerk's office may not have known specifically that the complaint was forthcoming (more likely, they were expecting a default judgment to come across their desk since the City had not responded to the initial petition), but there was clear premeditation to obstruct anything I filed. Coen had to have known she had an obligation to issue summons and knew that refusing to issue the summons would obstruct my capacity to ever claim a judgment in the case. This was deliberate sabotage, but quite frankly, I had no choice but to accept the determination of the clerk's office. So I set about to have the complaints served.

Incidentally, this particular sabotage only affected the defendants added to the lawsuit, ie, Garner, Wilson, Overman, Kukolski, Kennedy and Hickle. The City of Kalispell, City Attorney's Office and the Kalispell Police Department had all been served with summons that were issued when I filed the original lawsuit. Irregardless, I proceeded with service per the instructions given to me by April Coen, which was that there did not need to be new summons served with the complaint. Again, I knew this was improper, but at the time my rationality was that if this was how the clerk said to do it, then this was acceptable under some local rule or procedure.

Remember – at this point, I was not aware that the district court was acting in collusion with the City. I genuinely believed at this point in time that the corruption was still confined to city government, and had no reason to suspect duplicity from the County. Yet again, this just demonstrates the level of ignorance I had regarding exactly how entrenched the corruption of local government went. So when I accepted the clerk's explanation, I had no idea it was part of a premeditated effort to sabotage the lawsuit itself, nor that April Coen was committing more felony crimes.

With this sabotage in place, it would stand to reason that the corrupt players in this game would sit back and let it all proceed – laughing at me behind closed doors perhaps when I did not see their cheating hands at work. But either someone did not tell Frank Garner, or he could not let the sleeping dog lie, so to speak – because once again, Garner led the charge with more criminal misconduct.

Initially, I had a friend and employee of mine, Jeff Berna, perform service upon the defendants of the lawsuit. On the late afternoon of November 18, 2003, Jeff went into the Kalispell Police Department and announced that he was there to serve Frank Garner, Myron Wilson, Doug Overman and the Kalispell Police Department. By Jeff's report, he was rushed immediately into a back room and confronted by Frank Garner, who stood over him and threatened to have Jeff arrested for trying to serve him. According to Jeff, Garner told him that I was having Jeff commit a crime because he was not a licensed process server, and if he tried to serve him or anyone else named in my lawsuit, Garner would have him thrown in jail for it. Jeff said Garner got right in his face and asked, "Do you really want to go to jail for scum like Glick?" He also made a comment about how Jeff did not want to "take a fall because of Glick's little games."

This of course was a bold faced lie – Montana law allows for anyone over the age of 18 and of mental competence to perform service of process, only requiring someone to be a registered process server if they perform more than ten services in a year.[15] Jeff had only served the Nezats twice before for us, and even if he had served all the defendants in the case, he would still not have exceeded ten process services requiring him to be registered – and he had only been there to serve five, which would have brought his total services for that year to seven. This was an intimidating threat designed to scare Jeff and to obstruct lawful service.

And it worked – Jeff returned to Arcadia frazzled, terrified that he was going to go to jail. I could not believe what Jeff relayed, and when I heard the lies uttered to him, I took him to the back office and opened the actual law and showed him that what Garner had told him was a lie. He had not broken any law, nor could Garner arrest him for performing a service of process. But Garner's ploy had worked – Jeff refused to even try to go back and serve anyone with the complaint. And Jeff's story quickly spread, making everyone who heard too afraid to even try to perform service on the City or the KPD.

Incidentally, Garner called me immediately after, bragging about how he had scared off my "little errand boy", and telling me not to have people break the law for me. But Jeff had come back by then and I had the law pulled up for Jeff to see and read it off verbatim to Garner. Garner proceeded to call me a punk who was too big for his own britches, at which point I just hung up on him. Normally, I would have called the police to report a threatening phone call – but who does one call when the threat was coming from the Chief of Police Frank Garner himself?

It took until the next day for us to find someone willing to take the risk. One of our customers, Ian Chrisman, took up the

---
15 See Appendix 1, MCA § 25-1-1101(1).

challenge as something of a joke. He basically said, "Let them try to arrest me," laughing as he accepted the papers to serve.

Ian apparently went first to the City Attorney's Office (where Jeff went to the KPD first) and served City Attorney Charles Harball, who accepted service for the City Attorney's Office and Richard Hickle (though interestingly enough, refused to accept service for the City itself, even though Hickle had repeatedly said that his office was acting as counsel for the City).

Next, Ian went to the Kalispell Police Department and attempted to have the KPD defendants served. According to Ian, the court clerk spoke with Frank Garner after taking a quick look at the heading of the complaint, and then told Ian that Garner would not accept service, nor would he permit service upon his department or officers. Garner then instructed the receptionist to have Ian leave the city building or to have him escorted out.

Remember, this is yet more criminal misconduct – both for Garner's actions against Jeff and Ian – obstruction of service of process is still a crime, albeit a misdemeanor.[16] However, regardless of whether the crime is a misdemeanor or felony, it is still unlawful – and this triggers yet more compounded commissions of official misconduct. In this instance, Garner only triggered two violations of official misconduct per misdemeanor (knowingly committing an act known to be forbidden by law and doing so for the personal advantage of himself and others), but there were four misdemeanors committed here – obstructing service of four defendants. And he did it twice, which makes eight misdemeanors and sixteen separate violations of official misconduct. And that is not even including the deliberate threats and misrepresentations of law made against Jeff.

For anyone keeping count, by this juncture, Frank Garner had committed at least twenty felonies and eight misdemeanors in the

---

16 See Appendix 1, MCA § 45-7-302.

course of a month, all designed to obstruct a lawsuit being brought against himself and his department. And that is foregoing his making false reports to CFS and the threats made against Jeff Berna.

Ian left the window of the police department, but he did not leave the building. By his report, he next tried to serve Pam Kennedy, but she was not in her office. He next went to Chris Kukolski's office. According to Ian, Kukolski was very amiable and accepted the service without any hesitation. However, no sooner had Kukolski accepted service than his phone rang. Ian reported that Kukolski made a couple of affirmations, then said, "Yes, he's here now." Looking at Ian at this point, Kukolski then said, "I'll just come over there."

Apparently, Frank Garner had gone back directly to his office and called the City Attorney's Office to forewarn them of Ian's going to serve them, but Ian had already been there. He next tried to stave off Ian's service of Kukolski, who had just been served. Plainly, this demonstrates intent of Garner to commit even more crimes in obstructing service of the other defendants in the cause, but Kukolski – when he learned what Garner was doing – decided to get involved.

Kukolski then asked Ian to please have a seat in the front waiting area by the police station, telling Ian he needed to go speak with the police chief. Ian reported that he waited out in the waiting area for some twenty minutes. Garner came out of the police department and stormed past Ian several times, glaring at Ian as he went, though he did not say anything. My guess (from the layout of the building) was that Garner was on his way to the City Attorney's Office, but Ian said he did not try to figure out where Garner went. A few minutes later, Garner returned, equally upset and disappeared into the police department again.

Ian informed me that another ten minutes passed before Kukolski and Garner both emerged from the police department offices. Ian said that Garner's jaw was clenched as he came out and grudgingly said he would accept service on behalf of himself and the police department, and that he would make arrangements for the other KPD defendants to be present at 5pm to be served, as well. Kukolski said he had arranged for Pam Kennedy to be present at that time, as well. Ian accepted this and left. When he returned at 5pm, he was able to complete services upon everyone except the City of Kalispell itself, whom I had to ask one of our volunteers, James Valentino, to do later. As I recall, he just served the same person in the city planning area Mara had served before.

The service of the lawsuit however created an entirely new wave of retaliation. But this of course requires me to back up a little in time.

In August of 2003, during the course of the investigation, there was one point that Mara permitted Daughter 1 to go visit her birth family in Cut Bank, Montana. Specifically, she went to stay with her aunt, Memory Walters. The premise was that while the investigation was ongoing, it would do good for Daughter 1 to be away from the situation. To me, it seemed more like rewarding Daughter 1 for bad conduct, but I had no say in this issue. It turned out however to be a disastrous decision.

Memory had held a grudge against Mara for years, and blamed Mara for the death of her second daughter. She saw the opportunity of taking Daughter 1 as a means by which to dig up dirt and somehow use it to get Daughter 1 back into the folds of her father's family and away from Mara. Daughter 1 – finding a sympathetic ear, found she was encouraged to fabricate stories, learning very quickly that she was rewarded if she lied about things to her aunt. Amongst the falsehoods told to her aunt were that she was thin because her mom never kept food in the house, that she had no clothes at all, and that she and her sister were left for days at a time alone by Mara while she went out with her friends. Of course, every one of these were lies, and they were only told by Daughter 1 to get advantages – because of what she told her aunt, she got an entire new wardrobe, was allowed to eat any junk food she wanted (presumably under the pretense of "putting weight" on her), and was doted on by her aunt and other relatives.

Worst of all however, is that Daughter 1 felt compelled to once again expound upon her allegations against me. I can only presume that her aunt was not content with the allegation that I had supposedly only touched her one time, so Daughter 1 began telling her aunt and other relatives that it had happened several times and that it had been ongoing for a very long time. When she got back to Kalispell, this variation went away, but it surfaced when authorities questioned Daughter 1's cousin much later (after the investigation was reopened and my arrest), who wrote a poem about what Daughter 1 had told her, claiming that the molestation had been occurring over and over again.

In every recorded interview, Daughter 1 has insisted adamantly that this supposedly only happened once – but her entire family in Cut Bank were insisting that Daughter 1 told them it had been happening for a long time. Once again, this was another variation of the story tilted to give Daughter 1's audience the story they wanted to hear. In the end, Mara was forced to drive to Cut Bank to collect Daughter 1 because her relatives were threatening to do what the Nezats did the night of July 9, 2003 – they wanted to hold Daughter 1 and have her taken away from her mother, because of all the horrible "abuse" Daughter 1 had been reporting.

It was a couple months after Daughter 1 came back to Kalispell that we found out that the investigations were closed. Later, in October and November, Mara and I had reunited our households and were trying to somehow regain some semblance of normalcy. However, Daughter 1 had been finding new ways to act out, which were largely a return to the behavior she had demonstrated with her aunt.

Coming into the middle school in September, the staff had already been cued in (presumably by Overman) that Daughter 1 had reported being molested, and so she gained the attention of a school counselor, Mary Jane Foxx, almost immediately. Daughter 1 was never a slow child, and she quickly latched onto the attentions of someone who was willing to dote on her and give her attention – just as Memory had done – and getting out of class on a regular basis was an added bonus. Her friends that came around Arcadia would often complain that Daughter 1 would brag about how she did not have to go to class because she got to see Foxx instead, in fact. In essence, Daughter 1 had found someone new to get sympathy from, and once again began fabricating stories to get it.

Now something one needs to understand about Mary Jane Foxx – the woman has a messiah complex. I genuinely believe the only reason she got a job working at a school with teens was so she could find little children in need of "saving", and she certainly saw this in Daughter 1. And, as I mentioned, Daughter 1 was quick to find ways to take advantage of it.

Eventually, Daughter 1 found out that if she could have a "crisis" in class, she could even get extra time with Foxx. And this is when Daughter 1 began to make claims of wanting to kill herself.

Now I am not minimizing people who are genuinely distressed and are contemplating suicide. But Daughter 1 was always about getting attention – and considering how she escalated the need for attention between September and November, I cannot help but see this as her latest scheme for attention. Her efforts to accuse me of molesting her had waned, and Daughter 1 was looking for something new for people to pay attention to.

Daughter 1's claims of wanting to kill herself got her attention at the beginning, and would earn her an extra trip to Foxx's office if she did not want to be in class. After spending as much as a half hour to an hour's time talking about her feelings, Daughter 1 would be asked to sign a no-harm contract (essentially committing to not hurting herself) and be sent back to class. After awhile, Foxx began to see it for what it was – at least at first she did – and the trips to Foxx's office grew shorter until finally, Daughter 1 could not count on more than five minutes out of class.

Foxx's mistake here was giving Daughter 1 ammunition – when Daughter 1 complained about being sent back to class, Foxx told her that all she was doing was saying she wanted to kill herself, but she never actually had any plans on how to do it. Essentially, Foxx sent Daughter 1 back to class with a homework assignment, because the next time she showed up in Foxx's office, Daughter 1 now had a plan on how to kill herself in place – she said she was thinking about drinking one of the bottles of chemicals in the janitor's closet.

It was not all about killing herself though. Daughter 1 was a consummate story teller and more than once she would make up stories to Foxx, which only had Foxx calling either Mara and myself to rebuke us for how we were either "neglecting" or "mistreating" Daughter 1.

One incident that pretty much sums up this kind of thing was when Daughter 1 had told Foxx that she had to wear the same dirty clothes to school because she had no clean clothes at home. This was a blatant lie, of course – Daughter 1 had more clothes than any of the children because she kept having friends give her clothes. And I knew for a fact that Daughter 1 wore different clothes to school every day because it was an ongoing struggle with her every morning. Daughter 1 insisted on sleeping in her clothes from the day before rather than get dressed in pajamas, and she would always wake up grouchy and not want to actually change. And I do mean this was a *daily* struggle. It was standard practice every morning to see if Daughter 1 had changed out of her clothes into something new.

But of course, Foxx was more interested in "saving" *poor* Daughter 1, who was just so neglected that she just called me up at the store and began yelling at me over the phone that she was going to have our kids taken away from us because we insisted on sending them to school in the same "filthy" clothes every day. Apparently, teachers had noticed that Daughter 1 had been wearing the same outfit for three days or more in a row. I snapped back at Foxx that she had no idea what she was talking about, but I would get to the bottom of it.

When Daughter 1 got home, Mara and I sat down with her and asked what was going on. It took some pressure, but Daughter 1 finally admitted what was going on. She had been given a pair of faux leather pants from her friend Chelsey, and apparently a boy at school had liked her in them. So she devised a scheme where she would keep the jeans and a matching top in her backpack and change into them at school. When the teachers noticed her wearing the same clothes, she lied and said Mara and I would not get her any new clothes and all her clothes were dirty. And she almost had herself, her sister and my son taken away from us because of Foxx's insistence on believing whatever Daughter 1 told her – no matter how often Daughter 1 was caught in lies along the way.

At any rate, one morning, Daughter 1 got up in yet another grouchy mood (I believe it was November 13, 2003). We had arrived early at Arcadia as was our routine, and the kids had gone back to sleep before school. But Daughter 1 refused to get up – every time I turned my back, she was lying back down – not getting her homework together or even get her shoes on. So finally I went and stood over her while she packed her bag, and when she tried to lay back down, I sat down on the part of the couch she was trying to lie down on, ie, blocking her from lying back down on the arm of the couch.

At this point, Daughter 1 shouted, "You are making me feel uncomfortable!" Now, this was clearly something she had picked up from Foxx – it is a common counseling technique to tell victims of sexual abuse to speak up when their "offender" is making them uncomfortable. But I was not doing anything other than sitting beside her on the couch – there was not even any physical contact. I was just preventing her from lying down again, and she was throwing a tantrum.

I asked her, "How am I making you uncomfortable, [Daughter 1]? All I am doing is sitting here." Of course, all she could say is, "You just are." I genuinely believe she could get me to go away and she could lay back down again, but I stood (or sat as the case may be) my ground and stayed where I was, telling her I was not going anywhere until she got her shoes on and got out the door to school. In an angry huff, she finally threw on her shoes (literally growling at the top of her lungs as she did so), then grabbed her bag and started stomping towards the door.

At this point I had had enough and called Daughter 1 back. I then proceeded to tell her that I was not going to put up with another morning like this, that I did not have to (remember, I was having trust issues with Daughter 1 and was not really feeling I had to suffer through her abuse on top of it), and that when she got back from school, her mom and I were going to sit down and decide what to do about it. This only got Daughter 1 to growl all the louder, turn and slam the door behind her as she left the store.

Of course, when Daughter 1 got to school she was still in a rage and immediately pulled the, "I want to kill myself" card, which got her sent to Foxx. Reportedly, all she wanted to do was rage about how her mom was going to believe me when she got home, and that I had been the one wrong because I was making her uncomfortable. And of course, Foxx believed whatever Daughter 1 spun – she later came back and said that I was to blame for what happened that morning. At any rate, time eventually came when Daughter 1 was yet again asked to sign a no-harm contract, but Daughter 1 had learned from the past that if she escalated her "crisis", she could get extra time out of class. And so she made a critical mistake in her attention grab – she refused to sign the no-harm contract.

This immediately prompted Overman to be summoned, who of course wrote a report detailing how I had been alone with Daughter 1 (which was not true, since all three of our kids were present) – but at least he wrote in the report that Daughter 1 acknowledged that I had not touched her in any way. But because Daughter 1 refused to sign a no-harm contract, she was sent to Pathways, a local mental health treatment center, and put on suicide watch.

During the course of the next several days, all Daughter 1 could do was try to get her mom to have her released. I went to see her once in the facility when we could find someone to watch the store in the evening, but most nights (the only visiting time allowed), Mara went to see her. But Mara said early on that Daughter 1 wanted to see me again – and on the night of November 18 (the day the lawsuit had been filed), I agreed to do so the next night, which would have been November 19. Daughter 1 had wanted to see me alone, and to have her mom stay behind.

To this day I have no idea why that was. Mara said she believed Daughter 1 was going to try to get me to sign her out because I was "the softer touch" and Daughter 1 had always been able to manipulate me easier. To a certain degree, this had always been true – before the false allegation had been made. I had been far more lenient on Mara's girls than she was, and even covered for them at times with their mom. Before Daughter 1 had decided to make up this story about me in order to get her dad back with her mom, we had been really close. And I was still very close with Mara's youngest. I certainly did not agree that in the present state of our relationship, that Daughter 1 had any real ability to manipulate me like that, but I agreed to go out to see her while Mara watched the store.

However, roughly an hour before I was set to go visit, Daughter 1's doctor (whom name I seem to recall was Barnie Hauser) called, claiming that visitation had been called off for the night because someone had stolen a set of boots from one of the patients, so the facility was in lock down. I now know this was a made up story for other reasons, but it was what Mara had been told. However, also in the conversation, told Mara that someone from CFS had come to interview Daughter 1 and "badgered" Daughter 1 to the point of tears. According to Doctor Hauser, he wanted Mara to call CFS to make it clear that they should not do that – Daughter 1 was under suicide watch and this ran counter to Daughter 1's mental well-being.

It turned out that what had really happened on November 19, 2003, was that Kori Taylor – the intern from CFS – had come to Pathways to interview Daughter 1 related to the new investigation that Garner had sponsored. It was pretty obvious that Taylor's showing up the day after I filed the lawsuit against Garner – and in the afternoon of the day when Ian had actually successfully served him – was not a coincidence. Garner had been on the phone with everyone else – and that clearly included CFS, making sure that leverage was gained against me and soon.

Now, I should note that though I have seen Taylor's notes, the first was grossly redacted and the second was so clearly changed from the original that neither could be considered genuine documentation. Taylor's notes were clearly crafted to create an image that the authorities wanted conveyed – written in a word processor, not in any kind of actual record log – and everything from details told to her to dates were all skewed and disjointed. To be honest, it was plain this was a doctored record, but she was not even good enough to make it a *good* doctored record. There are pages and pages of supposed communications and investigations, but much of what she had written Mara and I were able to disprove – more than one person contacted said they never said what Taylor said they did in her notes. As I have said, the two disparate "records" Taylor produced were not only contradictory to each other, but they were also contradictory to the other people who were present.

Of particular note, Doctor Hauser confided later what really transpired that day – which without surprise contradicted nearly everything in Taylor's report. Doctor Hauser said that Daughter 1 denied repeatedly that I had done anything to her, but Taylor kept insisting that Daughter 1 was not being honest. When Daughter 1 began to cry, Taylor just pressed harder, trying to force Daughter 1 to renew her allegation against me. Daughter 1 continued to refuse, and Taylor just continued to badger her. Hauser said he felt helpless because since Taylor was with CFS, he had to let her interview Daughter 1, but he could not abide how Taylor was treating Daughter 1.

Finally, when Daughter 1 was allowed to leave, Taylor informed Hauser that she was filing papers to have Daughter 1 removed from her home, and she forbid Doctor Hauser from telling Mara or I. In fact, he was forbidden by Taylor to let either of us have contact with Daughter 1 before she could get the papers filed. This was why Doctor Hauser told us the story about the "lockdown" – because Taylor had forbidden him to let us have contact with Daughter 1, while also forbidding him to tell us why. He had hoped that by cuing Mara into the fact that CFS at least had *been* there, that she could somehow forestall what Taylor was trying to do. But Mara did not take any urgency away from the conversation, and by the time Mara got off work the next day, it had already been too late – Taylor had sprung her trap.

Chapter 7

The following is the context which appeared on my original website calling for public support, entitled "Another Case of Gov Abuse", and more or less picks up the story thread at this point. This website was originally posted on December 8, 2003. It has been edited to redact Daughter 1's name I am forbidden by court order to identify and Daughter 2's name (since she remains a minor), and I have provided links to Appendix 1 instead of the hyperlinks that were on the original site. I have also corrected for any grammatical errors. Otherwise, this is the original content of my public post.

Though I have no actual control over the original post any longer, since the host site, GeoCities, is no longer active, the site itself has been archived at http://www.oocities.org/ron_glick/ - so if anyone wishes to verify the validity of the original post, you can do so.

Some of this will be redundant, and that really cannot be helped without completely re-editing the site content to omit what has already been presented in the previous chapters. I had considered simply rewriting this content, but decided that presenting it as closely to its original content as possible was more important for the purposes of accuracy.

Additionally, for the purposes of full disclosure and accuracy, cited language for statutes contained in Appendix 1 come from the 2011 edition of the Montana code, simply because I could not locate a reasonable electronic copy of the 2003 edition originally cited. However, these laws have not changed substantially in the last ten years, so they remain accurate.

Keep in mind: some of this information as I presented it changed as other details emerged. For instance, I am now 45 as of this writing, and I don't necessarily ascribe to the belief that Daughter 1's recantation represents the full truth as I did then. But this original public appeal still remains largely accurate.

Another Case of Gov Abuse

We hear about it everyday. This government office is corrupt, or that elected official is dirty. But we always think that there are avenues to pursue, legal remedies to these people. That is what the US government is all about, right? Freedom from persecution, rights of the individual, the State not having absolute power over our lives. Well, I am a living example that when there is corruption in government, no one at higher levels truly cares enough to investigate.

Allow me to introduce myself. My name is Ron Glick. I am a 34 year old single father of a 12 year old boy who I have raised since he was an infant, since he was five on our own. Seven years ago, I set up a youth recreations program that focused on promoting educational games and activities amongst youth. And for the last two years, I have been dating Mara Pelton, who has two daughters of her own. We even set up a business together in our town of Kalispell, Montana, to allow for the youth program to have a full time facility. Life was on track until July of this year, 2003.

Jerry and Dixie Nezat are Mara Pelton's parents. And as it is ofttimes in relationships, Mara's parents do not like me. For whatever reason - I am not rich, I am not the "right" person for their daughter, whatever their reasoning - they decided to eliminate me from Mara's life.

On July 9, 2003, Jerry and Dixie asked to take one of the granddaughters, [Daughter 1], alone to their house. This had been a request made over and over again for over a week and a half. They wanted to have [Daughter 1] visit alone, allegedly to do house work for them. Each other time they had asked, Mara and I had been too busy to comply with their request, even though the request seemed rather odd in that they did not want the youngest granddaughter visiting, just the eldest. At any rate, on the above date, it was agreed to let [Daughter 1] go with her grandparents.

That evening, after spending six hours alone with her grandparents, [Daughter 1] made a sudden and unprecedented allegation - she claimed I had molested her! It took months to find out what really transpired that day, but one thing I knew to be true was that I had never molested [Daughter 1] and I knew Jerry and Dixie were somehow behind the allegation.

What came out months later was that when [Daughter 1] was three years old, she had witnessed her mother, Mara, nearly be raped by a man named Shane, a family friend. Something in things Dixie said to [Daughter 1] during the day triggered that memory, but the memory did not emerge completely. Instead, [Daughter 1] internalized the memory and saw herself as the victim. When she confessed this partial memory to her grandmother, Dixie insisted the memory was of me and convinced [Daughter 1] to press charges against me. When the full memory surfaced months later, [Daughter 1] was wracked with guilt over the harm she had caused and acknowledged I had never molested her.

To make a long story short, a report was filed and an investigation was launched on the initial night of July 9. As nerve wracking as a false allegation of this nature was, especially to a single father running a youth recreations business and nonprofit organization, it was made even worse - the reporting officer with the Kalispell Police Department, Myron Wilson, tampered with the witnesses, [Daughter 1] and Mara, by telling them I had a prior record for child molestation, when I have no record of any sort whatsoever. Additionally, threats were made to Mara that if she did not dissolve all ties to me, her children would be taken away. The intent had been to compel negative testimony against me and to discourage people who might testify on my behalf from allying with me by intimidating the witnesses into believing me a criminal by nature and to be afraid to continue to associate with me.

When I discovered the tampering, at least as was done to Mara since I avoided contact with [Daughter 1] during the investigation, I did what I thought was the proper legal action - I first asked of the presiding detective over the case, Doug Overman, why Myron Wilson would have done this. Doug Overman denied the officer would have done such a thing since it was obvious I had no prior record. Next, since it seemed obvious the Police Department would only continue denying that it happened, I sent a letter demanding damages for the action.

When an Officer lies to witnesses to coerce testimony, it is a felony. No one has the right to tamper with witnesses, not even law enforcement. Unfortunately, most people do not realize this and accept that Police lie and that's just a fact of life. A police officer can mislead, hypothesize, even make assumptions - but the moment that Officer tells a witness something that is not true or threatens a witness to compel the witness to change his or her opinion and/or testimony, it becomes a crime.[17]

In response to my demand, my business became swarmed upon by various government offices making demands of me and my business. Most of the demands were simple enough, if unwarranted in that no other business in my area was being asked to comply with these requirements. Finally, after months of inspections from the Fire Marshal that just continued to get more and more outrageous, I finally sent another letter to the City demanding the harassment stopped. That, at least, has happened.

---

17 See Appendix 1, MCA § 45-7-206.

Finally, in October, I was informed that the Police investigation was concluded. Detective Overman told Mara the case was closed and that no charges would be filed since his belief was that if it did happen, it happened while I was asleep (a point I did not agree with, but if it got the case closed, who was I to argue?). I confirmed additionally with the school counselor, Mary Jane Foxx, and the Kalispell Junior High School staff that they had also been told the same thing. Tana Ryggs with the Montana Municipal Insurance Agency, who was handling the claim for the city, had also been informed that the case was closed and no further action would be taken (in fact, her office could not process a claim until the investigation was closed and the reason she contacted me was to begin the claim process). I also called and confirmed for myself with the Police Department that the case was closed. Mara also received a letter from the Child Protective Services around this time that their investigation was also closed.

At this point, we thought all the criminal issues were over. We now only had to deal with the repercussions of what had been done to me. And so I made a request for the discovery in my case. I wanted to see if the statements made by Officer Wilson were on tape. Under MCA 2003 Section 44-5-214[18], an individual is entitled to any criminal history record information maintained about them by any criminal justice agency.

Imagine my surprise when my inquiry got the Police Chief himself, Frank Garner, to tell me he would not give me access to the files because the case was once again active and he was forwarding it to the County Attorney! As you will recall, no fewer than five separate people were informed by the Police Department that the case was closed and that no further action would be taken! Chief Garner further insisted that the case had never been closed and that while the case was open, I was not

---

18 See Appendix 1.

entitled to access the investigative information. Keep in mind - per the MCA Code of Authority listed above, there is no such restriction. Anyone who has information maintained about them by a criminal justice agency has right of access to their files - there is no restriction on whether the information is part of an active investigation or not.

I pointed this particular detail out to Chief Garner, telling him the Code did not allow him to use an active investigation as a bar to my access and attempted to show him a printed copy of the law. His response was, "You can put that away. I don't care what the Code says, you are not getting access to your file." When asked what legal authority he had to withhold the records, his only response was, "What legal right? Because I say so! That's what right!" So in other words, just because I asked for my records - a right I had under the law - now not only was my case open again, but now it was going to be prosecuted and I was still being refused my right to access the information!

At this point, I started a campaign contacting every supervisor I could within the City Government. I spoke to the City Attorney's Office, specifically to Adjutant City Attorney Richard Hickle, Mayor Pam Kennedy, and City Manager Chris Kukulski. I wrote new letters demanding my files that I was entitled to under the law. I even filed a Petition with the Court to order the files to be released, a Petition, I might add that was ignored by the Court! The only responses I received to the Petition were from Adjutant City Attorney Richard Hickle who provided a print out of my criminal offense record (ie, a list of crimes I have been convicted of, which I have no criminal record and all they have is identifying information) and a denial that I was entitled to anything else, claiming that the word "Complaint" in the MCA Code referred to a Complaint filed in a Court of law, in spite of the Code specifically stating that Court records were not included in criminal history record information.

In the end, I was forced to file a lawsuit against the City, Police Department, and all parties that had denied me my records, had tampered with witnesses and were responsible for harassing me during the investigation. I filed the lawsuit on November 18, 2003, and may be referenced through the 11th District Court of Montana as Case Number DV-03-572C.[19]

On November 20, 2003, Child Protective Services came and took my girlfriends daughters from her custody. This retaliatory act was based on new unfounded allegations from the Nezats (who had not had contact with the girls since July when they began their attack on me) and a made up allegation coming from the case worker, Kori Taylor, that had supposedly happened on the morning of November 13, 2003, in spite of there being a room full of witnesses who could dispute the entire incident.

The demand made by CPS is that Mara has to dissolve all contact with me or lose her girls forever. And since she and [Daughter 1] are my primary witnesses, if they testify for me, they are considered in violation of CPS. Very neat. Very convenient. And unfortunately, completely "legal" since District Court Judge Lympus, as of December 5, 2003, gave complete authority to Kori Taylor to make any demand of Mara that she felt like.

To date, Kori Taylor, CPS and the District Court have violated at least half a dozen laws.

MCA 2003 41-3-427(1)(c)[20], defining Petitions for immediate protection and emergency services, requires "the parents... must be given an opportunity to present evidence to the court before the court rules on the petition." Neither parent was notified of the petition at all, much less given an opportunity to respond or offer evidence.

---

19 A copy of this lawsuit, as well as documents leading up to its filing, are included in Appendix 2.

20 See Appendix 1.

MCA 2003 41-3-301(1)[21], defining emergency protective services, requires "the person or agency placing the child shall notify the parents... at the time of placement is made or as soon after placement as possible." No effort whatsoever was made to notify either parent that the girls had been taken into protective custody. A phone number was left at the youngest child's school for Mara to contact, but that was not discovered until after Mara sent someone to pick up her daughter from school. The father of the children was not notified until he received copies of legal papers four days later.[22]

MCA 2003 41-3-423(1)[23], defining reasonable efforts required to prevent removal of children from the home, requires CPS to make reasonable efforts including, but not limited to, voluntary protective services agreements and development of individual written case plans specifying state efforts. CPS made no effort whatsoever to prevent the children from being removed, have made no written statement of efforts between Mara and CPS to prevent removal of the children and in fact, removed the children before even investigating any of the [new] allegations at all.[24]

---

21 See Appendix 1.

22 It should be reiterated that Daughter 1 at this time was in Pathways Treatment Center for suicidal ideations; Daughter 1's treating physician had been forewarned by Kori Taylor on November 19, 2003, that Daughter 1 would be taken into State custody, and Taylor specifically forbid the doctor from informing Girlfriend or anyone else of this. Daughter 2 was in school when abducted on November 20, 2003, and Taylor ordered the school principal to not alert Girlfriend of this, leaving only a note to be collected when someone came to pick her up after school hours. So not only were the parents not notified by Taylor, she actually went so far as to order others to not inform the parents, either.

23 See Appendix 1.

24 I inserted "new" here, since in its current presentation this is somewhat inaccurate. The original allegations made in July, 2003, were investigated and dismissed by both the police department and CPS. It was the later allegations made by Girlfriend's parents – alleging that I had tickled Daughter 2 in her private parts and that I had "browbeat" Daughter 2 to recant her story (alleged abuse that neither could possibly have witnessed since they had not been around the children for over four months at that

MCA 2003 41-3-422(5)(a)[25], defining abuse and neglect petitions, requires that CPS has the burden of proof to prove probable cause for removal of the children from the home, which is to say they must prove they acted in good faith and adhered to the law in removing the children.[26] Section (4) of this Code also requires that the District Court must adhere to Montana Rules of Evidence. Inclusive in Montana Rules of Evidence as MCA 2003 Section 26-10-IV Rule 402[27], is the fact that all relevant evidence is admissible. In spite of this, District Court Judge Lympus refused to hear any evidence offered by the parents at the hearing which would have proven CPS did not have probable cause, that Kori Taylor's actions were premature, not based in good faith and that the reports made were false.

Additionally, Section (9)(a) of this Code [ie, 41-3-422] allows any person interested in any cause under this chapter of the MCA has a right to appear before the Court. Judge Lympus again denied the parents' rights to allow individuals to appear which could have disputed CPS' position.[28]

---

point in time), as well as the allegation of new abuse made by Kori Taylor that I had supposedly touched Daughter 1 inappropriately on November 13, 2003 – that were never investigated prior to the daughters' removal. Incidentally, neither daughter ever substantiated these new allegations of abuse, and it was a modified version of the original allegation – that had been investigated and dismissed by September, 2003 – that I was eventually prosecuted on. These new allegations were only used as an excuse to remove the girls, and when these false allegations could not be substantiated, Taylor defaulted to the allegation that Daughter 1 had already once made.

25 See Appendix 1.

26 Incidentally, the intake removal forms included in Appendix 2 clearly demonstrate that no good cause existed at the time of removal. Both daughters' referral forms have the box checked under good cause for removal checked as "Does Not Exist", which is essentially an acknowledgment by the caseworker removing the girls that there was no actual good cause to remove them in the first place. So I ask you – why were they taken if no good cause existed?

27 See Appendix 1, MCA § 26-10-402.

28 Of particular interest is that Judge Ted Lympus expelled me from the courtroom altogether. I was neither permitted to attend or to be heard whatsoever.

Additionally, for Rules of Evidence, MCA 2003 Section 26-10-VIII Rule 802[29], Hearsay evidence is not allowable. Hearsay is defined by MCA 2003 Section 26-10-VIII Rule 801[30] as "a statement, other than one made by the declarant while testifying at the trial or hearing, offered in evidence to prove the truth of the matter asserted." In the hearing regarding the petition of abuse, Judge Lympus allowed innumerable hearsay statements to be admitted as evidence by Kori Taylor alleging statements from [Daughter 1], the oldest of the two children.[31]

It should be noted that some exception exists to hearsay, wherein a person is unavailable for testimony. However the law again protects against someone preventing a person to be present for testimony as reason to allow hearsay, as per MCA 2003 Section 26-10-VIII Rule 804[32], which states "a declarant is not unavailable as a witness if [inability to be present] is due to procurement or wrongdoing of the proponent of the statement for the purpose of preventing the witness from attending or testifying." In this case, Kori Taylor abducted [Daughter 1] and [Daughter 2] with express purpose, amongst other causes, of denying access to her for purposes of testimony. In fact, as of the date of this writing (December 8, 2003), Mara has not been

---

29 See Appendix 1, MCA § 26-10-802.

30 See Appendix 1, MCA § 26-10-801.

31 To clarify, neither Daughter 1 nor Daughter 2 were present at this hearing. Taylor was permitted to allege that both daughters had made the allegations (specifically that I had tickled Daughter 2 in private areas and that I had touched Daughter 1 inappropriately on November 13, 2003) that Taylor had manufactured for this hearing, though neither daughter could ever be compelled to even make an official statement to police, either before or after this hearing. In other words, based upon allegations made solely by the caseworker, Judge Ted Lympus completely bypassed hearsay requirements to accept the statements made by Taylor about the alleged allegations made by both daughters as true, even though those specific allegations were never actually made by either, and the daughters were not allowed to appear in court to testify to the alleged accusations.

32 See Appendix 1, MCA § 26-10-804.

allowed any contact whatsoever with her children since the day they were abducted by CPS.

MCA 2003 41-3-433[33], which defines temporary investigative authority, states, "An order for temporary investigative authority may not be issued for a period longer than 90 days". In the abuse and neglect petition, Kori Taylor on behalf of CPS requested and was granted by Judge Lympus a temporary investigative authority extending for six months. Additionally, Kori Taylor has already expressed that she intends to extend that period by another six months if Mara has not complied with her demands in that time. Note - there is a demand for compliance, but no effort to actually investigate the allegations. There is no other way to see this - Kori Taylor is intentionally abusing her position to bully Mara into dissolving contact with me, without any investigation or corroboration of the alleged abuse. And for what purpose could there be, considering the timeframe involved, would she have to make such a demand? Since the abduction of the children occurred within 48 hours of a lawsuit in which Mara and [Daughter 1] were named as witnesses against the Police Department and the children are being held upon compliance of Mara dissolving relations with me, it is more than obvious what is going on here - dissolution of contact would mean no more lawsuit if the witnesses and parties abused are denied contact with me entirely.

MCA 2003 41-3-202[34], which defines actions CPS is required to perform upon receiving a report of abuse or neglect, investigation is a required step prior to removal of children from the home. In fact, CPS is required to promptly conduct thorough investigation into circumstances surrounding allegations of abuse and neglect. And if the reporter of the alleged abuse or neglect does so anonymously, Section (2) of this Code specifically states,

---

33 See Appendix 1.

34 See Appendix 1.

"Without the development of independent, corraborative, and attributable information, a child may not be removed from the home." No effort was expended to actually investigate the allegations made against me prior to removal of the children. No effort has been made since to even collaborate with the children whether the events alleged actually occurred. In fact, when asked in Court whether Kori Taylor reviewed information provided by Mara refuting the allegations, Kori Taylor's response was reportedly, "I have six months to review that". And since Kori Taylor has already declared an intention to extend the temporary investigative authority by another six months should Mara not comply with her demands, she has obvious intentions to not investigate these allegations at all and to simply use her position to hold the children hostage upon demands of compliance from Mara.

And what does Kori Taylor get out of this? Well, considering her current status within Child Protective Services is an intern and in Court reference was made that she would soon be a full fledged case worker, it would seem her pay-off is a nice fat promotion. Break the law, divide a family, help defend a corrupt local City government and get a promotion, which is probably accompanied with a pay raise as most promotions usually are. Combine this with Kori Taylor's being a self-confessed "survivor of child molestation" and you can easily see where Kori Taylor's motivations are from.

Essentially, as you can see, Child Protective Services had no authority to act as they did and the District Court made no effort to reign in an obviously out of control department. The response of taking the children was immediate upon filing of my lawsuit and the demands made of Mara are inconsistent with any credible investigative information that the department has. In fact, there has been no effort whatsoever expended to verify the validity of any statements and even Kori Taylor has admitted to not even questioning the alleged victims of the supposed molestation and abuse! This is purely a retaliatory act designed to bar me from witnesses in my lawsuit against the City and Police Department, which shows a collaborative level of conspiracy between the local City Government and the Office of Child and Family Services, of which Child Protective Services is a division of.

There is so much more to say and I will endeavor to enter more as I am able and as my research uncovers new areas of the law. I do not know what step this conspiracy of corrupt departments will take next against me. I could be arrested next on some new trumped up issue. They may force one of the girls to say something so they can see their mom. I don't know.
Needless to say, I cannot afford to hire an attorney. And even if I could, it would need to be an attorney outside my area since the local attorneys are too afraid of retaliation. I need help here and I am appealing to the public for that help! I have a couple of good leads for attorneys who specialize in this kind of false allegations, but we are looking at upwards of $10,000 to retain these kinds of people to aid in my defense.
Contact me at ron_glick@yahoo.com if you want more info or can offer help... I am also setting up a Legal Defense Fund through Paypal using the same address in hopes of raising money for legal aid. In the meantime, please contact your State Senators, Representatives, and also Shirley Brown[35], Child and Family Services Administrator, or anyone else who may be able to have pressure put on these people to intervene. And check back to this site as often as possible - additional details are provided all the time!
Please remember - We are nearly helpless in this fight and we need help from somewhere...

---

35 Originally hyperlinked to: shbrown@state.mt.us

As was mentioned at the beginning of this chapter, there has been some things that have changed. And my perceptions of what was going on at the time have changed, as well.

For instance, I now know that Ted Lympus – head judge of the Eleventh Judicial District Court of Montana – was complicit in the seizure of the girls, and that he was actively been involved in helping to undermine and sabotage my civil case, as well as later being an actor in my criminal prosecution. In this original post, I laid the blame primarily at the feet of CFS (which I repeatedly called CPS) and the court blindly accepting their actions as being in good faith. This was not the case – Lympus was only offering a pretense of a show cause hearing. Nothing conformed with how a show cause hearing should have proceeded that day – and Lympus' participation was as much part of the horse-and-pony show as was CFS and Kori Taylor.

I have since witnessed dozens of cases where Lympus blatantly defies the law on a whim. I have seen him rip children away from their families, seen him refuse on multiple occasions to recuse himself and even make derogatory statements in open court against anyone – expert or layman – from out of the Flathead Valley as having no voice in his court. I was an "upstart" from California suing his precious Good Ol' Boy network – where do you believe his loyalty lay?

There were also other issues there, as well. For instance, at the hearing, Mara had signed over a Power of Attorney for me to handle her legal affairs so I could speak for her at the hearing. Simply put, Mara could not understand law, nor could I effectively teach her the law that she needed to cite at the hearing – she just could not retain the information. So Mara granted me Power of Attorney – solely to handle her claims and litigations.[36] However, Lympus refused to permit me to use the POA, and

---

36 See Appendix 1, MCA § 71-31-3.

ejected me from the courtroom. Remember, Montana law states that anyone interested in the proceeding has the right to appear before the court – so Lympus ejecting me from the courtroom not only defied Mara's right to have assistance, but also violated the law that permitted me to be present as an interested party.

Additionally, please note that any party proceeding in this kind of case, ie, CFS removal of children, is entitled to counsel.[37] Mara made requests for representation, but she was repeatedly denied. This was why it was necessary for me to assume a Power of Attorney in the first place – because Mara needed help understanding the law and legal proceedings, and the district court refused to grant her assistance of counsel as required by law. But Lympus was dead set on Mara not having any legal assistance, even unprofessional assistance like what I could provide. Just like every measure taken along the way, Ted Lympus threw his lot in with protecting the Good Ol' Boy network rampant in Kalispell, and made sure Mara had no capacity to do anything about what was being done to remove and isolate her daughters.

This statement was the single solitary public plea I made prior to what fell afterwards. In short, I was eventually arrested while in Washington state, where I was setting up a satellite chapter of our youth program, and never again saw the light of day – much less access to a computer with internet access – from February, 2004, through 2009. But once I got out, I began to once again chronicle all that happened to me after this infamous posting in December, 2003.

The next chapters will present the contents of the online posts I made in 2009 following my release as I once again set out to plead my case to the court of public opinion. The postings, of course, only earned me more retaliation, but I will get into that later.

---

37 See Appendix 1, MCA § 41-3-422(11) and 41-3-425.

U.S. Political Prisoner Since 2004 / 183

Chapter 8

At first glance, this chapter will appear to have jumped over the story line that proceeded through the first chapters of this biography. However, I related those details in an online capacity in 2009, and rather than be repeatedly redundant, I am stepping forward in time to present the context of the posts I made then.

I was released from prison on February 17, 2009, and made it back to Kalispell by February 18, 2009. Immediately, I set about looking for a public forum where I could tell the story about what happened to me after my last public statement on December 8, 2003. So much had happened and though the general public had been fed a great deal of information about me, I felt the overwhelming need to speak out for myself – to set the truth on the page, so to speak.

And so I created an online blog (slang term for "bulletin log", essentially an online journal) where I planned initially to set forth some defective aspects of Montana legal practices. To be honest, at the beginning, I just wanted to get the corruption Montana as a whole exposed, and I was not out to necessarily tell my personal story. It was not until I found out that the Montana Supreme Court held off until the day *after* I was released from prison to deny my appeal that I realized I needed a forum for my own side, because there was certainly no hope within the so-called legal system.

Keep in mind – when this blog was originally written, it was with all the parties named, including Daughter 1. She was 18 years old by this point in time and, by my rationality, was not subject to protection a minor would have. But even with this in mind, her name was already publicized through the original

GeoCities site, as was her younger sister. I therefore felt no compulsion of making her anonymous in these postings. In spite of what has been said of me since by authorities seeking to discredit me, I did not post Daughter 1's name herein as a way of attacking her – it was because I had already publicly declared her name in the GeoCities posting – a posting that remained online as I started this blog – that I included her name in the Great Montana Conspiracy blog. As the expression says, the cat was already out of the bag, so what difference did it make?

Also remember that I am not excluding her name here because of any "sensitivity" to her – my legal and constitutional freedom of expression was stripped from me almost six years after I was originally sentenced. Originally, I was given an oral directive at the time of the order modification to remove all names from the blog, but the final written order only contained prohibitions of using any identifying information related to Daughter 1. If anyone visits the original blog site though, you will find that all names relating to Daughter 1 and her family have been stripped. And by the time I regained the right to mention others' names, Blogspot had barred my ability to edit this site, as I have mentioned earlier.

As with the original GeoCities post, the content of the Great Montana Conspiracy blog will be redundant of some information already presented. But I feel there is enough new content herein to justify these entries' inclusions into this volume.

I opened my blog, the Great Montana Conspiracy[38] and posted the following on February 21, 2009:

---

38 Originally posted at http://monspiracy.blogspot.com – this address was eventually blocked from permitting me to make new posts, though. Whether this was Blogspot deciding my material was too controversial or represented some clandestine effort of authorities to shut down the site, I never learned. Just one day I was no longer able to edit my blog, and so I changed to http://monspiracy.wordpress.com instead. Incidentally, both sites remain online as of this writing.

This is the site where the corruption within the State of Montana will be exposed. Or so I hope.

I know what a conspiracy theorist is. I know I will end up sounding like one. But I have lived this experience and I need to let someone else out there know about what I have been through and continue to go through...

For a foundation, please visit: http://www.geocities.com/ron_glick/[39]

This site was created in December, 2003, and precedes a lot. But it sets groundwork for what came after.

I haven't time in this blog to provide much detail, but stay tuned - I intend to type a great deal in here in coming weeks...

After this, I started to set up some foundation by explaining a couple of defective principles in Montana law, the first on February 24, 2009:

Before I get into a great deal of my own history, I thought it prudent to explain why it is a global Montana conspiracy that I am speaking of and not just something personal. Afterall, it is paramount that you recognize that I am not just spouting off paranoid delusions. The foundation for believability is credibility and I hope this post will set that groundwork.

First, let me play the Riddler: When is a justice system not a justice system? Answer: When it is not pursuing justice.

Okay, I know that's lame but it's vital to what follows. There are some fairly basic civil liberties that everyone who is U.S. citizen has by default - they are guaranteed through the United States Constitution. For instance, when you are accused of a

---

[39] Ironically enough, this address still worked for about two months after I posted this – but then GeoCities was permanently shut down and archived, so I no longer had any control over it.

crime, there are mandatory steps that the government must exhaust in order to prosecute you.

The first of these is as follows:

"No person shall be held to answer for a capital, or otherwise infamous crime, unless on a presentment or indictment of a Grand Jury..." Fifth Amendment to the United States Constitution.

Essentially, this right assures that noone will ever lose their freedom or liberty upon a baseless accusation - the allegation must be presented to a panel of citizens who review the allegation to determine whether there is a reasonable belief that a crime was committed by the accused. If not, the government cannot pursue prosecution.

The second of these is as follows:

"[N]o Warrants shall issue, but upon probable cause.." Fourth Amendment to the United States Constitution.

This one is a bit more vague, but it's been long established that it means that any individual accused of a crime has a right to challenge probable cause. In other words, the individual has the right to appear in court to challenge any allegation against them. This is typically done through a preliminary examination hearing. This hearing's purpose is for the Court to establish that there is probable cause that a crime was committed by the accused.

The difference between these two steps is crucial: the first establishes whether there are facts enough to support the prosecution, while the second establishes whether there is law to support it. These are both critical elements to permit an innocent man or woman from being wrongfully incarcerated.

However, Montana has unilaterally deprived its citizens of these basic civil liberties. Pursuant to Montana law, specifically MCA Section 46-11-201, " The prosecutor may apply directly to the district court for permission to file an information against a named defendant... If it appears that there is probable cause to believe that an offense has been committed by the defendant, the judge or chief justice shall grant leave to file the information..."

Essentially what this does is assure that noone in the State of Montana can have a grand jury hearing or opportunity to challenge probable cause. This strips Montana citizens of their civil rights and permits agents of the State to incarcerate anyone upon a simple signed statement alleging that a crime was committed, regardless of whether one was committed or not!

This system was not created to deal with me personally, but its existence permitted the corrupt officials of the City of Kalispell, MT, and Flathead County to imprison me to quash my legal claims against them. This is an ideal system for a corrupt authority to forever protect itself against ever being held accountable for its misdeeds - if an individual challenges them politically, imprison him or her. Hold him or her indefinitely until a conviction can be secured, and thereafter any claims he or she has against the corrupt authority can never be raised so long as that conviction remains - it becomes an underlying element of the conviction (ie, vexatious litigation) and civil remedies cannot be used to undermine a criminal conviction...

This is what happened to me - on Februrary 20, 2004, after almost eight months of fighting with the local authorities of Kalispell and Flathead County, it was deemed necessary to exercise their authority to imprison me. I was detained for sixteen months before I even saw trial, which permitted the authorities to tamper with and bury evidence and witnesses who could exonerate me, and to also manufacture their own witnesses against me. I was falsely convicted in July, 2005, of sexual assault, though there was an abundance of evidence to prove my innocence and the machinations of the authorities - yet I was assigned a public defender (Eduardo Gurtierrez-Falla, aka, Ed

Falla) who adamantly refused to in any way challenge the improprieties of the State.

Today, I remain a political prisoner of the State of Montana, even though I discharged a five year commitment to prison for a crime I did not commit! I remain now under fifteen year "probationary" and suspended sentences (more on that in my next post - ie, double jeopardy). My liberty remains restricted and though I have more freedom, I am not yet free...

I learned a few days ago also that the State supreme court finally got around to denying my direct appeal. No surprise there, since to reverse my conviction would be giving me free leave to attack the entire corrupt structure. The present state of affairs in Montana is that Montana is a rogue state, operating as a gestapo-style regime. Noone in this State is safe from the persecutions of the "Good Ol' Boy" system of "justice". And as such, this is why I have named this blog "The Great Monspiracy"...

Hopefully, I will be able to post more on all of this tomorrow...

Ciao for now,

Ron Glick
Political Prisoner since 2004[40]

This entry was followed on February 25, 2009, with the following entitled "Double Jeopardy":

---

[40] Incidentally, this was the first time I publicly represented myself as a US Political Prisoner since 2004 – I had been arrested, ie, taken into custody in retaliation for standing up to corrupt political entities on February 20, 2004, and have remained in the custody of the State of Montana ever since. Prior to this date, I had signed letters with this moniker, but this was the first time I actually made a public declaration that I was – and continue to be – a US Political Prisoner. All of my entries after this date are similarly signed, but I will forego printing this with each entry.

I don't have a lot of time to post today, so I thought I would try to get a quickrereassert explanation of the double jeopardy issue I discussed in yesterday's post.

As I mentioned, I have fifteen years remaining upon my falsely convicted sentence. I have discharged the first five years in prison and now have fifteen years "suspended" time remaining. Normally, suspended time means simply that if I do commit any more crimes within the designated period, I can get the entire fifteen year period re-assigned as prison time.

The issue here, and what makes this part of the Great Monspiracy, is that a suspended sentence, by definition, is a sentence not served at the time it is imposed. Contrariwise, a probation sentence is a sentence served in lieu of incarceration. The point here is that this is two separate sentences, and pursuant to the Fifth Amendment to the United States Constitution:

"[N]or shall any person be subject for the same offense to be twice put in jeopardy of life or limb..."

In other words, a person cannot be convicted twice of the same offense or be punished twice for the same offense. In a nutshell, I have been given a fifteen year suspended *and* probation sentence, just as every other person in Montana is when convicted. It's a violation of my civil liberties and is yet again an example of how this affects more than just myself...

Finally, following the presentation of this information, I at last elected to begin telling my own story again in detail. It began with a series of articles I entitled, "Another Case of Gov Abuse (ACGA) Continued", parts I, II, III and IV. These were intended to fill in the blanks of what was going on at the time of the original GeoCities post on December 8, 2003.

Keep in mind, these were posted during an hour's limitation at the local library, and were actually written quickly in about thirty minutes, since at the time I was also being pressured by my probation officer, Dave Edwards (you will read more of him later), to do job searches.

In the midst of posting these postings though, I inadvertently deleted the third page of the original GeoCities website. I had received notice that the pages would be archived, and I had gone in to see if they could be transferred. Somehow, in trying to save a back-up of the third page (thinking I was saving all three collectively), the third page was deleted. The contents of the page were saved in the buffer, but I could not rewrite the page contents to the GeoCities cite. Consequently, in the limited time I had, I had to save it as a separate blog entry, which cut into my time to actually write anything of great length that day. Consequently, the second entry is very brief.

Following is the complete sequence of this series in the order intended, with brief separations inserted between each entry, and minor grammatical corrections:

This will be my first update to the content of "Another Case of Gov Abuse", my original website posted in December, 2003. If you have not read that site, please feel free to go there NOW[41].

When I last posted my ordeal, it was with the forewarning that the Kalispell authorities could retaliate. Well, they did. They reopened the closed investigation on [Daughter 1], charged me with Sexual Assault and Witness Tampering (for allegedly making [Daughter 1] recant her allegation after the investigation was closed) and had me arrested on February 20, 2004. After that date, I was continuously incarcerated until February 17, 2009, since I was falsely convicted (following sixteen months of incarceration) of the Sexual Assault. Essentially, I became a

---

41 Originally, the word "NOW" linked back to the originals GeoCities site.

Political Prisoner in order to quash my objections to and claims against Kalispell authorities. Yet this Reader's Digest summary does not begin to detail the levels of depravity to which I have been subjected to in the last five years.

But what is certainly a long story of deprivation of civil liberties beyond imagining must begin where I left off on my recounting - what immediately followed my last post. But before I can get to that, I need to fill in some of the gaps that I left open when I originally typed the first website. At the time, I had planned to type more and fill in the gaps, but I was dealing with a limited amount of space on that server at the time and could only get the three pages worth of material online. Oh, what five years can change...

On December 8, 2003, it had only been a few days since the Eleventh Judicial District of Montana (by way of Judge Ted Lympus) endorsed the abduction of [Daughter 1] and [Daughter 2]. Mara Pelton (their mother) and I were still struggling with the idea that the court system was going to back up such a flagrant kidnapping by State authorities. We had been denied the opportunity to present any defense at the so-called "show cause hearing" and Judge Lympus would not permit me even into the courtroom to present the legal challenges to the State's action. In a nutshell, it became crystal clear that not only was the City of Kalispell corrupt, but that both Flathead County and State of Montana officials were also willing to abuse the law in order to protect the City. And it became questionable whether there was any hope at all of overcoming these atrocities.

Also at the point of writing "Another Case of Gov Abuse", [Daughter 1] had admitted that I had done nothing to her. In fact, with a friend, Carrie Beth Mountjoy as witness, I assisted [Daughter 1] in preparing a statement both recanting the allegation and providing her own information about circumstances which had surrounded the allegation. Originally, I had believed that [Daughter 1] had been coerced by her grandparents, Jerry and Dixie Nezat, to make a false allegation against me with promises of a scheme to supposedly get Mara and [Daughter 1]'s father, Jared Salois, back together. In [Daughter 1]'s recantation, which occurred around October 18, 2003, she said it had been a repressed memory. This is a story in and of itself, because it was prompted by a meeting between Mara, myself and two school counselors at the beginning of October.

Following the information that the official investigation with the Kalispell Police Department (KPD) was closed, the restrictions placed upon [Daughter 1] and I were lifted. The primary restrictions upon me were that I could not live with Mara or the girls. Once that investigation was concluded though, Mara and I decided to try to reintegrate our households. However, I had huge trust issues with [Daughter 1] and was reluctant to put myself back into a position where [Daughter 1] could concoct another lie and start the fiasco all over again. And so, as an effort to work toward resolution, we met with my son, John's, and [Daughter 1]'s counselors (Mary Jane Foxx was [Daughter 1]'s counselor - I cannot recall John's counselor's name) to try to work toward reestablishing a family life with all parties. This meeting occurred sometime around the first week of October, 2003.

The significance of this meeting was that during it, Mara suddenly had a recollection that she said she had previously not recalled. She said then that [Daughter 1]'s story had always sounded familiar, but she did not know why. During the meeting, she abruptly announced to everyone present that she remembered why [Daughter 1]'s story sounded so familiar - because what [Daughter 1] had described (ie, lying on the couch with me allegedly putting one hand up her shirt and the other down her pants) had actually happened to her, not [Daughter 1], though [Daughter 1] had actually <u>witnessed</u> it!

It turns out that when [Daughter 1] was three years old, shortly after Mara separated from Jared, Mara had a visit from one of Jared's friends (cannot recall his name at the moment)[42], supposedly to express his sorrow over the break-up of Mara and Jared. However, shortly after arriving, this "friend" assaulted Mara in the front room of their home, grabbing her from behind and forcing her down onto the couch, where he proceeded to try to force his hand up her shirt and the other down her pants! [Daughter 1] witnessed the entire assault, but sat to the side of the room through most of it crouched down, holding her knees and rocking back and forth. But [Daughter 1] did not stay there - in fact, the assault ended because [Daughter 1] took one of her toys (a hard plastic ball) and hit the assailant over the head with it. When he reached to push [Daughter 1] away, it gave Mara the chance to break his hold and she was able to overpower him and beat him (apparently pretty badly) before throwing him out the door. Mara never reported the assault, and she said she had mostly forgotten about it over the years...

When Mara mentioned this to the counselors, Mary Jane Foxx immediately said that [Daughter 1] would need to be talked to about it. Mara said she would do it and that is exactly what she did...

I am out of time at this computer, so need to wrap this up. I will hopefully continue this tomorrow...

Yesterday I was rushed, and I am again today, so I will try to get what I can in here as quickly as possible...

At any rate, after the meeting with the counselors, Mara and I put off immediately talking to [Daughter 1]. I did not really want to be a part of the conversation (considering the history

---

42 This was Jared's friend, Shane, whom I mentioned in a previous chapter.

involved) but Mara wanted me to. Instead, it all came out in a rather non-planned way on the night of October 15, 2003.

Mara, myself, [Daughter 1] and a couple of our friends/volunteers (Jeff Berna and Tasha Bordeaux) were sitting in the back room of the store (Arcadia) talking. John and [Daughter 2] (my son and Mara's youngest) were also there, but were asked to leave after the conversation turned. We were talking about something else entirely, something to do with [Daughter 1]'s problems in school, if I recall correctly, and I made a slip and mentioned something about the talk Mara and I had had with the counselors (forgive me that I don't recall more specifics about that part of the conversation, but it has been five years...).

At any rate, Mara decided to launch into talking to [Daughter 1] about the incident that she had recalled. I asked John and [Daughter 2] to leave the room when I saw where it was going, and made to leave myself, but was asked by Mara to stay. And truth to tell, I did want to hear what [Daughter 1] said. So I sat back and remained as quiet as I could while Mara talked to her daughter.

The first thing Mara did was ask [Daughter 1] if she recalled the incident that had happened when she was little. Mara asked her specifically if she recalled a man coming into the house (his name was Shane, by the way - I recalled that much) and assaulting her. [Daughter 1] looked dumbfounded and just shook her head, No. At this point, Mara began describing the incident in detail, starting with how Shane had come into the house and before long had pulled Mara down onto the couch from behind. In the middle of the telling though, [Daughter 1] began to fill in the details - in the presence of being told about the story, she suddenly recalled it in detail. In fact, [Daughter 1] began providing details that Mara did not recall herself!

Okay, time is up again... Hopefully I'll get to post more on this tomorrow... So little time, so much to tell...

First, I apologize for the break in sequence on Saturday's post. I spent my allotted computer time trying to fix the original website and had only a few minutes to upload the content of the corrupted third page before I lost it for good. This is actually a continuation of Friday's post (February 27, 2009), so please read that post in sequence with this one. Not that anyone as yet seems to be reading this blog, but I continue to hold out hope that someone will someday care...

Okay, as I mentioned last time, after Mara began to recount the story to [Daughter 1], [Daughter 1] not only recalled the incident but began to fill in details herself that Mara omitted. It became clear that [Daughter 1] recognized many similarities between what really happened to her when she was little and the alleged incident she had accused me of, including the fact (oddly enough) that the two couches in question had the exact same pattern!

After the recounting was finished, Mara asked [Daughter 1] if she had had any personal recollection of the incident before she had begun talking about it, to which [Daughter 1] said she had not. Then Mara asked [Daughter 1] if she knew anything about repressed memories, which again [Daughter 1] said she did not. Mara, having personal experience with repressed memories herself from periods of childhood abuse, explained to [Daughter 1] that a repressed memory occurred when something scary or traumatic happened and one's mind buried the memory as a means of self-defense, and that such a memory usually stayed buried until the mind felt the person was better able to deal with the pain associated with it. However, as Mara personally attested, such memories do not always return in one complete block and often it is easy to confuse an old repressed memory with something that happened recently since one only recently recalls the memory.

Mara then posed to [Daughter 1] that the two incidents (the one when [Daughter 1] was three and the one she accused me of when she was thirteen) had many similar details. Mara asked [Daughter 1] whether there was a possibility that the old memory could have been confused with some recent event, such as lying beside me on the couch being a similar enough incident to dredge up details (if not the full memory) of what [Daughter 1] had witnessed when she was little.

And [Daughter 1] immediately responded that the incident with me had not happened. In [Daughter 1]'s words, it could not have happened because the two memories were identical in every way. Once [Daughter 1] recalled the full memory of the assault on her mother, she recognized that the memory she had of me doing something like that was a false memory!

Again, keep in mind, this was all after the official investigations had been completed - there was nothing to be gained by getting [Daughter 1] to "change" her story at that point. In fact, the new version of events completely undermined the lawsuit Mara and I had filed against her parents (the Nezats) accusing them of coercing [Daughter 1] to make up a false allegation; if [Daughter 1]'s accusation was the result of a false memory, then this actually exonerated the Nezats of such wrongdoing. So for myself and [Mara], there was nothing to gain by getting [Daughter 1] to "change" her story in October, when all official investigations closed in September, and we had a lawsuit pending against Mara's parents that was completely undermined by this information!

I point this out to demonstrate that neither Mara nor I had any motivation to pursue this issue with [Daughter 1] other than for [Daughter 1]'s own benefit. Had [Daughter 1] said the two incidents were not the same, there would have been no gain nor loss. [Daughter 1]'s saying they were the same memory actually hurt our position against the Nezats, in fact. As one who read the original "Another Case of Gov Abuse" will know, this is a significant viewpoint to consider. And yet, that was completely overlooked late on down the line...

Following this conversation with [Daughter 1] (of which I had only listened), I asked [Daughter 1] if she would be willing to write up a statement of what she had said to both create a record and to act as testimonial discovery in the suit against [Daughter 1]'s grandparents. If my memory is correct, this occurred on October 15, 2003. [Daughter 1] said she would do this, but after three days she still had not done so.

On October 18, 2003 (again, if my memory is correct), I once again asked [Daughter 1] if she had written up the statement. [Daughter 1] responded that she did not really know what to write and asked me for help in doing so. I knew better than to sit down alone with [Daughter 1] to do this (I still had some significant trust issues with [Daughter 1], after all), and so we waited until later that day when Carrie Beth Mountjoy (a family friend, board member of both the youth program and business, and a shareholder in the business) came into the store. I asked Carrie Beth if she could act as witness for the preparation of this statement, and she agreed. And so the three of us ([Daughter 1], Carrie Beth and I) went to the back office to prepare the Affidavit of [Daughter 1].

Okay, running out of time again - hopefully I will be able to write more on this tomorrow...

Sorry, I got somewhat distracted yesterday and did not get a chance to finish this thread. It happens...

At any rate, as I attested last time, [Daughter 1], Carrie Beth Mountjoy and I went into the back office at Arcadia to help prepare what became the Affidavit of [Daughter 1]. [Daughter

1] had asked me to help her write up a statement and I had asked Carrie Beth to be present as a witness to confirm that what was typed was what [Daughter 1] was saying. Of course, later on, [Daughter 1] lied and said that it was only her and I and that I had typed up the whole thing and forced her to sign it. And even though Carrie Beth had later attested in an interview to the truth, I was never allowed to use this evidence at my trial... That will all come later though.

Basically, the meeting in the back office comprised [Daughter 1] as the attester, myself as the typist (asking occasional questions for clarification) and Carrie Beth as a largely silent third party. In hindsight, I suppose I should have had Carrie Beth sign the affidavit as a witness, but it simply never occurred to me at that time exactly how far-reaching the corruption in Flathead County, Montana, truly went.

As [Daughter 1] related her version of events, I placed the content of her statements into affidavit form (I worked as a paralegal for two years in California, so I knew legal format). I separated her individual statements and numbered each paragraph. As I needed to, I asked questions to get the information I wanted (ie, that specifically related to the lawsuit against the the Nezats – [Daughter 1] would have had a lot more in the statement that was completely irrelevant otherwise - though again in hindsight, I wish I had included [Daughter 1]'s opinion that she was frightened of her grandmother, Dixie), and when I actually typed anything, I always verified it with [Daughter 1]. When I finished, I printed out a copy for her to verify before signing. We actually revised the document three times after I printed out hard copies because she saw things she wanted to add or change.

In the end, I believe the document was three pages long (I lost my last remaining copy due to the duplicitous actions of one Tim Harris, who took custody of my legal papers upon my transfer to *prison - but that's another tale for another day....).*[43] *[Daughter 1] signed it and I sent a copy to the Nezats as discovery for the suit.*

Of course, the Nezats did not accept that at least part of their actions had been exonerated. They were still being sued for breaking into our home to steal Mara's dishwasher, for breaking the pipes under our house, for tearing down our address sign and other acts of vandalism, not to mention for their efforts to contact anyone and everyone they could to maliciously malign me as a "child molester" (They even called Arcadia's landlord to spread that false accusation!). Instead of accepting this, they instead called Child and Family Services (CFS) and alleged that I had "browbeat and tortured" [Daughter 1] into signing the statement and made up a new allegation, claiming I had supposedly tickled [Daughter 2] in her private areas![44]

Of course, [Daughter 2] denied this and to this day, [Daughter 2] has been the one person who has been unwavering in her support of my innocence; Even after [Daughter 2] was taken from her home, she refused to lie about me, even at the cost of not being allowed to be returned home. Which is an interesting

---

43 Incidentally, I did recover a copy of this affidavit, and a redacted copy is included in Appendix 2.

44 For anyone keeping track, this would make the fourth false allegation the Nezats had made against me. The first was Melissa Turner's daughter, the second was Daughter 1, the third was Chantel's daughter, and the fourth here was Daughter 2 (which, by the way, Daughter 2 has always denied). As I said early on, this was the Nezat's consistent pattern of behavior – to make up false allegations against men in Mara's life, and they did it over and again in my case. Jerry Nezat even accused one of my process servers, Tim Seymour, of being in trouble for molesting children at one point, which was yet another lie just to fling mud at yet another person – this time as an effort to prevent people from serving legal papers on them, since I suppose they believed that if people were afraid of being accused, they would not serve them. It did not work, but it just demonstrates how consistently they made this kind of false allegation against anyone they did not like or want around. In any other situation, their credibility would have been nonexistent; in this case, the authorities ignored all the false allegations the Nezats made in order to bolster their credibility.

story in and of itself. Remember, [Daughter 2] was six years old and [Daughter 1] was thirteen. [Daughter 2]'s older sister and even her mom, Mara, bent to the authorities' whims to help railroad me into a false conviction, yet the youngest of all of them, the one someone would think would be the easiest to manipulate, stuck to her guns and refused to lie for the authorities that had abducted her. In my mind, if there was ever someone deserving of honor and respect throughout all of this, it is little [Daughter 2]. I could not be more proud of her; I only wish I could tell her...

By the way, I know that CFS tried to convince her to lie about me because she told Mara in a couple of letters that the little genius managed to smuggle to her mom. [Daughter 2] had a reading coach in school, a teenage girl. [Daughter 2] convinced this girl to take letters to her mom to let her mom know what was being done to her. There were like two or three letters that Mara got before CFS found out about it and put a stop to it. But the letters, though actually written by the teenage girl, made it very clear what was going on: Kori Taylor, the CFS caseworker, was trying to get [Daughter 2] to lie about me and [Daughter 2] refused to do it. [Daughter 2] made it clear that she was mad at her sister ([Daughter 1]) because she was willing to say whatever Taylor wanted her to, and [Daughter 2] desperately wanted to come home, even at the cost of leaving her sister behind. She said she even had her suitcases packed and was ready to go anytime her mom came to get her.

I actually had to talk Mara out of going to get her daughter. Trust me, it was not an easy thing to do, but I knew that with the authority of the district court behind CFS, however unlawfully imposed that authority may have been, if Mara had gone and picked up [Daughter 2], it would have been considered kidnapping and Mara would have been on the run for the rest of her life. I could not let Mara do that, even if going after her daughters was the ethically right thing to do... Sometimes, it sucks being right....

Well, that's all the time I have for today. I will hopefully be here to type more tomorrow...

Following these four, I actually continued numbering as ACGA for awhile, but they fell into divergent threads, which is why I will be presenting their content somewhat separately in the next chapter. But I would like to provide another entry here at the end before I conclude this chapter.

This as written under the title of "An Aside", as it was originally posted between AGCA parts III and IV. I had seen a TV show that prompted me to make a statement, and though it is off-topic to the current history as it is being conveyed, I feel it is poignant enough that it does not recording:

I am going to set aside continuing the topic of [Daughter 1]'s affidavit for tomorrow. Instead, today I wanted to talk about something more general.

Last night, I was watching Heroes on NBC. Anyone following the show knows that the present storyline basically revolves around Peter's brother, as US Senator, forming an extra-legal organization to capture and contain people with powers, ie, the heroes. But Peter had a line last night that really struck home and I wanted to go off-topic today and talk about this a bit while it was still fresh.

Last night, Peter retrieved a video file that showed government officials taking US citizens, hooded and shackled, into custody without trials. The line that Peter says is something to the effect of, "What would people do if they knew they were abducting US citizens on US soil and holding them without trial?" Of course, that's paraphrased, but it gets across the general message. Ironically enough though, that is almost exactly what is going on in Montana and has been for decades at least!

As I have previously said, anyone who is charged with a crime in Montana immediately loses the first two safeguards of criminal justice: the rights to a grand jury and to challenge probable cause. But it's a bit more complex than that...

Essentially, the way it works in Montana is that any prosecutor can allege a crime was committed, submit that accusation before a judge and have that person arrested without that person even being forewarned that such an allegation has been made. It's the ultimate blindside. If John Doe is not liked by a prosecutor for any reason, all that prosecutor needs to do is submit an application to file an information and have the judge, acting solely upon the prosecutor's sworn statement (though the law actually requires that the statement be "supported by evidence", the courts in Montana consider the affidavit as the evidential requirement), can determine probable cause and have Mr. Doe arrested. After that, since the determination of probable cause has already been made, Mr. Doe does not get a preliminary examination of evidence hearing to challenge probable cause.

Of course, everyone thinks that a person arrested can bond out while waiting for trial. However, this does not happen properly in Montana. The Eighth Amendment of the US Constitution provides for no excessive bonds, which basically means that a person be permitted a bond which they can reasonably pay. Unfortunately, in Montana the entrenched system relies upon keeping accused people in jail and they routinely post excessive bonds upon people accused to keep them incarcerated. And I have personally witnessed the courts in Flathead County actually raise the bond amount if a person actually manages to raise the original bond amount! The idea here is that the system is designed to first deprive a person of his liberty without constitutionally mandated protections and then to keep that person incarcerated indefinitely in order to coerce them into accepting plea deals or to provide the State an exorbitant amount of time to railroad an accused into a conviction.

Take my own experiences. I sued the City of Kalispell and became a political enemy to those in power in local government. When it became clear that they could not really defend against my suit, the powers that be elected to remove me from my own support structure by charging me with a crime that had been previously investigated and dismissed. They filed for an information and got an arrest warrant issued on February 20, 2004, and then sent that warrant to Washington to have me arrested that night in Goldendale. A grand jury was never convened and my later pushes to get one convened were ignored. A week after I was arrested, the State did the same thing to arrest Mara Pelton, my girlfriend and business partner, and [Daughter 1]'s mother, upon a fabricated claim of witness tampering.

Keep in mind, Mara never supported [Daughter 1]'s accusation, except for the brief period following being told by Officer Myron Wilson that I had a "prior record" (which I proved through police and sheriff records to be untrue). She knew her daughter's penchant for lying and knew the background of the allegation well enough to know that [Daughter 1]'s story did not add up. As such, Mara was a staunch supporter of my innocence and as such I had entrusted all of the original documents that exonerated me into her care when I went to Washington. It never occurred to me that the authorities would go after her or that she would bow to threats if some kind of pressure was exerted. Proves how badly I misjudged Mara...

At any rate, the point here is that the local authorities were able to remove a political enemy and isolate him from his support structure without any constitutional prerequisites. After a week, when it became obvious that I would continue to have support from Mara (all outgoing communications from jail, both phone and post, are monitored and while I was in Washington, they were being conveyed to Kalispell authorities), the authorities trumped up a false charge on her and had her arrested. They released Mara after roughly a week in jail (I have never been able to get exact dates), but she was only released upon the very specific limitations that she would have no contact with me, direct nor indirect, and that she would not provide me any access to my personal or business records or assets. Effectively, the local authorities not only isolated me, but completely severed me from my primary source of external support.

After this, a rumor began circulating that got back to me that anyone who supported me in any way would go to jail, just like Mara. I heard this from Carrie Beth Mountjoy in a phone call shortly after Mara's arrest, and she said that the person who had started the rumor was James Valentino, a volunteer worker for the youth program, and another volunteer, Joe (whose last name I cannot recall)[45], joined in shortly thereafter. Conveniently enough, both of these "gentlemen" were engaged also in trying to court Mara (according to reports from another friend, both were publicly kissing Mara and being very physically affectionate within Arcadia). Joe, by the way, succeeded and Mara cheated on me with him within a month of my arrest. Irregardless, the rumor was devastating and led to every single person I ever knew turning their back on me - the explanation that was given to me by one such "friend" was that noone could afford to go to jail and lose their jobs and families and such.

After all of this, I ended up sitting sixteen months in jail prior to a trial that was little more than a kangaroo court. The assigned public defender worked for the State, not for me, and

---

45 This would be Joe Guiffrida.

refused to challenge any impropriety. And as a result, I was falsely convicted of a crime I did not commit.

The point of all of this is that the threat of US Citizens being arrested on US soil without constitutional protections is already going on. And everyone is ignoring it. So what happens when the public learns of these things? Well, so far, very little - the public either does not care or they simply choose not to believe that any of this is true. But I've lived through it and I can assure you that all of it, and much more, is tragically very, <u>very</u> true...

Benjamin Franklin said, "Let us all hang together, or surely we shall all hang separately." So why is noone else willing to hang with me to oppose this corrupt agency in our midst?

Okay, enough on this - tomorrow I will return to the account of [Daughter 1]'s affidavit...

As I said, certainly off point for chronology, but it is a significant summary of a very real underlying issue that persists throughout all of this. Consider it foreshadowing of things to come in this volume. And as the story continues to unravel, I am hoping the reader will keep this all in mind...

Chapter 9

The next entries in my blog that relate to this volume were an attempt to discuss Daughter 1's history. Having spent so much time on the wrongs done to me, and the actual *actions* that Daughter 1 had taken, I felt I really had not provided any real background on where Daughter 1's motivations – her fears, ambitions, etc. – came from. And so with this in mind, I presented a series of entries entitled, "[Daughter 1]'s Bio", which was subtitled as parts V-IX of ACGA (ie, Another Case of Gov Abuse), beginning on March 12, 2009.

As before, I am presenting the allowable text of all entries, divided by small separations:

There is one more bit of background I need to detail before getting into now material. Again, I left this information out of the original post primarily for space reasons - the Geocities site was a pain to work with back then... Still is, really, as the recent corruption of Part III of the original ACGA posting a couple weeks back showed... This blog works so much better for this purpose... At any rate, I need to give some background on [Daughter 1], especially as it was a contributing factor to how things went down.

[Daughter 1] admittedly had a difficult young life. Her mother, Mara, and father, Jared, divorced when she was somewhere around three years old. And when her mother remarried, she married an abusive, controlling man, Tim Pelton, who treated her like garbage. Of course, it did not start that way - as is common with most abusive people, Tim began by ingratiating himself to Mara and her daughter. But of course, the

ingratiation was all designed to get Mara to cede control of her life to him...

One of the things that Tim did was to insist upon adopting [Daughter 1]. This may not seem an inappropriate thing on the surface, save that Tim insisted on having the adoption finalized before he was married to Mara. Years later it would be learned that Tim actually went to Jared and threatened him in order to compel Jared to relinquish his parental rights. And that also requires some explanation.

This part is a little grey on specifics, but as I have it, Dixie Nezat played a part in Mara's divorce from Jared. She told Mara that Jared was cheating on her with a thirteen year old girl, and later Jared revealed that Dixie had told him that Mara was cheating on him with some young guy, as well. Mara insists she was never unfaithful to Jared and Jared insists that while he was with Mara, he was faithful as well. I am only a third party in all of that because it all happened years before I ever met Mara, but I tend to lean toward believing what someone tells me unless I have reason to believe otherwise. I only mention this part because of a similarity to what happened with Tim.

Now, as I understand it, Mara was single for a couple of years before she ended up with Tim. And Tim wasted little time in trying to replace Jared as [Daughter 1]'s father figure. He apparently was avid with Mara about letting him be [Daughter 1]'s father and to basically force Jared out of his own daughter's life. But Jared was the natural father and had full parental rights - as I was told, Jared was something of a lax individual, lazy and unmotivated, and Tim used this to his advantage in convincing Jared to give him premier status as father in [Daughter 1]'s life. And, conveniently enough, Jared had started seeing a new girl, a thirteen year old (irony or something else, I don't know, but this was years after Dixie's allegation that divorced them) who seemed to command all of Jared's attention. When Tim approached Jared about the adoption, Jared offered no resistance and signed over his parental rights to Tim. Shortly afterwards, Jared moved to Canada with his soon-to-be wife and Tim thought that was the last of that.

Years later, after I had started seeing Mara for several months, Mara ran into Jared at a grocery store in Kalispell. When Jared learned that Mara had left Tim, he revealed an interesting story - it turns out, prior to Tim going to Mara, Tim had gone to him and told Jared that he was going to report him as a sex offender for dating a thirteen year old if he did not sign over his parental rights. Jared panicked and complied, then moved to Canada to escape the potential threat of Tim reporting him anyway. In Canada, thirteen is legal age and Jared was able to marry his girl and settle down to have a family. But it was Tim who had initiated the whole thing, and of course, Mara knew nothing of the threat or the real reason for Jared signing away his parental rights.

I mention all of this to demonstrate that Tim Pelton was a dangerous control freak. As I said, he made a point of insisting that Mara help him adopt [Daughter 1] prior to their getting married - a hook that gave Tim absolute control over Mara's daughter. But once he had that control, his interest in [Daughter 1] began to wain. Once Mara married him, the interest became indifference. And once Tim had a new daughter with Mara ([Daughter 2]), Tim's interest turned to abuse. From that point on, [Daughter 1] was to blame for everything and [Daughter 2] was the favored child. But it did not end with favoritism - Tim did some horrid things to [Daughter 1] growing up, including bashing her head through a wall and putting a gun up to [Daughter 1]'s head threatening to shoot her! His abuse to [Daughter 1] in fact, by slugging her full strength in the stomach, was the final straw that led to Mara's divorce of Tim.

Tim had always been violent to Mara, though she had been able to protect herself from it, but she had never directly witnessed Tim strike [Daughter 1] until the slug in the stomach. And even after Mara witnessed it first-hand, still she wanted to try to make her marriage work. If not for the support of myself and Carrie Beth Mountjoy pointing out to her how unhealthy that kind of relationship was, Mara may still have been married to Tim to this day. But, thankfully, Mara saw the light and divorced Tim Pelton.

Unfortunately, the mental damage had been done to [Daughter 1]. Later counselors determined that [Daughter 1] had post-traumatic stress disorder. It resulted in [Daughter 1] acting out emotionally, doing poorly in school, having a compulsive habit of lying, seeking attention (even negative attention) and making innumerable suicide threats. These were problems that [Daughter 1] had long before I entered the picture, and I witnessed them first-hand many times, even before Mara and I started dating in 2001. Ironically, I was later blamed for all of these emotional problems of [Daughter 1]'s... It just made the corrupt officials' jobs easier to say I caused it all. And of course, the "attorney" working for me would not challenge the position of the State (That's too much to go into as yet, but I hope to get to it eventually in this blog...).

Basically, all of this is foundation for what happened next in the saga. Specifically, [Daughter 1]'s threats of suicide and her penchant for dishonesty fed right into the hands of those who wanted an excuse to bring me down... Hopefully, I will be able to get into all of that tomorrow...

This is a continuation of my post from a couple of days ago, providing some background on [Daughter 1], the person I allegedly "assaulted".

As I detailed in my previous post (March 12, 2009), [Daughter 1] was a troubled child. She had long-standing emotional issues that stemmed from her years of abuse at the hands of Tim Pelton, and everyone in and around her life knew of these issues. Mara knew [Daughter 1] had a tendency to lie about just about everything and that [Daughter 1] was not above lying about something to get attention for herself. A friend, Melissa Gamma, recently told me a story I was previously unaware of - how Melissa had seen [Daughter 1] slap her sister, [Daughter 2], then blame it on my son, John, and about how Mara believed [Daughter 1] and punished John. I point this out to demonstrate that, sometimes, even knowing [Daughter 1]'s penchant for dishonesty, that even Mara was not clear on when [Daughter 1] was actually lying.[46]

Another factor was that [Daughter 1] was more than a mediocre actress, as well. During [Daughter 1]'s growing up, Mara had had both of her girls in talent and beauty contests. One such contest when [Daughter 1] was younger (about eight, if I recall correctly), [Daughter 1] was invited to a Washington competition where, unbeknownst to Mara or [Daughter 1] at the time, [Daughter 1] had actually received an offer for an acting contract for her performance. No one learned of this until I uncovered a letter in Mara's home that Tim had concealed during their marriage making the offer. Of course, by this time (sometime in 2003), the offer had long-since expired. Tim had a

---

46 A better way of saying this is that Daughter 1 was very accomplished at lying. Even her mother, who knew quite well of Daughter 1's tendency to lie, could be deceived – and quite frequently was. It is therefore not too surprising that Daughter 1 could deliver a story designed to get sympathizers to believe her version of events – it was only those who approached Daughter 1's stories with a critical eye that could see through them. Also remember, no matter how accomplished Daughter 1 may have been at appearing believable, she was still a thirteen year old girl and she simply was not that sophisticated yet – which meant that the more complicated the lie, the more likely it was to fall apart under critical observation. But fast, short lies – like slapping her sister and blaming it on John – could slip under the radar...

problem with anyone else in the household being "better" than him at anything, and it can only be presumed that he hid the letter to make sure that [Daughter 1] did not "rise above her station". Yeah, Tim was a sick, sick man - this is a guy who hid the ashes of Mara's deceased daughter from her because Mara seemingly thought more of her deceased daughter than she did of him... Like I said, a very sick man...

At any rate, Mara knew full well what [Daughter 1] was capable of. She knew that, given a script, [Daughter 1] could perform admirably on just about any topic, even pull up tears as needed. In essence, [Daughter 1] was a perfect collaborator in creating a faux assault claim. Of course, [Daughter 1] was limited to what she was told and no one who helped her concoct the false allegation had any real experiences with actual assault cases...

In fact, [Daughter 1]'s original story fell apart within a week after she went to see a counselor, Edith Paxman. After interviewing [Daughter 1], Ms. Paxman noted that [Daughter 1] had no emotional attachment to her story (ie, she rattled off the details, but showed no genuine emotion in doing so), that [Daughter 1] used words she did not understand (the example provided to me was "fondled" – [Daughter 1] could not offer a definition of the word nor use it in another sentence, but freely used the word in her story) and that [Daughter 1]'s story had no actual ending (when prompted, [Daughter 1] created an ending, but it had to be pointed out that there was no actual resolution on how the alleged assault was stopped). All of this convinced Ms. Paxman that [Daughter 1] was not being honest. This interview was also what led to [Daughter 1] changing her story to claim I might have been asleep, and what ultimately led to the original police investigation being closed in September, 2003 (though the actual investigation stopped in July, 2003).

Specifically, when Ms. Paxman asked [Daughter 1] how the "encounter" ended, [Daughter 1] apparently acted confused and said she just got up and walked away. Ms. Paxman asked if I tried to stop her, and [Daughter 1] said I didn't. More questioning led to Ms. Paxman asking what I did do, and [Daughter 1] said I was just lying there, at which point she was asked if my eyes were open or closed, and [Daughter 1] responded closed. And when Ms. Paxman asked the ultimate question, "Could Ron have been asleep?", [Daugther 1] responded (disgruntledly, I was told) that I could have been. It was this statement to police in late July that ended the initial investigation - if the event *had* occurred and I was not conscious, it was not a willful act and not a crime.

Keep in mind, I have waffled back and forth on this point myself. Which is it: an involuntary act on my part, a concocted story with her grandparents' (the Nezats') collaboration, or a repressed memory that [Daughter 1] only imagined? In the end though, I had to ask myself - if it really did happen, why had [Daughter 1] changed her story so many times? And why were there so many questionable issues identified by Ms. Paxman? And why did [Daughter 1]'s second version of events, as told to Officer Myron Wilson of the Kalispell Police Department, include a claim that an arm that she was lying on had performed a physically impossible ninety degree move to "fondle" both of her breasts? I finally reached the conclusion that there is no way the event could actually have happened, but to this day I am not clear whether it was [Daughter 1]'s imagination or an actual repressed memory or a combination of both.

Personally, I lean more toward the idea that the the Nezats convinced [Daughter 1] to help create a story about me to break up Mara and I and that the details were created by the [Daughter 1], who drew upon her childhood memory for details. But since the assault on Mara never happened to [Daughter 1], and she had only been three years old at the time, [Daughter 1] was not able to create a solidly believable story that would hold up to scrutiny. Her story had holes, and [Daughter 1] was constantly changing details to try to fix them. This should have made my defense against the allegation a no-brainer, but as I have alluded, the attorney assigned to me, Ed Falla, was working for the corrupt officials who wanted me removed as a threat. He did his level best to suppress this information, refused to competently seek records and testimonies that would impeach [Daughter 1], and adamantly refused to breach the topic of contradictory stories to [Daughter 1] at trial. His big excuse was that he did not want to give [Daughter 1] a chance to break down and cry before the jury, that that would make us look like bad guys, but as I told Falla, the only way that would happen was if Falla acted like a bully - simply pointing out the inconsistencies and impossibilities in a civil, respectful manner would not do this. But Falla refused to actually defend me, and was a big part in the kangaroo court that convicted me...

Well, I'm once again out of time. I'll hopefully finish [Daughter 1]'s bio on Monday.

I would like to clarify something before I go on here. I left the impression, I think, that I hold a lot of resentment for [Daugher 1] in my last post, and though I do hold some resentment, I cannot say that I completely hold [Daughter 1] to blame, either. She was first manipulated into this whole scheme by her grandparents (the Nezats), then when she recanted, she was abducted by State officials who spent months threatening and intimidating her into saying what they wanted so she could go back home (not that apparently they ever delivered on that promise).

Do I believe that [Daughter 1] is to blame for what happened? Certainly, I believe a degree of blame needs to be laid at her feet. She was completely aware that the things she said were malicious and untrue. But does she deserve my hate and revilement? No, I do not believe she does. I am extremely disappointed that someone I loved and cared for would betray me the way she did, but she was only thirteen years old and was under a great deal of pressure from people she trusted and from legal authorities to do the things they wanted to do.

I have had the chance to read dozens of psychological papers on the subject of childhood susceptibility, and I understand that an adolescent can be misled by authority figures that she has trust in. That includes grandparents and law enforcement. So there's a lot of reasons to put what [Daughter 1] did into a different light and offer forgiveness for what happened. In the end, [Daughter 1] was just as much as a victim in this affair as I was, though not for the reasons that the State would have the public believe. [Daughter 1] was not sexually abused by me, but she was subjected to terror and deceit in order to make a case against me. [Daughter 1] may have proven herself untrustworthy and unreliable in the greater scheme of things, but I cannot bring myself to hate her for being the victim of these other people who should really be the ones that I hate.

At any rate, I had intended this to be the resolution of the background on [Daughter 1], but now with my aside, I may not have the time to finish, but I'll give it a good run.

As I last left off, [Daughter 1] was a troubled girl, with habits of lying and doing just about anything for attention, even if the attention was negative.

There was one point I remember that [Daughter 1] was given a pair of faux leather pants from a friend, and she really liked them. Then one day we got this call from Mary Jane Foxx (her school counselor) berating Mara for being an unfit mother for "making" [Daughter 1] wear the same clothes to school for three days in a row. Now, I personally knew that had not been true because this was a common problem for [Daughter 1] - getting up in the morning after sleeping in her clothes (yeah, good luck getting her to change out of those) and trying to wear the same ones the next day - and I had been personally involved in sending [Daughter 1] back into her room to change almost every morning. But still, Ms. Foxx was insisting [Daughter 1] was wearing the same clothes anyway.

Well, it turns out that [Daughter 1] was tricking Mara and I. [Daughter 1] told Ms. Foxx when confronted that her mom didn't do laundry and she had no clean clothes to wear. But of course, Mara did do [Daughter 1]'s laundry and [Daughter 1] easily had more clothes than any of the kids because of gifts from family, friends and such. So we knew that was a lie. Thing is, [Daughter 1] did not think Ms. Foxx would contact us about it. And when she got cornered in the lie, [Daughter 1] changed her story (sound familiar?) - now she admitted that it was her, that she had been wearing other clothes over the faux leather pants because a boy in school liked how she looked in them. Whether the boy part was true or not, I'll never know - personally, I think she just liked them and that was the only reason she needed.

The point of this story is that [Daughter 1] had no compunction against lying, especially to Ms. Foxx, and Ms. Foxx believed without question anything [Daughter 1] said. Ms. Foxx did not call us with a question about the clothes; she called with an accusation and threat to report abuse with CFS for neglecting [Daughter 1]. [Daughter 1] had a way of twisting people around to believe her, no matter what she said or how unreasonable her story might seem. And it was the perfect talent to make people believe she had been victimized by me once that idea had been put into her head.

Okay, clearly I need another day to wrap this up, so I'm going to close for now. Tomorrow, I will wrap this up and one and all will understand what all of this pretense over these last three posts in this thread have all been about. As much as I have sidelined on this, it really is all significant to the overall picture. And tomorrow, you will see why.

Hopefully, this will be my final input on [Daughter 1]'s background. Also, this should be the last bit of fill-in that I should have to do before moving into the details of what actually happened after the events attested to in the original "Another Case of Gov Abuse" posting back in December, 2003.

As I have said repeatedly in this thread, [Daughter 1] had many emotional problems stemming from her years of abuse at the hands of Tim Pelton: she had temper flare-ups, problems with honesty, issues with seeking unwarranted attention (even negative attention), suffered in her grades and she was completely amoral about consequences to anyone else when she would create scenarios to get people to pay attention to her. This is not to say that she had no feelings for anyone else, just that she never stopped to consider how what she did might harm other people and once done, stubbornly resisted setting things straight, because then people would stop paying attention to her.

All of this came to a head on November 13, 2003, a week before the penultimate intervention of Child and Family Services (CFS). As was common, Mara and I drove the children into town from our home near Bigfork (4234 Foothill Road, for anyone wanting geography)[47] early in the morning so [*] could go to her other job working a Wendy's (she worked the early AM shift). This usually involved [*] getting us all to Arcadia before 6 am, her leaving for work, and the rest of us camping out and catching some more sleep before we all had to go our various directions. In the school year, this meant the kids could get roughly an

---

47 This address has since been changed. 4234 Foothill Road apparently was completely removed after the Nezats drove their daughter from the property, and it was not renewed when the road's name was changed to Coyote Meadow Trail, though the neighboring address of the Nezats was.

hour's more sleep before getting up to go to school, and I could usually go back to sleep after they left for a little while before getting ready to open the store around 9 am.

[Daughter 1] was always a hard person to get motivated in the mornings. She was hard to get up to go into town, and once she laid back down, she was hard to get back up. Typically, unless she was watched, she would just lie back down and go back to sleep. [Daughter 1] was always irritable in the mornings, no matter how much sleep she had had and when she was irritated, she would lash out, both verbally and physically, at anyone else around her. This was pretty much the standard gamble any of us had to deal with in the mornings with [Daughter 1] - sometimes she would just be sulky, other times she could get downright violent. And never with any good reason.

On the morning of November 13th, it was pretty much one of [Daughter 1]'s worse mornings. She was agitated upon being woken up that morning to come into town, and she was still angry when she was woken up to go to school. She was yelling, stomping her feet, and basically acting out as much as she could. She was yelling at her sister and John, and I recall having to stop her from hitting her sister that morning (who, by the way, was almost always in a good mood when waking up - polar opposite to [Daughter 1]).

Now, as one may recall, [Daughter 1] had already gone through the initial stages of her allegation, had had it contradicted by counselor Edith Paxman, had actually recanted the allegation entirely, and we had moved to try reuniting our households. However, [Daughter 1] had also been seeing her school counselor, Mary Jane Foxx, who, as I had previously mentioned, pretty much took everything [Daughter 1] said as gospel truth, even when [Daughter 1]'s stories would more often than not end up proving to be untrue (see my previous posting for an example). But Ms. Foxx had a messiah complex, always looking to find someone to save, and she latched onto [Daughter 1] as a pet project, seeking to find reasons to believe that [Daughter 1] needed help all the time. Of course, [Daughter 1] ate up the attention and did whatever she could do to keep Ms. Foxx providing it. And, [Daughter 1] being the consummate actress she was, paid close attention to whatever Ms. Foxx told her, picking up on words and phrases that she could use to make her stories more believable.

On this particular morning, after I had gotten [Daughter 1] and the other two ([Daughter 2] and John) up, [Daughter 1] insisted on just sitting on the couch, not getting ready. She still had to get her shoes on and gather her things (she never got undressed or anything once we got to the store, though in [Daughter 1]'s case, she normally slept in her clothes anyway, even when Mara and I protested). John and [Daughter 2] were ready, but [Daughter 1] was not.

From previous experience, I knew better than to leave [Daughter 1] alone. But [Daughter 1] was upset that I would not leave the room. I sat down on the couch and tried to get her to calm down and get ready, but all she wanted to do was yell at everyone. Eventually, she yelled out that I was making her "uncomfortable". I recognized that this was not something [Daughter 1] would normally say, and knew this was something she had picked up. I asked her how I was supposedly making her uncomfortable and what she meant by that, but [Daughter 1] could not answer. She just kept saying that I was and that I should leave.

Since I was not touching her or in anyway doing anything inappropriate (and John and [Daughter 2] were also in the room), I saw this as an effort of [Daughter 1]'s to simply try ordering me around. I recognized that when [Daughter 1] could not explain what I was allegedly doing to make her supposedly uncomfortable, I knew she was just miming something Ms. Foxx had fed her. As with the "fondling" example with Edith Paxman, [Daughter 1] had been fed a term that she did not know the meaning to and when confronted about it, she just got angrier.

Eventually, I got [Daughter 1] to put on her shoes and get ready for school, but she did it with loud grunts and stomping of her feet, acting more like a three year old throwing a tantrum than anything else. By the time [Daughter 1] went to leave out the door, I had had enough. I stopped her (verbally, not physically) before she left the room and told her that this had gone too far and that when her mother came home that night, we would all have a long talk about this because I was not going to go through another morning like that. [Daughter 1] only growled, turned away and stomped out, slamming the door behind her.

[Daughter 1] was not done yet though. One of the many things [Daughter 1] had been doing over the preceding weeks to get Ms. Foxx's attention was to make threats of suicide (an old stunt she had been threatening to her mom since I had first known her, over a year before Mara and I were together - it was always yelled at her mom in such a way that I truly believe it was more an effort to hurt her mom than any real intent at self-harm). Ms. Foxx, unlike Mara, gave [Daughter 1] extra attention when she heard [Daughter 1] talk about suicide. But [Daughter 1] soon learned that if she just made threats alone, the attention waned. And so [Daughter 1] was always trying to escalate the threat to get more and more attention.

For example, when [Daughter 1] first made the threats, Ms. Foxx took [Daughter 1] out of class at the drop of a pin, and [Daughter 1] really enjoyed this special treatment. But after awhile, when [Daughter 1] only made threats, the attention slackened. Ms. Foxx asked [Daughter 1] if she had thought of how she was going to kill herself, and when [Daughter 1] had no answer,[48] Ms. Foxx took it as a sign that [Daughter 1] was not too serious about it. So [Daughter 1], being the quick study she was, thought up a way to kill herself (by drinking chemicals from the janitor's closet), and that got Ms. Foxx to start paying attention again. But Ms. Foxx would get [Daughter 1] to sign a "no harm agreement", in which [Daughter 1] promised not to harm herself, and Ms. Foxx would consider the crisis over and let [Daughter 1] go back to class.[49] Again, the attention had begun to wain and [Daughter 1] needed a way to escalate the attention.

On November 13th, she went to school in a rage, knowing she was facing punishment when she went home. [Daughter 1] wanted attention, and once again made the vocal threat to kill herself. Ms. Foxx took [Daughter 1] out of class, where [Daughter 1] raged about how her and I had gotten into a fight and she wanted to kill herself because her mom would believe me, not her, when she got home (forgetting that John and [Daughter 2] were also present to support what had really happened). Ms. Foxx asked [Daughter 1] to sign a no harm agreement, but [Daughter 1] knew that signing it would only get

---

48 Identical to Daughter 1's response to Edith Paxman when asked about a detail her story lacked – initial confusion, but always followed with something to fill in the gaps as soon as she thought of something, ie, made something new up.

49 I have always found the concept of a so-called "No Harm Contract" to be a completely irresponsible approach to suicidal ideations. Consider that if someone were genuinely considering killing themselves, how effective would be a signed promise not to hurt themselves? Do therapists genuinely believe that they can somehow sue a patient for breach of contract after they are deceased? To myself, the only effectiveness this kind of agreement provides is for people seeking attention, not for anyone genuinely considering suicide. That being said though, if it is used to somehow regulate people with genuine suicide ideations, it will ultimately lead to people getting what they actually want. In fact, some statistics show that as high as sixty-five percent of people in psychiatric hospitals who actually attempt suicide have actually signed no harm contracts (Barbara L. Drew, RN, Archives of Psychiatric Nursing, Vol 15, Iss 3, June 2001). Which only goes to further illustrate that Daughter 1 was never genuinely interested in suicide, only in the attention making threats gained her.

her sent back to class, and would not get her out of the trouble she was already in. And so she refused to sign anything.

What [Daughter 1] did not understand was that refusing to sign a no harm agreement triggered intervention. As school counselor, Ms. Foxx was able to have [Daughter 1] committed to suicide watch at the local treatment center, Pathways. The school had a police liaison (ironically, Doug Overman who had been the detective in the Kapispell Police Department investigation) who made a report and made it clear that [Daughter 1] was emotionally distraught and wanted to harm herself. He inquired into the argument and even [Daughter 1] stated that I had done nothing inappropriate, just that I would not let her get ready without supervision. [Daughter 1] was therefore committed to suicide watch at Pathways, where she was when I actually filed the suit against Kalispell on November 18, 2003.

Okay, still more to tell and I am running out of time. Guess I will have to finish this tomorrow...

Okay, hopefully this will be the final entry on this thread so I can move onto new material. It is looking like I may be running out of time on the limited amount of "freedom" I have left, so it's vital I get as much entered as I can over the next couple of weeks...

As I detailed in the last post, [Daughter 1] did not want to face the potential of punishment at home for her abusive behavior and she had a counselor at school (Mary Jane Foxx) who had been enabling [Daughter 1]'s whims as she sought inappropriate attention. Her last effort to play the suicide card though backfired and she ended up committed to suicide watch at Pathways here in Kalispell. This all happened on November 13, 2003.

[Daughter 1]'s commitment was pretty standard. Her therapist at Pathways, Dr. Barney Houser, believed she was suffering from emotional depression and agreed that her commitment was appropriate. Mara and I visited with [Daughter 1] and Dr. Houser and there was absolutely no issues from that meeting that had any real relationship to the former conflict over the false allegation. By this point, [Daughter 1] had recanted the allegation and everyone pretty much accepted (including myself) her most recent explanation that the accusation had stemmed from a repressed memory.

As for personal visits, Mara was the one who went to visit [Daughter 1] in the evenings, mostly because I still had trust issues with [Daughter 1] and I believed the trust issues went both ways.[50] As such, I did not believe she really wanted me to visit her. However, that was not true, as Mara came to me soon after [Daughter 1]'s commitment and said [Daughter 1] did want me to come see her. This was a problem for management due to meetings only being in the evenings and my commitments to organized gameplay at the store.

This was a complication because I was the official judge for every evening event that Arcadia sponsored - most of the game companies that promoted tournaments required a registered judge to oversee the games, and I was Arcadia's sole licensed judge for the games we promoted. This was a longstanding conflict I had with others helping me with Arcadia - I should not have been the only licensed judge, but noone else wanted to take up the responsibility... There were a couple of exceptions, one of those being Wednesday nights when we ran Warlord - Warlord did not require a registered judge and I was able to schedule a visit with [Daughter 1] for November 19, 2003.

Mara was convinced, by the way, that [Daughter 1] only wanted me to visit so she could play off of my sympathies to get her out of Pathways. [Daughter 1] hated being confined and was

---

50 Also, one of us had to keep the store open, since visiting hours were limited to evening hours, and I reasoned that I was the more logical choice to do so.

desperate to get out of suicide watch - Mara had stood firm and intended to have [Daughter 1] stay to get whatever treatment she needed – [Daughter 1], apparently, believed that I could be convinced to get her out, mostly because when it came to the kids, I had always been the "soft touch". Mara described it as [Daughter 1] and the other kids having me wrapped around their fingers - if they ever wanted anything, I was usually the one who would go out of my way to get it for them. I seriously doubt I would have been suckered into taking [Daughter 1] out of Pathways, but Mara was convinced that that was why [Daughter 1] had wanted me to visit, to saddle up to me with sweet talk and niceties to try to get her out...[51]

At any rate, while this was all going on, I and Arcadia were still being subjected to harassments by local officials. I had finally gotten the local "inspections" to stop, but I was still receiving harassing letters from Richard Hickle with the Kalispell City Attorney's Office. These started in response to my filed petition for production of police records which was filed back on October 30, 2003. But when they did not stop and it became clear that it was just another effort to obstruct my rights, I filed the full lawsuit on November 18, 2003.

This is the event that triggered everything else that followed. The next day, on November 19, Child and Family Services (CFS) intern worker, Kori Taylor, visited [Daughter 1] at Pathways. Of course, Mara nor I knew about what really was going on that day until later. Our first indication that anything was wrong was when Mara received a call from Dr. Houser around 5pm that day

---

51 Incidentally, this is another example of how Daughter 1 was never actually afraid of me – she only acted afraid of me when it could get her attention. And the opposite was equally true – when she saw advantage, she could just as easily act like she adored me if she wanted something. Just as she was clinging to me the morning of the accusation, she had once again taken on the approach of trying to endear me to her. But either way, asking to see me alone while in Pathways was not the conduct of someone who felt threatened by me, or of someone who was there because of me supposedly doing anything that had driven her to think of suicide.

telling her that visitation for that evening had been cancelled due to some unspecified lockdown. Since this was the evening that I had planned to visit, it was disappointing, but we accepted Dr. Houser's explanation.

But during that call, Dr. Houser also reported to Mara that [Daughter 1] had been visited by CFS and that [Daughter 1] had been subjected to a "very aggressive interview" by the worker that was "counterproductive to [Daughter 1]'s care". Apparently, the interview by Ms. Taylor had left [Daughter 1] in tears and Dr. Houser requested that Mara please contact CFS to ask that they not visit [Daughter 1] again.

What Dr. Houser did not say was that Ms. Taylor had come in and literally attacked [Daughter 1] (verbally, not physically) about the allegation that [Daughter 1] had already recanted. Keep in mind, both the police and CFS investigation had been closed in September, 2003, and this was two months later. [Daughter 1] had recanted the allegation in October and even when pressed by Ms. Taylor, [Daughter 1] insisted that nothing had happened with me, and that it had all been confusion with a repressed memory. Ms. Taylor would not accept this though and continued to berate [Daughter 1] until finally Ms. Taylor informed [Daughter 1] that she would be having her removed from her mother's custody. This is what caused [Daughter 1] to break down crying.

Ms. Taylor thereafter told Dr. Houser that he could not "forewarn the family" of her intentions to have [Daughter 1] removed, and apparently Dr. Houser was bound by that instruction to not alert Mara. He did however work around that instruction to place a warning call to Mara that evening to at least let her know something was in the wind. But by that time, without more information about the intent to remove [Daughter 1], there was nothing any of us could do.

Mara had intended to call CFS the next day, but planned to do so after she got back from work in the afternoon. She got back to Arcadia that day and I had to leave to run business errands, so she put off making the call until I got back. Had we known that there were machinations in the background, neither of us would have delayed following any of this up, but Ms. Taylor had made a point of hiding what she was doing from us (which, by the way, is a gross violation of state law - see the original ACGA).

Long story short, [Daughter 1] and [Daughter 2] were abducted by Ms. Taylor on November 20, 2003. No protocol was followed, no effort to "work with" the family was extended. This was an ambush - it was a surgical strike designed to kidnap and separate Mara's daughters to gain undue influence over them and to use this abusive control to intimidate Mara and myself. This may have been accomplished through the rubber-stamping of court proceedings, but it was nevertheless a grossly illegal action. This entire procedure was akin to the Nazi abductions of Jews during World War II. CFS was granted leave to act outside the law and used that illegal authority to intimidate witnesses against me and to coerce those who would otherwise support me from assisting me.

This was one of only several instances of this kind of behavior, but it was the first and by far the most harmful. As I previously accounted, the local district court judge, Ted Lympus, endorsed the abduction of the girls in the December 5, 2003, show cause hearing, and granted CFS authority to detain the girls for basically an indefinite period. There was no evidence, no justification for these actions – [Daughter 1] denied that I had ever harmed her and [Daughter 2] never accused me of anything, no matter how much pressure was put upon her. However, the effort of these corrupt authorities achieved success - following the show cause hearing, after it was made clear that CFS would not return the girls without their siding with the

State, [Daughter 1] finally agreed to reassert the allegation, even though in doing so she made critical changes (yet again) to her story.

Truth to tell, I cannot be sure how much time I have left on this system today, so I am going to end this here. Everything that needed to be filled in has been done so at this point, I believe, so tomorrow will start a new thread - what happened after the last posting I made in ACGA. I hope those who may be reading this post will stay tuned for what became an even greater transgression of civil liberties as I learned that the corruption I had been exposed to was not just limited to myself, but had existed for quite some time. It may not have started with me, but the status quo certainly gave the authorities the latitude to do as they wished to me without repercussions. So next, I need to explain what happened after [Daughter 1] reasserted her allegation on December 9, 2003.

Chapter 10

Having set forth the history of everything leading up to the original GeoCities posting, I next turned my postings on the Great Montana Conspiracy site to set forth what had come after. Specifically, what happened between the time that the Kalispell and Flathead County authorities had collaborated to make the felonious kidnapping and abduction of Mara's thirteen and six year old daughter a "legal" action and what ultimately led up to my arrest on February 20, 2003.

I would like to remind the readers of something at this point. A blog – to be genuine – is not subject to back-edits. And unlike most people who maintain a blog, I did not have a private computer where I could compose entries in advance – I was limited to a sixty minute window at the local library to manually enter whatever I could create in that period of time only. So there was more than once that I felt that I left out critical details – and sometimes, that required me going back on a topic after it was posted.

Eventually, I was compelled to go back and remove identifying information from the blog entries by an unconstitutional court order – but when I initially created this blog, my intention was to be as honest and up front as possible. And that included maintaining their integrity by leaving the entries as they were entered, and not going back to edit details.

This next series was entitled, "What Came After AGCA". The first entry of this series was posted on March 21, 2009, and it consisted of six parts, including two flashbacks that filled in details that were missed in the earlier presentations – ergo, why I mentioned the editing references earlier. With this series, I was finally able to start talking about what happened after the corrupt authorities of Kalispell and Flathead County rubber stamped the kidnapping of Daughter 1 and her sister:

The events that have previously been chronicled pretty much covers what happened leading up the writing of Another Case of Gov Abuse (ACGA) on December 8, 2003. I had always intended to update that site, but things just got away from me between work and all of the issues created by what happened next.

We were informed within days of my posting ACGA that [Daughter 1] had once again reasserted her allegation (on December 9, 2003, if I recall correctly) against me. I did not find out until months later what the actual contents of that reassertion entailed, but it represented yet another change in the specifics of the allegation.

Just as a reminder, [Daughter 1] changed the details of her story several times. Though she has continued to maintain that this allegedly only happened one time for a period of some ten or twenty seconds,[52] she has never been consistent on exactly what happened and in what sequence. Her first story, told to Carrie Beth Mountjoy and Mara Pelton (now Mara Nezatski) over the phone the night of July 9, 2003, was that I had supposedly put one hand (unspecified which) up her shirt, that she pulled it out, then I supposedly put the same hand down her pants. By the time she got to the police station that evening, it had only been one hand (my right, which had allegedly been on top of her) down her pants only, until the officer prompted her about the up the shirt part, at which point [Daughter 1] added that that had also happened a few seconds before the pants incident, but by my left

---

52 Technically, she originally said five seconds, and this became ten to twenty seconds in later revisions – yet another detail to keep the story growing and getting Daughter 1 more attention.

hand (which she was lying on) and that I specifically touched both of her breasts (keep in mind - it is physically impossible for the human arm to move in a ninety degree up and down fashion when held immobile beneath a body; in order for me to have physically touched both breasts, it would have required an action that defied the laws of physics). When Edith Paxman made the multiple observations of inconsistencies in [Daughter 1]'s story, she added details that ultimately led to [Daughter 1] claiming I may have been asleep, which is what ultimately led to the initial police investigation being halted in July, 2003, and closed by September 4, 2003 (the CFS investigation was thereafter closed on September 15, 2003, after the police department confirmed their investigation was closed). Later in October, 2003, [Daughter 1] recanted the entire allegation when her mom (Mara) confronted her with the fact that her details matched exactly an assault [Daughter 1] had witnessed happen to Mara when [Daughter 1] was three years old.

All of these changes should have been sufficient to impeach [Daughter 1] later on, but of course, the attorney assigned to me by the local authorities (my so-called public defender, Ed Falla) refused to try to impeach [Daughter 1]'s credibility at trial.

When [Daughter 1] reasserted her allegation in December, 2003, she changed critical details. In an effort to remove the physical impossibility of her claim made to police on July 9, 2003, [Daughter 1] now insisted that it had been the hand beneath her that had been put down her pants and that the hand on top of her went up her shirt, touching only one breast. To counter her signed affidavit recanting her original allegation, [Daughter 1] insisted that I had written the statement solely on my own and forced her to sign it.[53]

---

[53] This particular modification to her story did not occur until her February 4, 2004 interview – I mistakenly ran the interviews Daughter 1 had been subjected to while under CFS influence together here.

Incidentally, months later Carrie Beth was interviewed and confirmed that she was, in fact, present during the preparation of the affidavit and that I had in no way visibly threatened nor intimidated [Daughter 1] to say or do anything. Later, when [Daughter 1] was asked what she would say if Carrie Beth had made such a statement, [Daughter 1] flatly said that Carrie Beth would be lying. I have already provided extensive details of [Daughter 1]'s history of deception and lying, so I do not feel I really need to comment too much on which of the two should be believed. However, I should note that during her interview, Carrie Beth made it pretty clear that she no longer supported my innocence and that she was now inclined to believe whatever the authorities said I had done. This was also sprinkled with statements like, "I can't believe he fooled me since I'm usually a much better judge of character..." and such. But the point here is that even though Carrie Beth had decided to go along with any story that would not put herself in harm's way, and that she was clearly not a supporter of mine, she still verified the details I had provided to the letter. Carrie Beth collaborated my version of events and [Daughter 1]'s should have been impeached quite readily - again, save for Ed Falla's refusal to impeach the credibility of [Daughter 1].

Well, I will continue this thread more tomorrow. I have other things to type up this morning.

First, let me apologize for not posting yesterday. I do not have access to a computer on Sundays, and when I logged in yesterday, I had a lot of emails to respond to. So I ended up not having time to post. Considering that I am under constant threat of being revoked and sent back to prison, this needs to be a priority, but I find I do not have enough time to do everything I need to do each day... I have barely started in logging the events of the last five years and I fear I will not get anything close to enough published in here before I once again lose access to the internet (Montana prisons do not permit internet access by inmates). So I will try to get what I can in, but if this all stops suddenly one day, it will because I have once again lost what liberty I have...

At any rate, as I noted last time, [Daughter 1] had delivered five separate versions of the alleged events claiming I had allegedly assaulted her. The details kept changing every time someone pointed out a flaw in her story and, in at least the last instance, the details of the changed story were provided by a state representative (Kori Taylor of Child and Family Services (CFS)).

After it became clear after December 5, 2003 (the show cause hearing) that the local courts were giving carte blanche authority to CFS to do whatever they wanted (even though at that time there was no outstanding allegation against me at all), Mara's and my relationship started feeling some serious strain. Kori Taylor used her endorsed authority to continue to exceed her lawful authority by making demands of Mara that she dissolve all contact with me, including putting my son, John, and I out of her home and evicting me from our shared business.

I kept showing Mara the actual laws of the State[54] that showed that what Taylor was doing was illegal and tried to encourage her to fight against this misconduct, but Mara was simply too afraid to stand up for herself. She stressed constantly that if she fought, she would never get her girls back at all. As contrary point, I pointed out to her that if Taylor was not following the rules to begin with, that Mara would not get her girls back at all if she cooperated. I told Mara then that so long as I continued to fight the local authorities' improprieties, that CFS would never relinquish their control over Mara's girls, that it did not matter whether Mara cooperated or not, that CFS would never give up

---

54 See the extensive citations of state statutes in Appendix 2.

their leverage that could be used to try to force me to back down. Essentially, [Daughter 1] and [Daughter 2] were kidnapped by the State of Montana and used as blackmail against Mara to coerce her to withdraw her support from me.

In the end, CFS proved stronger in their bullying than I proved to be with simple reasoning.

Mara would not immediately evict John and I from her home or from the business, but she made it clear that we needed to find some kind of plan and to work toward that. Taylor had made several promises to permit visitation between Mara and her girls and had cancelled all three promises (these occurring all prior to [Daughter 1]'s "new" allegation on December 9, 2003) allegedly because Mara had not complied with the demand of evicting me from her life.[55] Only after [Daughter 1] reasserted her allegation did Mara start to get limited, monitored visitation, but she was not allowed to discuss the situation, ask the girls anything relevant to what they were going through or where they were staying, or even to hug her own children. This method of first complete deprivation of contact and later in such stringent control was a form of psychological torture for Mara. It was bad enough not being allowed to see her kids, but when they were dangled at her, one at a time, like carrots that she could not fully embrace, it became worse for her. Bit by bit, the abusive nature of Taylor's control over the girls wore Mara down to the point that she came to feel that she could only get what she wanted (the

---

55 I now know Mara not complying was an excuse – Daughter 1 and Daughter 2 were being isolated under threats that they could never again see their mom unless they said what Kori Taylor wanted them to say. Daughter 2 made this very clear in the letters she had smuggled to her mom while in CFS care. Only after Taylor was able to coerce Daughter 1 to reassert a twisted version of the original allegation was contact permitted, and then only in the most draconian capacity – no physical contact, never together and the girls were not permitted to say anything about what Taylor had been putting them through. Essentially, the girls were being abused – and CFS was the abuser, threatening more harm if the girls said anything about the abuse.

return of her daughters) by at least offering some token of cooperation with CFS.

Keep in mind, the deprivation of contact was designed for more than just control of Mara - it was a control element over the girls as well. [Daughter 1] was deprived all contact until after she reasserted her allegation, and then she was "rewarded" with a visit to her mom shortly thereafter. The period of deprivation lasted over three weeks and in that time, Taylor apparently used this time to wear [Daughter 1] down. [Daughter 1] had never been someone who considered others' feelings when she wanted something, and [Daughter 1] wanted to go home. That much had been obvious when she was held only a week under suicide watch. After three weeks of being told she would not be able to go home without reasserting her allegation, presumably using the same kind of aggressive interviews (as reported by Dr. Barney Houser), and [Daughter 1]'s clear desire to just go home, she gave in and reasserted her allegation, albeit with modifications to "fix" her previous mistakes. This, by the way, violated every pretense of law - but the law, as has been the consistent problem throughout this affair, was set aside to permit the authorities unrestrained leave to undermine my actual innocence.

At any rate, as CFS continued pressuring [Daughter 1], and [Daughter 1] herself began to buckle under the pressure, it became clear that Mara was not going to permit John and I to stay much longer, which would place Mara and I at legal odds as well over the business. I did not want this - I loved Mara deeply and I was hurt all the more by how much my war was costing her. We had had plans of expanding the youth program, plans that had preceded the allegations made in 2003. It had always been something we had planned for "down the road" - in fact, our most recent plan had been to try to set up a satellite youth program in summer of 2004. The situation though with Mara *being forced to make a decision between her girls and myself moved up this schedule. Out of love for Mara and in an effort to try to help her get back her girls, I agreed to move up the calendar and try to set up a satellite program right away. And since the plan had always been to set up such a program out of state, I began searching for a community that would work out for such a project.*

The plans to do this were rushed - I agreed to move up the schedule shortly after Taylor began cancelling Mara's visitations with her girls in late November, 2003, prior to [Daughter 1] reasserting her allegation in December, and found a site rather quickly - by the middle of December, 2003 - in Goldendale, Washington. I made a point of checking with the Kalispell Police Department once we had a target site and confirmed that there was no active investigation in their office that prohibited my leaving the State, and when I learned there was not, made plans to move to Goldendale. The move occurred on December 23, 2003.

This is enough for today, as my hands are hurting. Tomorrow, I will discuss the move to Goldendale and all it entailed.

As I mentioned in my previous post, Mara convinced me that to help her in cooperating with Child and Family Service (CFS) worker, Kori Taylor.[56] Mara's girls had been abducted through a

---

56 I want to reiterate – I did not *agree* that Mara's actions were proper, nor did I volunteer to abandon my entire life on some belief that Mara would ever get her girls back. But all I was doing was adding more stress by trying to convince her that she was wrong. In the end, she was wrong -she never got got her girls back. Even after I was in prison, CFS never returned her girls. They just made up one excuse after another. But the end underlying reason was always the same – they needed to keep Daughter 1 under their control. She had recanted her accusations once before, and – knowing the entire issue was fabricated to begin with – they could not afford to have Daughter 1 return to the safety of home and hearth and spill the beans on what had really gone on after Daughter 1 had been removed from her home. They had committed too many criminal actions themselves to permit their bullied accomplice to expose them. And therefore, they kept Daughter 1 under their thumb and away from

massive violation of state laws, but Mara believed that fighting against this misconduct would take longer than if she cooperated. I did not agree with her position - in fact, I had told her that cooperation would only strengthen their position, not weaken it, and that the authorities would not relinquish their undue influence until and unless I withdrew my own legal challenges against them, which I refused to do. But I could not convince Mara of this. And I felt that sooner or later, Mara would be forced in her conflict between myself and her girls to try to evict me from my home and business to try to comply with Taylor's demands. This was a legal struggle I could not afford, as it would undermine my support from Mara, and so I agreed to advance my plans to set up a satellite youth program, and made arrangements to move to Goldendale, WA.

This was not an easy thing to do, either. We had not had an opportunity to budget for this sudden move and our business had taken some serious financial hits from the defamation from city officials as well. So I went to Goldendale without any financial support. I had to actually apply for social services while I was there, which I should not have had to do when expanding a business like that. But I had agreed to move away to provide distance for Mara to try her direction with cooperating with the corrupt actions taken by CFS. Essentially, I went into voluntary exile with my son because I loved Mara and the girls enough to let them try to work things out Mara's way, even when I disagreed with her plan entirely.

The original plan had been to spend between six to twelve months in Goldendale establishing the satellite program and to secure a staff to operate it independently of my own direct involvement. I was only given less than two months though.

I was more or less successful in Goldendale. I was well into making inroads with local organizations - I soon had the support

---

Mara.

of the local chamber of commerce and had received support from a local nonprofit organization who agreed to let the Outpost CCG (the youth program) work under its nonprofit umbrella in Washington to solicit grants. Things were well on the road toward establishing the center I had planned on.

Unfortunately, the legal issues still ongoing in Kalispell put an abrupt end to my efforts there.

Prior to leaving for Goldendale, I had filed a motion for default judgment in my lawsuit against Kalispell. The city representatives had not filed a response to either the original petition (filed October 30, 2003) nor the complaint (filed November 18, 2003), so that by the end of December, there was no other proper legal recourse than to seek default judgment. I filed for default on December 23, 2003, the same day I left for Goldendale.

Sometime in the first week of January, Mara informed me of a letter that had been received at Arcadia's address in Kalispell from the local court clerk, Peg Allison[57] (to date, I have never actually seen the physical letter, by the way). In the letter, Allison stated that the default judgment could not be granted because the action had not been properly served. In a phone conversation I had with Ms. Allison immediately after this, she claimed that there had been no proof of service filed. Now, I knew that there had been because I had walked into the clerk's office and filed all three proofs myself - I had had Mara serve the city defendants with the original petition in October, 2003, and had had two different people (James Valentino and another patron of Arcadia[58]) serve the complaint in November, 2003. So I knew that

---

57 This would be Peg Allison, Clerk of the Eleventh District Court of Montana.

58 When I originally wrote this, I could not recall Ian Chrisman's name – I have since recovered his original affidavit, which provided me the name I could not record in this original blog entry.

Ms. Allison was lying, but I told her that I could provide copies of the proofs for her to prove that they had been served.[59]

As soon as I said that though, Ms. Allison changed her story and said that no, it was the fact that no summons had ever been issued[60] that was the reason for not granting the default judgments. In other words, she was intentionally obstructing the filing and fishing for excuses to not let the default judgment go through...[61]

There is more to this that I will have to finish later... Out of time for today. Hopefully I will get a chance to post more tomorrow...

---

59 By way of explanation, a proof of service is a sworn statement that service was performed upon a named defendant. In this case, it would be Mara's, Ian's and James' sworn statements that they had served the parties personally. I had taken these directly to the court myself, so knew full well they had been filed. This was a falsehood of Allison's – and she panicked when I said I could provide the proof of services.

60 In a previous chapter, I explained that a summons was a cover sheet issued by a clerk of court that is attached to an initial filing of a complaint or served to a new defendant informing them that they are being sued and the consequences of failure to file a response. As one might remember, the original filing in this action was the petition on October 30, and three summons were issued and served by Mara. The expanded action filed on November 18 did not have summons issued because the assistant clerk, April Coen, refused to issue summons and I mistakenly accepted this as a "local rule".

61 One other note here: it is not a court clerk's job to present a defense of why not to grant a default judgment – she is not a party to the action, nor is she a judicial officer charged with deciding contested legal matters. The law is specific – when a party does not respond to an action, the clerk *must* enter a default judgment, not find legal reasons to not grant it. It is the defendants in the cause who must present such a defense or it is a judge's duty to rule upon the motion if it is contested. Peg Allison, by actually making a decision to not permit the default judgment to proceed, was both usurping the power of the court itself, ie, the judge, as well as acting in excess of her lawful duties under law. In other words, Peg Allison was committing the felony of official misconduct, violating all three tiers just as Garner had done previously, as well as tampering with official records. And this was all done in defense of the corrupt authorities in Kalispell whom I was suing.

As a quick recap, I ended the last post with the first efforts of Peg Allison, the Flathead County District Court Clerk, to obstruct my legal actions. As I explained, I filed for a default judgment on December 23, 2003, when well over twenty days had passed without any filed response from the City of Kalispell[62] to my lawsuit. By law, any action that is not responded to is considered uncontested, which is to say that the responding party has no objection to the filed action. In the instant case, when I filed first a petition (on October 30, 2003) and then a complaint (on November 18, 2003), and no response was filed to these actions, by law a default judgment must be granted in favor of the pleading party. This is not a discretionary choice - the court is required by law to grant relief to a pleading party when no response is received from the defending party.[63] And yet, Ms. Allison had begun to obstruct the cause of action in an effort to block the default judgment I had filed for.

But this goes beyond what I described in my last post. Simply put, I ran out of time before I could detail the whole scenario. But before I finish this part, let me back up just a moment to clarify the earlier events.

As I mentioned in my last post, I filed the initial petition against the City of Kalispell, Kalispell Police Department (KPD) and the Kalispell City Attorney's Office on October 30, 2003. This followed a face-to-face confrontation between myself and then-Chief of Police, Frank Garner, on October 28, 2003. I had been told that the police investigation was closed (which was, in fact, closed on September 4, 2003, though I was not informed until the first week of October, 2003), and had confirmed this through no less than five sources. Since my letters requesting production of the records of the investigation were ignored, I had visited City Hall myself to request these documents. I first visited

---

62 Nor any defendant of the suit.

63 See Appendix 1, MCA § 25-20-Rule 55.

Richard Hickle of the City Attorney's Office, who claimed that the records could not be released for "confidentiality" purposes. After Mr. Hickle provided MCA statutes which he claimed set the restrictions for not releasing the records, I reviewed the same and found that they did not bar my rights to such records, though did set forth the requirement that I make the request through the agency holding the records. And so I went directly to the KPD.

When I went to the KPD's office, I was eventually referred to Mr. Garner (though he did not identify himself immediately). Mr. Garner stated very bluntly that he had no intention of releasing the records and, despite having verified through multiple sources, including CFS, the investigating officer, school counselors, the city's insurance agency, etc., that the case had been reported as closed, he suddenly insisted that the case had never been closed and that he was going to have the case sent to the county attorney with recommendations for prosecution. All because I wanted my records, and all because I had a pending claim against the KPD for their official misconduct. Clearly, Mr. Garner did not want me to have access to records that might incriminate his department. I later learned that in addition to his re-opening the KPD case, Mr, Garner called CFS to have their case re-opened this same day, as well.

One of the more interesting elements of this conversation was that Mr. Garner insisted that he did not have to turn over any files from an active case (his reason for re-opening the case to bar my request for records). I had had a copy of the actual law with me that day (MCA 2003 Section 44-5-214)[64] which clearly did not permit such a distinction. When I tried to show him the law, he refused to look at it. When I asked him then under what authority he was using to bar my access to the files, he stated, "Under what legal right? Because I say so. That's what right!" Clearly, this action was not a legal one - it was outside the

---

64 See Appendix 1.

boundaries of law, and Mr. Garner was not going to be compelled to follow the law.

For the record, it was four months later that I was actually prosecuted - not because of Mr. Garner's recommendation on that day, but as a follow-up to what later happened with Ms. Allison.

After consulting with a civil rights attorney in Helena, MT, I filed a petition for production of the police records on October 30, 2003. This is the action that actually initiated my suit against Kalispell proper.

Out of time again, so I will conclude this Flashback on Monday. I am being loaned the use of a separate computer on Monday, too, so I expect to get a lot typed in that day.

As I detailed in my last post, the conflict that led to my actually filing a legal action against the City of Kalispell was exacerbated by a face to face confrontation with then-Chief of Police Frank Garner. When I went to the Kalispell Police Department (KPD) to request the production of records from their investigation that had been closed, Garner acted to obstruct the production of those records by re-opening the investigation, and later placed a call to Child and Family Services (CFS) to have them re-open their own investigation. Prior to this, I had verified through several sources that all official investigations had been closed in September, 2003 (September 4 for KPD and September 15 for CFS). And all of this happened on October 28, 2003).

Following the confrontation with Garner, I consulted with a freedoms of information attorney out of Helena, MT. I confirmed with him that Montana law does not provide for a law enforcement agency to withhold records, even with an active, ongoing investigation. Therefore, Garner's actions to obstruct the production of records by re-opening KPD's investigation and having CFS re-open their own was yet another act of official misconduct. The attorney I consulted recommended that I file a petition with the local justice court to compel the production of the police records.

Pursuant to such advice, I prepared a petition for production of records and attempted to file it with the Kalispell Justice Court. However, that court refused to accept jurisdiction and referred me to the district court. It was at this point that I filed the petition with the Eleventh Judicial District of Montana, In and For Flathead County. This occurred on October 30, 2003.

Upon filing of the petition, which I filed in person, the court clerk issued to me three summons, one for each named defendant (City of Kalispell, Kalispell Police Department and Kalispell City Attorney's Office). I made a copy of one of the summons for my records, then personally stapled an original summons to each copy of the petition to be served. Mara Pelton (now Mara Nezatski) performed service that same day upon all three. Thereafter, I personally filed the proof of service signed by Mara with the court clerk.

The filing of this petition initiated a wave of harassing letters from Richard Hickle with the City Attorney's Office. It was also around this time that I learned that KPD officers were contacting clientele of my business, spreading the malicious rumor that I was a child molester (it turned out that this had been going on since the initial investigation had begun in July, 2003, but I did not learn of it until early November, 2003). In an effort to bypass these harassments, I began placing calls to the City Manager (Chris Kukolski) and the Mayor (Pam Kennedy). However, in spite of my best efforts to try to halt the harassments and defamations, they continued up until the point where I was forced to file an actual complaint on November 18, 2003.

When I prepared and filed this complaint, I did so again in person. I did so with the intent of having new summons issued by the court clerk since I had added several new defendants to the action (Pam Kennedy, Chris Kulkolski, Frank Garner, Myron Wilson, Doug Overman and Richard Hickle). However, the court clerk refused to issue new summons for the new defendants. I argued back and forth with the clerk for several minutes on this point – the clerk I spoke with insisted that since a summons had already been issued in the cause, that there was no need for a new summons.[65] I knew better – I knew that adding new defendants compelled the new defendants to be served with summons, too. Yet the clerk refused to budge on this issue, and I was forced to leave without the issuance of new summons.

Keep in mind, at this juncture, I was still unaware of the full breadth of the corruption in Montana or how far reaching the influence was to block my claim against the City. I started this fight believing that there had been a rogue police officer (Myron Wilson), and then later believed that his department was protecting him when I pursued claims against his misconduct. Likewise, when other branches of the City began to run interference and to extend harassments my direction, again I identified it as an extension of the City covering up for the potential liability they would inherit due to the official misconduct of its police department. At this point, I was not aware that the corruption and collaborative efforts to cover it up would also come to incorporate both the county and State governments. In a nutshell, I was truly naïve to the level of corruption that existed here in Montana, and ultimately I lost my entire life to this struggle because I simply did not know that there simply was no relief available to a person standing alone against it.[66]

---

65 This would be Deputy Court Clerk, April Coen.

66 Also note – none of us were aware up and through the filing of the lawsuit on November 18 that CFS had reopened their own investigation at Frank Garner's bequest. No effort was made to reach out to Mara or myself, much less to interview the children, prior to my filing the lawsuit – and then CFS came in with the ferocity of a sledge

Incidentally, I initially had a volunteer of my youth program, Jeff Berna, attempt to serve KPD and its officers on the night of November 18, 2003, but Frank Garner once again obstructed the legal process. When Mr. Berna went to the police department to perform service, Garner pulled Mr. Berna into his office and threatened to have him arrested if he actually tried to serve him or anyone in his department! The gist of the threat was the implication that Mr. Berna had no lawful authority to serve anyone unless he was registered with the State as a process server. Further, Garner went on to tell Mr. Berna that he did not want to "fall" because of "Glick's little games".

The applicable law, by the way, stated that anyone performing more than ten services of process in a calendar year had to register as a process server with the State; Mr. Berna had acted as a process server in two other instances, and his service of the KPD, Frank Garner, Myron Wilson and Doug Overmen would have brought his total services to seven. Mr. Berna was not in fact violating any law – Mr. Garner simply used his position of authority to threaten and intimidate Mr. Berna to avoid being served with legal process!

Needless to say, Mr. Berna took Garner at his word and would not perform the legal service. Mr. Berna told me directly that he could not afford to get arrested and that if I wanted to have KPD served, I would have to find someone else. Garner subsequently placed a call to me where he tried to threaten me as well, but while on the phone I referenced the applicable law online and proved that Garner was lying about his authority. However, Garner had succeeded in blocking service for the day since I did not readily have someone else to perform service that day.

The next day, I did find someone else to attempt service again upon the police department and the other city defendants, a client

---

hammer immediately after on November 19.

of my business, Ian Chrisman. He took up the service as a challenge and went to perform service upon the city defendants the next day, November 19, 2003. What Mr. Chrisman told me later was that he attempted to serve the KPD clerk, but that service was declined – the clerk told Mr. Chrisman that Garner had specifically instructed her not to accept service from Ron Glick.[67] He thereafter went to perform service upon the City Attorney's office and Richard Hickle, but the clerk there told him he would have to serve Hickle directly and he was not in the office.[68] Mr. Chrisman then served the city itself by serving the City Recorder and tried to serve the mayor, but she was not in her office. Next, Mr. Chrisman went to Chris Kukolski's office, and served him. Kukolski accepted the service without complaint and, according to Mr. Chrisman, was very polite about the whole issue.

However, right after he was served, Kukolski received a phone call while Mr. Chrisman was still in the office. As reported to me, Kukolski responded, "Yes, he is here", followed by, "Yes, I accepted service". The rest of the conversation was apparently little more than affirmative and negative responses, and ended by, "I'll come over and talk to you". Kukolski informed Mr. Chrisman that the call had been from Garner, who it seems had been calling the named defendants and trying to encourage that

---

67 This is a greatly truncated version of what happened, as I recounted earlier the full discourse – understand, I was on a limited schedule for these blog entries and I rushed through the presentation here, even though I had more time on this particular entry because this was prepared by the loan of a friend's laptop for a day. I was feeling pressured and needed to get as much down as I could, and out of necessity I was not nearly as complete in this recounting as I was previously in this volume.

68 When I was recounting this from memory, I got the details out of order. I now have Ian Chrisman's own affidavit signed on December 23, 2003, in which he declares he first served the City Attorney's Office, then tried to serve the police department. See Appendix 2 for a copy of this affidavit. It was also Jeff Berna who served the City Recorded the next day, not Ian. The City attorney defendants were served, not the *City*. With all the details running around in my mind, I got these a little jumbled.

no one accepted service. Kukolski then told Mr. Chrisman that he was going to meet with Garner and asked him to wait out in the front lobby.

Mr. Chrisman reported to me that he spent roughly twenty minutes in the lobby as Kukolski disappeared into the police department. As he sat there, Mr. Chrisman reported that Garner (who he did not immediately know at the time) made several trips past him and down the hall to the city attorney's office, apparently glaring at Mr. Chrisman at each pass.

Finally, Kukolski re-emerged from the police department with Garner at his side, and Garner, in what I am told was a very resentful tone, agreed to accept service for himself and on behalf of the police department. He also agreed to have the other defendants who had not yet been served to be available that evening for service, I believe around 8pm, if I recall correctly.[69] When Mr. Chrisman appeared at the scheduled time, defendants Pam Kennedy, Myron Wilson and Doug Overman were there to accept service – only the City Attorney defendants remained to be served. But Mr. Chrisman would do no more, which required me to find yet another person to complete service on the City Attorney the next day, James Valentino. As I understand it, Valentino had no trouble making that service.[70]

Upon completion of the services, I again personally filed the proof of services with the court clerk on November 20, 2003.

As an aside, these events happened over five years ago. My memory on some of the details may be slightly askew for this reason, but I have attempted to detail the events as accurately as I recall them. Certain things, especially the actions that I personally took, are indelibly imprinted in my mind. However, my memory may not be as clear on issues that were told to me by others. If there is a minor detail or two out of place, the rest of

---

69 I did not recall correctly – according to Ian's affidavit, it was 5pm, not 8.

70 Again, James served the City Recorder, not the City Attorney.

the details should not be discounted. The essential elements though – that three summons were issued directly to me by the clerk of court, that service was performed upon all parties, with summons in service of the petition, and that I personally filed all three proofs of service with the court is absolutely a fact. There is no discrepancy in these details – it is only a possibility that issues and sequences of events as reported to me by others may not be entirely accurate. On this issue, I simply have no control. However, I do believe that what I was told is accurate, or I would not be detailing it herein.

This wraps up this flashback. My next post will detail the events that began in January, 2004, and the reason for this flashback will become more relevant.

As I detailed in my previous post in this thread, I had initiated a suit against the City of Kalispell and several agencies and officials thereof, but no response had been filed to either the initial petition (filed October 30, 2003) nor to the actual complaint (filed November 18, 2003). Pursuant to Montana law, a party has twenty days to file an answer to a legal action, otherwise they are in default and the issues raised in the action are considered uncontested. I provided an even greater period for response that the twenty days – I did not file for default judgment until December 23, 2003, the same day I left for Goldendale, Washington, to set up a satellite youth program modeled after the one I had run in Montana for seven years.

By the way, for anyone seeking to verify any of this, the cause number in question for my suit against Kalispell is DV 03-572, Eleventh Judicial District of Montana, Glick v. City of Kalispell, et al.

Shortly after setting up in Goldendale, Mara Pelton (now Mara Nezatski), then my girlfriend and business partner, informed me that a letter had been received at the Kalispell address from Clerk of Court, Peg Allison. I believe this letter was dated January 4, 2004, though I have never actually seen a copy of the letter (despite requests to have a copy mailed to me, Mara never did). The essence of the letter was that the default judgment filed for would not be granted because service had not been "properly performed" upon the defendants of the cause.

As an aside, it is not the position of a court clerk to make this determination. The party being defaulted against needs to file an objection to the motion for default judgment in order for the court to consider such a defense. The clerk of court, nor the court itself, can lawfully presume to assert the defense of a party in a legal action. Since the parties in question had been lawfully served with a copy of the motion for default judgment, it was the parties' obligation to raise this defense. Allison's raising this obstruction violated due process. But this issue is minor compared to the innumerable unlawful acts Allison has taken against me through capacity of her office over the years.

At any rate, as I previously attested, I called Allison and asked for clarification. I had worked as a paralegal previously in California for two years and I knew I had performed service properly, so I needed to know what she was claiming was not done properly. Initially, Allison insisted that there were no proof of services in the file to validate that service had been performed. As one will note in my flashback posts, I knew this not to be true because I had personally filed the three proofs of service in the file.

When I told Allison this and offered to have copies forwarded to her from my Kalispell files though, she completely changed her story. When confronted with evidence that disproved her position, Allison then insisted that she had been thinking of another case and that the problem with my case was that there was no summons issued in the cause.

Again, one reading my flashback posts will note that there had been summons issued – three summons had been issued on October 30, 2003, when I filed the initial petition, though the clerk had actually refused to issue additional summons on November 18, 2003, when I filed the actual complaint and added six new defendants. So though there might have been grounds to say the additional defendants had not been properly served (though this was the fault of direct obstruction from the court clerk's office), three valid summons had been served at the outset of the cause. Therefore, at the very least, default judgment should have been issued against the initial three defendants: City of Kalispell, Kalispell Police Department and Kalispell City Attorney's Office.

However, when I told this to Allison, she insisted that there was no record of a summons in the court file (Note: I have requested on numerous occasions for a copy of the docket to this cause to confirm or refute Allison's claim, but Allison has ignored each of my requests).[71] *At the time of the phone call, I could not recall whether I had actually made a copy of the summons, and Allison played off this uncertainty. She insisted that since her office had not issued a summons, any service that had been performed would not be legal, and as such, no default could be granted.*

Remember, I knew three summons had been issued and knew that I had personally stapled a certified copy of the summons to the front of each copy of the petition that I had had Mara serve. Therefore, I knew that what Allison was saying was untrue. I could not be sure who had tampered with the court file, but it was obvious that, if I assumed Allison to be telling the truth, that someone had. And also remember, that at this point, I was not

---

71 Just to clarify, now over ten years later, I have still never been granted access to my own court file in this cause. After this date, Allison barred me from accessing copies, docket sheets, anything. All that I have recovered have been from third parties who had copies in their own files – but none of them had a docket sheet.

aware that the county court would aid and abet the city in unlawful conduct. So, at least at first, I had taken Allison at her word.

Without being able to recall initially whether I had made a copy of the summons, I reverted to statutory law that a sworn oath of someone conducting service was sufficient to establish that service had been performed. Therefore, I proposed to Allison that I would call Mara and have her attest to the service of the summons. Allison agreed and told me to have Mara call her.

Immediately after getting off the phone with Allison, I called Mara and asked her what she recalled from serving the initial petition. I asked her if she remembered serving a summons with each copy, and she said that, though she did not know exactly what a summons was, that she did remember a cover page being stapled onto the petition that was titled "Summons" that did not look like any of the rest of the filing (ie, the cover sheet was not printed off a computer like the rest of the petition was). This was sufficient to satisfy whether a summons had been served since I personally did know what a summons was and that I had personally stapled those to the front of the petitions, this would satisfy the chain of evidence. That Mara was willing to attest that these documents had been attached to the documents she served and that she did in fact serve these upon the defendants should have been enough to satisfy the legal prerequisites. Had someone tampered with the court file and removed the summons, there were now myself and Mara to attest that not only was a summons issued, but it had in fact been served as well.

Unfortunately, this would require that the rules of law were being followed.

After speaking with me, Mara called Allison to inform Allison that she had served summons upon the defendants on October 30, 2003. Unfortunately, Allison was actually the one working to obstruct the cause and instead of accepting Mara's attestment *(or alternatively requesting a signed affidavit for the court file), Allison instead chose to threaten Mara with perjury charges if she tried to testify that she had, in fact, served valid summons! The gist of what Mara later told me was that Allison told Mara that, as court clerk, she was the only one who could attest whether a valid summons had been issued or not and that if Mara tried to attest that there had been one issued, Allison was prepared to have perjury charges brought against Mara!*

When Mara called me back, she was in tears. Allison had scared her into thinking, much like Garner had done with Mr. Berna previously, that if she tried to make an official statement about her service of the summons, that she would be arrested! I tried to tell Mara that Allison's threat was meaningless, but to no avail. I tried to tell her that first of all, she would not be attesting to whether the summons were valid, I would, since the summons had been issued to me; the only thing Mara would be attesting to would be whether she had served the summons that I had provided. Also I told her that even if Mara had been the one to attest to the summons authenticity, she could not be charged with perjury unless she willfully made a statement she believed to be false under oath; if Mara believed the summons to be valid at the time she had made the service and attested to such, there could be no perjury charge! But Mara could not be dissuaded – she believed what Allison had told her and refused to sign an affidavit attesting to her service of the summons for fear of being arrested!

This, by the way, is another form of witness tampering, and is a felony under Montana law. Allison could not lawfully intimidate a witness to withhold her testimony or to attest to something she did not believe to be true. Mara believed that I had provided her certified copies of the summons because they were each embossed. She believed that the summons she served were valid and Allison's threats and intimidations were specifically designed to tamper with Mara as a witness. It was at this point, when I heard what Allison had told Mara that I recognized that it was not some unknown person tampering with the court records either – it was Peg Allison herself. And that implied that agents of the county were willing to commit crimes themselves to cover up the official misconduct of the city and its agents, even though the entities were supposed to be separate under the law.

    I spent the next couple of weeks trying to convince Allison to grant the default judgment. I confronted her over the fact that what she had done was felonious, that she was herself making herself a party to the action and that she could be named as a defendant herself. None of that mattered to her, and she refused to budge on the issue. And Mara, intimidated by the threat of being arrested, would not forward me a copy of my file that I had left in her care to produce the copy of the summons I had by then recalled was there.

    Finally, on January 28, 2004, I took the penultimate action that would lead to my arrest: I wrote a letter to Peg Allison informing her that if she did not immediately halt her unlawful obstruction of my cause and have the default judgment granted within thirty days of the letter, I would have no choice but to move my suit to the federal court pursuant to 18 USCA Section 1983, and adding herself, as well as the district court, the county attorney's office and CFS as defendants for their separate actions in abducting Mara's daughters, as defendant to the cause.

    At that point in time, a letter could travel between Washington and Montana within five days. It was like clockwork. Which meant that Allison received my letter by February 2, 2003. On February 4, 2003, [Daughter 1] re-entered the picture as she was subjected to another interview wherein she once again reasserted the allegation against me (which she had already done on December 9, 2003), but also added that when she had recanted her story, that I had forced he to sign a statement that I alone had prepared and that she had had nothing to do with! Further, she claimed that the reason she signed the statement, even though she had had nothing to do with it, was because Mara had told her she had to change her story!

As one might recall from my previous postings, I had asked [Daughter 1] for a statement following her recantation of the allegation in October, 2003, the month after the official investigations had been closed. Initially, I had wanted [Daughter 1] to do it on her own, but after a few days, [Daughter 1] asked me to help her put the statement together. However, I did not do this with [Daughter 1] alone – I asked Carrie Beth Mountjoy to sit in as a witness to confirm that what I typed in was what [Daughter 1] told me to. Later, when interviewed about this, Carrie Beth confirmed that she had been present in the room, but [Daughter 1] actually insisted that Carrie Beth was lying about it. Ironically enough, Carrie Beth had demonstrated in her interview that she was no longer a supporter of mine and that she had come to believe [Daughter 1]'s story to be true. As such, clearly Carrie Beth was not trying to help my cause by lying for me – which means that the only person lying in this scenario was [Daughter 1] herself.

Also I should reiterate that though I have said several times that [Daughter 1] has lied about not only the initial allegation and the subsequent events thereafter, I do not completely blame [Daughter 1] for this. [Daughter 1] was under undue influence, first from her grandparents and later from CFS officials who had abducted her from her home. [Daughter 1] was a young girl trapped in a circumstance that she honestly believed she could not get out of without cooperating with those who had authority over her. I have had the opportunity to read quite a few psychology articles on this subject and I believe that [Daughter

1] was not entirely to blame for all that she did. I believe that, like so many other young people, she had been indoctrinated to believe in the purity of authority figures and would do whatever an authority figure pressured her to do, even if she knew that what she was doing was wrong. So though I make allusions to [Daughter 1] lying, I do not mean in doing so to impugn her character beyond what the circumstances entailed.

Of course, that being said, it did not help matters that [Daughter 1] had a long-standing propensity for lying in the first place. She had never been the most honest child even before this fiasco, so it was likely easier for her to tell lies as she was required to because that kind of behavior was already part and parcel of her character beforehand. In contrast, her younger sister, regardless of the amount of pressure placed upon her, to this day has refused to make a false allegation against me. Just goes to show the level of credibility that I am talking about when it comes to [Daughter 1]'s independent integrity.

At any rate, the important factor about this second interview was that, like the one in December, it had been conducted not by a Kalispell police officer, but by a Columbia Falls officer named Brandy Arnoux.[72] Arnoux, it turns out, is a known sympathizer with CFS and their less-than-lawful tactics used to abduct children from their home, and could be relied upon to ask the questions that Kori Taylor (CFS's case worker) wanted asked. With Arnoux guiding the interview, [Daughter 1] was asked about specific elements of the affidavit she had signed and provided [Daughter 1] the chance to outright lay the accusation that she had been tampered with by both Mara and myself.

Of course, none of this was true, but it gave Kalispell the pretense to come after me with full barrels. It did not matter that [Daughter 1]'s then-current story contradicted her original

---

[72] Incidentally, Arnoux now works for the Flathead County Sheriff's Office, which by local standards is considered a promotion.

allegations, nor was there an effort to actually investigate what was being said. All the authorities wanted was an accusation on tape that they could act upon. And they did.

On Februrary 20, 2004, an information was filed in the Flathead court and a warrant issued for my arrest upon the charges of sexual assault and witness tampering. There was no grand jury indictment nor review, since in Montana that is not required to bring felony charges. I was provided no notification of the charge being filed nor an opportunity to respond to the filing, since again, under Montana law this is not required. And though typically a warrant is issued and delivered to law enforcement to have the individual arrested if he should be encountered by law enforcement, this warrant was faxed immediately to Goldendale, WA, where I was arrested that very same evening at my home there. The warrant was not even lawful in Washington since it was specifically worded to law enforcement of Montana, but still I was arrested. And I was not even Mirandized. And I remained incarcerated continuously thereafter.

A week following my arrest, Mara Pelton was also arrested on a witness tampering charge, though she was shortly thereafter released upon threat that if she aided me in any way, directly or indirectly, that if she had contact with me or provided me access to my business assets, that she would be re-arrested and remain incarcerated until I saw trial. Again, Mara folded under this threat like a house of wet cards. And others who were less than scrupulous took even further advantage by using Mara as an example, saying that anyone that helped me would suffer a similar fate – they would be arrested and face felony charges. And once the threats were made and with Mara proving that such a thing could be done, every iota of personal support I had simply vanished. I was locked away, my access to court completely severed, and with no resources to aid me in my fight against the corruption that had been leveled against me.

 This ends this thread, as it wraps up what happened to me prior to my arrest. I will start a new thread to discuss what happened to me in Goldendale and throughout the process that ended with my extradition back to Montana. That should be a relatively short thread (for me) and hopefully I will be able to start the next thread detailing my treatment once I returned to Flathead County. Finally, I will try to detail what I experienced once I was actually committed to the Montana State Prison.

 Essentially, this end of the story is in sight...

Chapter 11

My original posts in the Great Montana Conspiracy blog regarding what happened in the past did not continue much longer after this. In fact, of the last few remaining posts, there was only one more that is relevant to this volume published on March 31, 2009, entitled "After the Arrest, Part I". I had always intended to return to that thread, but threats ongoing at the time from my then-probation officer, Dave Edwards, shifted my focus more and more so that between April 1 and April 22, 2009, I only made ten blog entries, and over half of them were dedicated to responding to information and threats being directed at me by Dave Edwards.

Ultimately, the threats proved genuine, as on April 23, 2009, Dave Edwards attempted to violate my probation and send me back to prison for fifteen additional years. From Edwards' own mouth, this was retaliatory for my refusal to admit to a crime I did not commit and to abandon my appeals. Following this arrest, I spent six additional weeks in jail until I could overcome this newest effort to imprison me – but the message had been delivered: my daily entries were being monitored and if I continued to use the blog to make daily accounts of what had been done to me, I would continue to be thrown into jail, if not prison.

Incidentally, Edwards' actions led to a lawsuit against him and other officials which is still pending in the courts. But to continue this vein would digress too much, and not accomplish the primary purpose of this particular biography. Perhaps – assuming I am not retaliated against so that my voice is silenced – I may return with a new volume to detail what happened in the prison years and what has followed since in more detail. But suffice it to say that while Edwards remained my probation officer, I was under constant threat of being revoked for my speaking out, and as consequence, my posting to the Great Montana Conspiracy greatly shifted after I managed to get out of jail after six weeks.

This being said, there are some details that need to be filled in before I present the content of the final chronological entry that appeared in the Great Montana Conspiracy blog.

What would have been the content of the After the Arrest segment of my Great Montana Conspiracy blog ended up getting entered years later in the second incarnation of my blog. As I was not posting regular updates to the Blogspot site where the blog was originally posted – and in fact had abandoned the blog almost entirely for over a year to avoid further risk of incarceration – I do not have a specific date, but sometime between the final post there on July 27, 2010, and September, 2011, Blogspot decided to bar me from modifying the content of the blog on their site. I sent several emails in the weeks after discovering this, but the best I ever received from Blogspot was an acknolwedgment that my site was "locked", meaning I could not post to it, but never an explanation as to why. But as consequence, I ended up creating a new version of the blog on Wordpress on October 1, 2011.

To this day, I believe Blogspot's reason for locking my blog was because of contact from authorities in Kalispell. By that time, Dave Edwards had succeeded in having my freedom of speech infringed through imposition of new court-imposed modifications to my sentence (five years after imposition of my original sentence) and though I went through the blog to redact the content, I believe that when the order came through a year and a half after being pronounced, that the reduced requirements (ie, being only restricted to not publicly identifying Daughter 1 as opposed to naming any member of Daughter 1's family) frightened someone enough that they sent a directive to Blogspot to remove my site. Blogspot's failure to communicate their reasons would support this, since the one response I did received was very guarded. But regardless the reason, I was blocked from posting on the old blog, so I created a new one.

In the time since the original blog and the creation of the new one, the atmosphere had somewhat changed though. Dave Edwards was on the hotseat and fast approaching a civil trial for his misconduct, which made the probation department seem more than a little leery of pushing the boundaries of the law. They began to hold me to the exact conditions of my sentence (modified though it was) – oftentimes to extreme dimensions – and made no new efforts to bully me or impose new conditions. I would say I began to be treated like a normal person under state supervision, if it were not for the extreme limits the department has continued to compel me to adhere to. What will happen once the lawsuit is finalized is anyone's guess, but I at least seemed to have more liberty to speak out again.

With this in mind, I returned to posting some of my history on the Wordpress version of the Great Montana Conspiracy – albeit sparingly and with great care to not post too frequently. And it is from these later postings that the following comes, posted originally on December 20, 2012, entitled "You Ask For Proof":

Possibly the biggest thing I ever hear from anyone is, "Prove to me that the prosecution against you was not legal." I tell people it was in response to my filing a lawsuit, that it was a week out from a deadline to transfer the lawsuit to federal court, even that my girlfriend was arrested under false charges, as well. But still people ask for proof.

Well, here you have it. I recently recovered these documents when the court turned them over to my current attorney. Mind you, efforts to have any records produced from my former attorney, Eduardo Gutierrez Falla, aka, Ed Falla, have gone ignored now for over three years – and even longer from the clerk of court, Peg Allison – so it was something of a surprise to be given these.

Information
Order Granting Leave (Information)[73]

When I originally discovered these records and their significance, I was incarcerated and wrote immediately to the court (I also have my original letter now, in all its naivety), informing the court that I needed to meet with the judge immediately, as I had evidence that proved the charging documents filed against me were fraudulent, and that the signatory judge – Ted O. Lympus – may actually not have known they were even filed initially, ergo, without giving him an opportunity to even review them. Needless to say, I was ignored.

So you look at these documents, and at first glance they appear legitimate. I know when I first saw them, the critical details escaped me, too. It took looking at these documents for months before the detail popped out at me – and then I could not avoid it. My eyes gravitated to it each time I looked at the pages. Can you see it? Take a moment and try.

Okay, do not be surprised that you cannot see it – like I said, I missed it for months, mostly because I did not know exactly how far afield the corruption went. Let's face it – when you do not think in duplicitous nor criminal manner, you just don't think that they would do anything that breaks the law. You don't look for ways they could have broken the law, because you assume

---

[73] Originally, the texts "Information" and "Order Granting Leave (Information)" contained links to view these documents online. For this volume, they may now be viewed in Appendix 2.

they are following the law, even if it's an abuse of the system. But in this case, there was no law followed. Not only did they not follow the law, they literally went outside the legal system to file these documents.

Okay, I have give you long enough to figure it out, so let me tell you where to look: look at the time/date stamp in the upper right hand corner. Note the time each of these documents was filed. See it? At this point, it should jump right out at you, but let me lay it out anyway.

Every court clerk's office in this country has a set session for court hours and filings. Typically they range around the hours of 9am to 5pm. In the case of Flathead County, Montana, they are Monday through Friday from 8am to 5pm (see http://flathead.mt.gov/clerk_of_court/ – in the lower right hand corner are the posted hours for the Flathead County Clerk of Court). By law, these are the only lawful hours of court operations. A court of law may not initiate any proceeding outside its posted hours, and any court business conducted outside these hours its considered outside the jurisdiction of the court. Why? Because a judiciary is a public entity subject to review by the people, and operating during clandestine hours would forego this public scrutiny.[74]

So now you are looking at the time/date stamp in a new light, maybe? For those of you who may not be able to review these documents for some reason, let me clarify: The two documents are the Information and the Order Granting Leave To Final An Information filed on February 20, 2004 – at 4:33 am and 4:44 am, respectively. And the order was not even signed by the judge!

---

74 This is admittedly an over-simplified statement. Of course the clerk and court are considered open for emergency actions such as orders of protection, search warrants and the like. My point here was that the prosecutor could not initiate a prosecution outside business hours since this does not constitute any kind of urgency for which an after-hours filing would justify nor necessitate.

Under what reasonable measure of law – and under what lawful authority – could a clerk of court file documents – much less obtain judicial approval – before 5 am on a Friday morning? And since the judge did not even sign the document, there's not even any evidence that the judge even knew about it at the time the order was issued.

Mind you, anyone who knows me knows I despise Ted Lympus, and that he has performed quite a few acts of malfeasance specifically to knowingly aid and abet the crimes committed against me, but you must also know that I am a champion of truth above and beyond all else. So take this for what it is worth, butI have no reason to believe that Ted Lympus was involved during this unlawful filing and issuance of judicial order for my arrest. He certainly conspired after-the-fact, but in this particular act, I must acknowledge that Ted Lympus might well be innocent of duplicity.

All this being said, the matter was simple – these officials (who at the very least consisted of Lori Adams from the County Attorney's Office and someone from the court clerk's office, if not the court clerk herself) were so desperate to have me off the street – knowing it would take time to accomplish this since I was working in Goldendale, Washington, at the time – that they made a special trip into the court clerk's office before 5 am on a Friday morning and either with or without the court clerk's cooperation, filed and date-stamped the documents so they could get them to the sheriff's office and off to Washington before the end of the business week, knowing they would have to be sent to Washington to act upon.

Mind you, it's extremely rare to send an extra-jurisdictional warrant out of state to arrest someone immediately, as most of the time, warrants simply go into the system and wait for a law-enforcement individual to come across them. This kind of procedure is reserved only for the most dangerous felons, the *ones that present a real and present danger to the general public. I was accused of a one-time inappropriate contact with a minor over eight months previously (and alleged witness tampering, though this charge was dropped), so I clearly was not a real and present threat, because I had been out in the public without any incident for eight months. So why act with such haste?*

Simple – they needed to stop the lawsuit being sent to the federal courts. They knew if I managed to do that – without a conviction for the alleged charge – that I would shut them down. Flat. Cold. And they could not allow that. They were already too far invested in their own criminal conspiracy.

Whether you agree with my supposition or not, it is inescapable that these documents were filed in the clerk of court's office outside the legal hours of court operation. As anyone knows, any act that proceeds upon fraudulent grounds may not proceed beyond the act of fraud. Consequently, all actions, including my subsequent conviction – whether you agree or disagree with the means by which it as achieved – were illegal, since they were founded upon fraudulent documents.

So I say again, you ask for proof? The proof, in this instance, are in the court's own records...

Basically, the sequence went like this: I sent a letter to Peg Allison objecting to her blocking the default judgment providing a thirty day period that expired on February 27, 2004; a new interview with Daughter 1 was rushed through two days after Allison received this letter to fix the errors in Daughter 1's prior statements; and Lori Adams with the Flathead County Attorney's Office went into the Eleventh District Court of Montana Clerk of Court's office to file an action initiating prosecution at 4:33am on February 20, 2003, in an effort to rush a warrant to Washington to have me arrested before the expiration of my deadline.

Remember, Lori Adams waited eleven minutes and then stamped Ted Lympus' name to the warrant at 4:44am. It is clear there was a rush here – not only to get the documents in before the clerk's office opened that day, but to "authorize" my arrest. It is obvious that this was something someone had doubts about – otherwise they could have rushed this through first thing in the morning after the clerk's office opened. But someone wanted this pushed through in the manner to escape *someone's* scrutiny. And there are only three people who this might involved: County Attorney Ed Corrigan, Clerk of Court Peg Allison or Judge Ted Lympus.

Considering all of these people have been involved to one degree or another in what happened to me, I cannot imagine any of them nay-saying this, but clearly there was some fear that one of them – or some other unknown influential person in Flathead County – would not agree with the filing of this criminal charge. This is the only reason that would have necessitated filing this document hours before the clerk's office was even open – Lori Adams was trying to hide this from someone. Something was going on behind the scenes between the time Officer Brandy Arnoux interviewed Daughter 1 again on February 4, 2003, and the filing of the information on February 20. I just have never been able to find out what.

I may never know who or what made it necessary to slip my prosecution under the radar like this, but regardless of who it was, it did not bring the person out of the shadows to defend me after the process was started. And so I found myself incarcerated on the night of February 20, 2003, and was never saw the outside of a jail cell without iron shackles for the next five years as consequence.

This being said, I have received several anonymous criticisms of this position. The most poignant defense raised was the statute that defines that the clerk of court's office is always considered open for the purposes of filing papers.⁷⁵ But this is a misconstrued statute – this is a statute designed to reflect that an individual has until midnight of a deadline date to make a legal filing, and that if the document is received – even after business hours – that it must be considered timely. This is a prominent issue with such things as facsimile machines that provide clear date and time of when something is received by the clerk's office. This also provides an allowance for any urgent matters such as search warrants, protection orders, etc. that may need to be filed after hours. But it does not provide that *anyone* can file a document in a docket, assign a case number or issue a judge's order twenty-four hours a day – it is just designed to prevent time sensitive responses or filings from being entered as received on their proper dates.

In this instance, Lori Adams – a deputy county attorney, *not* a deputy of the court clerk's office – entered the Eleventh District Court Clerk's office at 4:30am and filed, date-stamped and created a file for the prosecution of the State of Montana against me. No clerk was present (no signature on the date stamp of a receiving clerk), nor was the judge, Ted Lympus, whose name she stamped as "authorizing" the pursuit of prosecution. This was a highly fraudulent and criminal act – and it has been vehemently defended by every level of government ever since I discovered it.

Incidentally, Lori Adams is presently seated as the judge of the Kalispell Municipal Court. Corruption has its rewards...

Just so I am clear, the governing law in this instance states that filing of papers under the Montana Rules of Civil Procedure is made by filing them with the *clerk of court*, not just filing them in the clerk's office.⁷⁶ Even if a document is received after hours, it still requires being *filed* by the clerk of court. The prosecuting

---

75 See Appendix 1, MCA § 25-20-Rule 77(a).

76 See Appendix 1, MCA § 25-20-Rule 5(e).

documents against me were filed in the record and a court file opened by Deputy County Attorney Lori Adams, not by any deputy of the court clerk's office.

Incidentally, there is no rationality that has ever been offered to explain how Lori Adams had authority to issue orders in Judge Ted Lympus' name, either – every time I have raised this issue, it has been ignored. Simply put, there is no evidence that Judge Lympus was present at 4:44am alongside Adams in filing these documents – which means that Adams usurped the constitutional power of a judicial officer as well as that of the court clerk to have the information (prosecuting document) approved and a warrant issued for my arrest.

Based upon all of this, the argument that the filing of information and issuance of an order compelling my arrest on February 20, 2003, was illegal. Or to put it another way, the entire foundation for the prosecution against me was based on fraud. And for those of you not aware, there is a legal principle that any conviction founded upon an unconstitutional act warrants immediate reversal. So ask yourself – if this is such a blatant violation of law, how is it that my conviction still stands and how Lori Adams not only escaped criminal prosecution for such blatant misconduct, but also earned herself a promotion to being allowed to take a judicial seat herself?

Having said all this, I would like to now present the final relevant chronological entry from my original Great Montana Conspiracy blog, posted on March 31, 2009, entitled as, "After the Arrest":

As I detailed up through my previous post, I had been set up pretty handily by authorities in Kalispell, Montana, who did not want to answer for their official misconduct. What started as a malicious scheme by my girlfriend's parents, who had a history of creating such false allegations over twenty years, ended up falling into the jurisdiction of a corrupt government authority where their official misconduct led to an ongoing state of conflict between themselves and me. The problem was that Montana had been corrupt at every level for so long without being challenged that the officials felt themselves immune from repercussions no matter how far outside the law their conduct went. Of course, I had no idea of what I had been up against when I set out to challenge the misconduct directed against me during the police department's initial investigation of the case, but I came to realize that corruption was not isolated to just Kalispell, Flathead County or even to the State of Montana – it included, perhaps to a more isolated degree, to the criminal justice system as a whole, even to that operating within Goldendale, Washington.

I have to say at the outset of this that I cannot say how much of this is typical of authority in Goldendale or how much was just some level of cooperation with Montana as some kind of perverted professional courtesy. All I know is what happened to me and that was only during a very brief period that did not provide me the opportunity to compare my treatment to that of anyone else...

Immediately upon arrest, I began making calls to my business in Kalispell. Of course, these calls were recorded, and I have every reason to believe that the contents of those calls were relayed to the Kalispell authorities, at the very least to the Flathead County Attorney's Office. I say this because of two things:

First, as I noted in previous posts, Mara Pelton (now Mara Nezatski) was arrested exactly one week to the day after me on February 27, 2004. The information charging Mara was not filed at the same time as mine, nor was the warrant for her arrest issued then either. Yet something within the week following my arrest warranted the Kalispell authorities to include her within their net. Since the allegation against Mara stemmed from the same accusation of [Daughter 1]'s on February 4, 2003, any genuine prosecution upon the same charge would have been filed at the same time as my own. But it was not. Clearly, it had been an afterthought to go after Mara. The question then would be why?[77]

The answer I believe stems from the content of my recorded conversations from the Goldendale jail. Specifically, I was requesting for Mara to send me copies of files I had left in her care at our mutual business upon the possibility that Kalispell would attempt to take some illicit action against me. Included in those records were documents proving that the original investigations with the Kalispell Police Department (KPD) and Child and Family Service (CFS) had been closed in September, [2003,] including records supporting that the two agencies had communicated these details between them. I had also requested that Mara request [Daughter 1]'s medical records to prove the inconsistencies between her various stories, of Edith Paxman's observations about [Daughter 1]'s untruthfulness, and most importantly the records of Dr. Barney Houser that would reflect that Kori Taylor of CFS subjected [Daughter 1] to an overly aggressive interview when [Daughter 1] refused to reassert the false allegation, an interview that had left [*] in tears. Further, I had been discussing with Mara about liquidating assets to aid me in my legal battle.

It is my belief that upon learning of my intentions to obtain these records that would exonerate me, and in the potential of liquidating assets to retain a private attorney,[78] that Kalispell officials took steps to bar my access to any resources I could

---

77 Just as an aside, I have never seen Mara's charging documents, so I have no way of knowing whether there was anything improper in how they were filed.

78 For the record, this would have been a *Washington* state attorney, not one licensed in Montana. This would have removed *any* potential undue influence Kalispell authorities had over controlling my defense or what could be presented to a jury.

draw upon, specifically by arresting Mara and putting her under threat of harm should she aid me in any way. So long as I remained incarcerated, I had no hope of accessing these things myself – and if Mara could be made to not supply them, then these authorities would have complete control over what did and did not come to light in my defense, and further had control over the attorney that I would be forced to work with.

Keep in mind, the original allegation against me was on July 9, 2003. I was not actually charged and arrested for this alleged offense until February 20, 2004, almost eight months later. The investigation had been closed and only re-opened to bar my access to the police records. When I had sought default judgment, the court clerk had tampered with the file to bar my rightful legal relief. And my subsequent arrest only occurred when it became clear that the local authorities were going to lose the ability to block my suit if I could successfully move the suit to federal court, a week from the deadline of the thirty day time limit I had set, in fact. If all of these things could be perpetuated to stop me, it is not too much of a stretch to recognize that when I could have conceivably obtained evidence that would have once again removed me from their control that they would once again exert their authority to block such an effort by any means.

Coming after Mara was a coup. Not only could they bar my access to records that could exonerate me while I was still in Washington (and consequently outside of their direct control), but it also deprived me any chance of possibly liquidating my assets to retain a private attorney. This was not part of their original plan, or it would have happened at the same time that they arrested me. Apparently, Kalispell authorities believed that I no longer had support in Kalispell, perhaps thinking I had fled to start a new life. Afterall, this was exactly what Kori Taylor had insisted of Mara – that she dissolve all contact with me and evict me from my home and business in Kalispell. When they learned that I actually did retain my interest in the Kalispell business and still had Mara's support, they took action to sever that support more directly – by arresting Mara on yet another false charge. However, they were successful in intimidating her enough that she finally did what they had wanted from her all along – she completely cut me off from my assets and from any outside support.

As an aside, I would like to say that, though I hold little resentment toward [Daughter 1], as I have commented on extensively in previous posts, I hold a great deal more toward Mara. [Daughter 1] was kidnapped and placed under extreme demands with absolutely no way of knowing what was really going on. She did not know the law, did not know that what was being done was illegal, nor that she had any right to challenge what was being done to her. [Daughter 1] was only a thirteen year old girl who was easily intimidated and undereducated about what the government could and could not do.

Mara, on the other hand, did not have this excuse. Mara knew that what CFS had done was illegal. I had shown her the specific laws that CFS had violated. She also knew from her own personal life experiences what the proper procedures were for CFS to respond to allegations of abuse – she had been a foster mother herself years earlier! She knew what was being done was wrong but in the end, to save herself, she collaborated with those that she knew were acting illegally, knowing that in doing so she was committing an innocent man to ongoing imprisonment and abuse.

Mara Pelton (now Mara Nezatski) sold - me - out. **Period.** And this is not something I can so readily forgive.

This is not to say that I do not in some way feel that Mara was a victim as well. She was put under threats and intimidations the same as [Daughter 1] was – my fault in her lies in the fact that she, unlike [Daughter 1], made an informed choice to betray me.

And that is not something I can see to completely be okay with. And of course, Mara did more than turn her back on me with the authorities – she also cheated on me, but that's something I will detail later.

The second reason I believe this was directly related to my phone calls to Mara was that immediately after Mara was arrested, within a couple of days, the Goldendale jail put a block in on my business' number. I could not call back to Kalispell to work on obtaining the records I needed nor maintain my support base.

At the time this happened, I had no reason to believe that the block had been created on Goldendale's side - I thought that there must have been some kind of disruption on Kalispell's side, such as the bill not getting paid or too much toll charges on the phone (all calls from jail are collect and phone companies tend to cap toll charges to a line after a certain amount). It was only toward the end when the block was suddenly removed two days before I left Goldendale, as they prepared for my extradition, that I realized the block had been put in by Goldendale jail officials.

The only reason for such a block would have been to bar my access to Mara and my support structure in Kalispell. And since that access had absolutely no impact upon the proceedings in Goldendale, I can only presume that the block was placed at the request of the Kalispell authorities...

At any rate, I am running out of time on this post, so I am going to end this thread for today. Most of it was actually written before I started today, but I spent a lot of time re-editing the posts I wrote yesterday, so I did not have time to type much more on this post. I will continue this thread hopefully tomorrow.

As I have mentioned, this was the last entry in which I made an effort to relate what had happened to me in the past on my original Great Montana Conspiracy blog. Pressure from Dave Edwards was making me more and more concerned for my liberty, and direct threats had been made against me by Edwards about my using the blog to write about my history. It was a nebulous gray period for the next three weeks, and it was out of fear of retaliation that I curbed these posts – a fear that was obviously founded in fact, since Edwards did try to send me back to prison in April, 2009.

Had I known that no matter what I did, Edwards would still have tried to send me back to prison, I might have continued this personal history – but I did not, and my choice to not continue at that time was impacted. This does not mean I did not continue using the site to express my opinions, but the continued thread of "After the Arrest" did not continue because of these threats.

However, there is still much to be said about what happened after my arrest – both in Goldendale, Washington, and once I returned to Kalispell. But I want to make something clear – though a significant amount of events happened, when you are locked behind bars with next to no contact with the outside world, one tends to lose track of time. Dates lose almost all significance, while time periods tend to merge together.

Looking back on my time incarcerated, the best description I can give is that without intellectual stimulation of the real world going on around me, my mind literally became lethargic, even sluggish. I think anyone who has been incarcerated can identify with exactly how your mind just shuts down when you have nothing to stimulate it but look at a concrete wall for sixteen hours a day. Sleep becomes an escape from boredom, and the more one sleeps just to cope with no activity, the more impaired your capacity to think and reason become.

After a few months, I can honestly say that I recognized my brain becoming enfeebled – not even able to recall things that had been part of my day-to-day routine. I found myself trying to recite lists of things just to try to keep my mental acuity up, but failing miserably. After the twenty months spent in county jail, even with access to a limited number of books and television programming, my capacity to think at all was crippled. And after five years, my memories of the world beyond prison had very little reality to me.

It would have been helpful for this accounting if I had been able to keep all of my legal papers throughout my incarceration, but every time I was forced to change facilities – and many times due to searches within a single facility, key documents were lost. For example, when I was extradited from Washington to Montana, I could only take the equivalent of an inch's height of paper (what I could force into a small manila-sized envelope), which meant I was able to take maybe a fifth of the papers I had accumulated in the six weeks in Goldendale's jail. And most of the those papers had been kept in storage – outside my regular access – until I was transported, and then I was given only a few minutes to sort out what to take.

Similar circumstances existed each time I was transferred – from Flathead County Detention Center, to the Montana State Prison, and between the various regional prisons. There was also instituted limits on how many records a prisoner could maintain and what subject matter, so legal papers were always subject to confiscation throughout the prison experience. Needless to say, the records that *could* have helped me during all of this were constantly compromised, and I repeatedly found myself trying to recall records, notes, dates, etc – and each time I was forced to do so, my mental fatigue would make me recall less and less.

So when I talk about my time while being imprisoned, the longer I was incarcerated, the less specific my memories become and therefore I have to reference things in generalities rather than the specific details which I have provided so far. I have managed to recover some of the pre-incarceration records, but well over ninety percent of the records pertaining to my prosecution and the research I was able to accomplish from inside have been lost and I have not been able to recover them. With this in mind, please forgive that the accounts following this point are going to be far less detailed.

At the point where my last Great Montana Conspiracy blog entry left off, I was still in the Goldendale jail. I was arrested the night of February 20, 2004, the same day that Lori Adams had filed the fraudulent documents in the Eleventh District Court of Montana. There was no secret where I was – I had maintained regular contact with Mara and law enforcement while I was in Goldendale, so Adams knew precisely where to send the warrant she alone had issued and filed – to the Klickitat County Sheriff in Goldendale. The only thing she did not have was my address, since in the county, mail was not delivered so all my correspondence was going through a post office box. This was not an effort to hide – as demonstrated by how quickly the Klickitat Sheriff located me, my residential address was well known – since I had been working with local law enforcement and city officials to establish the new youth program there.

The evening, as I recall sometime around six or seven in the evening, a sheriff deputy showed up at my door to arrest me. He did not have a warrant in his possession, nor did he Mirandize me[79] – he simply *said* the sheriff had a warrant for my arrest and took me into custody. It was not until I reached the jail that I was shown a copy of the warrant – and specifically, was permitted to read the language.

---

79 Just to clarify, to "Mirandize" means to provide a verbal Miranda warning, which is to say to inform me that I had the right to be silent; that if I gave up the right to be silent, anything I said could be used against me in a court of law; the right to have an attorney and to have that attorney present during questioning; that if I could not afford an attorney, one would be provided; and a general question of whether I understood these rights. This is a legal prerequisite to taking anyone into custody since the case of *Miranda v Arizona* in 1966.

Of particular note, the original warrant was addressed *only* to authorities in the State of Montana, which is to say that it only directed Montana officials to arrest me, not any law enforcement agency. This is of particular interest since under this warrant, the Klickitat County Sheriff could not have arrested me, and I could have refused to submit to arrest. But once already in custody, the sheriff's department had no intention of releasing me.

This brings up two important points:

First, this warrant was not sent to Washington seeking my arrest, but instead to sabotage what I was doing there, ie, communicate to Washington authorities that I was a sexual offender in another state (accused is the same as convicted to law enforcement, no matter what the Constitution says, I came to find out). Essentially, I believe Adams issued the warrant she did for two reasons: to continue to ward me against returning to Montana and to make sure I did not gain a support base in Washington.

Second, Washington authorities were never meant to actually arrest me. In fact, once they *did* arrest me and made it clear that I had complained about the language of the warrant, a *new* warrant was issued within a few days (unheard of, considering I was already in jail on the first warrant) that gave Washington authorities permission to detain me by redirecting the warrant to *any* law enforcement agency.

Irregardless, the authorities in Washington violated my rights from day one. First, they arrested me under a warrant that they were not empowered to act under, and second, they never Mirandized me. By not Mirandizing me, they could not have legally used the information gleaned during my arrest – ie, my complaint over the validity of the warrant – in order to obtain a new warrant. It should first have been a legal challenge presented by my attorney. In effect, the new warrant I was detained under was issued because of information I provided in a court of law after *not* being Mirandized.

This being said, Goldendale was dead set on running me out of town, and they did not end their efforts with the tainted arrest. They quickly sought to have me waive my rights to an extradition hearing, but I knew enough about extradition that I should have been protected – since an extradition could not be instituted as a means to quash a civil cause at the time,[80] and I knew that was precisely what was happening, I refused to waive extradition.

Now, before I proceed, I need to explain how extradition from Washington was supposed to work. The first step is to request a waiver of extradition, and if the waiver is refused by the person arrested, then the court has the right to hold someone for one thirty day period to await the issuance of a governor's warrant from the claiming state, and thereafter one additional sixty period may be applied for should the complaining state not have yet produced one. If there is no governor's warrant issued, then Washington releases the detainee. If a governor's warrant is issued, if the detainee chooses to contest its legality, then Washington provides the detainee a habeas corpus proceeding upon which to challenge the legality of the governor's warrant. If this fails, then Washington releases the detainee into the custody of the requesting state, who then escorts the detainee back to the state where the charge originated.

In my case, however, things went somewhat differently. I refused to waive extradition, and my attorney – astonished that I actually had a copy of the civil complaint against the very authorities seeking my extradition – informed the court that I was

---

[80] This is one of the notations I referenced earlier that I was not permitted to take with me from Washington – I had a near verbatim notated record of Washington's Uniform Extradition Act (I believe the edition at the jail was 2000), and there was specific language forbidding an extradition for an act taken to quash a civil claim. I have searched online for this text, but apparently Washington updated their laws in 2010, and the desired text is no longer in the law as far as I can find, and therefore I cannot provide it here. Therefore, when it comes to issues pertaining to extradition from Washington State, I will have to beg the reader's forbearance as I offer explanation without citations to support them.

contesting extradition on the grounds that it was an attempt to quash a civil complaint. The initial thirty day period elapsed, and the court renewed my detention order for the additional sixty days upon the assurances of prosecution that Montana was waiting on a governor's warrant. This took approximately another two weeks to arrive.

However, where this diverges significantly, I was extradited immediately upon receipt of the governor's warrant – I was denied any habeas corpus proceeding or to challenge the legality of the governor's warrant. Conveniently, my public defender went on vacation just before the warrant came in, and no one in the public defender system would respond to my complaints. Over vehement objections, Washington officers escorted me to the border of Idaho and turned me over to Idaho authorities at the state line, who then drove me to Montana.

Remember, not only was I allowed by law a chance to challenge the governor's warrant, but in order for the warrant to be effected, *Montana* officials needed to be the one to arrive to take me into custody and transport me back to Montana. Washington officials had no legal authority under law to escort me out of their state. Essentially, Klickitat County Sheriff officials were so anxious to see me evicted from their jurisdiction (I would guess fearful that my claim of retaliation for my civil suit might actually prevail in court) that they immediately extradited me through the same procedures as they would someone who had waived their extradition rights.

Remember, only if I had *waived* my rights to extradition to Montana could they have transported me – otherwise, having not waived my rights, I was requiring Montana to come collect me *after* I had exhausted my right to challenge the governor's warrant. The law is very specific on this – a waiver foregoes all rights under extradition, including compelling officers of the state making the accusation to retrieve the person charged. The only way Washington authorities would have the right to expel me from their state through extradition was if I waived those rights, which I did not.

Keep in mind – this is actually a crime in Washington, as it is in most states where extradition laws exist. The holding state cannot extradite a prisoner without adhering the the extradition laws of their state, and the officials in Washington committed criminal misconduct to rush me out of the state like they did.

Therefore, upon entering Montana, I was already being illegally detained, since I came into Montana's custody through an unlawful extradition from Washington State. This was one of the first issues I raised when I was assigned counsel once back in Flathead County, but the public defender assigned to my case was Ed Falla – and this is the man who set out to deliberately sabotage my case on behalf of the corrupt authorities from day one. So much so, that the entire next chapter is largely dedicated to what he did to assure my conviction.

Incidentally, I have been informed from an unconfirmed source that even if Washington had prevailed upon extradition, Montana would not have been able to drive me across the territory of Idaho without a new proceeding there – because neither Washington nor Montana can govern whether a person is extradited from within the borders of Idaho. There is allegedly a precedent to this effect, but I lack the legal resources to do the research. There are also considerable gray areas of extradition law – such as the fact Montana did not appear to take me into custody, or that the arresting state can only hold me for thirty days under the federal Uniform Extradition Act on which Washington's model is based, amongst others – that remain unexplored simply because I lack the legal resources.

Just as an aside for clarification, I am more than capable of doing legal research if I am afforded the proper resources, ie, Westlaw database access, Shepard's Index, etc. But I have been barred by the Clerk of the Eleventh District Court from using the public law library located in the Eleventh District Court building (one must register with the clerk to use the library, and I have been told by a deputy clerk that I am on a "revoked permission" list). I am completely convinced there is no such list, or that if there is, it is not a legal action to bar someone from a public law library. But it is what it is, and I have no choice in the matter.

This is the drawback to being a layman without money to hire an actual attorney – much of what is being done to me cannot even be objected to because simple legal research is something I cannot do.

Chapter 12

Eduardo Gutierrez-Falla, aka, Ed Falla – the leading public defender of adult criminal cases in Flathead County, Montana. And the bane of my existence for the eighteen-plus months that I was incarcerated in the Flathead County Detention Center. Though he was not the head public defender of the county (that would be Robert Allison, who handled only juvenile cases personally), Falla was the go-to public defender of the courts because he was by far the most efficient individual in running criminal defendants through the so-called justice system with a complete indifference to their actual civil liberties. While Mark Sullivan perpetuated the so-called defense of Mara – which largely just constituted enforcing the fear of going to prison if she helped me in any way – I was stuck with Falla.

To understand how Falla operated, you must first understand a little of how the legal system worked in Flathead County in 2004. Though presently there is a statewide public defender system (arguably no better than the earlier system under an only slightly different organizational structure), in 2004, each county had its own public defender system – and all public defenders were hired and fired by the head judge of the Eleventh Judicial District Court, Ted Lympus. On paper, Robert Allison was in charge of firing them, but everyone knew it was really Lympus controlling the office. If Lympus did not want an attorney as a public defender, he was *not* a public defender. Period.

You see, judges are always former attorneys (it is a requirement of the job to be a licensed attorney), but in Flathead County, all the judges save one were former prosecutors. Worse, the head judge, Ted Lympus had not only been a prosecutor at both the state and county levels, but he had also served on several crime and jail boards. In effect, Ted Lympus has always been a "hanging judge" even before he was an *actual* judge, very much in the belief of exacting the harshest possible penalties upon anyone accused of crimes. From the bench, he has exercised open bigotry, prejudice and a flagrant disregard for the law so long as it advances his own Good O'l' Boy brand of justice. Note – I say his *own* brand of justice – in other words, he could care less what the law says. I have personally witnessed the man violate law after law, liberty after liberty, based solely upon his own whims and xenophobia.

With this man presiding as head judge over Flathead County, there was little doubt that his take-no-prisoners approach would be exerted over the entire legal process. He went into the judicial position wanting to exact retribution and harsh penalties upon the accused, and he erected a system to make sure he could do so without restriction. He hand-picked the public defenders, and made it clear he did not want his "time wasted" by "frivolous" criminal defenses – to Ted Lympus, the job of a public defender was to convince defendants to accept plea deals, and if a public defender had a mind to file motions like suppression of evidence or general motions to dismiss, they would not be public defenders any longer. And since he controlled who got the job and who did not, his word held.

Lympus essentially maintained a policy – adopted by the other seated judges, as well – that if an attorney "rocked the boat" in "how things were done", none of their clients would ever prevail in a Flathead court. In effect, Lympus instituted a blacklist of attorneys who could not expect to ever win a single motion in the courts in this county – and you got on this blacklist by challenging the status quo, actually defending your clients and not helping the prosecutor and court convict more people, regardless of whether they were actually guilty or not.

Now one might ask why the public defender job was so sought after. Well, under Lympus' guidelines, a public defender literally got an automatic paycheck per client he could rush through the system following Lympus' guidelines. The more defendants the public defender could push through, the larger his return. And since the head judge created an environment where defense motions that were common everywhere else were actually prohibited, public defenders really just had to put up a pretense of representation, urge their client to take a plea deal, and sit back and take on more clients.

In law, this is known as a pretense of representation, and constitutes ineffective assistance of counsel. Under constitutional law (Sixth Amendment), a criminal defendant is not only entitled to assistance of counsel, he is entitled to an attorney who aggressively defends the rights and liberty of his client and who maintains an adversarial relationship with prosecutors and the court on his client's behalf. But in Flathead County, public defenders are only hired and retained if they agree to forego this precept and act as factory workers, rushing defendants down the assembly line to appear in court ready to lead guilty no matter what.

Criminal defendants are then held under incredibly high bails (a violation of the Eighth Amendment) that no average reasonable person could raise[81] while the public defenders – most often the *only* person a defendant meets with who alleges to understand law – work on convincing the defendant that they need to plea. The common fear tactic perpetuated by these public defenders is that these poor people accused of crimes have no

---

[81] In my case, my bail was $50,000. But I knew one person, Kerry Garner, who had a similar bail, met it – and Ted Lympus raised the bail to $75,000 – and when Kerry met that amount, Lympus raised it to $100,000. Needless to say, the bail amounts were not set to provide assurety that a defendant would appear for trial; they were set to act as a barrier of being released so that a person accused would have no choice but to eventually take a plea bargain.

chance of winning, and if they take their case to trial and lose, they will suffer an exponentially greater penalty for making the county "work for the conviction".

In 2002, the American Civil Liberties Union sponsored a lawsuit against Montana[82] over its public defender system (or lack thereof), naming defendants Flathead County, its commissioners and even public defenders from the county in its suit. In fact, ironically enough, the only three public defenders named in the suit were Ed Falla, Mark Sullivan (Mara's "attorney") and David Stufft (who was later assigned as co-chair on my case). According to the facts presented in the case, unlike public defenders in other counties, Stufft and Sullivan had requested twice the case load of indigent defendants that would normally be assigned, while Falla had requested three times as many. Out of the dozen or so private attorneys retained by Ted Lympus' court, these three were the most entrenched within the corrupt system in Flathead County, and were provided these extra case loads as rewards for their complicity with fast-tracking criminal defendants through the Eleventh District Court.

This lawsuit was settled out of court in 2004 with the agreement that Montana would institute a statewide public defender system that would not be answerable to the counties or their courts. And though this system was erected, not much has changed in Flathead County. Attorneys retained by the public defenders office use this department as a spring board for private practice, and rely upon their success in this department in order to gain credentials. But if they go against Lympus' doctrine and actually defend their clients, their clients receive harsher penalties from the courts. Essentially, the attorney still becomes blacklisted and none of their clients ever see leniency from the court. And should they ever try to go into private practice? The

---

82 See White v Martz, CDV 2002-133, Montana First Judicial District, Lewis and Clark County.

blacklist against that attorney's clients stands – effectively barring them from practicing in Flathead County, or by reputation any court in Montana.

The effect on people actually accused is psychological warfare upon helpless people – confined, undernourished and mentally exhausted by the constant fear they are subjected to (not to mention the constant strain of worrying about losing family, employment, property, etc. while incarcerated). All of this adds up to these people coming to the conclusion that they have no hope – and certainly no other choice than to accept a plea bargain, because they are convinced in short order that there is no way to win.

Remember – in Flathead County, there are no grand juries, no chance to challenge probable cause and no actual evidence ever required to have someone arrested and detained indefinitely under an impossibly high bail. I was detained for sixteen months without a trial, hearing or grand jury indictment. And the only evidence that was ever proffered in my case (even with Lori Adams filing her own action that was never screened by the actual court) was Lori Adams' sworn affidavit that a crime had occurred.

Believe me, the Founders of our country would be rolling over in their graves over this. They fought and died because England was doing this exact thing to colonists – magistrates would accuse people of crimes without evidence and throw them into jail until a confession could be coerced from them. This is why the civil defenses were put into place – to avoid this *exact* thing, ie, a government having a citizen arrested without cause and detained as a political prisoner at the whim of corrupt authorities. And that is precisely what happens every day in Flathead County, Montana. Worse – it was the system used to validate my own arrest to stop a lawsuit brought against the authorities within the jurisdiction detaining me.

From another perspective, if one were to take a look at the prosecution success rate of Flathead County, you would be astonished. Literally 99.9% of people accused in this county are convicted. And I only add the .01% because the only person I have *ever* known to have been accused and not convicted was Mara, and then only because her charges were dropped before my trial so my attorney could not allege she was coerced. Keep in mind, she was still being coerced and I demanded of Falla to put this before the jury, but e refused. The charge against Mara (witness tampering) were dismissed without prejudice, which is to say, they could be brought back at any time – So Mara was still under coercion, it just was a verbal threat at the time I saw trial instead of one written down.

But I am absolutely serious – I have spent over ten years within the criminal system of Montana, and of all the people I have met who were convicted out of Flathead County, not a single one of them could ever recall an instance where someone they met who was accused and somehow managed to get free of the accusation. To a man, every person I have ever known who has been accused of a crime has either folded under the threat of harsher penalties or gone to trial and had their case sabotaged by their public defender.

This is an absolutely impossible percentage to maintain in the real world. This essentially says that every time the prosecutor in Flathead County has ever prosecuted a crime, they have been right. That is just not possible. It is insanely impossible. No one is that perfect. And certainly not the Flathead County Attorney's Office. And yet the conviction rate speaks for itself.

And Ted Lympus presides over it all. He literally runs the entire courthouse like a puppeteer. And he has made certain that he is surrounded at every level by other officials who will further his agendas.

In Flathead County, there was effectively a triumvirate of power within the criminal justice system in 2004. Judge Ted Lympus controlled the judges and public defenders, County Attorney Ed Corrigan controlled the prosecutions, and Court Clerk Peg Allison handled the paperwork, acting as the glue holding the entire system together. And to be honest – the system does not work much different today. Just another illusory public display offering a pretense of justice – when the truth is, there is none.

Now having explained the harsh and incredibly corrupt system I found myself deposited in, I believe it will be easier to understand how and why Ed Falla was assigned to my case. I was the "problem child", the "upstart" who had the audacity to stand up to the entrenched powers-that-be in Flathead County, and Ed Falla – being the single most trusted of the public defenders and the one with the largest caseload of defendants for his capacity to rush them through the system – was seen as the absolute best hope to wear me down and get me to buckle under.

To accomplish this, Falla would routinely cuss at me, berate me, insult me and otherwise demean and degrade me at every opportunity. As just one example, I am of Apache decent and wear my hair long in recognition of my heritage – but Fall would routinely tell me that my long hair made me look like a pervert. In fact, he would tell me repeatedly that if I even thought about going before a jury looking like this, they would convict me from the moment they saw me because I even "looked like a sick child molester". Keep in mind, this is supposed to be *my* legal defender – but he spent a considerable amount of time trying to tear down my self-confidence and personal self esteem.

From what I am told, this is what he did with all his clients – he was just more aggressive with me because, first of all, I was a priority target to get to bend the knee, so to speak, and second, I would not bend. For almost seventeen months, Falla berated me

– time and again. And when I complained about it to the court, the judge at the time, Katherine Curtis, told me that I was a "grown man" and she did not need to "hold [my] hand".

Once again, remember that this was illegal – it is verbal assault. It *is* a crime. And to assault a prisoner is a felony. And reporting it to the seated judge only got *me* rebuked.

At any rate, this was what I had to put up with right up throughout Falla's representation. I had no advocate in court acting for me – I had another opponent I was constantly fighting with. And I complained as much on four separate occasions to the court. And in each instance, the court ignored me.

Of course, when I first met Ed Falla, I had no idea about how destructive he would be to my case. I went into the attorney-client relationship with the ideal that this was *my* attorney, who would work for me. But from the very beginning – when I wanted to explain the case and about how I was innocent – he told me he did not care whether I was innocent or not. He insisted that was not his job. He asked me point blank, "Why the f*** would I care or not? It's not my job to care. It's my job to get you the best deal I can for what you did."

I suppose I should have known right then what he was like. I know I was flabbergasted by what he said. Here was the man who was supposed to be defending me, and he did not *care?!*

I went from this point to trying to insist on what I needed for my defense. I told him about the extradition issues, and he said it did not matter – I was already there. I told him that Daughter 1 was under undue influence and I wanted to file a motion to dismiss, and Falla responded that was not done in this jurisdiction. I next told him I wanted to challenge the probable cause, ie, a preliminary hearing on the evidence, to which he responded that was not going to happen because probable cause had already been decided.

After throwing all of this at him and having him shoot down every single suggestion, I asked Falla how none of this could matter. I had had the chance to do legal research before I met with Falla initially and I had the Montana statutes governing preliminary hearings and informations, but Falla simply told me that none of that mattered. I even told him I wanted to file a habeas corpus to bring these issues out, and he only said, "they don't do that here." Keep in mind, a habeas corpus is a *federally* protected right that cannot be taken from anyone detained, but as was typical, Falla unilaterally denied me any pretense of civil liberty or access to the court. "That's not how law is practiced in Flathead County, and I am practicing law here," he told me on one occasion. "What do I care how it's practiced anywhere else?"

At this point, I should discuss a little in how and why all of this was unconstitutional. The Founders of our country instituted the right to grand jury for any felonious crime in the Fifth Amendment to the United States Constitution. Later, states – believing themselves independent of the limitations of the Constitution – created their own complaint and information systems. One of those was the "information", which was a simplified version of bringing a criminal complaint against a person. This method of criminal indictment was challenged in a famous US Supreme Court case in 1884 and was upheld conditionally, though it actually preceded an even broader case forty years later (1925). The problem was that even though the broader context overruled the former, it was not *specifically* addressed in the latter decision and so state governments have continued to rely upon the 1884 case.

At one point, I wrote an article about this issue that provides a significantly better background. I wrote this for a local paralegal, Jerry O'Neil, who had expressed an interest in the topic of challenging the absence of grand juries in Montana. Of course, he never did anything with it, but the information is still valid:

The argument presented in <u>Hurtado v. California</u>, 110 U.S. 516 (1884) specifically addresses one issue: Does a state's enacting an information system, as opposed to the constitutionally mandated grand jury, violate the <u>due process clause</u> of the Fourteenth Amendment (in relevant part, "...nor shall any State deprive any person of life, liberty, or property, without due process of law..."). However, it does not answer the question as to whether the states have the right to overwrite the constitutional prerequisite, only as to whether the denial of grand jury is a due process issue. Though it can certainly be argued that the High Court was incorrect in its conclusions, it does not address the question of whether the States have the right to deny the privileges of grand jury indictment.

The true issue that should have been addressed to the High Court was whether other language of the Fourteenth Amendment (in relevant part, "No State shall make or enforce any law which shall abridge the privileges or immunities of citizens of the United States...") prohibited the States from depriving the privilege of grand jury.

However, the High Court issued a blanket ruling in <u>Gitlow v New York</u> (268 US 652 (1925)) that specifically bypassed the precepts set in <u>Hurtado</u>. In that case, the High Court determined that the States <u>were</u> bound to the Bill of Rights through the due process clause of the Fourteenth Amendment. Though this case did not specifically overrule <u>Hurtado</u>, as that case dealt with whether an information system specifically violated due process protections, <u>Gitlow</u> did declare that the States were bound collectively to not violate citizens' rights guaranteed under the Bill of Rights by virtue of the due process clause of the Fourteenth Amendment, in effect trumping the decision in <u>Hurtado</u>, even though this case has not been specifically revisited by the High Court.

However, the issue of due process aside, this decision also relies upon certain presumptions, first and foremost being that the information system incorporates a probable cause determination hearing, specifically:

"*[W]e are unable to say that the substitution for a presentment or indictment by a grand jury of the proceeding by information, <u>after</u> examination and commitment by a magistrate, certifying to the probable guilt of the defendant, with the right on his part to the aid of counsel, and to the cross-examination of the witnesses produced for the prosecution, is not due process of law.*" <u>Hurtado</u> at 538 (emphasis added).

Clearly, the High Court determined that if an information system was to be used, the presumption was that an individual would still be permitted a preliminary challenge to the evidence, one in which he had the aid of counsel and the opportunity to cross-examine witnesses, <u>before</u> issuance of an information.

This is <u>not</u> the procedure adopted nor practiced in Montana. In fact, Montana State law specifically provides that an information can be issued by a court solely upon filing for leave of information by the prosecutor's office (MCA § 46-11-101, et seq), and that the only prerequisite for leave to file an information is that such request be by affidavit "supported by evidence" which <u>only</u> the judge or magistrate may require. There is <u>no</u> opportunity for an individual to challenge an accusation nor cross-examine witnesses prior to issuance of the information.

Further, citizens arrested in Montana are not even provided a probable cause determination hearing <u>after</u> issuance of the information. In fact, individuals are literally jailed solely upon the information issued by the court and then detained until either they are coerced by extensive incarceration under excessively high bails to confess or they can be brought to trial.

This is one of the more damaging decisions of the Supreme Court, setting a terrible precedent. The issues were set forth well by Justice Harlan, whose dissenting opinion is correct. Unfortunately, the majority did not agree with him:

"What all of them seem to have missed, including the litigants, is that the issue [sic] not just whether grand jury indictment is part of "due process", guaranteed by the Fifth and Fourteenth Amendments. The Fourteenth also provides:

"'All persons born or naturalized in the United States, and subject to the jurisdiction thereof, are citizens of the United States and of the State wherein they reside. No State shall make or enforce any law which shall abridge the privileges or immunities of citizens of the United States;'

"This language was made the opening statements in the Fourteenth for a reason. They were not without force and effect. They were intended by the framers of the Fourteenth to extend the jurisdiction and protection of federal courts to all rights recognized by the Constitution and Bill of Rights against actions by state government.

"First, 'any law' includes the state constitution, which is its supreme law, subject to the U.S. Constitution.

"Second, 'immunities' includes all those rights recognized and protected by the Constitution and Bill of Rights, including those of the Ninth and Tenth Amendments. The framers of the Fourteenth used 'immunities' because the rights recognized and protected by the Constitution and Bill of Rights are rights against action by government, which are 'immunities', as distinct from nonvested rights of business.

"If there is any doubt as to what the framers of the Fouteenth meant by their words, here are some more of their words, taken from debates in Congress and the press during the drafting and ratification debates on the amendment (See "Intent of the Fourteenth Amendment was to Protect All Rights", by Jon Roland): [sic]

"From the legislative history of the Fourteenth it should be clear that all of the rights recognized by the U.S. Constitution are not only rights against state action, but that the Fourteenth Amendment authorizes Congress to legislate protection of such rights against state action, and grants jurisdiction of the federal judiciary over cases between citizens and their states involving them. Among those rights are the right to keep and bear arms and the right to a grand jury indictment. While the Supreme Court might reasonably have confirmed this in any given case by only declaring such rights as are minimally needed to render a decision, it is important that they not fail to do so for all the rights that are issues before the court, and the precedent of the Hurtado case needs to be reversed."

Essentially, my point of this dissertation was to point out what I had observed from my time within the legal system of Montana. Going in though, I only knew what how a legal system was *supposed* to work, ie, grand jury investigates and indicts, then challenge of probable cause, then entry of plea, and finally defense motions (motions to dismiss or suppress evidence and habeas corpus, for example). Of course, in Flathead County – even though each of these were provided for in Montana state law, they were *not* provided to criminal defendants in Flat head County. And Falla had no trouble depriving me of those basic liberties at every opportunity.

This was pretty much how all of our meetings went. I would research defenses, present them to him, and Falla would tell me how none of it mattered. From April, 2004, when I first arrived in Flathead County through around the end of May, Falla refused to listen to any defenses I presented and yet refused to come up with any of his own.

Early on, I insisted that Ted Lympus had a conflict of interest over my case because he was presiding over Mara's custody hearings. I wanted him removed for cause, but of course, Falla refused to challenge Lympus' integrity. Instead, he claimed we could use a one-time replacement statute to remove him, and then the case would be randomly reassigned. And, in all fairness, that part was true, except that when Lympus was dismissed, *he* decided who got the case. In an order written by his own hand, he assigned the case to Katherine Curtis who, of the three seated judges at the time, was by far the most aggressive besides Lympus – and she had a particularly aggressive stance against sex offenders. In fact, she is well known for imposing considerably harsher sentences than even Lympus himself. In effect, Lympus made sure that if I were to get another judge, that it would be the next worse he could throw at me.

Now, the reason why this is significant is two-fold. First of all, a recused judge has no place deciding who his replacement is. If he is being recused, he is done with the case and is forbidden by law to do anything further – much less assign the new judge. But more importantly, Falla's insistence on not having Lympus dismissed for cause wasted my one replacement option. I had cause to remove Lympus – he had a conflict of interest. But I had no cause to remove Curtis. If it had gone the way I had requested, Lympus would have been removed and I could still have removed my case from Curtis' court. But Falla made certain to line it up so I would end up in the least favorable court I could.

Keep in mind – though the third judge, Stuart Standler, was seen publicly as the most lenient and open, he was sleeping with Curtis. As consequence, there was no way to assure that if Curtis were removed, she would not have exercised some control over Stadler through their inter-office romance.

Yes, two judges were having a relationship with each other that exceeded judicial ethic limitations. I have had more than one attorney confirm this fact to me – this was no secret. However, a judge must always be above impropriety, and when two judges in the same district are involved sexually, there can be no assurances of separation between their courts. Both the law and the canon of judicial ethics prohibit a judge to preside over a case in which his "spouse" is engaged; sans the marriage component, one judge could not sit over a case the other has also sat over without a conflict by this definition.

For the record, both Curtis and Stadler resigned as judges at the same time, so they are no longer presiding judges of the Eleventh Judicial District. But they were both in power in 2004.

At any rate, there came a day when Falla came to me with a waiver of speedy trial. As I recall, this was the end of May. The trial schedule called for a late June trial, as I recall, and he insisted he had not been able to conduct any research in my case because the State had not provided him access to any witnesses. Mind you, I had provided him a list of two dozen witnesses, but he had made no effort to contact anyone, including Mara, who had all of my records on the prior investigations. But at this point, he insisted that he could not be expected to go to trial without preparation, but that the court would not give him an extension if I did not sign a waiver of my speedy trial rights.

Now I knew better than to sign something open-ended. I knew about consent and waivers, and I told Falla this. He returned that he only needed one three month extension and he assured me we would go to trial by the first week of October. I then asked him, "So you're sure we will go to trial by October?" And his response was, "I guarantee it."

In spite of the fact that we butted heads and could not agree on anything, I *still* believed he was acting as my advocate and that he was essentially being honest with me. I knew he could not prepare for a trial if he had no witnesses interviewed nor access to any of my paperwork, and I felt at the time that three more months versus a for certain conviction was the least of two evils. And so, upon Falla's guarantee, I signed the waiver.

What I did not know, of course, was that Falla was lying. Falla never had any intention of going to trial in October – he had plans to leave the country on vacation for three weeks in October, so he was certainly not going to prepare for a trial to happen then. But he got my signature, and that was what he had been after. With a waiver, he could have me held indefinitely. And he did – for sixteen months I sat in jail waiting for trial, all while Mara and others continued to be threatened and those who had once supported me being more and more convinced that I must be guilty if I were still in jail.

What the reader needs to understand here is that Falla's waiver form had no effect. Once he revealed a few weeks after I signed this that he was leaving the country for three weeks on vacation in October, I immediately challenged his having me sign a waiver. His response was to shrug and say, "You signed it, that's all anyone needs."

Of course, this is not true and I knew better – in order for any waiver of rights to have effect, it must be signed freely without coercion, deception or lack of knowledge. In this case, Falla only got me to sign the waiver under the "guarantee" that it was only for three months and we would be going to trial in October. Since Falla knew full well that he would not even be in the country at the time he had "guaranteed" we would be in trial, he only gained my consent through deception. This would, in any other situation, have voided the waiver.

As I had on so many occasions, I raised this objection to Katherine Curtis in open court at a hearing designed to substitute out Ed Falla as my attorney. I informed her that though I had signed a waiver, it had been done under deceptive representation by my attorney, and that I withdrew my waiver. Falla – acting against me as he so often did – presented the waiver with my signature and said that it was clearly a voluntary act, and of course, Curtis agreed. Needless to say, I suppose, but Curtis compelled me to keep Falla as my attorney and granted his request for a second extension of the trial date.

This was not the first or only time that I raised this objection, by the way. I did so repeatedly, at every chance I could get, in letters and in open court, insisting that I was being denied my speedy trial rights because my waiver was obtained through deception. And each time, I was ignored.

As time progressed, it also became clear that things Falla had been telling me were lies. For instance, at our first meeting, he told me Mara now believed the allegation against me and that she was cooperating with the prosecutors; Yet in November of that year, I received discovery that included a recent paper prepared by Kori Taylor of CFS stating that Mara still insisted that her daughter had made up the allegation against me. Falla continuously made excuses for not interviewing witnesses, and even by the time I reached trial, most of the witnesses had not been interviewed. Daughter 1 had, as had Mara and Carrie Beth – and I am told the Nezats were, though I never saw any actual evidence of this.

But as this was going on, the Kalispell Police Department were busy making their own contacts – trying to track down anyone who could give them some kind of substantiating allegation against me, ie, desperately seeking new evidence. They contacted family members of mine as far away as Kansas in an effort to find out any former allegations against me that they could.

I will admit that it was extremely disheartening how unsupportive my family proved to be at this time. None of them wanted to be involved, and even my own mother, Sharon Mejak, was willing to fabricate a story about me having sued people my whole life – just because the police were bothering her at work and she did not want to lose her minimum wage job. Keep in mind – I have never initiated a lawsuit against anyone prior to 2003, but Sharon insisted I had.

Falla used my mother's statements as reason to not permit me to bring character evidence into trial, by the way. To better frame this for the reader, character evidence is that which shows what someone's behavior is like – and I had over seven years of impeccable service working with children running a youth recreations program. The corrupt authorities certainly did not want me to parade parents into court to provide this, so Falla barred my using this kind of evidence at my trial by insisting that if my mother got on the stand for the prosecution, that it would make my look like a terrible person. I of course disagreed – I told Falla to deposition Sharon and find out where I was supposed to have filed previous cases and then go to those jurisdictions to prove I had never filed anything. With this evidence, Sharon would have been impeached before the jury, and it would have shifted to what kind of a woman would lie in court against her own son. But, as I have said repeatedly, Falla's job was to sabotage my defense, not to help it – and he refused to permit character evidence at my trial.

Of course, the most damning thing that Falla did was to help the prosecutors manufacture witnesses against me.

By February of 2005, I was still incarcerated and Falla could not get me to confess. His efforts to fast-track me through a prosecution had failed, and the police had not been able to obtain anything else that substantiated any other criminal behavior against me. And so in absence of any real evidence, Falla collaborated with prosecutors to *create* more evidence.

At the time, I was being detained in a cell with other inmates accused of sexual crimes. Two of those individuals were Larry VanAlstine and Frank "Ray" Allen, who were both clients of Ed Falla's as well. Falla, motivated to accomplish the task assigned to him by the corrupt officials used these individuals to secure my conviction.

Now, I was obviously not privy to conversations between VanAlstine, Allen and Falla, but the content of their conversations, interviews and other information were relaid piecemeal over time to me that has permitted a fairly accurate accounting of what happened. And it is that assembled and logically concluded history that I will relate, because it is what I believe happened.

Sometime prior to February, 2005, VanAlstine – who was facing a new felony charge of sexual intercourse without consent – approached Falla about finding a way to make a deal to offer the prosecutors, including testifying against anyone in jail with him. Falla leaped on this opportunity and began to collaborate with VanAlstine to act as a witness against me, feeding him information specific to my case and to another of his clients, Kimberly Neise, who was awaiting trial on charges of prostitution with a local business man, Dick Dasen.[83]

Within weeks, VanAlstine was taken to the Kalispell Police Department where he made a statement claiming that I had "confessed" to molesting Daughter 1, and that I had been working with Dick Dasen to collect underage, virgin girls and sell them to Dasen for anywhere between three to five hundred dollars per girl.[84] It was fabricated of course, but it laid the

---

[83] This conclusion is based on two factors: one, that VanAlstine's statements to police included information only available on recorded interviews (not paperwork I had in my cell), unedited transcripts (of which mine were edited) and from information specific to Neise's accusations against Dasen that no one currently incarcerated would have had access to. This information came from content of prosecution discovery, which meant it was either prosecutors or Falla himself who provided this information to VanAlstine, but since Dasen had several accusers and only information specific to Neise's case was used by VanAlstine, it limits where the information could have come from.

[84] Incidentally, this latter was the information that came uniquely from Kim Neise – that she was offered three to five hundred dollars per girl she brought to Dasen for prostitution. Again, no one not involved with that specific prosecution knew of that

foundation to pressure me to really confess to molesting Daughter 1 as a means of avoiding the prostitution charge.

Of course, none of us in jail with VanAlstine knew what he had done. But after a week or so of continuing to be jailed within the same cell as me, VanAlstine became more and more anxious that I would find out what he had done. A jailhouse snitch is the worst possible thing someone could be, but even worse is when a snitch makes up details to become a snitch. Because of this, VanAlstine was becoming fearful of retaliation.

One night, VanAlstine confided in Frank Allen (who was in jail on a probation violation) what he had done, and about his fear that I would find out. Apparently, after a week of nothing happening, VanAlstine was afraid authorities would not use the information. Allen decided to use this to his own advantage and went to tell Falla that he also wanted to testify against me, that I he had heard me my "confession" to VanAlstine. VanAlstine did not know what Allen was doing at first, but after Allen had made his own recorded interview, he told VanAlstine not to worry, because he had gone in and "backed up" what VanAlstine had said.

The problem was, because Allen had not really been primed as VanAlstine had, and VanAlstine had not confided everything into his admission to Allen, Allen did not have the details to collaborate VanAlstine's story properly. Therefore, Allen's statement was across the map with inaccuracies and contradictions to VanAlstine's. Nevertheless, it gave the authorities material to work with.

Personally, I do not believe Falla planned on VanAlstine making a jailhouse confession to Allen, and Allen's sudden involvement upset his careful coaching of VanAlstine. Fearful that he would suddenly find himself berated with people claiming to back up VanAlstine's story, he began to distance himself. And

---
detail.

his first step was to find new counsel immediately for Allen (though interestingly enough, he continued to represent Allen).

A month later, both VanAlstine and Allen were taken in for second interviews. By that point, their stories had come into sync – whereas before it sounded like two interviews contradicted each other repeatedly, now their stories backed each other up. Either Allen and VanAlstine spent that month working to sync up their stories or – as I believe more credible – someone worked with them outside the cell to make sure their stories were the same before bringing them back in for new interviews.

Remember, this was similar to what had been done with Daughter 1 – when her earlier interviews were contradictory, they simply coached her and then gave her a new interview. In the instance of VanAlstine and Allen, there was no need for secondary interviews – if the allegation was that they had both been privy to the same conversation, there was no need for a secondary interview, since the facts should have been presented at the first interview. But VanAlstine and Allen were brought in a second time, and their interviews were now much more collaborative than they had been before. Whether it was Falla, another attorney or prosecutors who groomed VanAlstine and Allen for this second interview, I cannot tell from the contents of the interviews – I can only say that it was very obvious that someone had worked with them together, and there was not enough privacy in the jail cell to allow for this kind of in depth collaboration since neither could let anyone else know what they were doing.

At any rate, Falla kept me completely uninformed that his own clients were being groomed to be witnesses for the prosecution. He had a clear loyalty to me to inform me of new "evidence" he had come across, but he waited until after the second interviews were actually *transcribed* before he informed me that "two jailhouse informants" had come forward against me.

By that point, I was isolated in a medical isolation cell because I had been attacked and had a fractured hand, so I suppose Falla believed I would not realize that the two people who had supposedly come forward on their own were actually his clients. But I knew, and I also knew that it was far too convenient that the two men who had "come forward" were also Falla's clients. And when I read the transcripts, I also knew the details had come from information the two could only have gotten from either Falla or the prosecutors.

Another convenient circumstance in my favor was that shortly after that time, Dick Dasen had also been convicted and was being kept in a medical isolation unit because of his high profile status, which meant when we did get recreation time, we went out together. I had previously sent a letter to his attorney (whom the guards at the jail helped me identify) about what was being said, but I did not get any response from him. But speaking with Dasen confirmed something vital: the three hundred to five hundred dollar figure was a unique and specific allegation made by Kim Neise, who had been a client of Ed Falla's. Which meant that this specific part of Allen's and VanAlstine's story had come from confidential information that Falla possessed. But since no other accusations made against Dasen were included, it was pretty obvious that Allen and VanAlstine had only been privy to the information Falla had, which narrowed down the source for their information to Falla alone.

Upon learning of this conflict, I of course sought to dismiss Ed Falla. I knew he had sabotaged my case from the beginning by this point, but now I had evidence that he was actually helping prosecutors make up an entirely new charge against me. But, as was typical, Judge Curtis would not dismiss Falla as my counsel – even with this blatantly clear conflict of interest. Even assuming that I had been wrong about where VanAlstine and Allen got their information, both of his former clients had been declared as state witnesses and he could not cross-examine them or even participate in a strategy involving them in my case without foregoing the loyalty he owed to both of them as their attorney.

Curtis elected to appoint a co-counsel to my case to bypass this conflict, and selected David Stufft. Of course, this did not really solve anything, since Falla remained the lead counsel on my case – and now the prosecution was building a defense based around the supposed jail house informants. And though this issue was raised on appeal, the Montana Supreme Court never ever responded to it when they denied my appeal.

In the end, the state decided they would rather work with Allen (who was only in on a probation violation) than with VanAlstine (who was facing a new felony), and VanAlstine was completely cut out of the deal he had tried to set up.

I spoke of this issue in my original Great Montana Conspiracy blog when I received word that the Montana Supreme Court had denied my appeal, and after my appellate defender refused to challenge that the High Court had refused to even address the issues raised. On March 6, 2009, I posted a brief blog post entitled, "Enemy of the State":

Well, today I heard from my appellate defender, William Hooks out of Helena, MT. He filed my appeal for me over three years ago. And though he didn't make all the arguments I wanted him to, I did feel he made a couple very strong arguments to overturn my conviction. A couple of weeks ago the Montana Supreme Court ruled on my appeal, affirming my conviction and ignoring most of the issues that had been raised in the appeal to do so. And now, Mr. Hooks informs me that he will not be filing a motion for reconsideration because he does not believe they overlooked anything. In a nutshell, Mr. Hooks has apparently sold me out to remain in favor with the powers that be.

Let me talk briefly about only one of the issues that the supreme court failed to review and which Mr. Hooks decided was "not" overlooked. And I mention this one because it is, in my humble opinion, the strongest of all the arguments. There is a case called State v. Finley (276 Mont. 126) in which the Montana Supreme Court agreed with prior US Supreme Court precedent that a person is entitled to effective assistance of counsel at all critical stages of his defense, and if that person challenges the effectiveness of his counsel, he is entitled to separate counsel during a hearing to determine the merit of such claims; otherwise, the person is left without representation during a critical stage of his defense. The case says a lot more than that, but that's the gist of it.

One of the many things I was exposed to during my prosecution was an attorney (Ed Falla) who worked very much for the corrupt powers-that-be, and who did everything he could to sabotage my defense and to make evidence that exonerated me unavailable for my defense. And I sought to dismiss him as counsel on several occasions. Two of those occasions resulted in hearings, and at both hearings I was forced to fight my own counsel, alongside the prosecution and the court. Effectively, I was left without counsel and was actually openly opposed by counsel at both hearings.

In September, 2007, the supreme court issued a preliminary order to fix this mistake with the latter of the two hearings, but did nothing to address the previous three day hearing that occurred between November and December, 2004. In the final order issued by the supreme court, it completely ignores this critical issue in order to affirm my conviction. And my own attorney, Mr. Hooks, is cooperating with this blatant disregard of my constitutional rights!

Let's face it - I am an enemy of the state of Montana and so long as I continue to fight these people, I will forever be deprived of all reasonable rights and privileges under the law. I am supposedly a US citizen, so when do I get rights like everyone else?

Needless to say, the argument against Ed Falla and his consistent conflicts of interest were never properly addressed in my appeal, either.

Regardless, now armed with a supposed witness who would testify that I had confessed to the crime, the state was finally ready to take me to trial. And so on July 11, 2005 – sixteen months after I had been arrested and two full years after the initial allegation – I was paraded in front of a jury in my jail clothes and shackles. I was not allowed to wear normal clothes, so the jury saw me from the outset as a criminal, and though this had supposedly been a strategy of Falla's to gain sympathy of the jury for how long I had been held already, he made no objection when Lori Adams moved to forbid Falla from mentioning this detail. Further, I was told by Judge Curtis that if I tried to speak up and interrupt the proceedings, I would be removed from the courtroom and the trial would continue without me.

The trial lasted three days and was a mockery, of course. Frank Allen testified and got almost every detail wrong, but Stufft refused to impeach him. The prosecutors, Lori Adams and Tim Wenz, had concocted a new version of the events alleging that I had patted the couch and tried to get Daughter 1 to come back and lie down, but when Daughter 1 took the stand and would not collaborate this, Lori Adams actually threatened her in open court.[85]

But by the end, I was convicted – primarily because Ed Falla and David Stufft offered at best a pretense of defense. The jury

---

[85] The trial transcripts were doctored to conceal certain things at the trial, including the threat made against Daughter 1, and every effort I have made to obtain the original minutes of the trial to have an independent transcript prepared have been blocked.

was not allowed to know about the lawsuit more than in a cursory capacity, they never heard of Daughter 1's contradictory statements, nor of the threats made against Mara or other witnesses. In essence, the jury was only given the information the state wanted them to see – and with Falla only willing to present a defense that I was asleep during the affair, it was a defense that primarily relied on discrediting Allen. But there was no effort genuinely made to impeach Allen or discredit him in front of the jury to undo his claim that I had confessed to the crime.

Just for point of fact, I did not testify at my own trial because of Falla's defense. I did not agree that the event had happened at all, and I refused to endorse Falla's strategy. It was not my strategy and I had no say in what Falla would present to a jury. And I could not in good conscience take the stand and lie by telling Falla's version of events. I knew Falla was sabotaging my case, but I also knew that if I got up on the stand and contradicted what my own attorney had spent two days telling the jury, that what slim chance I did have would be surrendered. And so I would not take the stand.

I wanted to – I genuinely did. But I could not lie, and if I took the stand, I felt I would have been begging the jury to convict me. In hindsight, knowing that I would not have won anyways, I wish I had taken the stand and obliterated the defense Falla had created. But I was still holding onto a measure of hope, and I was too afraid to let go of even that small sliver. And in the end, the authorities proved they would just rewrite the script anyways, so it would likely not have mattered.

Then, within ten days of the conclusion of my trial, Frank Allen was dead. Frank Allen was discovered in the front room of his parent's house, supposedly overdosed on his prescription pain pills. There was no note and there had been no discussion of killing himself, yet his death was pronounced a suicide without ever conducting an autopsy. Considering the time frame involved, I have always found his death to be downright incriminating of the system.

As part of his agreement to testify, Allen was released from jail and was staying with his parents. The state would not discuss a deal with Allen prior to the trial so the incentive could not be used to undermine his integrity. But after the trial, after they had gained the conviction they wanted, the state was no longer willing to give Allen what he wanted – specifically, a free pass on his probation violation. The state apparently intended to renege on its good faith offer of amnesty to Allen once the had me convicted. And Allen, being the consummate con artist that he was, would likely have threatened himself to expose that he had lied and who had helped set him up to prosecute me.

To this day, I have always maintained my belief that the one thing keeping me alive was that I had always been very outspoken, and that if something untoward happened to me, even if it silenced me, it would validate my accusations against the corrupt authorities in Kalispell and Flathead County. Keeping me alive, in essence, acted as a counter to my claims that the authorities were committed to destroying me – since killing me outright would be the most logical means to dispose of me. If I lived, it was a strange defense the authorities could use to displace suspicion from themselves.

Frank Allen however had no such protection. He worked through duplicitous and covert manipulation, not outspoken protest. The fact that no one would care who Frank Allen was not only worked against him, but aided the very authorities committed to silencing me. When given a choice of losing the conviction over me and my gaining validation that the prosecution against me had been staged, or alternately keeping my conviction intact but remove Allen, the corrupt authorities chose the only path open to them to pursue the latter path – they killed the man they had manufactured to testify against me and staged it as a suicide.

Of course, I have no way of knowing who specifically did this. But I do know that within days of it happening, one deputy in the jail told me that Allen was now dead. It was a deadpan statement, with no explanation – only that Allen was dead. To this day, I believe it was a warning – telling me that the same thing could be done to me. Whether the jailer telling me intended it as a threat or a warning that I needed to be careful, I will never know. But the fact that it was relayed to me almost immediately only proves that Allen's death was not a suicide – and there were people within the political system who wanted me to know.

At any rate, I had to wait an additional five months to be sentenced, and almost immediately after sentence was pronounced. On December 1, 2005, I was sentenced to twenty years, with fifteen of those years suspended and within less than a week, I found myself en route out to prison.

Prison, in and of itself, is another story entirely. As I have said before, perhaps someday – assuming I survive the publication of this expose – perhaps I will detail those years. But for now, the sequence that I have set out to tell has been told.

And this is where my story ends.

I will use the next chapter to provide some closure to this story. My insights, my motivations, and where I plan to move forward to. But now – to the best of my current ability – you know what happened to me, and the reader has been forewarned. This may be the United States, but no one – and I do mean *no one* – has any real rights. It is all a mask, one that can be torn away far too easily, and you too might one day find yourself where I have.

Because any of this could just as easily happen to you.

Chapter 13

Many things have been said about me over the years, and roughly ninety percent could probably be traced back to members of law enforcement or someone answerable to one official or another in Flathead County, Montana. There are simple hate mongers out there who will run with a hateful story without ever considering whether the information is true or not, but I have to say that the majority of perverted and misdirected information about me has at one time or another been linked back to the very people who started this affair in 2003 – if not directly to them, then certainly to information they initially propagated. It has been hurtful, and it has been malicious.

But what it has not done is change the truth.

The Nezats started this rash of accusations, but to be honest, they were spiteful, malicious people who had been doing this kind of thing for years. No one of any significance believed them nor listened to them for long. They had too many past examples of false accusations. But once the city and county officials backed them up, suddenly their far-fetched accusations gained credibility.

But still, it did not make what they said true.

And this is the truth: in 2003, I did not molest Daughter 1, nor have I ever before or since molested anyone. Period.

I would hope that anyone having read this volume will have realized that something very, very wrong went on here. If I had been genuinely guilty of a one-time, five second inappropriate contact with a thirteen year old, why was so much effort expended to vilify me? There are people in this county having actual sex with their own children – repeatedly – who have not had so much effort expended to make sure they fall. And yet all of this – just because I supposedly copped a feel?

I am not saying that if I had actually committed this crime that the police should not have been involved or that an investigation should not have been conducted. It was in this case, and it cleared me. It was only reopened in retaliation.

This brings up a point of criticism that I am sure will get raised again by the anonymous supporter of the local corrupt authorities – one person online tried to sway the wording I use to suggest that one can only be cleared of a crime through a court of law. That is the most ridiculous statement that ever existed. To be found *legally* innocent or guilty of a crime under state or federal law requires a court, but to be cleared of wrongdoing can be done by simple examination. If a person is accused of a crime, but they have an alibi that proves they could not have committed a crime, one does not need to take the issue to a court of law to say that person has been cleared of suspicion or of the crime. Just imagine how bogged down a court of law would be if every time someone is suspected of wrongdoing, every single instance of clearing them must be taken before a judge. That is just insane.

And yet this is the kind of reasoning and rationality these people try to confuse the issue with. They play word games and imply truths that do not exist. Sometimes it feels like I am defending myself against a legion of Mad Hatters – all speaking gibberish, but still needing to explain away their nonsense because the Hare is taking it all in as true.

I mention all of this for a reason – one of the things that Dave Edwards initiated about me, and which has been mimicked by many people in positions of authority over me, is that I have no empathy for Daughter 1. That by speaking of my side of this issue, I am somehow "re-victimizing" her. I assure you, the reader, that this is the furthest from the truth. I have said repeatedly herein that I hold no resentment towards what Daughter 1 did leading up to my arrest and conviction – I only hold some lesser degree of resentment that she has not come forward with the truth since she turned eighteen, but after five years of conditioning, that resentment is tempered by pity that she was forced to endure all she did because I would not relent and confess to a crime I did not commit.

Yes, I do feel guilty that Daughter 1, Mara and all the rest were made to suffer because of me. But as guilty as I feel, I know I was not the one actually causing them pain – it was the terrorists who call themselves authorities in Flathead County and Kalispell city government who are the real criminals here. And no matter how badly I have felt in the past or will continue to feel until the day I die, I know in my heart that I was not the one causing them harm. Just as I know that anything said in here – presented as true and forthright – could not harm them if they were equally truthful and forthright in their own actions.

I am sure that Mara, Daughter 1 and all the others who collaborated with the gestapo-style tactics of the Flathead County and Kalispell authorities feel some degree of shame – but just as with a child caught with the hand in the cookie jar, they are turning their shame into overzealous defense and attacks on me. Much easier to deflect blame for one's own actions than to actually accept responsibility for them.

And for the record, I *am* to blame for everything that happened to Daughter 1, Mara and the rest. I did not commit the harm, but I know that I could have stopped it at any time. All I had to do was lie, surrender my principles, my integrity, and my honor – and they could have gone on with their lives. My refusal to abandon my principles is responsible for the harm – indirect though it may be – suffered by all the victims of this tyrannous regime operating in the northwest corner of the State of Montana.

But regardless of whether I share blame or not, it all pales to one point that is far more prudent:

I am and remain a good man. And that is the one thing these people can never take away from me unless I let them. And I refuse to let them.

Remember what I quoted earlier from Edmund Burke? Allow me to paraphrase it here: The only thing necessary for evil men to succeed is for a good man to do nothing. I did not do nothing – I stood up and said no. And the consequence is that my entire life, past and future, was obliterated, and innocent victims were caught in the path of the shrapnel for my arrogance.

But I am not saying this here for the first time. In the last few weeks of my original Blogspot posting of the Great Montana Conspiracy blog, I posted several statements explaining this. The first, published on March 31, 2009, was entitled simply, "An Aside", and consisted of the following:

Last week during a meeting with my probation officer, he expressed to me that he felt it was not perhaps in good taste to name [Daughter 1] as the person who accused me of sexual assault. Primarily, his reasoning was based upon the fact that [Daughter 1] had been a minor at the time she made the allegation and that, if the accusation is presumed to be true, that she is a victim deserving privacy. Though I certainly can see his point of view, I cannot say that I agree with it. But I felt that an aside might be appropriate to discuss this issue.

First, I want to point out that, had this accusation been true, had I actually committed a crime against [Daughter 1], there would certainly be a privacy issue to consider. Had [Daughter 1] been actually molested, raped or otherwise assaulted, it could be considered unfair to publicize her identity, regardless of her age, and subject her to further emotional duress. Had there not been the underlying elements behind her charge, had the initial investigation stayed closed, or she had not so blatantly contradicted herself between versions of her stories, it might never have been necessary to even discuss this issue. Any of these scenarios could have provided [Daughter 1] the privacy that some might suggest she would thereby entitled to.

However, this is not the case. [Daughter 1] was not molested or otherwise assaulted by me and the only consistency in her story has been its inconsistency. The local authorities exceeded their authority and used [Daughter 1] as a weapon against me and in so doing made her a primary element to discussion of their improprieties. And though this position is admittedly my own, and these same officials have manipulated the legal arena to convict me of an offense that makes the allegation legally true and the circumstances legally irrelevant, none of this changes the true facts. I have maintained now for over five years, in spite of being deprived of my liberty and freedom as consequence, that I did not do what [Daughter 1] accused me of and, simply put, the actual facts support my position. That the Kalispell authorities have succeeded in keeping these factual elements out of court in order to railroad me into a false conviction is what is genuinely relevant. No matter how much these corrupt officials like to play at being gods, the truth is they cannot change reality. They can certainly control the perception of reality, but they cannot change the actual events as they really happened.

I have said upon many occasions throughout this ongoing oration that I do not hold [Daughter 1] entirely accountable for what has happened. I recognize that she had been placed under extreme duress and that others had exerted undue influence over her to gain their desired goals. That [Daughter 1] was easily manipulated is inconsequential to the larger scheme of things. That she has had a history of lies and deceptions is not at issue either. These are just the means by which those truly to blame exerted their control over her, not the underlying cause of her actions.

I raised [Daughter 1] for over two years as my own daughter. To this day, I still have a special place in my heart for the young woman that I took under my wing, just as I hold a special place for her sister, [Daughter 2], as well. I am deeply hurt by her betrayal and disappointed that she could be manipulated in this way against me, since I had thought she had returned my affections, but the truth is she is her own person, and she made her own decisions. I do not agree with them, and I have been hurt far worse than a simple betrayal of confidence alone could be responsible for, but I know the ideas were not hers alone – there were others pulling her strings. But it does not make the pain of that betrayal any less.

All this being said, [Daughter 1] has made some serious mistakes, and in making those mistakes, regardless of whether she acted alone or at the direction of others, she has nevertheless caused great harm to others. And not just to me – to her mother, her sister, my son, John, and to our mutual friends and families. Her actions led, indirectly, to the loss of our business and way of life. Regardless of whether I hold a personal grudge against her or not (which I do not, by the way), the fact is that [Daughter 1]'s actions have had consequences, and I do not believe that she should be completely sheltered from those consequences by some pretense that claiming to be a victim of a faux crime somehow provides her immunity from the fallout of her misdeeds. There are repercussions to what [Daughter 1] has done and I do not feel that she should be entitled to shelter from her own sins while everyone else around her has suffered.

This girl sent her own mother to jail – and could have had her sent to prison. All because she did not have the moral fortitude to stand up to people who were making her do things that she knew were wrong. She destroyed lives, and I do not feel that she should be sheltered from the consequences of her actions.

However, none of this is the reason that I have continued to use [Daughter 1]'s name in these posts. The real reason, and it has nothing to do with morality, is that as far as I was concerned, the cat was already out of the bag by the time the charges were filed against me and [Daughter 1] became an "official" victim. I posted the original "Another Case of Gov Abuse" in December, 2003. I was not charged and arrested until February, 2004. At the time I wrote the original public plea for help, there was no need to shelter [Daughter 1]'s identity.

The original allegation had not only been investigated and dismissed by that time, but [Daughter 1] herself had recanted her false accusation. Though she had been abducted by CFS, she had maintained the truth when Kori Taylor insisted she reassert the lie. I had no reason to believe at that time that [Daughter 1] would reassert the false allegation nor that it could be used to bring a charge against me in light of all the overwhelming evidence at that point in time exonerating me. I did not believe that my support structure could be so critically undermined or that [Daughter 1] could be compelled to place her own mother in jeopardy of harm.

In a nutshell, I had absolutely no reason to believe that I would be faced again with [Daughter 1]'s false accusation and therefore had no reason to withhold [Daughter 1]'s name from my original posting in 2003. At that point, I had believed that my sole fight was against [Daughter 1]'s kidnapping by state authorities and in the possibility that the local authorities might manufacture a new false charge to arrest me under. There had been no reason to consider withholding [Daughter 1]'s identity as a victim of assault and so I did not. But as a consequence of openly discussing an allegation I had thought dead and buried, I openly spoke of [Daughter 1] by name. And in doing so, any future posting that omitted her name would be pointless.

In other words, I did not name [Daughter 1] to cause harm to her nor to redirect some kind of hostility her way. I am not attempting to vilify her nor am I attempting to shift blame to her for anything that she is not accountable for. On the contrary – I believe I have gone out of my way to divert unnecessary hostility toward her by defending her on more than one occasion, including within this very post. I named [Daughter 1] at a time when such issues as whether she was an alleged victim of a crime were not at issue, and as such there had been no need to consider omitting her name.

[Daughter 1] is now eighteen years old,[86] by the way, and reportedly in the US military. She is no longer a minor and is no longer under the undue influence of state agents, at least she should not be. As a legal adult, [Daughter 1] could now step forward and tell the truth, tell her side of the story, tell about how her and her sister were kidnapped and how she was coerced into making false statements under the fear of never being returned home. She could take a major step in righting the wrongs that she was forced to commit. But personally, I have little hope in such an event occurring.

It would require an act of great courage and integrity to step forward at this juncture and admit to all she has done. Likely, she feels a great deal of inner pain and anxiety over what she has done. I know the authorities did their level best to convince her that I would hurt her if given the chance. This could not be further from the truth, of course, but these people are empowered by these kinds of lies, and I fear that their having over five years to embed these fears in [Daughter 1] has made hope of this kind of thing impossible. And I cannot seek her out in any way to ask if she would even consider this because I am compelled by court order to have no contact with her directly or indirectly.

---

86 As of this writing, she is now twenty-four.

In the end, all I can say is that [Daughter 1] will never have anything to fear from me. Regardless of whether the truth ever comes out, regardless of whether I ever clear my name or not, I recognize that [Daughter 1] has been made as much of a victim of the cruel machinations of corrupt officials as much as I have. Perhaps she was not the victim of a sexual assault, but being torn from your family and be made responsible for all that has happened must have a profound impact upon her. My heart goes out to all that she has suffered through the years, just so she could be used as a weapon against me. But none of this makes [Daughter 1] a target of my indemnity. She was used as a tool, as a means to an end that was not her own. And I cannot bring myself to hold any anger toward her for that...

At any rate, I hope this post answers any underlying concerns about my using [Daughter 1]'s name so publicly. As always, I welcome any comments...

Of course, posting this explanation only earned me more ire and condemnation from Dave Edwards, but I now realize that the attacks on me for this were never about Daughter 1 as any kind of victim. Edwards was intent upon forcing me to "accept responsibility" for the crime, and for me to be putting out appeals to Daughter 1 in this fashion only made his work all the harder.

After failing to convince me to "accept what [I] had done to [Daughter 1]", Edwards turned to a new tactic – he now insisted that Mara had contacted him, fearful of me. Later, Lara would attest to what really happened, that Edwards called her, warned her I was out and "looking for her", and she needed to be careful. The obvious inference was that I was looking to hurt her – even though Edwards knew I had a pending claim in court for the business assets that Mara had taken for herself when I was arrested.

Simply put, Edwards was working hard to undermine any defense I might have of proving my innocence – at that time, I had been free of incarceration for mere weeks and was trying to get in touch with people whom five years of imprisonment had barred me from, people who were witnesses in my case and who could help me overturn the conviction. Edwards was dead set on making certain that I would not be able to contact these potential witnesses, and kept exerting more and more pressure on me, and continued to search out these people – like Mara and Daughter 1 – so he could convince them that I intended them harm. Of course, that was never true, but fear had always been the tactic of the corrupt local officials, and for whatever reason, Dave Edwards was in bed with those that had falsely convicted me.

At any rate, once Edwards claimed that Mara had contacted him fearful of harm, I once more tried to reach out with an appeal and expression of my opinions of her. On Aprile 14, 2009, I wrote a new blog entry entitled, "Dear Mara", in which I set forth both a personal appeal to Mara directly, as well as a copy of the letter sent to her in my efforts to make contact. The point of this post was to prove that my efforts to contact her were not malicious, but also explain my reasons and feelings relating to her efforts to collaborate with corrupt officials to save herself:

As anyone who reads this blog will know, Mara Pelton, aka Mara Nezatski, was once my girlfriend and business partner. When I was arrested in February, 2004, she collaborated with the corrupt officials (who had had me arrested to stop my lawsuit against the City of Kalispell) after she herself was arrested on a false charge of witness tampering (that was subsequently dismissed four days before my trial in July, 2005), and barred me from my personal and business assets. Also, she betrayed me even further by cheating on me with Joe Guiffrida.

As I posted yesterday, someone has been manipulating Mara into believing that I am a threat to her.[87] *The only conceivable reason for this (at least to me) is that someone has a vested interest in keeping Mara from even speaking to me, and is terrorizing her under my name as a means of controlling her.*

Had this been a recent occurrence, I could conceive that this was a game of the local authorities who continue to deprive me my civil liberties. But this started back after I was arrested and continued throughout my trial and sentencing in 2005. At that point in time, the authorities already had a measure of control over Mara - they had a false charge hanging over her head with threat of being returned to jail. This intimidation was all they needed to keep Mara under their thumb.

Therefore the threats came from a different source, someone who had an interest in both controlling Mara and assuring that she would betray my faith. As I have said, I had nothing to gain from terrorizing Mara and a lot more to lose, not to mention that I did not even know she had a cell phone, much less had her number.[88] *As such, the only person who had access to Mara (ie, opportunity and means) as well as something to gain from this (ie, motive) was Joe Guiffrida.*

---

87 At this time, I did not know it was Dave Edwards – the very person who "reported" that she was afraid I would harm her. It was not until months later, in the course of appellate proceedings on a restraining order Edwards compelled her to file that she made the admission that it was Edwards who contacted her, not the other way around.

88 This is reference to details mentioned in a separate blog entry. When I was incarcerated in Flathead County Detention Center, someone was calling Mara's cell phone – either claiming to be me or claiming to be making threats on my behalf (that part was never precisely clear). Either way, Mara believed I was behind these calls and that I wanted to harm her. However, when I was arrested, Mara did not have a cell phone, and deprived of all contact with her after being arrested, I had no way of learning this, much less what her number was. Remember, I had zero support outside of jail, so there was no one outside "helping" me harass Mara – and considering I needed her for both her witness statements and the evidence of mine that exonerated me, threatening her made absolutely no sense.

I am explaining this only to flesh out what I said yesterday. But all of this is important in what I am going to say next, as well.

As of yesterday, my probation officer, Dave Edwards, has ordered me to have no direct contact with Mara. He is utilizing a part of my order that says he can restrict my contact with people who have a negative influence over me. This is not applicable here, and I have filed a grievance against the action. But I have already been told that the grievance will be denied, which means I am just going to be fighting through appeal to try to overturn this - but anyone who has been following this blog will know, I have no rights and this so-called grievance system is little more than a pretense of justice. I have dealt with Montana Department of Corrections grievances for over three years now and I can assure you that, being an enemy of the state, my objections will be denied, regardless how illegal the measures taken against me are.

If Mara genuinely felt threatened, she could have filed a restraining order, and I would have welcomed the chance to face her in court to tell her what was going on. But she did not - she attacked me through the corrupt authorities who have control over my life. If this was really Mara who made this complaint and not just someone Mara put up to it, she has fallen incredibly far from the woman I once loved with so much of my heart...

Therefore, I am powerless to try to correct these falsehoods. I do have permission to have Mara served, as I had planned to, with the copy of the motion removing the civil cause to federal court. Originally, I had written a two page cover letter to accompany the documents, but after the events of yesterday, I re-wrote the letter, hoping to resolve this conflict. Then I realized that I could not deliver such a letter with the documents, since I am quite certain that a complaint would be made that I had used the service to attempt direct contact, and I would most assuredly be arrested. I have therefore re-written it again to be a brief letter explaining what I am doing, that I am forced to withdraw my offer to settle this issue out of court by Dave Edwards' order, and that if she wants to resolve this out of court, she will need to contact Edwards to have the instruction rescinded. In other words, the barest minimum legal position I can take.

This being said though, there are things in the letter I have abandoned that I would like Mara to see one day. She probably will not, but since I believe that I will be soon re-incarcerated over all of these faux reports of making threats, I want the letter entered here at least for prosperity.

Everyone who has read this blog knows that I hold no malice against Mara. I have gone to great lengths to set the record straight on that. I regret that I lost her, I am pained by her betrayal, but I hold no ill will toward her. I do not, nor have I ever, wished her harm. But, as has been the case from the beginning of this fiasco, no one wants to believe the truth when a lie is so much easier to believe. I believe it was Mark Twain who said that a lie is far easier to believe than the truth because it can be molded to fit what the speaker wants to be heard, and that the truth, by comparison, is far more rigid and less likely to be believed.

The truth is that I have been working hard to prove my innocence for nearly six years now, and that effort is not helped in the least by terrifying Mara. Regardless of whether anyone believes that I could not hold some deep hatred for Mara, common sense says that terrorizing her works contrary to my objective. Only someone with a suicide wish would think to scare away one of his greatest resources. None of this makes sense, but I cannot reach Mara to reason with her. And so I am going to type here what I wanted so badly to say to her in my letter. And hope that some day after I am gone that she may possibly learn the truth...

Dear Mara,

Please find attached a copy of the motion to remove the civil cause I told you about in my last letter to the U.S. District Court. For reference, that court's address is 201 E. Broadway, Missoula, MT 59802. I am providing this copy to you, along with a copy of the original suit and current cause docket, to provide you the opportunity to object to this action if you so choose.

I regret that I have had to proceed in this manner, but you have left me little choice, especially after what was perpetuated today. I tried to approach you equitably by letter sent to your old address, which I sent over three weeks ago; Since it was not returned, it was clearly delivered to wherever you are. Yet instead of trying to settle this issue, you have aggravated the circumstances, since today I was told by my probation officer, Dave Edwards, that you had registered a complaint against me, claiming you were "terrified" of me and that I was a "threat" to your safety. At this point, it is fairly obvious that you have no intent of settling these issues out of court, and so I must proceed with the suit against you, as much as I may hate doing so.

This breaches another area that must be addressed though: clearly you are under the misapprehension that I intend you harm. Nothing could be further from the truth.

James Valentino informed me in December, 2005, that someone claiming to represent me had been making threatening calls to you on your cell phone since shortly after my arrest. You should know that I did not even know you had a cell phone until days before my trial in July, 2005, and only then because Carrie Beth mentioned it in a transcribed interview - but the number was not included. Further, thanks to James' and Joe's spreading the rumor that anyone helping me would go to jail like you did, I had no support outside the jail, and I could not call a cell phone from the jail if I wanted to. All these points show that I could not have been behind the threats against you back then. Someone else was playing the fear card against you, but it was not me. And there's only one other person who actually benefited from you turning away from me in fear: Joe. Tim played the same game with you, if you recall: alienate you from all other support so you would rely solely on him. You resisted ; why do you embrace the lies Joe has spun so readily?

Let me set the record straight: I have never, nor would I ever, wish you harm, threaten to harm you nor victimize you in any way. I have nothing to gain by it, and much to lose. I need your allegiance in my war for my identity, not your enmity. How could terrorizing you possibly help me clear my name or recoup my rightful property from you? If you will set aside this fear that has been inbred into you and think logically about this, you will see that the pretense of my threatening you neither makes sense nor matches the personality of the man you lived with for over two years. And, despite what you have been told, prison did not fundamentally change who I am: I did not turn gay, and did not adopt a criminal mentality. I am still the compulsively truthful man of honor I have always been. And I have suffered through nearly six years of hell because of it.

You should remember that CFS claimed I was physically abusive to you, as well; but you know that was not true then. Why are you willing to believe such malice of me now?

You should know me well enough to know that I would never harm an innocent; I spent my life protecting people, not hurting them. Even when I had cause to, I never did. No matter how badly I had been hurt by people - Melissa, Paul, your parents, the board of directors for Prime Station - I never retaliated. And you know I have lived a life of being betrayed. Remember the curse I told you about? "Destined ever to be loved by those you do not love, and unloved by those you do"? I've lived with that curse my whole life and still never retaliated outside the law, even when I was sorely tempted. So why would I change now?

Regardless of how much pain you have caused me, no matter your betrayal of my trust and love, in spite of your abandonment, I still see you as a victim in all of this, along with myself, [Daughter 1], [Daughter 2] and John. We were all victims of cruel, malicious people who acted above the law. And from where I sit, that still makes you an innocent in this conflict. Your actions were motivated by self-preservation and not a small amount of deception and deceit, but that did not make them malicious. I do not condone what you did, cheating on me and turning your back on me, but I've lived with that kind of treatment my whole life. You were not the first nor likely will you be the last. But it does not mean that I would wish you ill. I still love you, [Mara]. And I always will. I can just never trust you ever again.

Remember how we had this conversation time and again about Melissa? You could not understand how I could still love someone who had betrayed me and left John and I homeless, of how I still held no ill will against her. When we met again at the VFW, you were convinced that my lingering love of her would mean I would leave you to return to her. But you didn't listen, no matter how much I explained it, though maybe you will understand it better now: Once I love someone, I can't stop loving them. My relationship with Melissa or any of my other girlfriends did not end because I stopped loving them - they stopped loving me and ultimately cheated on me. And you did the same thing - you stopped loving me and cheated on me. But that betrayal did not stop me from loving you. I never lost that feeling. And I will live with it for the rest of my days. But there's no going back - I could never trust you not to betray me again. You have shown yourself unfaithful to me, and to me, that hope of happiness with you is forever lost.

The point of all of this is that I have no real desire to prolong this contact. If you had not absconded with the business assets and the Magic cards belonging to the youth program, or you were not a key witness I still need to prove my innocence, I would have left you to your life. You cannot possibly comprehend the amount of pain I deal with every day that this issue remains unsettled. I cannot bear to think of Joe having stolen you away through lies and deceit. terrorizing you in my name to have you for himself. As you have stolen my property, he has stolen you from me. I would prefer to have been able to walk away entirely, but my need to recover what is rightfully mine and clear my name make it necessary to prolong my pursuit of you. And your resistance to settling all of this only makes my agony worse. But this is where my interest in you ends: once I have my property and my good name restored, you can go on and live your life built on lies and misdirection. I will have no further need to contact you ever again.

I will never understand how you could possibly trust Tim, whom you personally witnessed beating [Daughter 1] and had tried to beat you, yet you are too terrified of me to even speak to me, when I have never raised a hand to you or yours?

Regardless what lies you believe though, the truth is unchanged: my sole interest in you is for return of my property and to clear my name. And both issues are being addressed through legal channels, as this is the only option you have left to me. I gain nothing by your being afraid of me. And Joe is only playing the same nonsense game your parents did - remember how they kept claiming I was going to their home to wreck their vehicles and property, even when you knew I had never left your side? You're only falling for Joe's version of the same manipulative game: make up some heinous act to blame on me to make me look like a threat. For crying out loud, Mara, you should know me well enough to know that I do not rely on others to do things anyway - if I had a way to contact you myself, wouldn't I be doing that? I have no legal reason not to after all... Or at least, I did not before today. If I were this threat that you have come to believe me to be, why have I not shown up at your work, or your door, or at places I know you would be? Why would I even be filing through court? In an investigation, one looks for three things: means, opportunity and motive. If you honestly believe I had means and opportunity, you still lack motive because I honestly have nothing to gain. On the other hand, Joe always has - he gains you.

But I know you. None of this will make a difference. Joe will deny it and you will believe him. I can't change that, no matter how I might long to protect you from harm. It's your life and it is yours to live. Just do not expect me to ever be civil with Joe, anymore than I was to when Tim came around to harm you. I want nothing to do with him, so do not send him as a messenger - ever. I will not speak to him or deal with him. And, if after reading this you decide to work this out, I am still not able to talk to you directly because of your game in calling Dave Edwards today. If you ever want to resolve this in person, you will need to undo the limitations you have had placed upon me by calling him to set the record straight.

I may have meandered a bit here, but this letter's purpose is still legal in nature. I needed to clarify certain issues that have impeded my efforts to settle this issue out of court. You are under a gross misapprehension if you believe I mean you harm or that my purpose for trying to contact you was for any otter purpose than to settle the legal issues discussed herein. And once those issues are settled, you can continue to live in your fantasy world all you want - my reasons for needing contact with you end with the legal affairs. You should never have trusted in Joe's deceptions to begin with, and you should have questioned his motives from the beginning, especially when his version of events *so drastically contradicted what you knew before. And even if you did not know Joe to be behind this, you should still have known me incapable of what I was supposedly doing...*

Whatever. So be it. I hope this letter will set things right, though I doubt it will...

The reason I present this herein should be plain – I am not publishing this volume to cause harm to either Daughter 1 nor Mara. I have never had a reason to seek harm against them – and I certainly have had an abundance of opportunity to do so. Kalispell is not that big – I met people who knew Mara who told me where she lived, worked and hung out recreationally. Yet never once did I seek her out. The same was true of Daughter 1 – if I had wanted to find her, I could have. I ran into her friends from school and could very easily have backtracked through them to her if that had been my intent. It was not, and therefore I never even tried. I even discouraged people from doing it on my behalf.

So here we are, finally arrived at the end of this volume. I have presented a great deal herein, and I hope I have done a job sufficient enough to prove the premise I set out to establish. I set out at the beginning of this not only to profess my innocence – and to prove it through documentation, records and laws – but also to warn anyone and everyone of the real criminals operating in Kalispell and Flathead County.

I said at the beginning that the corruption goes all the way to the state level here in Montana, and I certainly experienced that first-hand once I was in the prison system. But I do not believe that going into those details herein serve a purpose towards my objective. Those details are far more general – aimed at inmates and citizens as a whole rather than at me personally – and if I do set them forth, I do not believe they belong in a volume dedicated to my own struggles for liberty and identity.

In closing, I want to make something crystal clear – this corrupt regime in Kalispell and Flathead County did not come into existence just to fight me. This is not a case of political opponents setting aside their differences to fight a common enemy. This power block of corruption was already in place and had been operating under the radar for at least twenty years (I have heard much through rumor that it has always been this way, just with different figureheads at different points in history). All that needed to be done was for Frank Garner to throw out his flares for help, and the rest of his corrupt mafia rushed forward to defend him and his misconduct.

The bottom line is that all of this started with Frank Garner. Yes, there were the Nezats and their false accusations. There was Daughter 1 and her propensity to lie. There were city and county officials harassing my business. But all of that were passing annoyances. They all would have passed and life would have continued. But Frank Garner went further. He went beyond just harassing to outright destruction.

Ultimately, Frank Garner is primarily responsible for the escalation of this to a lawsuit, to Daughter 1 and Daughter 2 being kidnapped, to my arrest and conviction, and to all I have suffered since. If he had not vindictively gone after me and my family, there would never have been a lawsuit – the insurance company was ready to settle. If he had not had Mara's daughters kidnapped, or called upon his court friends to block the default judgment, the issues could easily have resolved themselves even after the suit was filed.

But Frank Garner was an egotist. He had to exert his power and prove he alone was in power and that I was powerless. He had to flex his muscles and show exactly how much corrupt influence he had, and precisely how ruthless he could be to exact revenge against someone trying to hold him or his department accountable for wrongdoing.

Yes – though there were other actors who preceded Frank Garner is getting the ball rolling, so to speak, the ball would have eventually come to a stop on its own. But Garner had to load the ball into a cannon and fire it through the wall of my house – just to prove he was above the law. And he proved it quite effectively. He proved he could commit any atrocity, any crime, any unethical or immoral act and not only get away with it – but revel in the sheer joy of getting away with it.

Power corrupts, and absolute power corrupts absolutely. And Frank Garner was a man with absolute power who was not afraid of causing malicious harm to anyone who did not let him do whatever he wanted, legal or otherwise. And the irony that he was actually the Chief of Police – charged with serving and protecting citizens – only makes this all the more sadistic on his part.

So this volume is not directed at Garner alone – I am wanting this to impact *all* corrupt officials in Kalispell and Flathead County government. This being said though, as I write this, Garner's potential elevation to a position of state power is by far the most urgent matter that needs addressed.

I am here. I remain. For now. I can only hope that what I say does not get buried by the mountains of garbage that will now be thrown my way to discourage people from even looking at this...

Remember the Robert Heinlein quote I opened with – do not let these people tell you what you can see, hear or know. Do not let these people be the tyrants they model themselves to be. Look, listen and – above all else – think for yourself.

If one person can walk away from this with a new understanding of how things truly are, then perhaps I can go to my grave knowing that maybe, just maybe, I may have made a difference. If not in my own life, which at the point you read this may already be lost, then perhaps in yours, the reader.

Do not allow my liberty to be sacrificed for the pretense of your own safety. Please do not let the spirit of liberty die with me...

Those who would give up essential Liberty, to purchase a little temporary Safety, deserve neither Liberty nor Safety.

- Benjamin Franklin, 1755

Afterwards

I conclude this volume on September 7, 2014. As of today, I have been a U.S. Political Prisoner of the State of Montana for over ten years.

Most will not understand the significance of this, because I am no longer in prison. But whether I am in a cell or not, I remain in state custody. I am unable to travel beyond a four county range, and I certainly cannot move away. Though my sentence called only for fifteen years of suspended time after my prison sentence, I am committed instead to both a probationary and suspended sentence simultaneously, making me subject to conditions of custody and supervision.

This likely needs some degree of explanation, as most will likely not understand the difference here. A suspended sentence is a sentence not served at the time it is imposed, while a probation sentence is one served in lieu of incarceration. In essence, a suspended sentence is not served in custody, but the full time suspended can be returned if one is convicted of a new crime, while a probation sentence is spent in custody with restrictions on liberty and does count against the time of your sentence. Pursuant to the Fifth Amendment of the United States Constitution, Double Jeopardy protects both against being twice tried for the same offense *and* not being punished twice for the same offense. Consequently, having two simultaneous sentences imposed for the same offense is a double jeopardy violation.

This being said, this is a failing of the entire Montana criminal justice system, not something manufactured against me alone. Montana uses this violation to keep convicted persons in their system indefinitely – and in many cases, for the rest of their natural lives. Since a suspended sentence is not counted off as time passes (until the full period expires) and is only returned upon the offender when a new crime is imposed, Montana uses probation violations (essentially considered misdemeanors under the law) to count as new criminal conduct in order to return convicted people back into the system for perpetual eternity.

As an example, my own sentence is twenty years with fifteen suspended. Since I am serving probation and suspended time, if a probation violation is brought against me, instead of serving thirty, sixty and ninety days as the law requires for first, second and third probationary violations, I instead would have the entire fifteen years returned to me, regardless how much time had passed. In effect, Flathead County could wait for the last day of my suspended sentence, arrest me upon a trumped up violation, and have the court condemn me to another fifteen years of probation/suspended time. It is an unending loop, and one Montana has been using for at fifty years – yet no one does anything about it, because – especially in the modern prison-for-profit system – it is just good business to keep people in the system.

I heard a statistic repeated the other day that I have heard consistently over the last ten years – the United States has more people in prison or jail than any other country in the world, roughly 1 out of every 100 citizens. We *are* a police state – and Montana takes that status and raises it to a gestapo level. Plain and simple.

I only take the time in explaining this now to make one point clear – unless something unforeseen transpires, I will likely remain a political prisoner for the rest of my days. These people manufactured a full-fledged felony against me once – how hard does one think it would be to frame me for a simple probation violation? Oh, guess what – this guy over here who does not want to go to jail says he saw you in a bar drinking, so now you are going back to prison for fifteen years! And yes, it is that simple.

Oh, and yes – I cannot drink or frequent bars or casinos while on probation. I also cannot go to churches, parks, the county fair or any public place where children might be congregating. And those are just conditions related to everyone who has committed a sex offense in the state. I actually have had conditions placed upon me that are on not a single other person in Flathead County - I cannot date anyone with children (not just minors, adult children, as well) – and at 45, how easy does one think it is to find someone my own age who does not have children? I cannot go to McDonald's or Dairy Queen, nor can I go to the physical therapy pool at the local gym that – by the way – is owned by the hospital as a physical therapy center (remember, I have a chronic joint pain disease, and aquatic therapy is part of my medical treatment plan). I was even forbidden to even try to find employment working with the general public, because – as was rationalized to me – if a child entered a place of business, I would be in a position of authority over them. I have even been forbidden to take over full power of attorney over my elderly grandmother.

Keep in mind – I was not accused or convicted of stalking children in public, nor even with recidivistic behavior. Nothing in the accusation contained elements of alcohol abuse nor gambling problems. And certainly none of this ever suggested that I was a danger to anyone elderly. But these impositions are imposed over me nevertheless, and most of them are put upon me alone. For instance, I rank as what is known as a Level 1 sex offender, the lowest risk of reoffense (because there is no such thing as a Level 0) and am not allowed to even enter McDonald's, while Level 2 offenders are allowed to work there. I am not allowed to act as power of attorney for my grandmother, but I know a Level 2 offender who caretakes two elderly relatives in his own home.

I have said over and again – this has never been about me committing a crime. My penalties are grossly disproportionate to anyone else's convicted of even worse things – even people convicted of incest and rape have less restrictions upon them than I do. And the probation department is always finding new ways to tweak the restrictions I have to further limit what I can do and how I can function in life.

And, unlike other offenders, I will never be permitted to leave this region ever again; in spite of pretense to the contrary, the expressed "concern" is that because I resisted returning to Flathead County once, if I were permitted to leave, I would flee and they would have to waste time finding me and returning me to Flathead County. I can go through the process – pay the fee (yes, they charge for permission to transfer) and have the application rejected every time, because I have been told – quite bluntly – that Flathead County will never let me go.

And so, after spending five years in prison, I am now confined to living an impoverished life under the thumb of the very people who manufactured this crime against me in the first place. Ironically enough, I was eligible for parole before I even saw trial, since one becomes eligible for parole after a fourth of your sentence, and for me that was at fifteen months (I spent sixteen months waiting for trial) – but then had to wait still an additional year because Montana would not release me without completing sex offender classes (that could have been completed in community). I then was passed over twice by the parole board because I would not "take responsibility for [my] crime", meaning I spent my entire five year sentence behind bars. When I was released, I was subjected almost immediately to a new threat of incarceration, spending six more weeks in jail.

Now I have been out for five years, and I remain under constant fear of the authorities deciding they have had enough of me and either returning me to prison or just doing away with me as they did Allen. Though the authorities these days do not actively throw obstacles in my way, their work of the past still has me boxed in a corner. And these people have spent so much time vilifying me in this community, that more often than not, I *do* get recognized. I even had someone posting regular comments publicly on Craigslist warning people to stay away from me. Yes, by name, ie, "Beware of Ron Glick – he is a dangerous rapist" type messages.

Whereas once I lived a life of confidence and upward mobility, I now have to be fearful every time I am in the grocery store if a child walks into my aisle, or every time I go to dinner and children sit by me. I used to run a youth recreations program and loved being around children – now I have to be afraid. Not of them, but of their parents or anyone else in this community who might recognize me and accuse me of something. And worse, I know there never actually has to be anything close to a real event – just scare someone enough, child or adult, give them an incentive, and they will readily make up a story to save themselves. So even being the most careful I can possibly be, I am still subject to being accused again. And that fear is not good for my health, considering my disease. But I live with it every. Single. Day.

This being said, I have not let this affair completely defeat me. I have begun to pursue my writing again. I presently have six novels and eleven trivia books published (this will make my eighteenth unique publication, in fact). I continue to help people in whatever way I can, whether it is helping them with filing legal papers as an advocate, a computer tech, or just general assistance in whatever area I can. I never bill for my help, and my books do not sell hardly at all (marketing is an incredibly hard thing to work on without money, I have found out).

As I have mentioned before, I am disabled, so I live on a measly seven hundred, twenty-one dollars a month, with a paltry seventy-eight dollars in food stamps added on. After bills are paid each month, I am lucky to have thirty to forty dollars disposable income a month, which is generally gone by the middle of the month. I used to run businesses and help the community – now I barely help myself financially. But as I have said, I continue to help where I can.

Part of the destitution is because of my disability – spending five years imprisoned without any form of treatment and now being denied even physical therapy on the outside takes its toll. But a larger part are the restrictions imposed upon me. I am unable to travel, which means I cannot go to events across the nation to promote my books. In the last year, I have received four separate invitations to appear at conventions around the country, one as a featured author, and I have to decline all of them because I am not allowed to travel or be at a gathering where children congregate. I am not allowed at a fair, does one honestly believe these people would let me go to a science fiction convention to promote myself? I am forbidden to even work in the public or at a call center – how could I ever be permitted to sit at a table and sign books for people at a convention?

I have been telling people this story for a decade now. And every time I tell it, one detail or another keeps drawing out the comment, "They can't do that." They could not keep someone in jail for sixteen months without a trial, but they did. They cannot keep someone from going to a fast food restaurant, but they have. They cannot keep you from medical treatment, and yet I am forbidden to go where it is provided.

And in each instance, I say the same thing – But. They. Have.

Perhaps during the course of this volume, the reader might have asked something similar, such as, "How is it possible that so many crooked people could exist?" or perhaps, "How is it that one person is right and insist that so many others are wrong?" All I can say to these is that when there is no checks and balances enforced against corruption, it breeds more corruption. When abuse and racketeering become common practice within government and no one punishes them, the people who are in power have no reason to curb their misconduct. And corruption draws others who support the ideals of corruption, bringing people from outside the area to reinforce the preferred status quo. And should anyone try to stand up, they just get run off the field.

When children have no boundaries and have no accountability for what they do wrong, they become uncontrollable – and this is really no different. These people gain power, money, influence and more through maintaining a criminal empire hidden behind the doors of government – and no one dares to stand up for fear of having their lives destroyed. Just like what happened to me.

Remember – Frank Allen died because he tried to work the system for his own advantage. There was nothing protecting him, and so he was an easy target to just kill. My voice – being loud and outspoken – until now has been my only shield. Who knows if it will keep me from harm after this, though.

In my case, this has never been about what is legal, what is right, nor even about punishing me for an actual crime. Oh, it *is* about punishment – it is about punishing me for standing up under my First Amendment rights to bring complaint against government without molestation. And yet, I am living proof that this so-called liberty does not truly exist. Not for me, and not in Kalispell, Montana.

I do the best I can. I continue to speak the truth and help make a difference where I can. It is all I can do. Be myself, and not be the person these true criminals would have others believe me to be. No matter what people like Frank Garner, or Dave Edwards, or Lori Adams, or anyone else says – I *am* a good man. And I will not let these lying Mafiosos change who I am by telling others lies about me.

The reason I emphasize this here at the end has purpose. As I write this, Frank Garner is presently running to be the House Representative for District 7 in the Montana Congress. He is a man of unscrupulous ethics and decrepit moral caliber – yet he has prevailed through the primaries and stands poised to take the election because this is a largely Republican district, and he is running as a Republican.

I am hoping that this volume will do more than prove my innocence – I am also hoping that it will help to dethrone people like Garner, to keep them from positions of power and authority where they can continue to use their power to hurt rather than protect the citizens of Montana.

As I said – Garner is not alone in this. He did not act alone, nor did he start this, though he was the primary reason this escalated beyond a point where it could be quietly settled, and whom I place primary blame in initiating the vendetta against me that ruined my life. There were other players involved, people who took up the charge in order to shelter him from harm later, just as there were lesser opponents before he got directly involved. I say that all the major effects happened because of Garner – and that is true – but his evil could not exist without others bolstering him up, people who not only ignored his criminal misconduct in office, but rewarded him for it in return.

This is why I am putting this volume out at this time. I had hoped to hold off and publish this story one day when and if I cleared my name. After all, in putting this out while I am still within this corrupt authorities' power and control, I am taking a huge risk. I am literally begging these people to eliminate me.

But considering the consequences if I remained silent – well, I just could not do that in good conscience.

And this is not the complete, unabridged edition either. This volume is already exceeding 400 pages, and there comes a point when I have to stop. There are more records, pleadings and records that I could have referenced and included – but I would have had to literally publish a set of these books that would just have been impossible to put forth at once. I was selective – I chose each record here with care – but please understand that this is not even close to a full accounting of the records I have. And anyone wishing to review what I have is more that willing to ask for them. I just cannot possibly include everything here.

I implore to whomever reads this – do not ignore what I have said. Do not let my example fall of deaf ears. Stand up and do something about this – if not here in Kalispell, then in your own city, county, state or country. Doing this – taking this step in speaking out in this way – is possibly the most terrifying thing I have ever done. I have definitely placed a huge target on my back.

But I need to get up every day and look myself in the mirror. And I have to answer to the man looking back at me. And quite frankly, I just cannot face that man if I knew I had the power to speak out and did not.

It is as I have said – the one thing these people cannot take away from me is that I am a good man. I can only hope that when this settles, that will have been enough.

For anyone who might wish to use this volume for legal purposes, I do hereby declare, under penalty of perjury, that by affixing my name hereto that the contents of this volume are true and correct to the best of my ability to present.

/s/ Ron Glick
September 7, 2014

Appendix 1

Following are relevant areas of Montana law, published in codice form as Montana Code Annotated (MCA). For the purposes of this appendix, the redundant language of "MCA §" has been omitted, but each entry should be assumed to start with this legal reference. Also, Montana Rules of Civil Procedure (MRCP) are in the code as Title 25, Chapter 20, which would translate to MCA § 25-20-101, et seq., and Montana Rules of Evidence (MRE) are in the code as Title 26, Chapter 10, which would translate to MCA § 26-10-100, et al., so where references to MRE are made, the original citation address is listed herein for organizational purposes, and are not identified as MRE specifically. Where possible, areas not relevant have been redacted with […] to conserve space.

The codes herein are presented numerically, as opposed to the order they are introduced in the preceding content of this volume. I am hoping this will be an easier way to reference them.

25-1-1101. Registered process server...: (1) ...[A] person who makes more than 10 services of process... within this state during 1 calendar year must be registered under Title 37, chapter 60.

25-20-Rule 4: Persons Subject to Jurisdiction; Process; Service.

[…]

(c) Summons.

(1) Issuance. [...] Upon request, the clerk must issue separate or additional summons against any parties designated in the original action or any additional parties who may be brought into the action...

25-20-Rule 5(e): Filing with the court defined. The filing of papers with the court as required by these rules shall be made by filing them with the clerk of the court, except that the judge may permit the papers to be filed with the judge, in which event the judge shall note thereon the filing date and forthwith transmit them to the office of the clerk.[89]

25-20-Rule 55: Entering a Default. When a party against whom a judgment for affirmative relief is sought has failed to plead or otherwise defend, and that failure is shown by affidavit or otherwise, the clerk must enter the party's default.

25-20-Rule 77(a) District courts always open. The district courts shall be deemed always open for the purpose of filing any pleading or other proper paper, of issuing and returning mesne and final process, and of making and directing all interlocutory motions, orders, and rules.

---

[89] This particular rule has been rewritten since the dates at issue in this volume. It is now innumerated as Rule 5(d) and is greatly simplified, but the context is identical to the law presented here that was in effect in 2003. Montana law still requires that documents must be filed with the court clerk or with a judge who then shall transmit them to the clerk.

26-10-402 [MRE Rule 402]. Relevant evidence generally admissible; irrelevant evidence inadmissible.

All relevant evidence is admissible, except as otherwise provided by constitution, statute, these rules, or other rules applicable in the courts of this state. Evidence which is not relevant is not admissible.

26-10-801 [MRE Rule 801]. Definitions.

The following definitions apply under this article:

[...]

(c) Hearsay. Hearsay is a statement, other than one made by the declarant while testifying at the trial or hearing, offered in evidence to prove the truth of the matter asserted.

(d) Statements which are not hearsay. A statement is not hearsay if:

(1) Prior statement by witness. The declarant testifies at the trial or hearing and is subject to cross-examination concerning the statement, and the statement is (A) inconsistent with the declarant's testimony, or (B) consistent with the declarant's testimony and is offered to rebut an express or implied charge against the declarant of subsequent fabrication, improper influence or motive, or (C) one of identification of a person made after perceiving the person; or

(2) Admission by party-opponent. The statement is offered against a party and is (A) the party's own statement, in either an individual or a representative capacity, or (B) a statement of

which the party has manifested an adoption or belief in its truth, or (C) a statement by a person authorized by the party to make a statement concerning the subject, or (D) a statement by the party's agent or servant concerning a matter within the scope of the agency or employment, made during the existence of that relationship, or (E) a statement by a coconspirator of a party during the course and in furtherance of the conspiracy.

26-10-802 [MRE Rule 802]. Hearsay rule.

Hearsay is not admissible except as otherwise provided by statute, these rules, or other rules applicable in the courts of this state.

26-10-804 [MRE Rule 804]. Hearsay exceptions: declarant unavailable.

(a) Definition of unavailability. Unavailability as a witness includes situations in which the declarant:

(1) is exempted by ruling of the court on the ground of privilege from testifying concerning the subject matter of the declarant's statement; or

(2) persists in refusing to testify concerning the subject matter of the declarant's statement despite an order of the court to do so; or

(3) testifies to a lack of memory of the subject matter of the declarant's statement; or

(4) is unable to be present or to testify at the hearing because of death or then existing physical or mental illness or infirmity; or

(5) is absent from the hearing and the proponent of the declarant's statement has been unable to procure the declarant's attendance by process or other reasonable means.

A declarant is not unavailable as a witness if exemption, refusal, claim of lack of memory, inability, or absence is due to the procurement or wrongdoing of the proponent of a statement for the purpose of preventing the witness from attending or testifying.

(b) Hearsay exceptions. The following are not excluded by the hearsay rule if the declarant is unavailable as a witness:

(1) Former testimony. Testimony given as a witness at another hearing of the same or a different proceeding, or in a deposition taken in compliance with law in the course of the same or another proceeding, (A) in civil actions and proceedings, at the instance of or against a party with an opportunity to develop the testimony by direct, cross, or redirect examination, with motive and interest similar to those of the party against whom now offered; and (B) in criminal actions and proceedings, if the party against whom the testimony is now offered had an opportunity and similar motive to develop the testimony by direct, cross, and redirect examination.

(2) Statement under belief of impending death. A statement made by a declarant while believing that the declarant's death was imminent, concerning the cause or circumstance of what the declarant believed to be impending death.

(3) Statement against interest. A statement which was at the time of its making so far contrary to the declarant's pecuniary or proprietary interest, or so far tended to subject the declarant to

civil or criminal liability, or to render invalid a claim by the declarant against another or to make the declarant an object of hatred, ridicule, or disgrace, that a reasonable person in the declarant's position would not have made the statement unless the declarant believed it to be true. A statement tending to expose the declarant to criminal liability and offered to exculpate the accused is not admissible unless corroborating circumstances clearly indicate the trustworthiness of the statement.

(4) Statement of personal or family history. (A) A statement concerning the declarant's own birth, adoption, marriage, divorce or dissolution of marriage, legitimacy, relationship by blood, or family history, even though the declarant had no means of acquiring the personal knowledge of the matter stated; or

(B) a statement concerning the foregoing matters, and death also, of another person, if the declarant was related to the other by blood, adoption or marriage or was so intimately associated with the other's family as to be likely to have accurate information concerning the matter declared.

Other exceptions. A statement not specifically covered by any of the foregoing exceptions but having comparable circumstantial guarantees of trustworthiness.

41-3-201. Reports. (1) When the professionals and officials listed in subsection (2) know or have reasonable cause to suspect, as a result of information they receive in their professional or official capacity, that a child is abused or neglected by anyone regardless of whether the person suspected of causing the abuse or neglect is a parent or other person responsible for the child's welfare, they shall report the matter promptly to the department of public health and human services.

(2) Professionals and officials required to report are:

[...]

(g) a peace officer or other law enforcement official;

[...]

41-3-202. Action on reporting. (1) Upon receipt of a report that a child is or has been abused or neglected, the department shall promptly assess the information contained in the report and make a determination regarding the level of response required and the timeframe within which action must be initiated. If the department determines that an investigation is required, a social worker, the county attorney, or a peace officer shall promptly conduct a thorough investigation into the circumstances surrounding the allegations of abuse or neglect of the child. The investigation may include an investigation at the home of the child involved, the child's school or day-care facility, or any other place where the child is present and into all other nonfinancial matters that in the discretion of the investigator are relevant to the investigation. In conducting an investigation under this section, a social worker may not inquire into the financial status of the child's family or of any other person responsible for the child's care, except as necessary to ascertain eligibility for state or federal assistance programs or to comply with the provisions of 41-3-446.

(2) An initial investigation of alleged abuse or neglect may be conducted when an anonymous report is received. However, the investigation must within 48 hours result in the development of independent, corroborative, and attributable information in order

for the investigation to continue. Without the development of independent, corroborative, and attributable information, a child may not be removed from the home.

The social worker is responsible for assessing the family and planning for the child. If the child is treated at a medical facility, the social worker, county attorney, or peace officer, consistent with reasonable medical practice, has the right of access to the child for interviews, photographs, and securing physical evidence and has the right of access to relevant hospital and medical records pertaining to the child. If an interview of the child is considered necessary, the social worker, county attorney, or peace officer may conduct an interview of the child. The interview may be conducted in the presence of the parent or guardian or an employee of the school or day-care facility attended by the child.
Subject to 41-3-205(3), if the child's interview is audiotaped or videotaped, an unedited audiotape or videotape with audio track must be made available, upon request, for unencumbered review by the family.

(5) (a) If from the investigation the department has reasonable cause to suspect that the child suffered abuse or neglect, the department may provide emergency protective services to the child, pursuant to 41-3-301, or voluntary protective services pursuant to 41-3-302, and may provide protective services to any other child under the same care. The department shall:

(i) after interviewing the parent or guardian, if reasonably available, document its determination regarding abuse or neglect of a child; and

(ii) notify the child's family of its investigation and determination, unless the notification can reasonably be expected to result in harm to the child or other person.

(b) If from the investigation it is determined that the child has not suffered abuse or neglect and the initial report is determined to be unfounded, the department and the social worker, county attorney, or peace officer who conducted the investigation into the circumstances surrounding the allegations of abuse or neglect shall destroy all of their records concerning the report and the investigation. The destruction must be completed within 30 days of the determination that the child has not suffered abuse or neglect.

(c) (i) If the report is unsubstantiated, the department and the social worker who conducted the investigation into the circumstances surrounding the initial allegations of abuse or neglect shall destroy all of the records, except for medical records, concerning the unsubstantiated report and the investigation within 30 days after the end of the 3-year period starting from the date the report was determined to be unsubstantiated, unless:

(A) there had been a previous or there is a subsequent substantiated report concerning the same person; or
(B) an order has been issued under this chapter based on the circumstances surrounding the initial allegations.

(ii) A person who is the subject of an unsubstantiated report that was made prior to October 1, 2003, and after which a period of 3 years has elapsed without there being submitted a subsequent substantiated report or an order issued under this chapter based on the circumstances surrounding the initial allegations may request that the department destroy all of the records concerning the unsubstantiated report as provided in subsection (5)(c)(i).

(6) The investigating social worker, within 60 days of commencing an investigation, shall also furnish a written report to the department and, upon request, to the family. Subject to subsections (5)(b) and (5)(c), the department shall maintain a record system documenting investigations and determinations of child abuse and neglect cases.

(7) Any person reporting abuse or neglect that involves acts or omissions on the part of a public or private residential institution, home, facility, or agency is responsible for ensuring that the report is made to the department.

41-3-301. Emergency protective service. (1) Any child protective social worker of the department, a peace officer, or the county attorney who has reason to believe any child is in immediate or apparent danger of harm may immediately remove the child and place the child in a protective facility. After ensuring that the child is safe, the department may make a request for further assistance from the law enforcement agency or take appropriate legal action. The person or agency placing the child shall notify the parents, parent, guardian, or other person having physical or legal custody of the child of the placement at the time the placement is made or as soon after placement as possible. Notification under this subsection must include the reason for removal, information regarding the show cause hearing, and the purpose of the show cause hearing and must advise the parents, parent, guardian, or other person having physical or legal custody of the child that the parents, parent, guardian, or other person may have a support person present during any in-person meeting with the social worker concerning emergency protective services.

(2) If a social worker of the department, a peace officer, or the county attorney determines in an investigation of abuse or neglect of a child that the child is in danger because of the occurrence of partner or family member assault, as provided for in 45-5-206, against an adult member of the household or that the child needs protection as a result of the occurrence of partner or family member assault against an adult member of the household, the department shall take appropriate steps for the protection of the child, which may include:

(a) making reasonable efforts to protect the child and prevent the removal of the child from the parent or guardian who is a victim of alleged partner or family member assault;
(b) making reasonable efforts to remove the person who allegedly committed the partner or family member assault from the child's residence if it is determined that the child or another family or household member is in danger of partner or family member assault; and
(c) providing services to help protect the child from being placed with or having unsupervised visitation with the person alleged to have committed partner or family member assault until the department determines that the alleged offender has met conditions considered necessary to protect the safety of the child.

(3) If the department determines that an adult member of the household is the victim of partner or family member assault, the department shall provide the adult victim with a referral to a domestic violence program.

(4) A child who has been removed from the child's home or any other place for the child's protection or care may not be placed in a jail.

(5) The department may locate and contact extended family members upon placement of a child in out-of-home care. The department may share information with extended family members for placement and case planning purposes.

(6) If a child is removed from the child's home by the department, a child protective social worker shall submit an affidavit regarding the circumstances of the emergency removal to the county attorney and provide a copy of the affidavit to the parents or guardian, if possible, within 2 working days of the emergency removal. An abuse and neglect petition must be filed within 5 working days, excluding weekends and holidays, of the emergency removal of a child unless arrangements acceptable to the agency for the care of the child have been made by the parents or voluntary protective services are provided pursuant to 41-3-302.

(7) Except as provided in the federal Indian Child Welfare Act, if applicable, a show cause hearing must be held within 20 days of the filing of the petition unless otherwise stipulated by the parties pursuant to 41-3-434.

(8) If the department determines that a petition for immediate protection and emergency protective services must be filed to protect the safety of the child, the social worker shall interview the parents of the child to whom the petition pertains, if the parents are reasonably available, before the petition may be filed. The district court may immediately issue an order for immediate protection of the child.

(9) The department shall make the necessary arrangements for the child's well-being as are required prior to the court hearing.

41-3-422. Abuse and neglect petitions -- burden of proof. (1) (a) Proceedings under this chapter must be initiated by the filing of a petition. A petition may request the following relief:

(i) immediate protection and emergency protective services, as provided in 41-3-427;
(ii) temporary investigative authority, as provided in 41-3-433;
(iii) temporary legal custody, as provided in 41-3-442;
(iv) long-term custody, as provided in 41-3-445;
(v) termination of the parent child legal relationship, as provided in 41-3-607;
(vi) appointment of a guardian pursuant to 41-3-444;
(vii) a determination that preservation or reunification services need not be provided; or
(viii) any combination of the provisions of subsections (1)(a)(i) through (1)(a)(vii) or any other relief that may be required for the best interests of the child.

(b) The petition may be modified for different relief at any time within the discretion of the court.

(c) A petition for temporary legal custody may be the initial petition filed in a case.

(d) A petition for the termination of the parent-child legal relationship may be the initial petition filed in a case if a request for a determination that preservation or reunification services need not be provided is made in the petition.

(2) The county attorney, attorney general, or an attorney hired by the county shall file all petitions under this chapter. A petition filed by the county attorney, attorney general, or an attorney hired by the county must be accompanied by:

(a) an affidavit by the department alleging that the child appears to have been abused or neglected and stating the basis for the petition; and
(b) a separate notice to the court stating any statutory time deadline for a hearing.

(3) Abuse and neglect petitions must be given highest preference by the court in setting hearing dates.

(4) An abuse and neglect petition is a civil action brought in the name of the state of Montana. The Montana Rules of Civil Procedure and the Montana Rules of Evidence apply except as modified in this chapter. Proceedings under a petition are not a bar to criminal prosecution.

(5) (a) Except as provided in subsection (5)(b), the person filing the abuse and neglect petition has the burden of presenting evidence required to justify the relief requested and establishing:

(i) probable cause for the issuance of an order for immediate protection and emergency protective services or an order for temporary investigative authority;
(ii) a preponderance of the evidence for an order of adjudication or temporary legal custody;
(iii) a preponderance of the evidence for an order of long-term custody; or

(iv) clear and convincing evidence for an order terminating the parent-child legal relationship.

[...]

(6) (a) Except as provided in the federal Indian Child Welfare Act, if applicable, the parents or parent, guardian, or other person or agency having legal custody of the child named in the petition, if residing in the state, must be served personally with a copy of the initial petition and a petition to terminate the parent-child legal relationship at least 5 days before the date set for hearing. If the person or agency cannot be served personally, the person or agency may be served by publication as provided in 41-3-428 and 41-3-429.

(b) Copies of all other petitions must be served upon the person or the person's attorney of record by certified mail, by personal service, or by publication as provided in 41-3-428 and 41-3-429. If service is by certified mail, the department must receive a return receipt signed by the person to whom the notice was mailed for the service to be effective. Service of the notice is considered to be effective if, in the absence of a return receipt, the person to whom the notice was mailed appears at the hearing.

(7) If personal service cannot be made upon the parents or parent, guardian, or other person or agency having legal custody, the court shall immediately provide for the appointment or assignment of an attorney as provided for in 41-3-425 to represent the unavailable party when, in the opinion of the court, the interests of justice require.

(8) If a parent of the child is a minor, notice must be given to the minor parent's parents or guardian, and if there is no guardian, the court shall appoint one.

(9) (a) Any person interested in any cause under this chapter has the right to appear. Any foster parent, preadoptive parent, or relative caring for the child must be given legal notice by the attorney filing the petition of all judicial hearings for the child and has the right to be heard. The right to appear or to be heard does not make that person a party to the action. Any foster parent, preadoptive parent, or relative caring for the child must be given notice of all reviews by the reviewing body.

(b) A foster parent, preadoptive parent, or relative of the child who is caring for or a relative of the child who has cared for a child who is the subject of the petition who appears at a hearing set pursuant to this section may be allowed by the court to intervene in the action if the court, after a hearing in which evidence is presented on those subjects provided for in 41-3-437(4), determines that the intervention of the person is in the best interests of the child. A person granted intervention pursuant to this subsection is entitled to participate in the adjudicatory hearing held pursuant to 41-3-437 and to notice and participation in subsequent proceedings held pursuant to this chapter involving the custody of the child.

(10) An abuse and neglect petition must:

(a) state the nature of the alleged abuse or neglect and of the relief requested;
(b) state the full name, age, and address of the child and the name and address of the child's parents or guardian or person having legal custody of the child;

(c) state the names, addresses, and relationship to the child of all persons who are necessary parties to the action.

(11) Any party in a proceeding pursuant to this section is entitled to counsel as provided in 41-3-425.

(12) At any stage of the proceedings considered appropriate by the court, the court may order an alternative dispute resolution proceeding or the parties may voluntarily participate in an alternative dispute resolution proceeding. An alternative dispute resolution proceeding under this chapter may include a family group decisionmaking meeting, mediation, or a settlement conference. If a court orders an alternative dispute resolution proceeding, a party who does not wish to participate may file a motion objecting to the order. If the department is a party to the original proceeding, a representative of the department who has complete authority to settle the issue or issues in the original proceeding must be present at any alternative dispute resolution proceeding.

(13) Service of a petition under this section must be accompanied by a written notice advising the child's parent, guardian, or other person having physical or legal custody of the child of the:

(a) right, pursuant to 41-3-425, to appointment or assignment of counsel if the person is indigent or if appointment or assignment of counsel is required under the federal Indian Child Welfare Act, if applicable;
(b) right to contest the allegations in the petition; and
(c) timelines for hearings and determinations required under this chapter.

(14) If appropriate, orders issued under this chapter must contain a notice provision advising a child's parent, guardian, or other person having physical or legal custody of the child that:

(a) the court is required by federal and state laws to hold a permanency hearing to determine the permanent placement of a child no later than 12 months after a judge determines that the child has been abused or neglected or 12 months after the first 60 days that the child has been removed from the child's home;

(b) if a child has been in foster care for 15 of the last 22 months, state law presumes that termination of parental rights is in the best interests of the child and the state is required to file a petition to terminate parental rights; and

(c) completion of a treatment plan does not guarantee the return of a child.

[...]

41-3-423. Reasonable efforts required to prevent removal of child or to return -- exemption -- findings -- permanency plan. (1) The department shall make reasonable efforts to prevent the necessity of removal of a child from the child's home and to reunify families that have been separated by the state. Reasonable efforts include but are not limited to voluntary protective services agreements, development of individual written case plans specifying state efforts to reunify families, placement in the least disruptive setting possible, provision of services pursuant to a case plan, and periodic review of each case to ensure timely progress toward reunification or permanent placement. In determining preservation or reunification services to be provided and in making reasonable efforts at providing preservation or reunification services, the child's health and safety are of paramount concern.

(2) Except in a proceeding subject to the federal Indian Child Welfare Act, the department may, at any time during an abuse and neglect proceeding, make a request for a determination that preservation or reunification services need not be provided. If an indigent parent is not already represented by counsel, the court shall immediately provide for the appointment or assignment of counsel to represent the indigent parent in accordance with the provisions of 41-3-425. A court may make a finding that the department need not make reasonable efforts to provide preservation or reunification services if the court finds that the parent has:

(a) subjected a child to aggravated circumstances, including but not limited to abandonment, torture, chronic abuse, or sexual abuse or chronic, severe neglect of a child;

(b) committed, aided, abetted, attempted, conspired, or solicited deliberate or mitigated deliberate homicide of a child;

(c) committed aggravated assault against a child;

(d) committed neglect of a child that resulted in serious bodily injury or death; or

(e) had parental rights to the child's sibling or other child of the parent involuntarily terminated and the circumstances related to the termination of parental rights are relevant to the parent's ability to adequately care for the child at issue.

[...]

(4) A judicial finding that preservation or reunification services are not necessary under this section must be supported by clear and convincing evidence.

(5) If the court finds that preservation or reunification services are not necessary pursuant to subsection (2) or (3), a permanency hearing must be held within 30 days of that determination and reasonable efforts, including consideration of both in-state and out-of-state permanent placement options for the child, must be made to place the child in a timely manner in accordance with the permanency plan and to complete whatever steps are necessary to finalize the permanent placement of the child.

(6) If reasonable efforts have been made to prevent removal of a child from the home or to return a child to the child's home but continuation of the efforts is determined by the court to be inconsistent with the permanency plan for the child, the department shall make reasonable efforts to place the child in a timely manner in accordance with the permanency plan, including, if appropriate, placement in another state, and to complete whatever steps are necessary to finalize the permanent placement of the child. Reasonable efforts to place a child permanently for adoption or to make an alternative out-of-home permanent placement may be made concurrently with reasonable efforts to return a child to the child's home. Concurrent planning, including identifying in-state and out-of-state placements, may be used.

(7) When determining whether the department has made reasonable efforts to prevent the necessity of removal of a child from the child's home or to reunify families that have been separated by the state, the court shall review the services

provided by the agency including, if applicable, protective services provided pursuant to 41-3-302.

41-3-425. Right to counsel. (1) Any party involved in a petition filed pursuant to 41-3-422 has the right to counsel in all proceedings held pursuant to the petition.

(2) Except as provided in subsections (3) and (4), the court shall immediately appoint the office of state public defender to assign counsel for:

(a) any indigent parent, guardian, or other person having legal custody of a child or youth in a removal, placement, or termination proceeding pursuant to 41-3-422, pending a determination of eligibility pursuant to 47-1-111...

41-3-427. Petition for immediate protection and emergency protective services -- order -- service. (1) (a) In a case in which it appears that a child is abused or neglected or is in danger of being abused or neglected, the county attorney, the attorney general, or an attorney hired by the county may file a petition for immediate protection and emergency protective services. In implementing the policy of this section, the child's health and safety are of paramount concern.

(b) A petition for immediate protection and emergency protective services must state the specific authority requested and must be supported by an affidavit signed by a representative of the department stating in detail the alleged facts upon which the request is based and the facts establishing probable cause or, if the case is subject to the federal Indian Child Welfare Act, clear and convincing evidence that a child is abused or neglected or is in danger of being abused or neglected. The affidavit of the department representative must contain information, if any, regarding statements made by the parents about the facts of the case.

(c) If from the alleged facts presented in the affidavit it appears to the court that there is probable cause or, if the case is subject to the federal Indian Child Welfare Act, clear and convincing evidence to believe that the child has been abused or neglected or is in danger of being abused and neglected, the judge shall grant emergency protective services and the relief authorized by subsection (2) until the adjudication hearing or the temporary investigative hearing. If it appears from the alleged facts contained in the affidavit that there is insufficient probable cause or, if the case is subject to the federal Indian Child Welfare Act, clear and convincing evidence to believe that the child has been abused or neglected or is in danger of being abused or neglected, the court shall dismiss the petition.

(d) If the parents, parent, guardian, person having physical or legal custody of the child, or attorney for the child disputes the material issues of fact contained in the affidavit or the veracity of the affidavit, the person may request a contested show cause hearing pursuant to 41-3-432 within 10 days following service of the petition and affidavit.

(e) The petition for immediate protection and emergency protective services must include a notice advising the parents, parent, guardian, or other person having physical or legal custody of the child that the parents, parent, guardian, or other person having physical or legal custody of the child may have a support person present during any in-person meeting with a social worker concerning emergency protective services. Reasonable accommodation must be made in scheduling an in-person meeting with the social worker.

(2) Pursuant to subsection (1), if the court finds probable cause or, if the case is subject to the federal Indian Child Welfare Act, clear and convincing evidence based on the petition and affidavit, the court may issue an order for immediate protection of the child. The court shall consider the parents' statements, if any, included with the petition and any accompanying affidavit or report to the court. If the court finds probable cause or, if the case is subject to the federal Indian Child Welfare Act, clear and convincing evidence, the court may issue an order granting the following forms of relief, which do not constitute a court-ordered treatment plan under 41-3-443:

(a) the right of entry by a peace officer or department worker;

(b) the right to place the child in temporary medical or out-of-home care, including but not limited to care provided by a noncustodial parent, kinship or foster family, group home, or institution;

(c) the right for the department to locate, contact, and share information with any extended family members who may be considered as placement options for the child;

(d) a requirement that the parents, guardian, or other person having physical or legal custody furnish information that the court may designate and obtain evaluations that may be necessary to determine whether a child is a youth in need of care;

(e) a requirement that the perpetrator of the alleged child abuse or neglect be removed from the home to allow the child to remain in the home;

(f) a requirement that the parent provide the department with the name and address of the other parent, if known, unless parental rights to the child have been terminated;

(g) a requirement that the parent provide the department with the names and addresses of extended family members who may be considered as placement options for the child who is the subject of the proceeding; and

(h) any other temporary disposition that may be required in the best interests of the child that does not require an expenditure of money by the department unless the court finds after notice and a hearing that the expenditure is reasonable and that resources are available for payment. The department is the payor of last resort after all family, insurance, and other resources have been examined.

(3) An order for removal of a child from the home must include a finding that continued residence of the child with the parent is contrary to the welfare of the child or that an out-of-home placement is in the best interests of the child.

(4) The order for immediate protection of the child must require the person served to comply immediately with the terms of the order and to appear before the court issuing the order on the date specified for a show cause hearing. Upon a failure to comply or show cause, the court may hold the person in contempt or place temporary physical custody of the child with the department until further order.

(5) The petition must be served as provided in 41-3-422.

41-3-433. Temporary investigative authority. The department may petition the court for authorization to conduct an investigation into allegations of child abuse, neglect, or abandonment when necessary. An order for temporary investigative authority may not be issued for a period longer than 90 days. The petition must be served as provided in 41-3-422.

44-5-214. Inspection or transfer of criminal history records. (1) An individual or the individual's agent may inspect any criminal history record information maintained about the individual or transfer copies of that information to any other person upon the presentation of satisfactory identification to the criminal justice agency maintaining the criminal history record information. Fingerprints may be required for identification. An agent must also submit a notarized authorization from the agent's principal or an authorization order from a district court.

[...]

(3) (a) An individual may request inspection or transfer of copies, or both, of criminal history record information only during normal working hours.

(b) Copies of records may be made by or at the request of a properly identified individual or the individual's authorized agent. If a machine for making copies is not reasonably available, the individual or the individual's agent may make handwritten copies.

A charge may be made by the agency for the cost of supplying the copies. Each copy must be clearly marked to indicate that it is for inspection only.

(c) An agency employee should be available to answer questions concerning record content. A record of each request to inspect records under this section must be maintained.

45-2-101. General definitions. Unless otherwise specified in the statute, all words must be taken in the objective standard rather than in the subjective, and unless a different meaning plainly is required, the following definitions apply in this title:

(1) "Acts" has its usual and ordinary meaning and includes any bodily movement, any form of communication, and when relevant, a failure or omission to take action.

[…]

(15) "Conduct" means an act or series of acts and the accompanying mental state.

[…]

(33) An "involuntary act" means an act that is:
(a) a reflex or convulsion;
(b) a bodily movement during unconsciousness or sleep;
(c) conduct during hypnosis or resulting from hypnotic suggestion; or
(d) a bodily movement that otherwise is not a product of the effort or determination of the actor, either conscious or habitual.

[…]

(35) "Knowingly" – a person acts knowingly with respect to conduct or to a circumstance described by a statute defining an offense when the person is aware of the person's own conduct or that the circumstance exists. A person acts knowingly with respect to the result of conduct described by a statute defining an offense when the person is aware that it is highly probable that the result will be caused by the person's conduct. When knowledge of the existence of a particular fact is an element of an offense, knowledge is established if a person is aware of a high probability of its existence. Equivalent terms, such as "knowing" or "with knowledge", have the same meaning.

[…]

(65) "Purposely"--a person acts purposely with respect to a result or to conduct described by a statute defining an offense if it is the person's conscious object to engage in that conduct or to cause that result. When a particular purpose is an element of an offense, the element is established although the purpose is conditional, unless the condition negatives the harm or evil sought to be prevented by the law defining the offense. Equivalent terms, such as "purpose" and "with the purpose", have the same meaning.

[…]

(74) "Tamper" means to interfere with something improperly, meddle with it, make unwarranted alterations in its existing condition, or deposit refuse upon it.

[…]

(76) "Threat" means a menace, however communicated, to:

(a) inflict physical harm on the person threatened or any other person or on property;

(b) subject any person to physical confinement or restraint;

(c) commit a criminal offense;

(d) accuse a person of a criminal offense;

(e) expose a person to hatred, contempt, or ridicule;

(f) harm the credit or business repute of a person;

(g) reveal information sought to be concealed by the person threatened;

(h) take action as an official against anyone or anything, withhold official action, or cause the action or withholding;

(i) bring about or continue a strike, boycott, or other similar collective action if the person making the threat demands or receives property that is not for the benefit of groups that the person purports to represent; or

(j) testify or provide information or withhold testimony or information with respect to another's legal claim or defense.

[…]

(80) "Witness" means a person whose testimony is desired in an official proceeding, in any investigation by a grand jury, or in a criminal action, prosecution, or proceeding.

45-2-103. General requirements of criminal act and mental state. (1) Except for deliberate homicide as defined in 45-5-102(1)(b) or an offense that involves absolute liability, a person is not guilty of an offense unless, with respect to each element described by the statute defining the offense, a person acts while having one of the mental states of knowingly, negligently, or purposely.

45-7-206. Tampering with witnesses and informants. (1) A person commits the offense of tampering with witnesses and informants if, believing that an official proceeding or investigation is pending or about to be instituted, the person purposely or knowingly attempts to induce or otherwise cause a witness or informant to:
(a) testify or inform falsely;
(b) withhold any testimony, information, document, or thing...

45-7-208. Tampering with public records or information. (1) A person commits the offense of tampering with public records or information if the person:
(a) knowingly makes a false entry in or false alteration of any record, document, legislative bill or enactment, or thing belonging to or received, issued, or kept by the government for information or record or required by law to be kept by others for information of the government;
(b) makes, presents, or uses any record, document, or thing knowing it to be false and with purpose that it be taken as a genuine part of information or records referred to in subsection (1)(a);
(c) purposely destroys, conceals, removes, or otherwise impairs the verity or availability of a record, document, or thing...

45-7-302. Obstructing peace officer or other public servant. (1) A person commits the offense of obstructing a peace officer or public servant if the person knowingly obstructs, impairs, or hinders the enforcement of the criminal law, the preservation of the peace, or the performance of a governmental function, including service of process.

45-7-401. Official misconduct. (1) A public servant commits the offense of official misconduct when in an official capacity the public servant commits any of the following acts:

(a) purposely or negligently fails to perform any mandatory duty as required by law or by a court of competent jurisdiction;

(b) knowingly performs an act in an official capacity that the public servant knows is forbidden by law;

(c) with the purpose to obtain a personal advantage or an advantage for another, performs an act in excess of the public servant's lawful authority...

72-31-347. Claims and litigation. Unless the power of attorney otherwise provides, language in a power of attorney granting general authority with respect to claims and litigation authorizes the agent to:

(1) assert and maintain before a court or administrative agency a claim, claim for relief, cause of action, counterclaim, offset, recoupment, or defense, including an action to recover property or other thing of value, recover damages sustained by the principal, eliminate or modify tax liability, or seek an injunction, specific performance, or other relief...

Appendix 2

Following are documents leading up to and including the lawsuit in 2003. All of these documents are relevant and show a progression of events leading up to the day of suit on November 23, 2003.

Keep in mind as you read these documents that they are not originals – Mara Pelton retained all of my original copies after my arrest, and after intimidation from authorities, she refused to communicate with me, much less turn these documents directly over to me. Therefore, I have been left to my own devices and retrieval of copies from various parties' records to reproduce this appendix. The Eleventh District Court and my own attorney, Eduardo Gutierrez-Falla, have refused all requests to produce relevant documents, so I have no control over the quality of the reproductions. There are also notes on many of the pages that were not part of the original documents, which should be evident and are not intended to reflect what the original document contained. In most instances, simply disregard any handwritten notes appearing on the pages.

This being said, the records I have managed to recover are incomplete. They represent a significant portion of the record, but it is by no means complete. If in the future I am able to obtain more records, I will amend this book as I am able.

In presenting these documents, I am doing so in the interest of full disclosure. I did not write any of these records, and therefore the deliberate bias of my opponents comes out quite prominently in some of them. For instance, the police investigative reports deliberately misrepresent information given to them to effect a summary of the case more inclined to where they wished to go, and omit altogether any reference to my challenges of impropriety during the investigative process or threats made against witnesses.

In mentioning the police reports, it is also notable that the police investigation clearly ended and the reporting ended mid-page – later additions to this record (provided in later a later Appendix) were added on and start independently on new screens rather than continuing from this point. I am only providing the records up and through this point as this Appendix's purpose is to solely present information that led up to and included the lawsuit – the latter records were more designed to represent post-lawsuit actions.

Another issue of note is that the Complaint included in this index is not the initial filing in the case. This cause was initiated with a Petition for records filed on or about October 30, 2003, but the Eleventh District Court Clerk's Office has refused to provide me access to the court file (supposedly a public record) nor a copy of the document in question, and no attorney who allegedly represented me will obtain this record for me. Therefore, I am only able to provide the Complaint filed on November 18, 2003, which instigated the actual abduction of Mara Pelton's daughters on November 20, 2003.

One final note is that within the content of Daughter 1's affidavit are references to her Jerry Nezat's shirt and glasses, and Daughter 1's stereo and Mara's dishwasher. A couple of weeks after Daughter 1's allegations, Jerry broke into our trailer, vandalized the door and stole Mara's dishwasher and Daughter 1's stereo, leaving a shirt with his reading glasses in the front pocket on top of dismantled pieces of the dishwasher. When asked, Jerry readily acknowledged they were his, but claimed he loaned the shirt to Daughter 1 – which Daughter 1 denied in her affidavit. Just as with the felony assaults the night of July 9, in spite of leaving deliberately incriminating evidence at the scene, Jerry was never prosecuted for the thefts or break-in.

U.S. Political Prisoner Since 2004 / 373

Initial Demand Letter To City of Kalispell
(July 18, 2003)

Ron Glick
338 Main Street
Kalispell, MT 59901
(406) 257-4263

City of Kalispell
312 1st Avenue East
Kalispell, MT 59901

RE: Kalispell Police Department Witness Tampering

To Whom It May Concern,

On Wednesday, July 9, 2003, an allegation was made against me of child molestation. Though I am innocent of the charges, their having been fabricated by the alleged victim's grandparents, a repeating pattern extending back fifteen or more years, nonetheless an investigation and report needed to be made. However, in the course of the initial report, the officer taking the report took one potential witness into a room and proceeded to misdirect her in order to, I can only assume, sway her as a witness.

Essentially, the events of the evening progressed as such: After a week and a half of consistent requests to have their granddaughter (the alleged victim) alone at their house, Jerry and Dixie Nezat took their granddaughter for the day with plans of having her stay overnight on the aforementioned July 9. My relationship with the alleged victim's mother, Mara Pelton, meant they came to me for the request that day since her mother was at work. At the time, it seemed a little odd that the Nezats were requesting only one of their two granddaughters, but they masked this by saying they were needing her to help with different chores around their house (the actual chores helping with had changed with each request), and the youngest one was too small to be of much help. This had never been an issue in the past, but it was not enough of a red flag to raise any specific concerns. The Nezats did have a long standing history of manipulating people into believing fabricated stories they had created, as I found out later on, and an equally long history of making false allegations of child molestation against any man in their daughter's life, but though they had had a tumultuous relationship with me, I had no reason to suspect foul play at this request and granted it. This happened around 11am.

Around 4:30pm, Dixie Nezat called our workplace, Arcadia. Mara and I were out doing bank business, and Mara returned the call as soon as she returned around 5:15pm. Immediately upon returning the call, Dixie Nezat proceeded to tell Mara that the alleged victim, after six hours alone with her grandparents, had suddenly confided that I had molested her. There was an immediate threat placed upon Mara that unless she brought herself and her kids to the Nezats' house and moved in there (she was told in no uncertain terms that she would not be allowed to live even in her own house), that a police report would be filed against me. In addition, in spite of numerous demands made by Mara, the Nezats refused to release the alleged victim into her mother's care. Note should be made here that the Nezats never actually called the police, nor do I believe that was ever their intent.

After three hours of arguing by phone, Mara Pelton, at the recommendation of her counselor, finally called the Sheriff's Department and made a report, both of the alleged molestation and the fact her parents refused to release the alleged victim into her mother's care. The Nezats even refused to release Mara's daughter into the custody of the Sheriff's Department (in this additional time frame, the alleged victim had now suddenly become afraid of her mother as well, which was even more absurd that the initial allegation) and it took an additional three hours of arguing by phone for the Sheriff's Department to convince the Nezats to bring the alleged victim in for a statement.

Had this all proceeded in a professional and detached manner from this point on, I would not now be writing this letter and this would be an issue between the Nezats and myself for proving both my innocence and their modus operandi. But unfortunately, the officer taking the initial report, Officer Myron Wilson, was not content to be impartial and began to manipulate the witnesses. Whether he spoke alone to Jerry or Dixie Nezat or what might have been said if he did is unknown (though it will become known if there is a need to subpoena them to ask what was told to them by this officer); however, he did pull Mara Pelton into a solitary room. Though the officer had a notepad, according to Mara he never took a note, asked her identifying questions or in any way conducted a proper interview. Instead, the officer proceeded to tell Mara that I was going to jail, that I had "a previous record for this kind of thing". He also told her that neither her nor her girls could have any contact with me or my girls would be taken away. Mara of course believed all of this to be true (who questions something a police officer tells you?) and walked out of that office convinced of my guilt.

Mara left that night with only the basest explanation, that she could not risk losing her girls by staying. It took a full twenty four hours before Mara got back in contact with me and informed me of her belief of my guilt, based entirely upon the officer's statement. I have since proven to her by retrieving copies of my own criminal record (or lack thereof, truthfully) to convince her that the officer had lied to her (but it took the better part of an additional day to do this). However, the damage had been done and if she had remained out of contact with me as instructed by this officer, this would have critically damaged my ability to defend myself. As it is, it gave credibility to the allegation as she believed for that 24 hours of my guilt and informed anyone she spoke to during that period of her belief. Again, based *solely* on the misinformation provided by your officer.

I spoke yesterday, July 17, 2003, with Detective Doug Overman on this issue. He gave a fairly credible statement that none of the foregoing was in the file and expressed his personal disbelief that Officer Wilson would do such a thing, that it violated policy and that since my criminal record or lack thereof was in the file, he should not have said this.

In essence, not only was my case damaged by the tampering of this officer, but I very nearly lost contact with the single most important witness of my defense, someone who could testify to her parents' past activities of making false allegations of child molestation (none of which, much like this one, were ever reported by them) and their history of manipulating memories and ideas, someone who could put me in touch with other people who had been told similar stories by her parents, and the single strongest character witness I could have on my side, the alleged victim's mother.

I have been damaged by all of this. Whether true or not, child molestation has a nasty stigma and I have become as much a victim in this affair as the little girl who has been convinced by her grandparents that this event truly happened. But my ability to defend myself was placed in jeopardy by your duly appointed representative. Tampering with witnesses is a crime, one which was perpetrated against me. As such, I have been damaged, possibly irrevocably.

Therefore, you can consider this letter both notice and demand for restitution of these damages. I feel I have been damaged in a way that is beyond comprehension. The amount of anxiety, betrayal of trust from a law enforcement agency, everything that I have endured over this last week, all of it is component of this complaint. I have operated a youth recreations program for over six years and the damage this has done may well be irreversible and I may lose all I have invested in this over that time, even if I am found innocent of the charges. I was not allowed to properly defend myself and nearly lost the support of someone I care for very deeply. Not to mention, someone who has come to trust me and care for me as a father figure in her life has been further convinced that a story which was fabricated and forced on her to believe as truth has more credibility since I had supposedly done this to other little girls. My family has been torn apart by all of this and your officer has only made it that much worse.

I will give you this one opportunity to avoid public declaration of your officer's transgressions. I feel I have been damaged and I feel I am owed compensation for the emotional duress and the damage to my case caused by your representative. But if we can work this out, there's no need to file suit. I am hereby making a demand of $250,000 (two hundred fifty thousand dollars) against the City of Kalispell for damages done to my person through the inflammatory, defamous and highly illegal misrepresentation of my character to a potential witness in my defense. I also want the officer in question removed from active duty and dismissed from the police force. I am open to discussion on a reasonable settlement of this issue, but I am only giving you 15 (fifteen) days from the date of this letter to resolve this to my satisfaction. At the end of that time, if I have not received compensation or an adequate settlement, I will file a lawsuit against the City of Kalispell and call a press release of my actions and why. Mara Pelton is preparing a statement and will sign an affidavit testifying to her conversation with your officer on July 9, 2003 in the event this must proceed that far.

I am certain that whomever reads and responds to this demand will be as equally appalled at the actions of this officer as I am. Your officers are sworn to protect the citizens and uphold the law and to have a rogue officer tamper with a case in this fashion seriously violates the trust the citizens place in your government. Your officer has taken an already difficult situation and made it even more so.

I look forward to your response.

Sincerely,

Ron Glick
July 18, 2003

Letter From Child and Family Services
(September 18, 2003)

DEPARTMENT OF
PUBLIC HEALTH AND HUMAN SERVICES
DIVISION OF CHILD & FAMILY SERVICES

JUDY MARTZ
GOVERNOR

GAIL GRAY, Ed.D
DIRECTOR

(406) 751-5950
FAX (406) 751-5975

PO DRAWER 190
KALISPELL, MONTANA 59903-0310

September 18, 2003

Mara Pelton
4234 Foothill Rd.
Kalispell, MT 5990_

Dear Mara,

As you are aware the Division of Child and Family Services had received a referral concerning your daughter ▓▓▓▓. The result of my investigation into the allegations of exposure to ▓▓▓▓ substances, I do not believe that ▓▓▓▓ necessary. As our office to continue contact at this time. However, I urge you to ensure that ▓▓▓▓ attends school consistently.

Please don't hesitate to call if you have any questions.

Respectfully,

Maggie Barker

Maggie Barker
Community Social Worker
Division of Family and Child Services

Kalispell Police Department Reports
(July 9 – September 4, 2003)

KALISPELL POLICE DEPARTMENT
CASE REPORT - 203CR001019-

Sector 01 Level 0
NOT REVIEWED

CORE DATA

Case Report# 203CR0010194
Other# D-03-6091
Master CR#

Classification 45-5-502 SEXUAL ASSAULT
Ranking FELONY DOMESTIC

Reported As SEXUAL ASSAULT
Time Reported (WED) 07/09/2003 19:52
Taken By SIPPHILLI
Reported How PHONE

Time of Occurrence 06/24/2003 (TUE) To

Injuries
Weapons
Stolen Property$ Stolen Vehicles
Damaged Property$ Damaged Vehicles

Scene 378 MAIN ST DBA ARCADIA KALISPELL
Sector 01
Premise 24

Time Dispatched
Time On Scene 07/09/2003 20:27   4:28 WILSON MYRON L
Time Cleared Scene 07/09/2003 20:27

Assigned To DET   008BURNS
Cleared

MEMBERS

ASSIGNED BURNS GREG (008BURNS)

OFFENSES

07/09/2003 19:52 STATE 45-5-502 SEXUAL ASSAULT   FELONY (A)
Arrest#

NAMES

SUSPECT GLICK RONALD DWAYNE   M WN 510 160 34
Address 1842 AIRPORT RD #4 KALISPELL, MT 59901   Home Phone 406-250-6166
Employer ARCADIA   Occupation OWNER   Work Phone 406-257-4763
SSN/SNOKE   Arrest#   Deposed N
Gang   ID How/By

VICTIM   F WN 13 yr.
Address   Home Phone
Employer   Occupation STUDENT   Work Phone
SSN   Arrest#   Deposed N
ID How/By

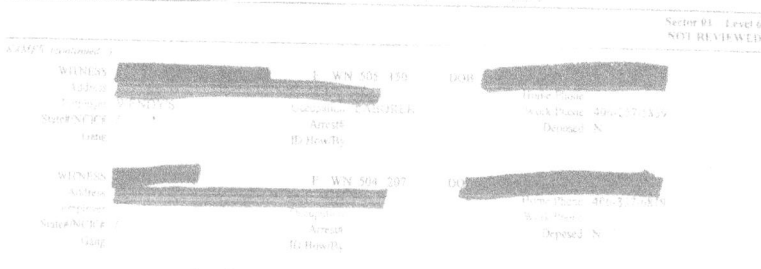

Ron Glick / 380

KALISPELL POLICE DEPARTMENT
CASE REPORT - 203CR001019

Sector 01 Level 6
NOT REVIEWED

INVESTIGATION REPORT WRITTEN BY 039WILSON ON 07/09/2003 (continued)

laying on the couch with ████ on her side near the front edge and Ronald behind her. ████ was laying on Ronald's left arm. While watching videos, Ronald began reaching his left hand under ████'s shirt. ████ was not wearing a bra and Ronald eventually fondled each of her breasts. Ronald then began reaching his right hand down ████'s pants. ████ stated that Ronald's hand was underneath her underwear. ████ asked Ronald to stop but he continued. Ronald continued reaching until his hand was hovering over her pubic hair. ████ stated that she repeatedly asked him to stop and, eventually, grabbed his hand. ████ then pulled Ronald's hand out of her pants, got up from the couch, and sat in another chair. According to ████, the entire incident took about 5 seconds. When I asked ████ if she was sure Ronald was wake during the incident, she stated, "Yes." ████ advised that Ronald had been talking to her.

According to ████, this was an isolated incident and at no other time, has Ronald made any sexual advances toward her. (Please refer to videotape for further details).

After concluding my interview with ████, I spoke to her mother, Mara. Mara described ████ as a very flirtatious teenage girl, who hugs and kisses Ronald all of the time. Mara was surprised by ████'s allegation and stated that ████ had not given her any indication that anything was wrong. ████, understanding her mother's interest in Ronald, chose to report the incident to her grandmother instead.

As of yet, I have not contacted Ronald Glick for an interview.

SUPPLEMENTAL WRITTEN BY 036GUERMA ON 07/11/2003

On July 11, 2003 I conducted an interview with Ronald Glick at the Kalispell Police Department. I read Glick his rights and he agreed to speak with me.

Glick advised he knew the nature of the interview and wished to state he did not touch ████ in an inappropriate manner and he believed he was being "railroaded" by the grandparents, Dixie and Jerry Nezat. Glick advised the Nezat's did not like him since had dated the girl's mother, Mara.

Glick advised me he and Mara had dated for approx. 1.5 years and were no longer seeing each other. Glick advised the relationship had ended in March. Glick further informed me he believes ████ cares for him deeply as a role model in her life.

Glick did admit they spend mornings together at Arcadia and they do watch cartoons together that he downloads on his P.C. off the internet. Glick further advised they had layed on the couch together. Glick continued to state he did not do it and he believed he was being framed by the Nezat's. Glick stated the Nezat's had done this before to other boyfriends of Mara's.

Glick declined submitting to a polygraph or voice stress analysis. Glick also stated any DNA on him would be just through "everyday" contact.

SUPPLEMENTAL WRITTEN BY 036GUERMA ON 07/14/2004

On July 14, 2004 I conducted an interview with Mara at the Kalispell Police Department. Pelton stated she believed her daughter was not being honest about the incident and believes she is being coached by her grand parents.

Pelton advised me she and Glick were in fact an couple but things were on "hold" at the moment.

U.S. Political Prisoner Since 2004 / 381

KALISPELL POLICE DEPARTMENT
CASE REPORT - 203CR00?0?0

Sector 01 Level 2
NOT REVIEWED

SUPPLEMENTAL WRITTEN BY [REDACTED] ON 0?/1?/2003 continued

while speaking with her, I could clearly see Pelton's checkbook was a joint account with Glick. Pelton advised me Glick had sold his share of the business, but could not state to who.

Pelton informed me she was no longer living on Foothills Rd., as her parents would not let her live there. Pelton advised me Glick was a "volunteer" at Arcadia, and received no pay as the business was not yet profitable. Pelton stated Glick had been living with them and they had been supported by her wages from Wendy's. Pelton advised me Glick was now living in Arcadia, transporting the rear to an apartment.

Pelton advised me she would bring [REDACTED] in for an interview on Wednesday.

SUPPLEMENTAL #1 WRITTEN BY [REDACTED] ON 0?/?/200?

On July ?6, 200? I conducted an interview with Dixie and Larry Nezat concerning the injury report made to them by [REDACTED].

Dixie informed me [REDACTED] had come to them last Wednesday and stated she had something she needed to tell them. [REDACTED] then told them she and Glick had been lying on the couch one morning at Arcadia watching TV. She alleged Glick started moving his hands over her breasts and down to her "private parts". Dixie stated [REDACTED] told them Glick tried to stop several times but he would not.

Both of the Nezat's advised the [REDACTED] was noticeably upset and crying very heavily while disclosing this information. The Nezat's both stated concern that Glick was very controlling of Mara and would try to either her to commit or on the alleged incident.

SUPPLEMENTAL WRITTEN BY [REDACTED] ON 0?/?/200?

On July 16, 2003 I conducted an interview with [REDACTED] at the Kalispell Police Dept. Mary Pelton, [REDACTED] mother was also present.

I asked [REDACTED] about the alleged incident with Ronald Glick. [REDACTED] advised that she and Glick had been lying on the couch together watching cartoons. [REDACTED] advised they had lived on the couch before together. [REDACTED] stated Glick was placed against the back of the couch and she was on the outside edge. She stated Glick then started feeling her up. She recalled Glick put his left arm up her shirt and his right down her pants, "feeling" her up. [REDACTED] informed me she informed Glick to stop several times. [REDACTED] advised this was the only time she had been inappropriately touched by Glick. [REDACTED] did not know if Glick was sleeping while he did this.

[REDACTED] stated that Glick had told her in the past that he loved her and he stated he believes that you should "marry people younger," and he "considers her to be a woman".

Mary also informed me [REDACTED] has been more upset [REDACTED] and was [REDACTED] also have had her into counseling against Glick.

Ron Glick / 382

KALISPELL POLICE DEPARTMENT
CASE REPORT - 203CR0010194

Sector 01 Level 6
NOT REVIEWED

SUPPLEMENTAL   WRITTEN BY 038OVERMA ON 07/17/2003

On July 17, 2003 I again spoke with Ronald Glick. Glick continued to deny that he had touched ▓▓▓ knowingly in any way. Glick did acknowledge they had spent time on the couch together.

When questioned if he could have done the touching while "sleeping" or otherwise unknowingly, Glick responded it was possible but did not believe it would be likely.

Glick continues to insist the Nezats are coaching ▓▓▓ in her testimony. (see video taped interview)

SUPPLEMENTAL   WRITTEN BY 038OVERMA ON 07/29/2003

On July 28, 2003 I conducted an interview with Chantel Beasley at the KPD. Beasely advised me she had never dated Glick but two of her friends had. Beasely advised her friend, Melissa Turner, had dated him and Mara Pelton is currently dating him. Beasley stated she did not personally know Glick and further advised she had heard of no allegations against him from her friends.

SUPPLEMENTAL   WRITTEN BY 038OVERMA ON 09/04/2003

Neither Glick nor ▓▓▓ and Mara Pelton would agree to take a polygraph test to help assist in confirming statements. This investigation is suspended pending further evidence.

U.S. Political Prisoner Since 2004 / 383

Civil Complaint Filed In Cause No. DV-03-572
(November 18, 2003)

Ron Glick
338 Main Street
Kalispell, MT 59901

IN THE JUSTICE COURT, FLATHEAD COUNTY, MONTANA

Ron Glick,

Plaintiff,

vs

City of Kalispell, Kalispell Police
Department, Kalispell City Attorney's
Office, Chief Frank Garner, Officer
Myron Wilson, Detective Doug
Overman, Mayor Pam Kennedy,
City Manager Chris Kukulski,
Adjutant City Attorney Richard
Richard Hickle, and Does I-XX,

Defendants.

Complaint for Witness Tampering;
Slander; Defamation of Character;
Harassment; Emotional Duress;
and Other Relief

CASE NO: DV-03-572C

COMES NOW PLAINTIFF to complain against Defendants and each as follows:

I

Defendant City of Kalispell is a legally incorporated municipality in the County of Flathead, State of Montana, and Plaintiffs recognize Defendant's governing authority over all City government offices, including Defendants' Kalispell Police Department and Kalispell City Attorney's Office.

II

Defendant Kalispell Police Department is a legally formed law enforcement agency located in the City of Kalispell, County of Flathead, State of Montana, and exists within

the government of the City of Kalispell.

III

Defendant Kalispell City Attorney's Office is a legally formed agency located in the City of Kalispell, County of Flathead, State of Montana, and exists within the government of the City of Kalispell.

IV

Defendant Police Chief Garner is the duly appointed Chief of Police of the Defendant Kalispell Police Department and does work within the City of Kalispell, County of Flathead, State of Montana.

V

Defendant Officer Myron Wilson is an employed officer of the Defendant Kalispell Police Department and does work within the City of Kalispell, County of Flathead, State of Montana.

VI

Defendant Detective Doug Overman is an employed officer of the Defendant Kalispell Police Department and does work within the City of Kalispell, County of Flathead, State of Montana.

VII

Defendant Mayor Pam Kennedy is the duly elected Mayor of the Defendant City of Kalispell and does work within the City of Kalispell, County of Flathead, State of Montana. Additionally, Defendant has been the authoritative superior of Defendant Kalispell City Attorney's Office and is currently the authoritative superior of Defendant City Manager Chris Kukulski.

VIII

Defendant City Manager Chris Kukulski is the duly appointed City Manager of the Defendant City of Kalispell and does work within the City of Kalispell, County of Flathead, State of Montana. Additionally, Defendant is the current authoritative superior of Defendant Kalispell Police Department and Kalispell City Attorney's Office.

IX

Defendant Adjutant City Attorney Richard Hickle is a duly appointed attorney of the Defendant Kalispell City Attorneys Office and does work within the City of Kalispell, County of Flathead, State of Montana.

X

Defendants identified herein as Does I-XX are believed by Plaintiff to be individuals and/or agencies who have, directly or indirectly, aided the Defendants with the actions against Plaintiff and does therefore hereby incorporate said individuals and/or agencies into this complaint. Plaintiff will endeavor to identify these individuals and/or agencies and amend this complaint as appropriate as the identities of such become known to Plaintiff.

XI

On or about July 9, 2003, Plaintiff is informed and believes and thereon alleges that a false allegation was made against Plaintiff for child molestation through the machinations of Jerry Nezat and Dixie Nezat, hereafter the Nezats, through their granddaughter, ████████ an action which amongst other malicious deeds led to a lawsuit filed by Plaintiff and Mara Pelton against the Nezats, a true and correct copy of said lawsuit available as Case No. DV-03-512B in Flathead County District Court,

Eleventh Judicial District.

XII

Plaintiff is informed and believes and thereon alleges that on or about said date, a Complaint was filed against Plaintiff with the Defendant Kalispell Police Department by ▮▮▮▮▮ mother, Mara Pelton. Additionally, Plaintiff is informed and believes and thereon alleges on or about said date, Defendant Officer Myron Wilson recorded said Complaint and performed initial interviews with ▮▮▮▮▮ the Nezats and Mara Pelton.

XIII

Plaintiff is informed and believes and thereon alleges that during the course of interviewing the alleged victim, ▮▮▮▮▮, Defendant Officer Myron Wilson did tell ▮▮▮▮▮ that Plaintiff had a prior record for child molestation, a statement Defendant Officer Myron Wilson knew to be untrue. Additionally, Plaintiff believes and thereon alleges that Defendant's action were intended to tamper with the witness to compel negative testimony against Plaintiff.

XIV

Plaintiff is informed and believes and thereon alleges that during the course of speaking with the alleged victim's mother, Mara Pelton, that Defendant Officer Myron Wilson did tell Mara Pelton that Plaintiff had a prior record for child molestation, a statement Defendant Officer Myron Wilson knew to be untrue. Additionally, Plaintiff believes and thereon alleges that Defendant's action were intended to tamper with the witness to compel negative testimony against Plaintiff.

XV

Plaintiff believes and thereon alleges that Defendant Officer Myron Wilson made a similar comment to the Nezats, which in turn incited the Nezats against Plaintiff and Mara Pelton and that led to malicious acts by the Nezats against Plaintiff and Mara Pelton, as set forth the aforementioned lawsuit.

XVI

Plaintiff is informed and believes and thereon alleges that the aforementioned Complaint led to an investigation by the Defendant Kalispell Police Department and said investigation was conducted by Defendant Detective Doug Overman.

XVII

Plaintiff is informed and believes and thereon alleges that during the course of the aforementioned investigation, a representative of the Defendant Kalispell Police Department did contact Tim Pelton, the legally adopted father of the alleged victim, ███████, and did proceed to tell Tim Pelton that Plaintiff was in fact a child molester, a statement known to be untrue by the Defendant Kalispell Police Department. Plaintiff believes and thereon alleges that Defendant's action was intended to tamper with Tim Pelton as a witness to compel negative testimony against Plaintiff.

XVIII

Plaintiff believes and thereon alleges that Defendant Officer Myron Wilson's and Defendant Kalispell Police Department's actions were intended to tamper with the beliefs of witnesses in an effort to compel negative testimony from witnesses and potential witnesses. Plaintiff further believes and thereon alleges that such actions endangered Plaintiff's potential defense and have led to innumerous hostilities against Plaintiff from the witnesses tampered with by the Defendants.

XIX

Plaintiff is informed and believes and thereon alleges that Defendants' actions have caused harm to Plaintiff, Plaintiff's relationships, and Plaintiff's potential defense against the false allegation of child molestation and that Plaintiff is entitled to damages in the amount of $250,000 (two hundred fifty thousand dollars) per instance, for a total accounting of $1,250,000 (one million two hundred fifty thousand dollars).

PLAINTIFF'S SECOND CAUSE OF ACTION

XX

Plaintiff does hereby incorporate by reference Plaintiffs' First Cause of Action, inclusive, into this Cause.

XXI

Plaintiff is informed and believes and thereon alleges that Defendant Officer Myron Wilson and Defendant Kalispell Police Department did knowingly and with malicious intent to cause harm to Plaintiff by informing ▓▓▓▓▓▓ Mara Pelton and the Nezats that Plaintiff had a prior record of child molestation and additionally by Defendant Kalispell Police Department by informing Tim Pelton that Plaintiff was a factual child molester. Plaintiffs are further informed and believe and thereon allege that Defendants' actions constitute slander, as defined by MCA Section 27-1-803, by publicizing false and unprivileged information charging Plaintiff with a prior criminal history which Plaintiff does not have and for the express purpose of maliciously causing harm to the Plaintiff.

XXII

Plaintiff is informed and believes and thereon alleges that Defendants actions have caused harm to Plaintiff, Plaintiff's reputation and Plaintiffs' relationships and that Plaintiff is entitled to damages in the amount of $100,000 (one hundred thousand dollars) per instance, for a total accounting of $500,000 (five hundred thousand dollars).

PLAINTIFFS' THIRD CAUSE OF ACTION

XXIII

Plaintiff does hereby incorporate by reference Plaintiff's First and Second Causes of Action, inclusive, into this Cause.

XXIV

Plaintiff is informed and believes and thereon alleges that Defendant Officer Myron Wilson and Defendant Kalispell Police Department did knowingly and with malicious intent to cause harm to Plaintiff's reputation by informing ███████, Mara Pelton and the Nezats that Plaintiff had a prior record of child molestation and additionally by Defendant Kalispell Police Department by informing Tim Pelton that Plaintiff was a factual child molester. Plaintiff is further informed and believes and thereon alleges that the aforementioned witnesses did convey belief of the information provided by Defendants to members of the general public and that such conveyance has significantly affected Plaintiff, Plaintiff's reputation in the community and Plaintiff's business and profession in youth recreations. Plaintiff is still further informed and believes and thereon allege that Defendants' actions constitute Defamation of Character, as defined by MCA 27-1-801, and that such Defamation was intentional and willfully executed by the Defendants and that such execution was committed maliciously with the express purpose of causing harm to Plaintiff.

XXV

Plaintiff is informed and believes and thereon alleges that Defendants actions have caused harm to Plaintiff, Plaintiff's reputation and Plaintiffs' business and that Plaintiff is entitled to damages in the amount of $100,000 (one hundred thousand dollars) per instance, for a total accounting of $500,000 (five hundred thousand dollars).

PLAINTIFF'S FOURTH CAUSE OF ACTION

XXVI

Plaintiff does hereby incorporate by reference Plaintiffs' First through Third Causes of Action, inclusive, into this Cause.

XXVII

Plaintiff is informed and believes and thereon attests that on or about July 18, 2003, Plaintiff made an initial demand for damages against the Defendant City of Kalispell and Defendant Kalispell Police Department, though the demand for restitution changed over the course of the next several months as new grievances became known to Plaintiff.

XXVIII

Plaintiff is informed and believes and thereon alleges that over the course of the following months, Defendants have made efforts to harass, annoy and intimidate Plaintiff and Plaintiff's business. Plaintiff is further informed and believes and thereon alleges that such efforts by the Defendants were specific as follows:

1) Plaintiff received a letter from the City of Kalispell citing a violation by Plaintiff's business of hanging a non-permanent banner from the front of Plaintiff's business. In spite of innumerous banners and other nonpermanent

decor hanging from businesses all along Main Street where Plaintiff's business is located, Plaintiff complied with the request and removed the banner;

2) Plaintiff was visited at Plaintiff's business by a police officer from Defendant Kalispell Police Department, who entered Plaintiff's business, asked for Plaintiff by name, and proceeded to meet with Plaintiff in the back room of the business, where the officer informed Plaintiff in a gruff manner that the Chief had told the officer to speak with Plaintiff about bicycles parked by patrons of Plaintiff's business on the sidewalk blocking passage of pedestrians. Plaintiff hereby attests that upon informing the officer that Plaintiff had made every effort reasonable to have bicycles placed outside of walk areas whenever they were noticed and had even made a request of the Defendant City of Kalispell for permission to place bike racks in front of the business, a request that had been denied the previous year, that the officer's behavior changed and the officer offered to put in a good word with the City and left without offering identification. Plaintiff believes and thereon alleges this officer's behavior suggested an effort to publicly humiliate Plaintiff in his business, to imply Plaintiff was in trouble with the Police and to intimidate Plaintiff;

3) Plaintiff was visited by a representative of the City Health Department, who entered Plaintiff's business with a prepared notice in hand, which the representative took with him when he realized he had no authority to inspect Plaintiff's business since Plaintiff's business does not serve open food to the general public. Plaintiff believes and thereon alleges that said representative had been planning to issue a pre-determined violation to Plaintiff but could not do so

since Plaintiff's business was not in violation of any code he could enforce; and
4) Plaintiff was called by Jim Stewart, who identified himself over the phone as the Fire Marshal, who again asked for Plaintiff by name, though Mr Stewart did not know Plaintiff's business name nor physical address. Mr Stewart later informed Plaintiff that a message was delivered to him to inspect Plaintiff's business, but was unwilling or unable to recall whom the message had been from. Jim Stewart conducted an initial inspection of Plaintiff's business and cited violations, which Plaintiff corrected. Jim Stewart inspected Plaintiff's facility on three separate occasions thereafter, adding new violations after each visit, making it impossible for Plaintiff to comply with all demands. Upon interviewing neighboring businesses, laintiff discovered that no other business Plaintiff could contact was ever held to such stringent standards as what was being asked of Plaintiff's business.

XXIX

In addition to the above, Plaintiff is informed and believes and thereon alleges Plaintiff has additionally been denied access to information entitled to Plaintiff under MCA Section 44-5-214, which permits any individual to inspect and have copied any criminal history record information maintained by a criminal justice agency, and Section 44-5-103, which defines criminal history record information as, amongst other things, the filing of complaints and information arising from the filing of such complaints, not including any court records, by Defendants Detective Doug Overman, Defendant Adjutant City Attorney Richard Hickle, Defendant Mayor Pam Kennedy, Defendant City Manager Chris Kukulski, and Defendant Chief Frank Garner. Plaintiff is further informed and believes and thereon alleges that Defendant Adjutant City Attorney Richard Hickle has attempted to cloud the issue by alleging "Complaint" is intended to reference a court filed document in spite of the MCA's specific omission of court records.

XXX

Plaintiff is informed and believes and thereon alleges that in or around October, 2003, Defendant Kalispell Police Department and Defendant Detective Doug Overman closed the ongoing investigation against Plaintiff. In addition, Plaintiff is informed and believes and theroen alleges that various representatives of the Defendant Kalispell Police Department informed several other parties besides Plaintiff, including Mara Pelton, members of the Kalispell Junior High School Staff, the Kalispell Junior High School Counseling Department and Tana Ryggs with the Montana Municipal Insurance Agency that the investigation was closed and that no further action would be taken.

XXXI

Plaintiff is informed and believes and thereon alleges that on or about October 30, 2003, Plaintiff renewed Plaintiff's request for information as allowed by MCA 44-5-100 et seq, with Defendant Adjutant City Attorney Richard Hickle and Defendant Chief Frank Garner, of which both requests were denied. Plaintiff is informed and believes and thereon alleges that, in response to the above request, Defendant Chief Frank Garner on behalf of the Defendant Kalispell Police Department re-opened the investigation against Plaintiff and reassigned Defendant Detective Doug Overman to begin contacting witnesses in the case again.

XXXII

Plaintiff believes and thereon alleges that Defendants are denying Plaintiff the aforementioned criminal history record information on Plaintiff, and subsequently reopened the investigation against Plaintiff to frustrate Plaintiff's efforts to review the criminal history record information, due to the incriminating nature against Defendants of said records and additionally to further harass and frustrate Plaintiff by refusing to comply with requirements under the law.

XXXIII

Plaintiff is informed and believes and thereon alleges that the foregoing details an extensive, concerted and premeditated effort by the Defendants to annoy, harass and intimidate Plaintiff and that Plaintiff has suffered harm from Defendants' actions. Plaintiff additionally believes and thereon alleges that Plaintiff is entitled to damages in to form of $25,000 (twenty five thousand dollars) per instance of harassment, for a total accounting of $250,000 (two hundred fifty thousand dollars).

PLAINTIFF'S FIFTH CAUSE OF ACTION

XXXIV

Plaintiff does hereby incorporate by reference Plaintiffs' First through Fourth Causes of Action, inclusive, into this Cause.

XXXV

Plaintiff is informed and believes and thereon alleges that Defendants' actions have caused personal grief, loss of trust and caused harm to the familial relations that still exist amongst and between the Plaintiff, Mara Pelton and their children. Plaintiff is further informed and believes and thereon alleges that the Defendants are directly responsible for the emotional distress, as defined by MCA Section 27-1-310 as "mental anguish or suffering, sorrow, grief, fright, shame, embarrassment, humiliation, anger, chagrin, disappointment, or worry", which the Plaintiff suffers from since Defendants actions were performed for the express purpose of causing harm to Plaintiff.

XXXVI

Wherefore Plaintiff is informed and believes and thereon alleges that the Defendants actions as set forth above have caused damage to Plaintiff and that Plaintiff is entitled to damages in the amount of $100,000 (one hundred thousand dollars) per afflicted family member, for a total accounting of $500,000 (five hundred thousand dollars).

PLAINTIFF'S SIXTH CAUSE OF ACTION

XXXVII

Plaintiff does hereby incorporate by reference Plaintiffs' First through Fifth Causes of Action, inclusive, into this Cause.

XXXVIII

Plaintiff believes and thereon alleges that Plaintiff may have been or will become during the course of this proceeding further damaged by Defendants and Plaintiff does hereby reserve the right to amend these pleadings to incorporate such damages should they become known to Plaintiffs.

Wherefore Plaintiff does respectfully request of the Court Judgment against the Defendants in the amount of $3,000,000 (three million dollars) and each as follows:

1) Damages in the amount of $250,000 (two hundred fifty thousand dollars) per offense of witness tampering by Defendants against Plaintiff, for a total accounting of $1,250,000 (one million two hundred fifty thousand dollars);

2) Damages in the amount of $100,000 (one hundred thousand dollars) per offense of slander by Defendants against Plaintiff, for a total accounting of $500,000 (five hundred thousand dollars);

3) Damages in the amount of $100,000 (one hundred thousand dollars) per offense of defamation by Defendants against Plaintiff, for a total accounting of $500,000 (five hundred thousand dollars);

4) Damages in the amount of $25,000 (twenty five thousand dollars) for each offense of harassment by Defendants against Plaintiff, for a total accounting of $250,000 (two hundred fifty thousand dollars);

5) Damages in the amount of $100,000 (one hundred thousand dollars) for each offense of emotional duress by Defendants against Plaintiff, for a total accounting of $500,000 (five hundred thousand dollars); and

6) Such other and further relief as the Court may deem appropriate.

Wherefore Petitioner does hereby attest under penalty of perjury that the above is true and correct to the best of his ability to present and that this is signed in the City of Kalispell, County of Flathead, State of Montana on November 18, 2003.

_____
Ronald Glick

Plaintiff will have hand delivered to all Defendants and/or Defendants' agents, true and correct copies of this complaint.

11, 18, 2003

Affidavit of Daughter 1
(October 20, 2003)

12/11/03   17:20   CHILD AND FAMILY SERVICES → 9P7587799   NO.015 020

Ron Glick and Mara Pelton
338 Main Street
Kalispell, MT 59901
(406) 257-4263

Ron Glick and
Mara Pelton,

Plaintiffs,

Case No: DV-03-512B

Affidavit of ▓▓▓▓

DIXIE NEZAT AND
JERRY NEZAT,
INDIVIDUALLY AND
AND COLLECTIVELY
AND DOES I-X,

Defendants.

Comes now ▓▓▓▓▓▓ to attest as follows:

1) I am a resident of the County of Flathead, State of Montana;

2) I am the natural daughter of Mara Pelton and the granddaughter of Jerry and Dixie Nezat;

3) I have known Ron Glick for nearly three years;

4) Since I am not that good at writing, I am having someone else help me type this so I know the right words to use and how to say them;

5) When I was three years old, I witnessed my mom being attacked by a man who I only knew as Shane, a friend of my Dad's, Jared Salois. I am told that what I witnessed was Shane tried to rape my mom, but I hit him in the back of the head with a toy, which

1

made him let go of my mom. My mom was then able to get away and fight off Shane, and then threw him out. Until very recently, I did not remember this memory;

6) Over the course of many years, I was physically abused by Tim Pelton. One of the many things Tim did to me over the years was when I was about seven or eight, Tim threatened to shoot me at gunpoint. When he was in the home, he beat me on almost daily basis. Tim has slugged me, pushed me, hit me and picked me up and threw me against walls;

7) For about two weeks around the first part of July and last part of June of this year, my grandparents, Jerry and Dixie Nezat, kept asking my mom and Ron to have me visit for a day so I could do work for them;

8) On July 9, 2003, my grandparents came into Arcadia and asked to take me for the day and night. While my Grandpa was in Arcadia, I noticed he was wearing his black-rimmed reading glasses. He was wearing them while he looked at some comics on the shelf and then sat down at the back table to read his book;

9) Ron agreed to my grandparents request to take me and I left with them;

10) On the way to my grandparents home, they were talking and gossiping about Arcadia, Ron and other things. During this conversation, they mentioned that Shane was back in town and made like Mom would be happy to see him;

11) At this time, I said I had something important to tell my grandparents;

12) When I got to the house, my grandparents did not put me to work. I went to my home, which is next to my grandparents home, to get my toothbrush and a book to read. Grandpa came with me, but I was the only one who went in, through the window. Grandpa did not help me get into the house because the bricks below my window made it

easy to climb in;

13) While in the house, I know I saw my stereo. In fact, I tripped over it. So I know it was there;

14) Then after this, we went up to my grandparents' house, where I spent the day chasing their cat and goofing off all day. During the day Grandma was talking to me, but I don't remember what she was saying. I was kind of tuning her out. I saw Grandpa using his reading glasses again as he read a newspaper;

15) About 5:30pm or so, my grandma asked me to tell her what I wanted to tell them. I told them that Ron had molested me. I now believe that what I thought was a recent memory was actually the memory of what Shane did to my mom, and because Grandma was talking about Ron and Shane in the car at the same time, my mind overlapped the memory. I understand this now because I have talked to Counselors and they have helped me realize that Ron did not hurt me;

16) Immediately after, my grandma called my mom and told my mom that she had to come out to my grandparents' place with my sister. I could tell my mom was wondering why because my grandma was explaining what happened;

17) I talked to my mom and Carrie Beth Mountjoy over the phone when my grandparents would let me, which was not very much because they kept me away from the phone for a long time. Carrie Beth offered to let me stay with her, but my grandparents would not let me go to town for any reason and kept saying they did not trust Carrie Beth. I asked lots of times to go stay with Carrie Beth, but my grandparents kept saying no;

18) I guess I don't know when the Police got involved but Grandma kept calling

someone, which was probably my mom, over and over again. My grandma kept saying over and over that she was going to keep me there and call the police and have my sister, Talisha, and I taken away from our mom;

19) Finally, I guess the police convinced my grandparents to bring me back to town for a statement. This was sometime around 10:30 or 11pm at night;

20) Carrie Beth met us at the Police Station and tried to hug me, but Grandpa grabbed me pretty hard by the arm, to where it hurt, and yanked me away. He said, "No, don't touch her. I don't trust you!" to Carrie Beth, which hurt my feelings because Carrie Beth is a really good friend of mine;

21) During the interview, I repeated what my Grandma and Grandpa had said, using words they had used, even though I didn't understand what the words meant. Also, during the interview, the Police Officer interviewing me said that there was a record of Ron molesting another child before;

22) After all this, I was returned to my mom and went home with her;

23) A few weeks later, I got a call from a Sheriff Deputy who told me that my grandpa had told him that I had been loaned Grandpa's shirt. This was not true, Grandpa never loaned me a shirt and I do not know how that shirt would have gotten into the house;

24) Also, in the next several weeks before that day, I had seen my radio in the house along with our dishwasher. I was really surprised when Mom called and told me they had been stolen.

Wherefore I do hereby attest that the above is true and correct to the best of my ability to recall and that by signing, I swear under penalty of perjury, that the foregoing is true

12/11/03 17:28 CHILD AND FAMILY SERVICES → 9P75A7799 NO.015 D24

and correct, and that it is signed on the 20th day of October, 2003, in the City of Kalispell, County of Flathead, State of Montana.

Signed:

Ron Glick / 402

Affidavit of Ian Chrisman
(December 23, 2003)

Ron Glick
338 Main Street
Kalispell, MT 59901

IN THE ELEVENTH DISTRICT COURT, FLATHEAD COUNTY, MONTANA

Ron Glick,

Plaintiff,

vs

City of Kalispell, Kalispell Police
Department, Kalispell City Attorney's
Office, Chief Frank Garner, Officer
Myron Wilson, Detective Doug
Overman, Mayor Pam Kennedy,
City Manager Chris Kukulski,
Adjutant City Attorney Richard
Richard Hickle, and Does I-XX,

Defendants.

Affidavit of Ian Chrisman

CASE NO: DV-03-572C

Comes now Ian Chrisman to declare as follows:

1. I am a legal adult and resident of Flathead County, State of Montana;

2. On or about November 19, 2003, I attempted to perform legal service against the Defendants named above;

3. During the course of my attempts to serve the City Attorney's Office, I was informed by an individual identifying himself as City Attorney Charles Harball, that the insurance company would need to be contacted as they were legal counsel for all Defendants in the above named suit;

4. Defendant Charles Harball accepted service for the Defendants City Attorney's Office and Defendant Richard Hickel, but would not accept for any other Defendant;

5. Additionally during the course of my efforts to serve the above named Defendants, Defendant Frank Garner also refused to accept service and would not permit service of Defendants Kalispell Police Department, Myron Wilson nor Doug Overman. In fact,

U.S. Political Prisoner Since 2004 / 403

when asked, Defendant Frank Garner instructed his receptionist to have me leave or I would be escorted out of the building;

6. After serving Defendant Chris Kukulski, said Defendant aided me in having Defendant Frank Garner accept service for Defendant Frank Garner and Kalispell Police Department and did additionally make arrangements for Defendants Myron Wilson, Doug Overman and Pam Kennedy to be present at 5pm of said date to receive service;

7. At or around 5pm of said date, Defendants Myron Wilson, Doug Overman and Pam Kennedy were made available for service, but none of said Defendants would accept service on behalf of the Defendant City of Kalispell;

8. After said efforts, I allowed the Defendant City of Kalispell to be served by another party.

Wherefore I hereby attest that the foregoing is true and correct to the best of my ability to present, and that this is signed in the City of Kalispell, County of Flathead, State of Montana on ~~October 27, 2003~~. December 23, 2003

_____
Ian Chrisman   DATE: 12/23/03

April J. Coen

Printed Name: April J. Coen
Notary Public for the State of Montana
Residing in: Kalispell
My Commission Expires: 09/23/2006

APRIL J. COEN
Notarial Seal
State of Montana

Child and Family Services Intake Form (Daughter 1)
November 21, 2003[90]

---

[90] Though this form is dated Nov 21, Mara's daughters were actually abducted Nov 20.

U.S. Political Prisoner Since 2004 / 405

Child and Family Services Intake Form (Daughter 2)

Ron Glick / 406

November 21, 2003[91]

CHILD SUPPORT ENFORCEMENT REFERRAL
See Instructions on back of form

Name of Child: ███████████████
SSN: ███████

Date of Birth: ███████ Sex: Female Race: Cauc

Name of Social/Placing Worker: Keri Taylor
Office Address: P.O. Drawer 310, Kalispell 59901
Phone Number: 751-5950
Referral is for: [ ] Father [ ] Mother [✓] Both

Referral is for: [ ] IV-E Foster Care [ ] CWS Foster Care [ ] Adjudicated Delinquent

Father's Name: Tim Pelton SSN: ███ DOB: ███
Mother's Name: Mara Pelton SSN: ███ DOB: ███

Date child was placed in care: 11/21/03
Monthly cost of foster care for this child: ___

Attach a copy of the court order or placement agreement.
Does Child Support Enforcement Division (CSED) have an existing case for this child?
Note: If unsure, call the local CSED office
[✓] Yes [✓] For FATHER, Case # ___ [ ] For MOTHER, Case # ___
CSED is hereby requested to redirect payments to: DPHHS, Fiscal Bureau, PO Box 8005, Helena, MT 59604.

Circumstances of this child have changed (includes address change, termination of parental rights).
[ ] No [ ] Yes
(Please explain): ___

Check if the parent is a minor? Mother [ ] Father [ ]
Have either or both parents been ordered to pay child support? [ ] Yes [ ] No [ ] Unknown
If yes, attach a copy of the order

GOOD CAUSE: As the placing worker, I claim that:
Good cause is claimed for the following reason (circle all that apply):
1. It is not in the best interest of the child (see CFS Policy Manual, section 306-2)
2. The case plan is to return the child within 90 days.
3. Parental rights have been terminated
4. Legal proceedings for adoption are pending
5. Parent is deceased (see CFS Policy Manual, section 306-1)(attach copy of death certificate)

[ ] Good cause for Father   [ ] Exists   [✓] Does not Exist
[ ] Good cause for Mother   [ ] Exists   [✓] Does not Exist

CFS Supervisor or designee: ___ Date: ___
County: ___ Eligibility Worker Initials: ___ TEAMS Case No. ___

---

91 Though this form is dated Nov 21, Mara's daughters were actually abducted Nov 20.

U.S. Political Prisoner Since 2004 / 407

Information
(February 20, 2004 – 4:33am)

```
Lori A. Adams, Deputy
OFFICE OF THE COUNTY ATTORNEY
Flathead County, Montana
P.O. Box 1516
Kalispell, MT 59903-1516
    Telephone (406)758-5630
Attorney for Plaintiff
```

FILED OF DISTRICT COURT
2004 FEB 20 AM 4:33
FILED
BY_____
DEPUTY

IN THE DISTRICT COURT OF THE ELEVENTH JUDICIAL DISTRICT OF THE
STATE OF MONTANA, IN AND FOR THE COUNTY OF FLATHEAD

STATE OF MONTANA,)
) Cause No. DC-04-064(A)
     Plaintiff,)
)
  vs.   ) INFORMATION
)
RONALD DWAYNE GLICK,)
)
     Defendant)

* * * * * * * * * * * * *

Lori A. Adams, Deputy Flathead County Attorney, charges that on the dates hereinafter set forth, in Flathead County, Montana, the above-named Defendant committed the offenses of: COUNT I: SEXUAL ASSAULT, a Felony and COUNT II: TAMPERING WITH WITNESSES AND INFORMANTS, a Felony.

The facts constituting the foregoing offenses are:

COUNT I: SEXUAL ASSAULT, a Felony

The Defendant, RONALD DWAYNE GLICK, between June and July, 2003, in Flathead County, Montana, knowingly subjected L.P., a minor (DOB: 5/03/90), to sexual contact without consent, contrary to Section 45-5-502, MCA. Because the victim was less than sixteen (16) years of age at the time of the offense, and the Defendant was three (3) or more years older than the victim, this offense is punishable under Section 45-5-502(3), MCA, by life imprisonment or imprisonment in the state prison for a term of not less than two (2) years or more than one hundred (100) years and may be fined a maximum of $50,000.00.

INFORMATION
Cause No DC-04-_____

DEFENDANT'S
EXHIBIT
3

Ron Glick /

COUNT II: TAMPERING WITH WITNESSES AND INFORMANTS, a Felony

The Defendant, RONALD DWAYNE GLICK, between July 2003 and October 2003, believing that an official proceeding is pending, he purposely or knowingly attempted to induce or otherwise cause a witness, namely, L.P., to withhold testimony by confronting her and telling her that she was wrong in her accusation of him sexually assaulting her and making her sign an affidavit stating that he did not sexually assault her, in Flathead County, Montana, all contrary to the provisions of Section 45-7-206(1)(b), M.C.A., and punishable under the provisions of Section 45-7-206(2), M.C.A., by a maximum term in the State Prison of ten (10) years and/or a maximum fine of $50,000.00.

All known possible witnesses for the State are listed as follows:

1. Officer Myron Wilson, Kalispell Police Department;
2. Corporeal Rod Myers, Flathead County Sheriff's Office;
3. Officer Doug Overman, Kalispell Police Department;
4. Lieutenant Greg Burns, Kalispell Police Department;
5. Lieutenant Roger Nasset, Kalispell Police Department;
6. Officer Brandy Arnoux, Columbia Falls Police Department;
7. Kori Taylor, DPHHS;
8. Jerry Nezat, witness;
9. Dixie Nezat, witness; and
10. L.P., victim.

DATED this 20th day of February, 2004.

OFFICE OF THE COUNTY ATTORNEY
Flathead County, Montana

By: _____
Lori A. Adams,
Deputy County Attorney

INFORMATION
Cause No. DC-04-_____

Ron Glick / 410

Order Granting Information
(February 20, 2004 – 4:44am)

IN THE DISTRICT COURT OF THE ELEVENTH JUDICIAL DISTRICT OF THE
STATE OF MONTANA, IN AND FOR THE COUNTY OF FLATHEAD

STATE OF MONTANA,)
　　　　　　　　　　) Cause No. DC-04-066A
　　　Plaintiff,)
　　　　　　　　　　) ORDER GRANTING LEAVE TO
　vs.　　　　　　　) FILE AN INFORMATION
　　　　　　　　　　)
RONALD DWAYNE GLICK,)
　　　　　　　　　　)
　　　Defendant.)

* * * * * * * * * * * * *

Having considered the State's Motion for Leave to File an Information, and there being probable cause to believe that the Defendant has committed the offenses of COUNT I: SEXUAL ASSAULT, a Felony and COUNT II: TAMPERING WITH WITNESSES AND INFORMANTS, a Felony, as alleged therein, the State is hereby granted leave to file an Information charging the Defendant with those offenses.

DATED this 20th day of February, 2004.

TED O. LYMPUS
Judge of the District Court

Appendix 3

I wish to say right at the outset that I do not include this particular record with any great zest. It is a necessary document as it is the first recorded interview of Daughter 1 on the night of July 9, 2003, but it is one that sickens me whenever I am forced to review it. And by necessity, I must review it for this entry. More than anything else, this document makes me feel like I am trying to get people to believe the lie – that by presenting this, I am somehow lending credibility to what was done to me. I know the truth, and I know this interview is actually so full of contradictions that it – as a whole – is exonerating. But the things said in this interview – to me – are abhorrent. They are descriptions of inappropriate contact with a girl I raised and saw as a child – and being forced to think of things like her breasts or vagina just makes me ill.

Yet this being said, I must present this document in the interests of full disclosure and transparency. I did not create the document, and when viewed as a whole, it should demonstrates how unreliable Daughter 1's details were even on that first night. Later interviews diverged even further, but this document is self-contained and no other document I possess demonstrates as effectively how contrary Daughter 1 is in her own interview.

Of course, there is a lot lost by reviewing this as a text document and not seeing the accompanying video. If watched, Daughter 1 can clearly be seen watching Myron Wilson for leads, hints at what he wants to hear. In many cases, her details change because she did not receive the response she wanted in the initial telling and so altered details to get a better reception. Anyone watching the video can tell that Daughter 1 is fishing through a great deal of the interview – looking to Wilson for guidance in what to say. To me, this comes across even in the written transcript, but I also have seen the video, so I am certain there are just ques I look for because I know they are there, also.

As the reader reviews this document, I ask that you mind certain details. For instance, when Daughter 1 is first asked on how long this occurred – with only the original allegation of putting a hand down her pants – that the incident supposedly lasted five seconds, but when she added the accusation later that I had also touched her breasts, she increased this timeframe to forty-five seconds; or how I supposedly first touched her vagina, but a few seconds later did not; or how initially she claimed we were talking, and then later said we were not. But most importantly, note how insistent she is after making the initial account of how I had only put my hands down her pants – she says repeatedly, and Wilson asks several times, if anything else happened and she said no over and again. Only after Wilson continued to prod – and you can see the confusion on Daughter 1's face in the video, like she is trying to guess what Wilson wants her to say – did she claim I had touched her breasts at the same time.

Also, pay attention to how Wilson leads the interview with suggestions of reaching over the top of her, feeding her lines of what to say, and that he is the one who ultimately – after being told that I supposedly only reached down her pants – continued to fish until Daughter 1 said I fondled her breasts, as well. Wilson was pushing for something more from Daughter 1, and if you were watching the video, you could see Daughter 1 hesitantly answer questions, gauging how Wilson was responding.

Remember, even Mara has said repeatedly that Daughter 1 was a consummate actress – and Wilson was her audience. She was looking for leads from him throughout the interview, and even in written form, one can see how she would far too often follow the line Wilson threw out.

This being said, I would reiterate that one needs to review this interview for themselves. It is very easy to look at what is said in individual statements and be repulsed – I know I am. But I ask that you take a genuine look at the overall scheme of the interview and how inconsistent Daughter 1 is throughout. Then remember that this is neither the story she originally told to Carrie Beth Mountjoy earlier that evening, nor the story she would continue to tell as time went on. The changes in her story in this one interview are notable – but her story between interviews varied so greatly that it could not even be seen as the same story.

One other point: the handwritten notations on this document are from Ed Falla's investigator, Rick Hawk, and are meant to clarify areas from the actual recording.

Daughter 1's Interview
(July 9, 2003)

Okay ▓▓▓ will you spell your first name for me, please?

▓▓ ▓▓▓▓▓▓▓

MW: And your last name?

▓▓: ▓▓▓▓▓▓▓

MW: What's your middle name?

▓▓ ▓▓▓

MW: What's your date of birth?

▓▓ ▓▓▓▓▓▓▓

MW: Okay. Do you know your social security number by any chance?

▓▓ Nope.

MW: Okay. What's your current address?

▓▓ Uh, ----------------------you asking where I sleep all the time, or where we might or like---
----

MW: Um, probably where you sleep.

▓▓ 4234 Foot Hill Road.

MW: 4234?

▓▓ Uh huh.

MW: So you're thirteen?

▓▓ Yes.

MW: Where do you go to school?

▓▓ Here, we go to school-------------

MW: I guess you're our for the summer now, aren't you?   Is that good or bad?

▓▓ Uh,

MW: Do you like school or hate school?

▇: I kind of like it.

MW: Do you? You like school? Well, that's good----------------. I hated school when was a kid, I just despised it. Uh, I spoke with a deputy today named Rod Meyers. He came into our office and he said the he had um, started an investigation and that you were a complainant of a possible sexual assault and realized that uh, the incident had actually taken place at Arcadia here in Kalispell. So that's why he turned it over to our agency. Alright? And that's why we are taking the primary role in the investigation at this point.

▇: Yeah, right here in -----------------

MW: ------that's within our jurisdiction, so that's why we handle it ----------- sheriff's office. Um, Rod expressed to me that you were possible the victim involved in this and provided me with your name and your mom's name and your grandma's name and phone numbers and that sort of thing. Okay? Um, that's about how much I know about the case. I don't know anything else about it. Um, what I'd like to do to begin with is establish um, I'm probably going to ask you some stupid questions, alright? So don't feel that I'm insulting you or talking down to you. Okay? Um, can you tell me what a lie is?

▇: A lie is when you're not telling the truth.

MW: Okay. So then express to me what telling the truth is.

▇: Telling the truth is tell what really happened.

MW: Okay. Um, if I was to say ▇ hair is blond. Would that be a truth or a lie?

▇: That would definitely be a lie.

MW: Okay. Alright.

▇: My hair might be turning blond, but it's still not blond yet.

MW: Okay. So if I was to say ▇ eyes were brown. Would that be the truth or a lie?

▇: True.

MW: Okay. So you know the difference between the truth and a lie?

▇: Yeah.

Ron Glick / 416

MW: Okay. Um, I know that there's some conflict here um, because your mom is, for the lack of a better description, associated with the person who is the suspect in this case which would be Ron Glick. She has an association with him, okay? And that's why I gave you the options of whether or not you wanted mom in the interview. Okay? Uh, I want you to be a comfortable as possible. Okay? And your mom, also, wanted you to be as comfortable as possible, you know. So I want you to feel at ease with that, uh, if at any point and time, though you would rather have your mom in here or grandma in here during this interview, um, say the word, we'll bring them in. Okay? I don't want you to feel uncomfortable. I want you to feel relaxed about this. It's going to be difficult for you to have to describe to me, but I want you to do it as best as you can and as accurately as you can. We don't want to exaggerate the truth, we just want the truth. We certainly don't want any false statements. Alright? Because, there's a heavier responsibility here. There could be some very serious consequences. And you seem like a very, bright, young girl. You do. You seem very bright. Okay. And very mature for your age. And that's why I ask you to bring in here. I ask you to be mature with me, try to understand that we're going to have to talk about some mature subjects. I don't want you to be embarrassed. Just talk to me. Okay? Try to feel as comfortable as possible. Okay, ▇▇▇ why don't you tell me what happened. Just give me a brief over flow of what happened.

▇: Well, me and Ron usually lay down on the back on the couch and just watch ———— instead of downloading on the computer.

MW: Um, Ron Glick?

▇: Yeah.

MW: Okay. And where is this at?

▇: Arcadia. 'Cause usually my mom has to be to work at seven and they don't open till ten. So, we usually watch videos.

MW: Oh, I see. So your mom drops you off at Arcadia on her way to work. Okay. And then you just spend the time with Ron in the back on the couch watching videos.

▇: Well, like sometimes, ----- just k ind of resting

MW: Okay.

▇: And I have------------------down there. -------------- and then wake up in there and go to work.

U.S. Political Prisoner Since 2004 / 417

MW: So, it's not that, it's certainly not that she needs somebody to watch you, that's just a place where mom takes you to drop you off on her way to work each morning and uh, so then you'd spend the time, how much of your day do you spend at the Arcadia?

■ Uh, usually, well, we open at ten and then we, then we, Monday through, or Sunday through Thursday, we close at ten and we open at ten and Friday and Saturday we open at seven and close at midnight. -------go home.

MW: So you spend the whole day there? — *Sentence missing from Transcript @1:50:46*

■ Uh huh.

Inaudible

MW: Okay, so while you're on the couch watching videos with Ron, did something happen?

■ ~~inaudible~~ *Nothi's said*

MW: Okay. Was it an isolated incident? Was it only once?

■ ~~Yeah~~ *Don't know*

MW: Or has it been several times?

■ It was ~~one incident.~~ *only once*

MW: Okay. Could you describe that incident to me?

■ He just started touching my body ---------- and I ---- Ron, stop and he didn't stop and I repeated it a couple of times and I give up because he wouldn't stop.

MW: Okay. When was this? Did he----------

■ Uh, quite a while ago.

MW: How long ago?

■ I don't remember the exact date, but it was not to long ago.

MW: Can you give me an idea? A week ago? Two weeks ago? A month ago?

■ Two weeks--------

MW: Two weeks ago?

So it was before the fourth of July, then obviously?

■ Yeah, it was ~~definitely before~~ the fourth of July.
(handwritten: definitely before)

MW: Okay. Can you remember back to any specific events that were happening in your life that you remember, help you remember that day. Like a birthday of a mom or bother or sister, grandmother, ~~anything~~ that can help you specifically remember the exact day?
(handwritten: There's nothing)

■ No.

MW: Okay. So about two weeks ago?

■ Yes.

MW: Okay. Um, were you on the couch?

■ Yeah.

MW: Is the is the back of Arcadia?

■ Yep, it's in the back office. We have a couch and a chair back there.

MW: Okay. Were you laying on the couch with Ron?

■ Yeah.

MW: Okay. Um,

■ (handwritten: Actually) We just lay down and watch videos all ~~day~~ (handwritten: morning).

MW: Alright. What led up to it?

■ I don't know.

MW: Okay.

■ It just kind of happened.

MW: You guys normally have a relationship where you are around each other quite a bit and you kind of push and shove and wrestle and things like that?

■ Yeah.

MW: That's a pretty accurate description of it? Kind of a playful —

■ Yeah.

MW: ---- relationship. Okay. So it's not uncommon for him to touch you. I mean, –

■ It's just that he was touching me in my private places.

MW: Oh, okay. So in other words he was touching you in a different way then?

■ Yes.

MW: Okay. There's a thing that we talk about anytime we do interviews like this, I talk to the person about it and I say um, there's a good touch, a bad touch and a secret touch. Okay? A good touch would be uh, when mom kisses you on the head, a bad touch would be like when your brother punches you in the eye and a secret touch would be like, when somebody touches you in a secret place where they don't want you to tell anybody about it. Which would one would you catagorize this touch ----------?

■ Inaudible Secret

MW: Okay. Describe to me, you're on the couch, you're laying there, you're watching v ideos, what happened?

■ He just started like, sliding his hand down my pants and, you know. stuff

MW: Okay.

■ I kept telling him----- M.W. Talk over her

MW: In front or in back?

■: In front.

MW: Okay. Were you laying down or were you sitting up?

■ Um, laying down.

MW: Okay, so you were laying on the couch, is he behind you or in front of you?

■ He was actually behind me ----------

MW: Okay, so you're laying in front of him on the couch?

███: Uh huh.

MW: He reaches over the top of you?

███: Yeah, kind of.

MW: Kind of. Just—Try & describe

███: Kind of, I was ———— we were both laying down and we just kind of, he usually rests his hand on my side, but he just kind of slid his hand down into my —pants

MW: Okay. So you were laying kind of on your side, not on your back and he just kind of reached over the top of you?

███: Yeah.

MW: Okay. And he started trying to slid his hand down your pants?

███: ~~Inaudible~~ um huh

MW: Okay. Did you tell him to stop?

███: Yes.

MW: Okay.

███: Over and over again, and then I stopped trying and then I tried pulling his hand out- and stuff

MW: Okay. Alright. Um, was he on top of your underwear or under wear

███: Under.

MW: He was under your underwear? Alright. So he continued trying to slid his hand down your pants and you told him to stop?

███: Yes.

MW: And you told him to stop, repeatedly?

███: ~~Inaudible~~ nods head

MW: Okay. And you reached down and pulled his hand out?

■ Yeah. *nod's yes*

MW: Did he touch your private parts? I don't mean to embarrass you, but the best way to talk about these kinds of things is very clinical, but that's what I'm going to. Okay?

■ Okay.

MW: Did he touch your vagina?

■ I don't, I don't *quite* understand.

MW: Okay. Um, a woman's private parts are called the vagina.

■ Yeah.

MW: That's - do you understand that?

■ Yes.

MW: Okay. Did he touch that?

■ Yes.

MW: Um, how long did this go on?

■ Like about five seconds. ----inaudible---- *Then I got his hand out*

MW: So you were eventually able to pull his hand out?

■ ~~Inaudible.~~ *Nods yes*

MW: Okay.

■ ------------I got up and I sat up in the chair.

MW: Okay. Did he try and stick his fingers inside of you?

■ Inaudible *Shake head No*

MW: No? How far down, it's important for us to know how far down, down your pants he went. Um, did he, he actually touched your vagina?

■ Not, almost, but [well inserted above "Not"]

MW: Almost, then. So he didn't actually touch your vagina then?

■ No, but he was really, really close.

MW: Okay. Um, I'm trying to thing of a way that you can describe to me how close he was. Okay? There's a bone right up on the top, right here. Do you know which bone I'm talking about? It's kind of, it's kind of like in here, your pubic hair on down to the tip and there's a bone right here, at the very top, it's like part of your pelvis. Do you know the area that I'm talking about?

■ ~~Yeah~~ [handwritten: shakes head NO]

MW [handwritten]: says NO

MW: Okay. Try you best to try and describe to me how far down was [handwritten: he put] his hand in your pants. Did he go around the corner and touch your actual vagina or was he, did he still have his hand above that area?

■ He had it, ~~----~~ [handwritten: kinda] above that area.

MW: Okay. So he was still in the area of your pubic hair then and he didn't go any further down then that?

■ Well, he went over my pubic hair.

MW: He went over your pubic hair?

■ Yeah.

MW: Okay. Like he lifted his hand up and went over the top of it?

■ No, he kind of slid his hand over.

MW: Over the top, over your pubic?

■ ~~Inaudible.~~ [handwritten: nods yes]

MW: But he stopped and didn't go actually around the corner------? Is that accurate? Is that true?

■ Yes.

MW: Okay. And afterwards you pulled his hand out of your pants. You got up and went-------

■ And I sat down in the chair.

MW: Sat down in the chair. Okay. Is that the only incident of this kind that you have experienced with Ron?

■ Yes.

MW: Is it. He's never made any sexual advances towards you in the past?

■ No.

MW: Okay. Well, I want you to know that it is not acceptable for him to do that. You understand that? Right? This is not your fault. Okay?

■ I ----inaudible was scared of coming

MW: Okay, that, you understand that's common and it happens a lot. Do you know that there's a lot of, there area lot of women out there that are victimized and even raped and they ---don't tell -- and it's because they're afraid. Okay? So that's natural. And it's nothing that you should feel ashamed of. Not at all. So don't. You didn't. So after the incident happened, after this incident happened, have you been around Ron since?

■ Yes.

MW: Okay. Has he made any other advances towards you?

■ Inaudible. shake head NO

MW: None?

■ No.

MW: Okay. Um, could he tell that you were upset about this?

■ I don't know if he could tell, but he, the time we didn't watch any videos, you know in the mornings, we just kind of, --------inaudible slept instead

MW: Did you sleep in separate in the apartment?

■ Yeah, he slept usually on the couch ------------inaudible + I had a sleeping bag in the basement

MW: Okay. Was Ron awake when this happened? He was fully awake?

Ron Glick / 424

■ Yes.

MW: Were you talking to him?

■ Yeah.

MW: Okay. So there's no question that he dozed off and thought that he was with somebody else at the time?

■ Yeah.

MW: Um, yeah, there's no question that he—

■ Yeah, there's no question.

MW: He was awake? Did he say anything to you?

■ No.

MW: Nothing at all? [*she talk but it inaudible*] What about when you got up and walked away? Did he say anything to you about, anything at all?

■ Well, [*he kinda so?*] ----- after that he said, do you want to come back and lay down.

MW: And what did you tell him?

■ I said, no, ---- [*I'll sit here*]

MW: Okay. Did he ever touch you up on top?

■ Yeah.

MW: He did?

■ Uh huh.

MW: When?

■ At the same time he was trying to ---- [*go down my pants*] inaudible

MW: Okay.

■ Inaudible

MW: ▓▓▓ let me ask you a question. Do you feel kind of guilty about this?

▓▓ ~~Inaudible~~ Nods yes

MW: Okay. Alright. That's, that too, is something that is very understandable. Um, and is often the case that, let me explain something to you, you're thirteen years old. Okay? You're thirteen years —

▓▓ Yeah, I know I'm thirteen years old.

MW: Well, I just want to explain it to you. No, but you're thirteen years old, he's an adult. He is the one that is making the decision here to be irresponsible. Okay? And it's really easy for a thirteen year old girl to be intimidated by an adult. And to allow something to have to continue even when she doesn't feel right about it, to continue just because she feels intimidated. Can you understand that?

▓▓ Yeah.

MW: Okay. So, so when did he touch you, when did he touch your breasts? Was it before this incident?

▓▓ No, it was at the same time of this incident.

MW: Okay. Can you describe that to me? Was it before he tried to put his hand down your pants?

▓▓ A little bit before, then he tried going down my pants.

MW: Okay. ------ did he reach up underneath your shirt?

▓▓ Yes.

MW: Okay. Were you wearing a brasserie?

▓▓ ~~Yes.~~ No + Shake head NO

MW: Okay. So, you're laying on the couch, you're laying in front of him, he's behind you, he's on his side, you're on your side, he reached over your side and what did he do?

▓▓ He well, first with his other hand, which I'm laying on top of, he's trying, he was getting under my shirt and then he started putting his other hand down my pants.

MW: I see, so, he uses his right hand to try and stick his hand down your pants, but his left hand that you were actually laying on, he was reaching up underneath your shirt at the same time?

▇: Well, he was sort of reaching up my shirt first and then he started to put his hand down my pants.

MW: Okay. Was he able to put his hand up underneath your shirt?

▇: Yes.

MW: Okay. And did he actually touch your breasts?

▇: Yes.

MW: Okay. Um, did he just rub over the top of them?

▇: No, he just rubbed on them.

MW: Both of your breasts?

▇: Well, one of them and [inaudible]

MW: Okay. And this was kind of happening, happening simultaneously, while he was trying to put his hand down your pants?

▇: Yes.

MW: Okay. And you asked him to stop?

▇: Yes.

MW: Okay. How long did this whole event take place?

▇: I'm guessing about forty-five seconds.

MW: Okay. Um, okay. Finally you just got up and walked away from him. Did he try kissing you?

▇: No.

MW: Not at all?

■ ~~Inaudible~~ No

MW: And you've never experienced an incident like this before?

■ No.

MW: Okay. Never made any advances towards you?

■ No.

MW: Alright. How do you ~~fell~~ feel about —— this

■ I have felt confused, scared, and then I don't know how to explain this, like kind of like a guilty --confused------

MW: Do you know what I want you to do?

■ No.

MW: Okay. Do you have any recent pictures of yourself?

■ Uh, no.

MW: None at all?

■ None.

MW: You got to get one. You got to get one. Because you know what happens in cases like this? Um, right now you look at everything from the perspective of being a thirteen year old young lady. Okay? When you get to be twenty-five, if this sort of thing ever comes up and bothers you, which I hope it doesn't, um, but if it does, you need to be able to look back at that picture of you when you were thirteen.

■ I have my year book picture.

MW: There you go.

■ In my year book.

MW: There you go. You need to be able to look back at that picture of you and say, but, just a minute, that's how old was. Okay. Because when you're twenty-five, you know what, you're going to look at it from the perspective of a twenty-five year old and you're going to say, I should have done more. And that's not the case. You're a thirteen year old. Okay. And you're a very nice young lady. But you're still thirteen. And I don't, I'm not talking down to you, I'm just telling you that you don't have a lot of life experience right now.

▇ You made me cry.

MW: You don't have a lot of life experience right now and you have to realize that it is very easy for a thirteen year old girl to be intimidated by this. That's why the States, State of Montana steps in and says anybody under the age of sixteen years old cannot, CANNOT have sexual intercourse. They can't consent to it. Okay? And the reason for that is, because the State says they don't have the maturity before that age to be able to consent to that decision. Alright. And there's good reason for that. You know. You're a very mature young lady, I'm not say that, but what I am telling you is that you're still thirteen. Okay? So, don't blame yourself for this and don't beat yourself up over it. It is not your fault. Okay?

▇ Ron Glick is also accused of molesting a five year old.

MW: Do you feel in anyway, because you feel, you told me you felt guilty, do you feel in anyway that you egged Ron on?

▇ I don't—inaudible understand

MW: Do you feel in anyway that you encouraged Ron to do this?

▇ Not really.

MW: Did you ask him to do this?

▇ No.

MW: Did you suggest to him in anyway to do this?

▇ No.

MW: Did you rub up against him in any special way to try and encourage him to do it or to make him think that you wanted him to do this?

▇ Inaudible shake head no

MW: I don't think you did either. Alright? And I don't want you to think that I think that. But I have to ask you that. Alright? Is that the only incident that we're talking about? Is there any other incidents which you can think of where he touched you on top of your clothes, underneath your clothes, anywhere? Any other incidences?

▇ No.

MW: Okay. Do you have anything else that you'd like to tell me?

▇ No, ----- inaudible [handwritten: I hope I did not make you feel uncomfortable]

MW: Okay. I'll ----- inaudible. Alright. Just don't blame yourself. Remember that year book picture, right? Okay. If it ever comes up, I want you to look back at that year book picture and I want you to think, but I was thirteen years old. Alright?

▇ Inaudible

MW: Alright. Well, I'm going to bring your mom in here and I'm going to talk to you mom and I'm going to have you sit out here and talk with your grandparents for a second. Okay. It was really nice to meet you. Inaudible

▇ Okay.

MW: And if you ever need, if you ever need to talk to me about any thing, um, I'll give you my business card, you can call anytime, dispatch will put you in touch with me. Alright?

▇ Inaudible [handwritten: will do]

MW: There you go. If I can help you out in anyway you get a hold of me. Alright?

▇ Okay.

MW: Okay. Thanks a lot.

MW: There's some good news and bad news, unfortunately. Um, good, there's no sexual intercourse, ------ let me stop the tape.

About the Author

Ron Glick (born January 20, 1969) is a community activist, and is presently active in several charitable enterprises. He was born in Plainville, KS. After living in various states, he currently lives in Kalispell, MT. He is unmarried, with ambitions to someday change that. He is the author of The Godslayer Cycle, Chaos Rising and the Oz-Wonderland series, as well as having compiled several volumes of Ron El's Comic Book Trivia. He is also the creator of the Golden Age Preservation Project, converting golden age comic books for a modern audience. He is presently working on the third novel of the Oz-Wonderland series, *The Wonderful Alice of Oz*. He loves contact and welcomes input on his work through his website at: http://ronglick.com

www.ingramcontent.com/pod-product-compliance
Lightning Source LLC
Chambersburg PA
CBHW060232290526
45789CB00001B/11